Chapter 84:
Confirm the Truth

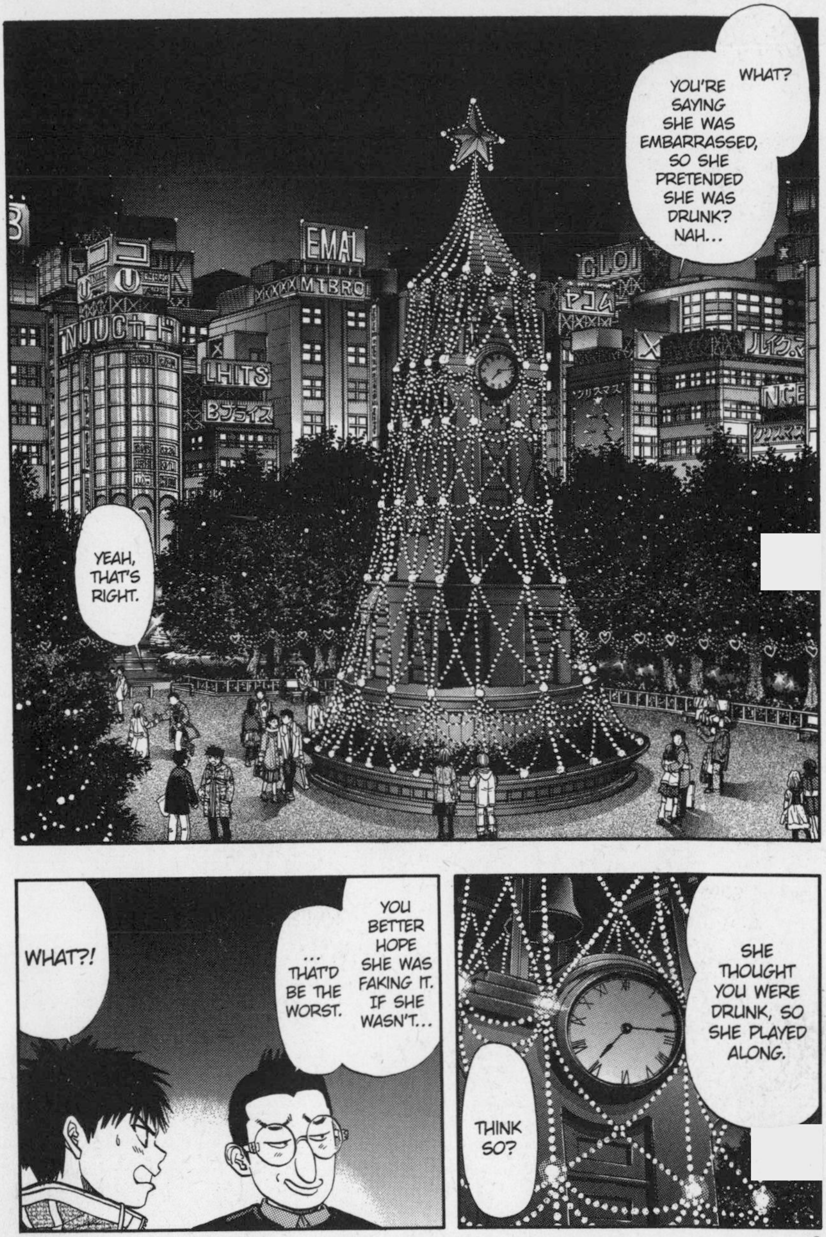
WHAT? YOU'RE SAYING SHE WAS EMBARRASSED, SO SHE PRETENDED SHE WAS DRUNK? NAH...
YEAH, THAT'S RIGHT.
SHE THOUGHT YOU WERE DRUNK, SO SHE PLAYED ALONG.
THINK SO?
YOU BETTER HOPE SHE WAS FAKING IT. IF SHE WASN'T...
...THAT'D BE THE WORST.
WHAT?!

I"s
VOL. 10: TO YOU
The SHONEN JUMP ADVANCED Manga Edition

STORY AND ART BY
MASAKAZU KATSURA

English Adaptation/Arashi Productions
Translation/Arashi Productions
Touch-up Art & Lettering/Deron Bennett
Design/Hidemi Sahara
Editor/Jonathan Tarbox

Managing Editor/Frances E. Wall
Editorial Director/Elizabeth Kawasaki
VP & Editor in Chief/Yumi Hoashi
Sr. Director of Acquisitions/Rika Inouye
Sr. VP of Marketing/Liza Coppola
Exec. VP of Sales & Marketing/John Easum
Publisher/Hyoe Narita

Printed in the U.S.A.

Published by VIZ Media, LLC
P.O. Box 77010
San Francisco, CA 94107

SHONEN JUMP ADVANCED Manga Edition
10 9 8 7 6 5 4 3 2 1
First printing, November 2006

www.viz.com

THE WORLD'S MOST
CUTTING-EDGE MANGA
SHONEN JUMP
ADVANCED
www.shonenjump.com

Masakazu Katsura

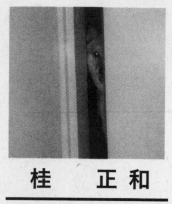

桂　正和

Recently, because I haven't taken any pictures of myself, I'm having this rascal take my place again. Third time, isn't it? Well, this dog was in volume 1, so what the heck? It's sort of a turning point. The last time the dog appeared, I asked if anybody could guess its name. Now, it's time I revealed the answer.

Her name is Alfred. I'll bet the sharp-witted among you can guess why. Since she's a female, I call her Alfreko.

When Masakazu Katsura was a high school student, he entered a story he had drawn into a manga contest in hopes of winning money to buy a stereo. He won the contest and was soon published in the immensely popular weekly manga anthology magazine *Weekly Shonen Jump*. Katsura was quickly propelled into manga-artist stardom, and his subsequent comic series, *WINGMAN*, *VIDEO GIRL AI*, *DNA²*, and *SHADOW LADY* are perennial fan favorites. *I"s*, which began publication in 1997, also inspired an original video series. Katsura lives in Tokyo and possesses an extensive collection of Batman memorabilia.

SHONEN JUMP ADVANCED MANGA

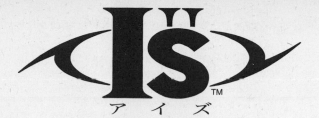

I"s™

アイズ

Vol. 10
TO YOU

STORY & ART BY

MASAKAZU KATSURA

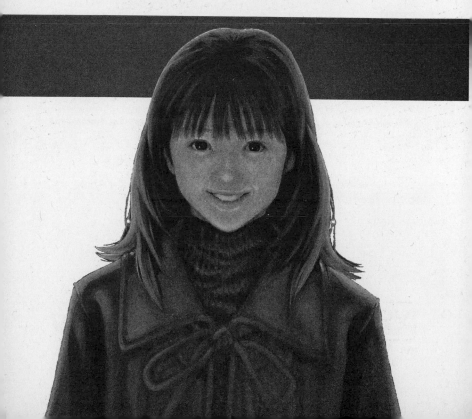

I"s

アイズ

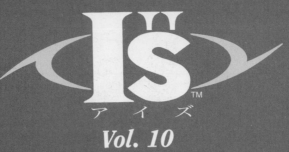

Vol. 10

CONTENTS

READ THIS WAY

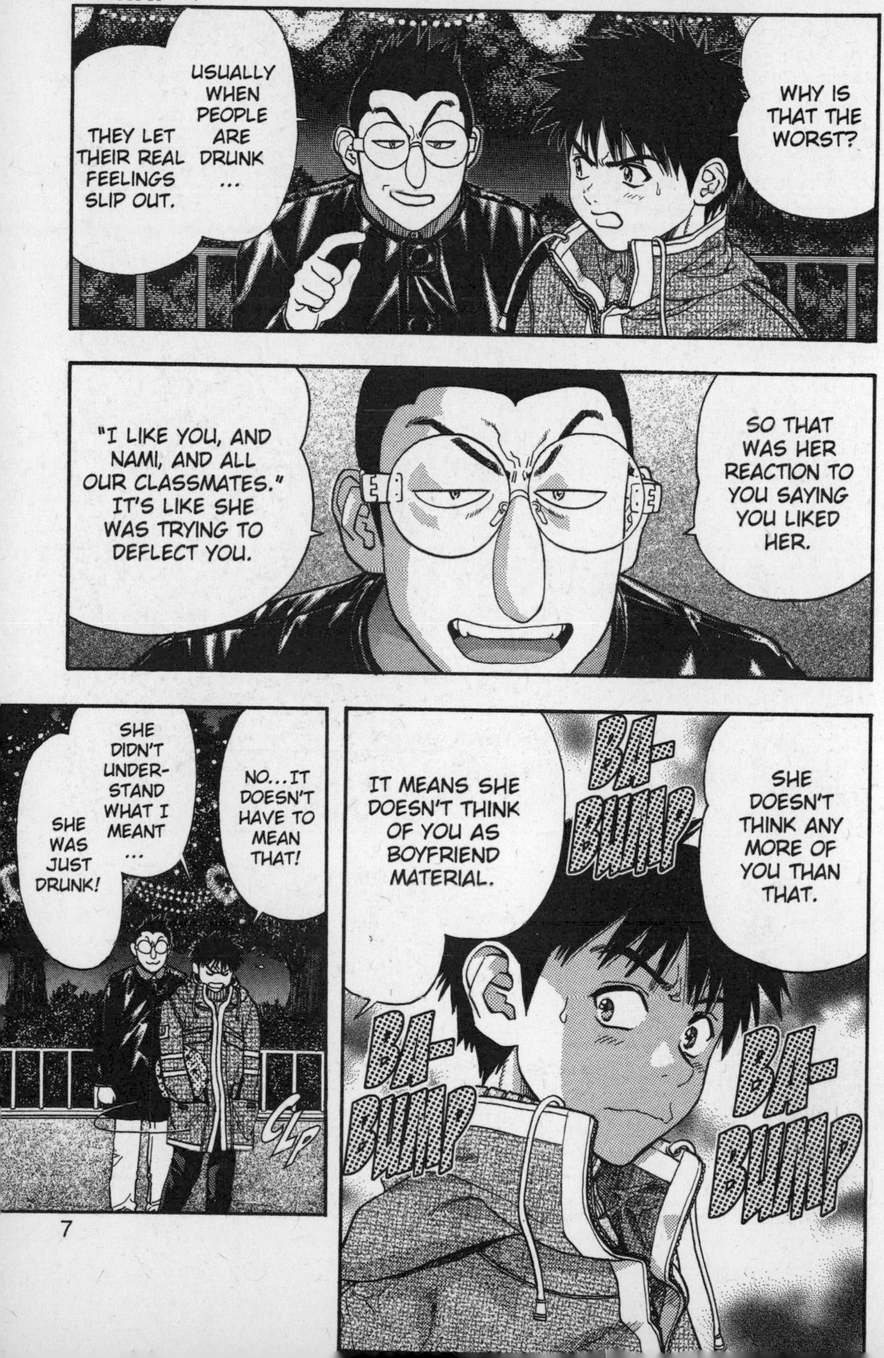
WHY IS THAT THE WORST?
USUALLY WHEN PEOPLE ARE DRUNK...
THEY LET THEIR REAL FEELINGS SLIP OUT.
SO THAT WAS HER REACTION TO YOU SAYING YOU LIKED HER.
"I LIKE YOU, AND NAMI, AND ALL OUR CLASSMATES." IT'S LIKE SHE WAS TRYING TO DEFLECT YOU.
SHE DOESN'T THINK ANY MORE OF YOU THAN THAT.
BA-BUMP
IT MEANS SHE DOESN'T THINK OF YOU AS BOYFRIEND MATERIAL.
BA-BUMP
BA-BUMP
NO...IT DOESN'T HAVE TO MEAN THAT!
SHE DIDN'T UNDER-STAND WHAT I MEANT...
SHE WAS JUST DRUNK!
GLP

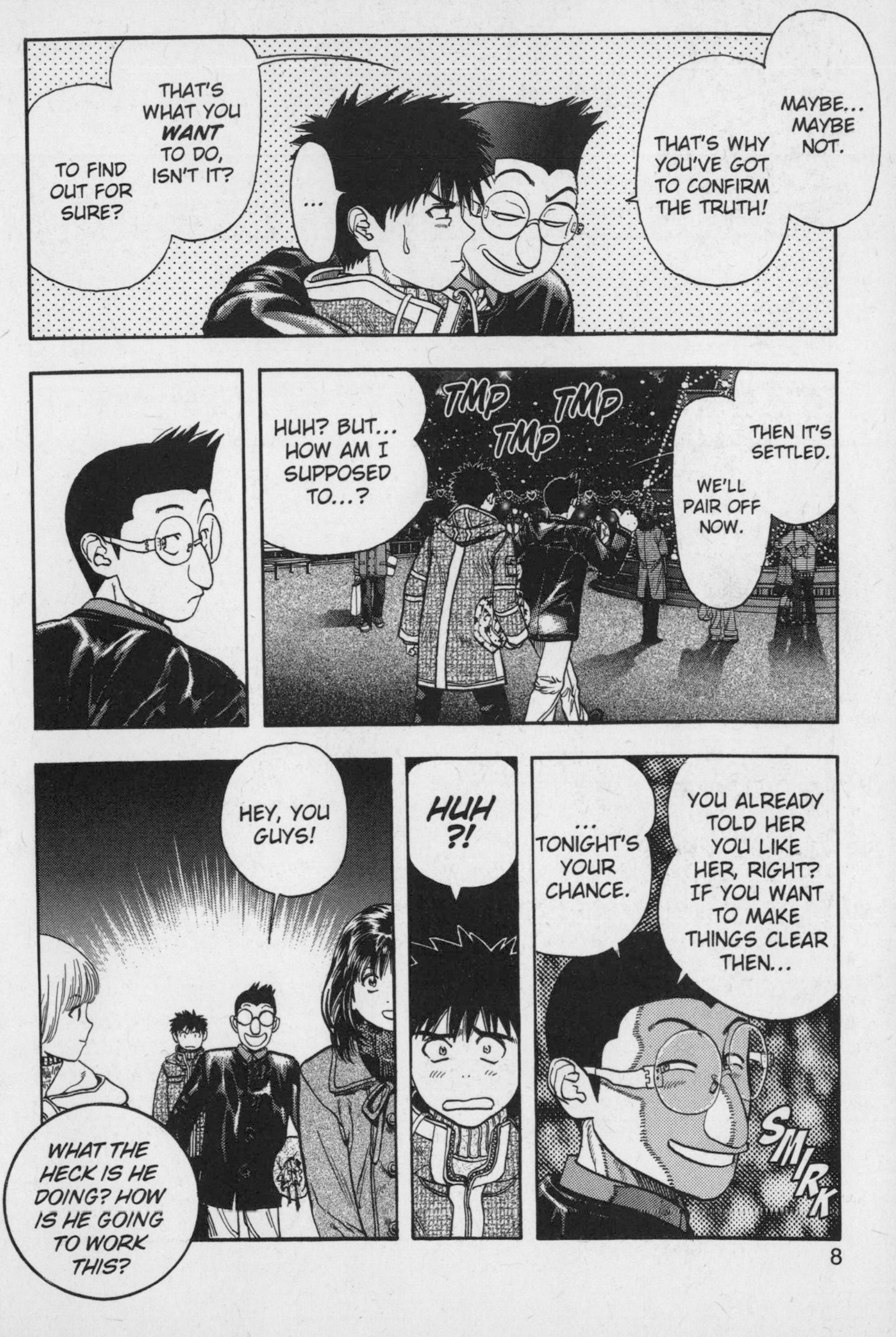
MAYBE... MAYBE NOT.
THAT'S WHY YOU'VE GOT TO CONFIRM THE TRUTH!
...
THAT'S WHAT YOU WANT TO DO, ISN'T IT?
TO FIND OUT FOR SURE?
THEN IT'S SETTLED.
WE'LL PAIR OFF NOW.
TMP TMP TMP
HUH? BUT... HOW AM I SUPPOSED TO...?
YOU ALREADY TOLD HER YOU LIKE HER, RIGHT? IF YOU WANT TO MAKE THINGS CLEAR THEN...
...TONIGHT'S YOUR CHANCE.
SMIRK
HUH?!
HEY, YOU GUYS!
WHAT THE HECK IS HE DOING? HOW IS HE GOING TO WORK THIS?

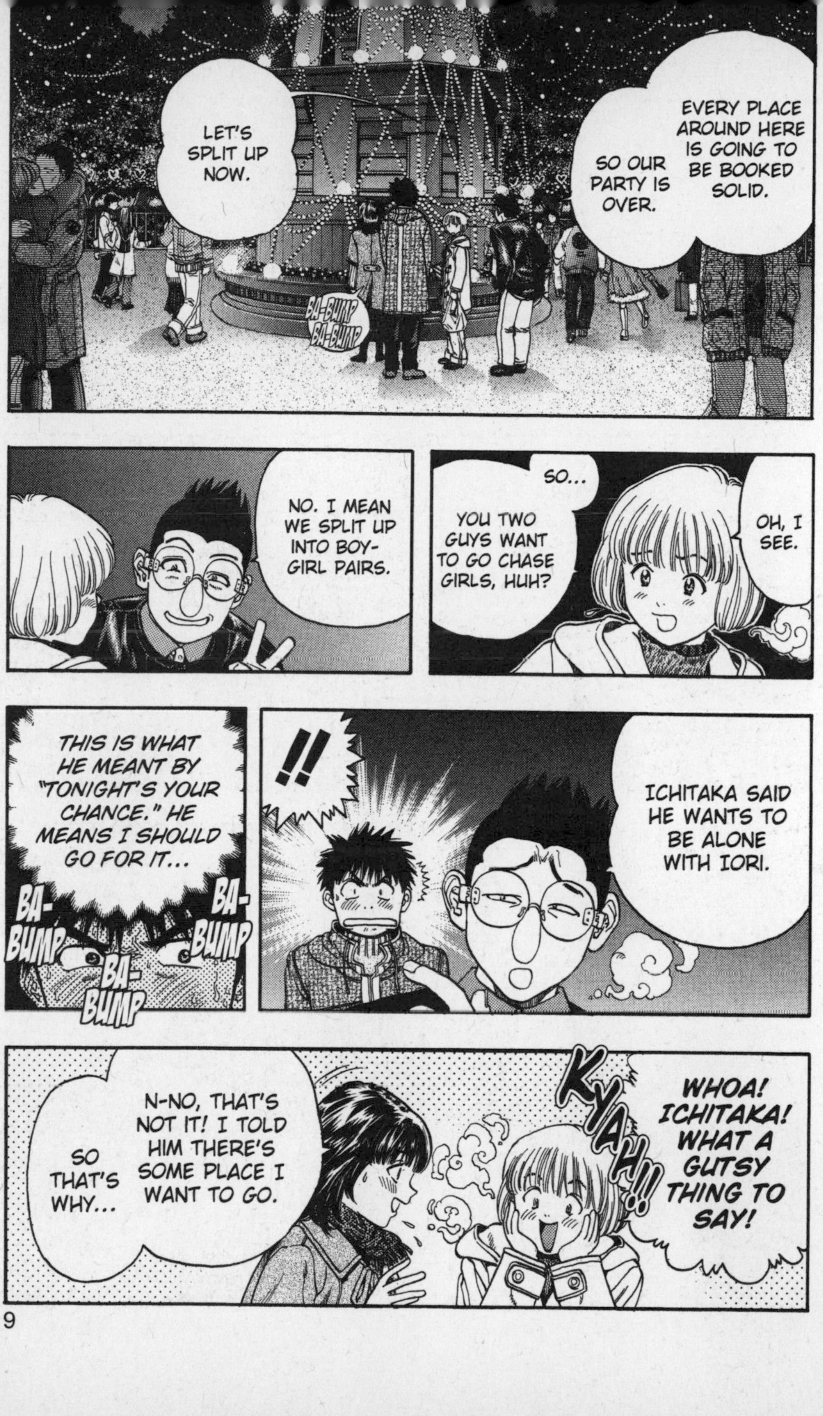
EVERY PLACE AROUND HERE IS GOING TO BE BOOKED SOLID.
SO OUR PARTY IS OVER.
LET'S SPLIT UP NOW.
BA-BUMP BA-BUMP
OH, I SEE.
SO...
YOU TWO GUYS WANT TO GO CHASE GIRLS, HUH?
NO. I MEAN WE SPLIT UP INTO BOY-GIRL PAIRS.
ICHITAKA SAID HE WANTS TO BE ALONE WITH IORI.
!!
THIS IS WHAT HE MEANT BY "TONIGHT'S YOUR CHANCE." HE MEANS I SHOULD GO FOR IT...
BA-BUMP
BA-BUMP
BA-BUMP
WHOA! ICHITAKA! WHAT A GUTSY THING TO SAY!
KYAAH!!
N-NO, THAT'S NOT IT! I TOLD HIM THERE'S SOME PLACE I WANT TO GO.
SO THAT'S WHY...

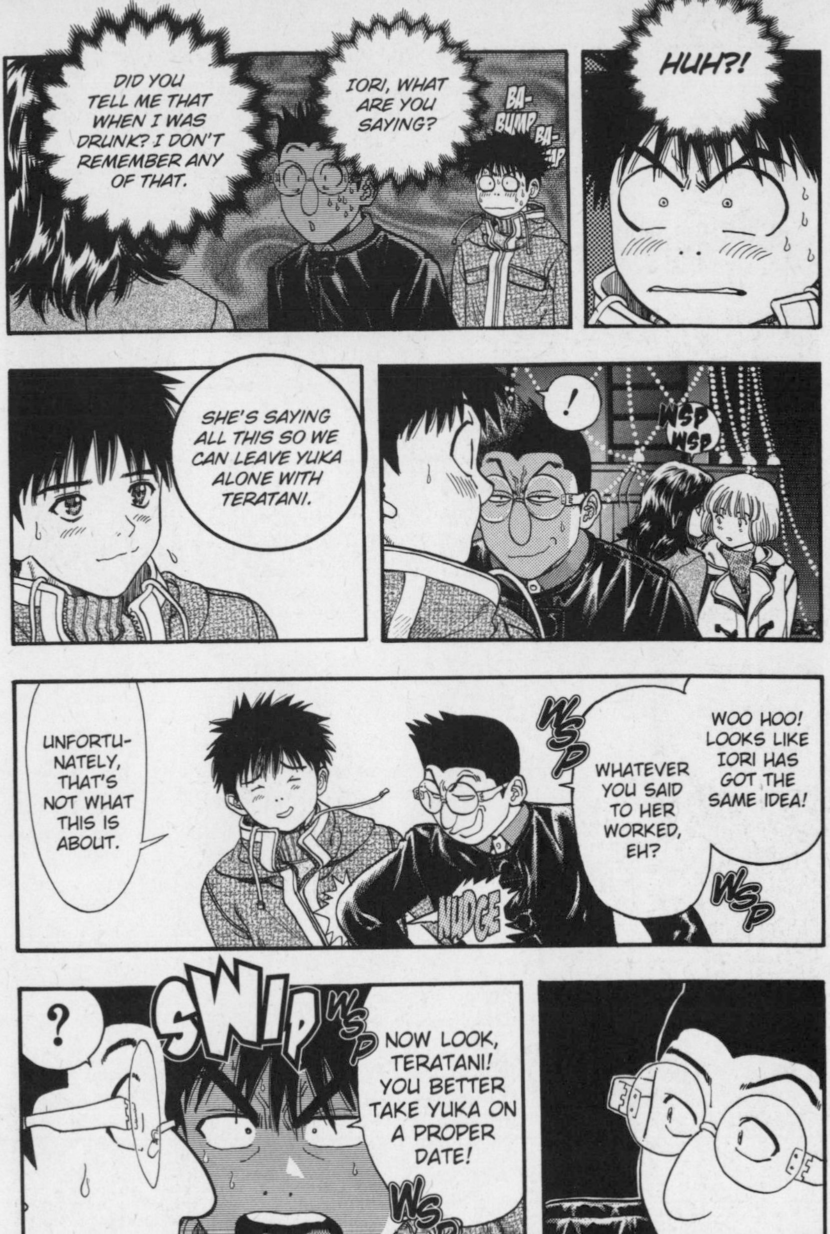
HUH?!
IORI, WHAT ARE YOU SAYING?
BA-BUMP BA-BUMP
DID YOU TELL ME THAT WHEN I WAS DRUNK? I DON'T REMEMBER ANY OF THAT.
!
WSP WSP
SHE'S SAYING ALL THIS SO WE CAN LEAVE YUKA ALONE WITH TERATANI.
WSP
WOO HOO! LOOKS LIKE IORI HAS GOT THE SAME IDEA!
WHATEVER YOU SAID TO HER WORKED, EH?
WSP
NUDGE
UNFORTUNATELY, THAT'S NOT WHAT THIS IS ABOUT.
NOW LOOK, TERATANI! YOU BETTER TAKE YUKA ON A PROPER DATE!
WSP
SWIP
WSP
?

READ THIS WAY

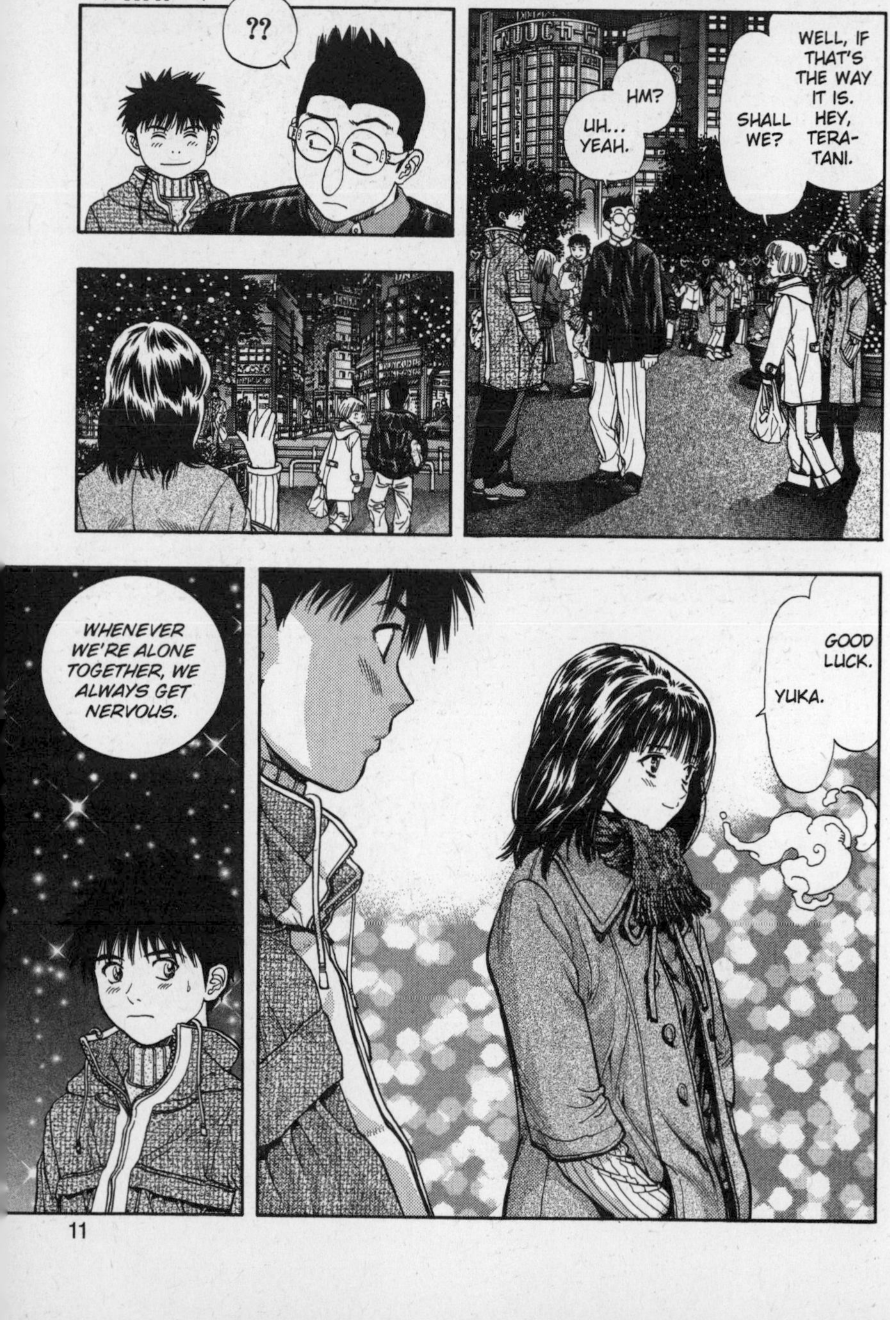
WELL, IF THAT'S THE WAY IT IS. HEY, TERA-TANI.
SHALL WE?
HM?
UH... YEAH.
??
GOOD LUCK.
YUKA.
WHENEVER WE'RE ALONE TOGETHER, WE ALWAYS GET NERVOUS.

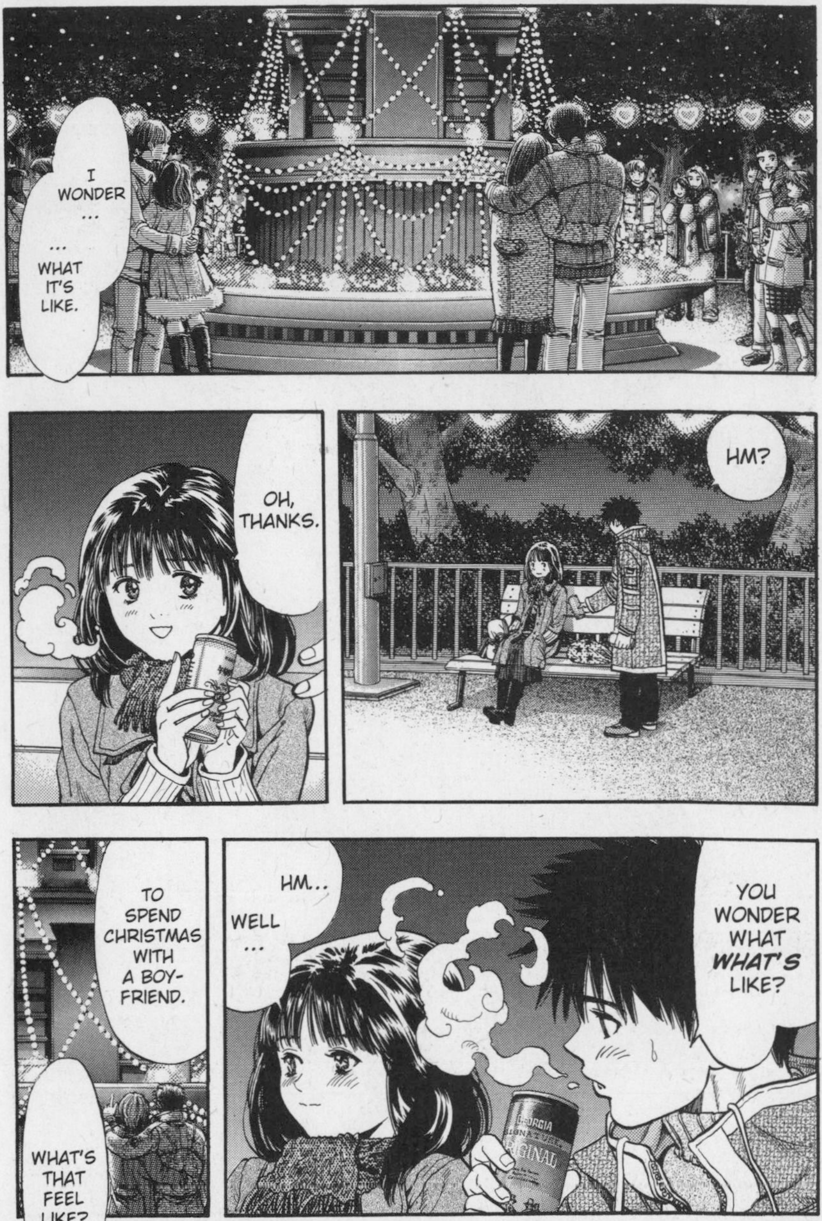
I WONDER ...
... WHAT IT'S LIKE.
HM?
OH, THANKS.
YOU WONDER WHAT *WHAT'S* LIKE?
HM... WELL ...
TO SPEND CHRISTMAS WITH A BOY-FRIEND.
WHAT'S THAT FEEL LIKE?

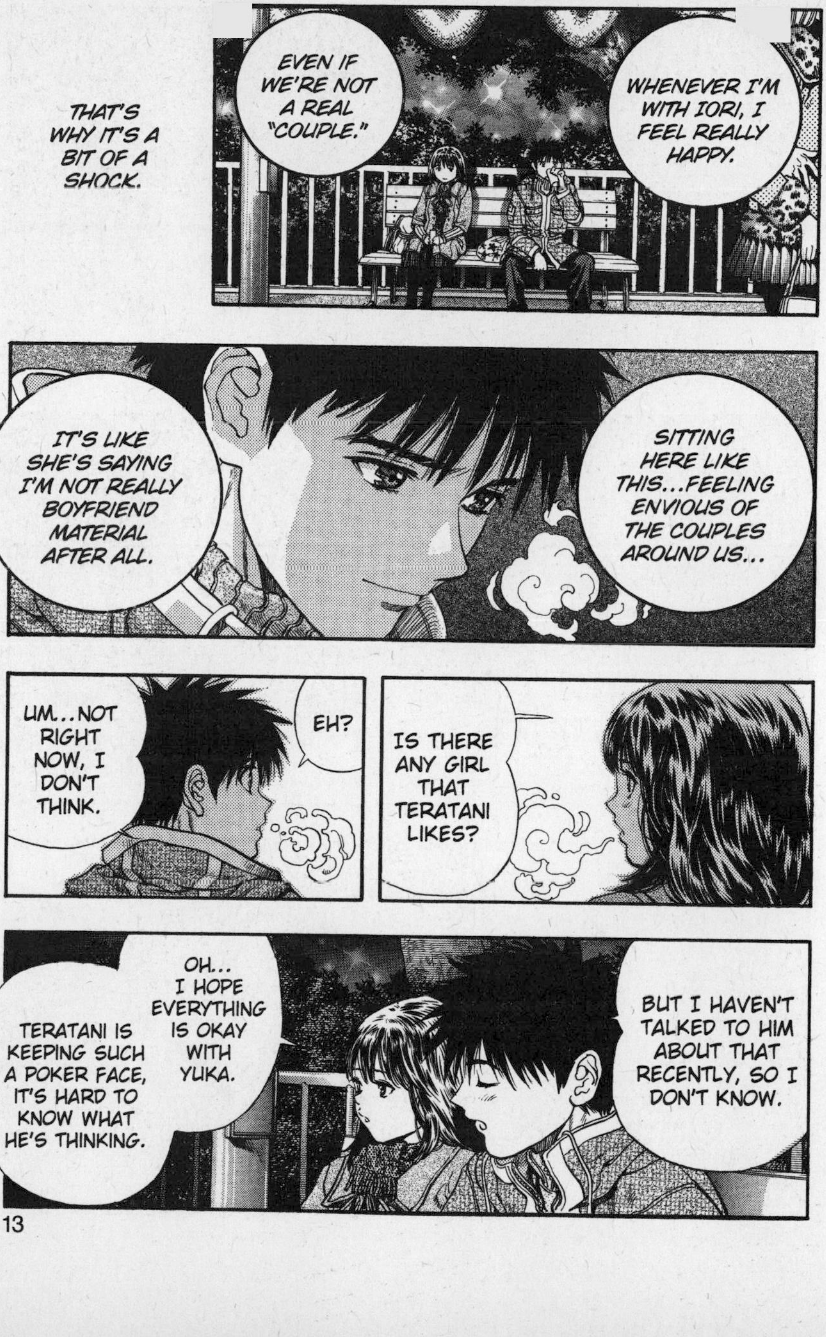
WHENEVER I'M WITH IORI, I FEEL REALLY HAPPY.
EVEN IF WE'RE NOT A REAL "COUPLE."
THAT'S WHY IT'S A BIT OF A SHOCK.
SITTING HERE LIKE THIS...FEELING ENVIOUS OF THE COUPLES AROUND US...
IT'S LIKE SHE'S SAYING I'M NOT REALLY BOYFRIEND MATERIAL AFTER ALL.
IS THERE ANY GIRL THAT TERATANI LIKES?
EH?
UM...NOT RIGHT NOW, I DON'T THINK.
BUT I HAVEN'T TALKED TO HIM ABOUT THAT RECENTLY, SO I DON'T KNOW.
OH... I HOPE EVERYTHING IS OKAY WITH YUKA.
TERATANI IS KEEPING SUCH A POKER FACE, IT'S HARD TO KNOW WHAT HE'S THINKING.

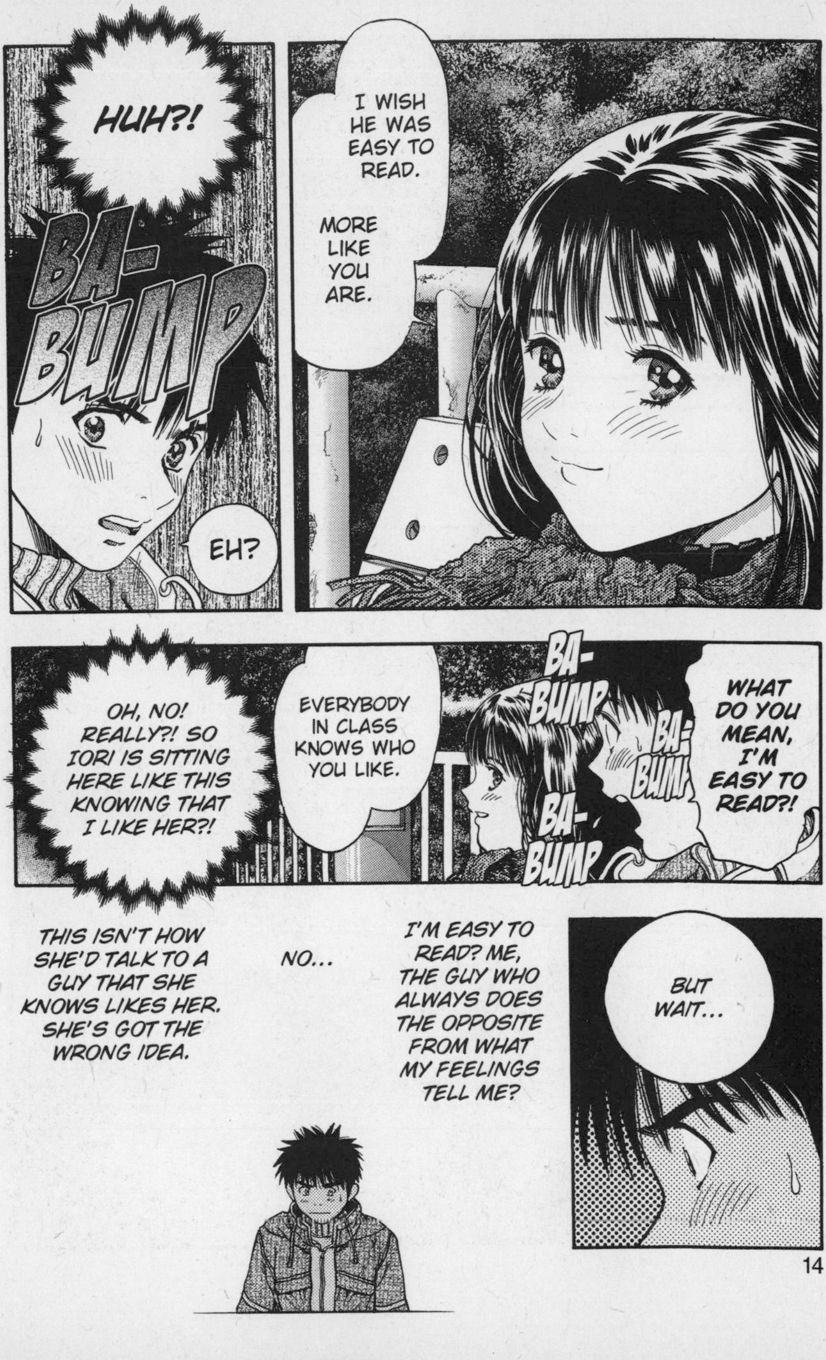
I WISH HE WAS EASY TO READ.
MORE LIKE YOU ARE.
HUH?!
BA-BUMP
EH?
WHAT DO YOU MEAN, I'M EASY TO READ?!
BA-BUMP
BA-BUMP
BA-BUMP
EVERYBODY IN CLASS KNOWS WHO YOU LIKE.
OH, NO! REALLY?! SO IORI IS SITTING HERE LIKE THIS KNOWING THAT I LIKE HER?!
BUT WAIT...
I'M EASY TO READ? ME, THE GUY WHO ALWAYS DOES THE OPPOSITE FROM WHAT MY FEELINGS TELL ME?
NO...
THIS ISN'T HOW SHE'D TALK TO A GUY THAT SHE KNOWS LIKES HER. SHE'S GOT THE WRONG IDEA.

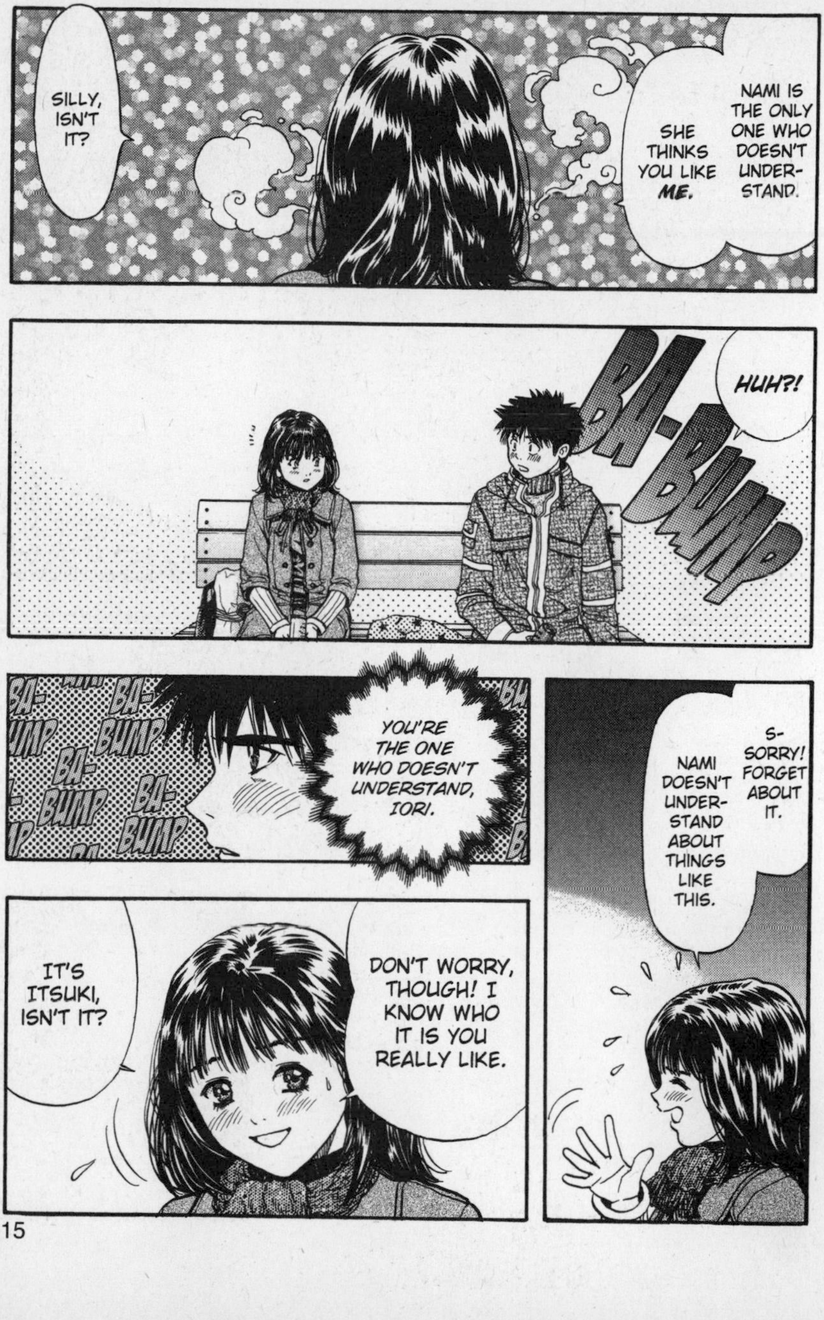
NAMI IS THE ONLY ONE WHO DOESN'T UNDER-STAND.
SHE THINKS YOU LIKE *ME.*
SILLY, ISN'T IT?
HUH?!
BA-BUMP
S-SORRY! FORGET ABOUT IT.
NAMI DOESN'T UNDER-STAND ABOUT THINGS LIKE THIS.
BA-BUMP
BA-BUMP
BA-BUMP
BA-BUMP
YOU'RE THE ONE WHO DOESN'T UNDERSTAND, IORI.
DON'T WORRY, THOUGH! I KNOW WHO IT IS YOU REALLY LIKE.
IT'S ITSUKI, ISN'T IT?

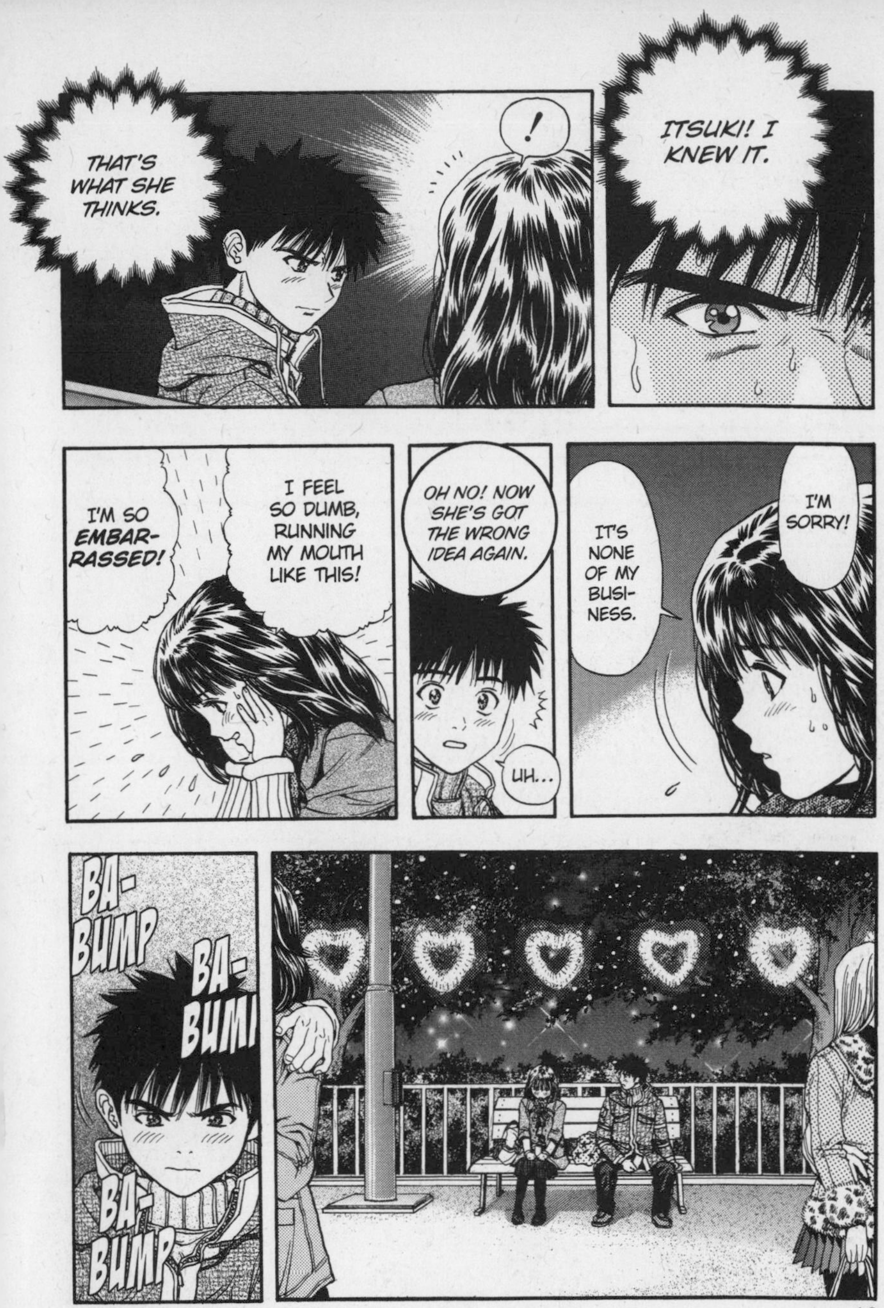

ITSUKI! I KNEW IT.
!
THAT'S WHAT SHE THINKS.
I'M SORRY!
IT'S NONE OF MY BUSI-NESS.
OH NO! NOW SHE'S GOT THE WRONG IDEA AGAIN.
UH...
I FEEL SO DUMB, RUNNING MY MOUTH LIKE THIS!
I'M SO EMBAR-RASSED!
BA-BUMP
BA-BUM
BA-BUMP

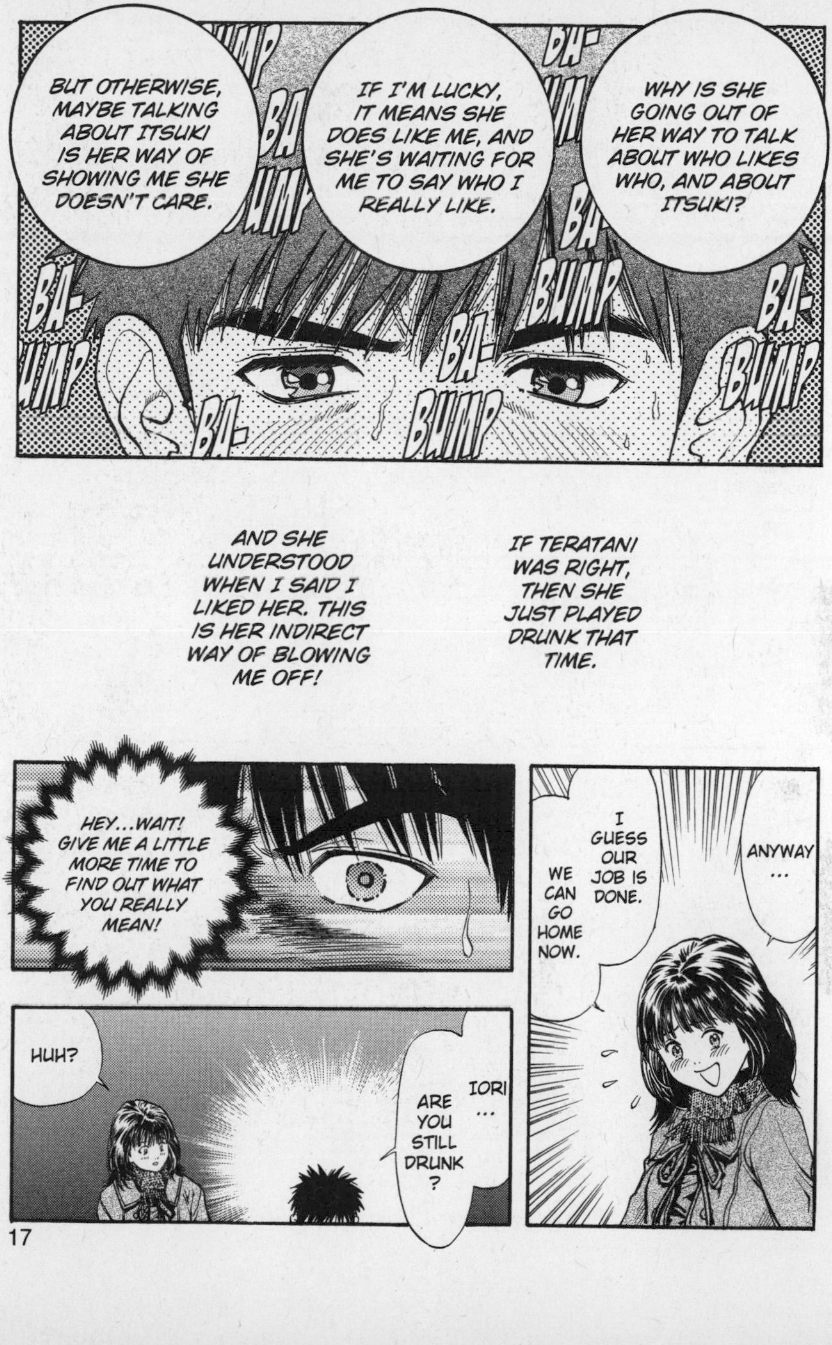
WHY IS SHE GOING OUT OF HER WAY TO TALK ABOUT WHO LIKES WHO, AND ABOUT ITSUKI?
IF I'M LUCKY, IT MEANS SHE DOES LIKE ME, AND SHE'S WAITING FOR ME TO SAY WHO I REALLY LIKE.
BUT OTHERWISE, MAYBE TALKING ABOUT ITSUKI IS HER WAY OF SHOWING ME SHE DOESN'T CARE.
BA-BUMP BA-BUMP BA-BUMP BA-BUMP BA-BUMP BA-BUMP
IF TERATANI WAS RIGHT, THEN SHE JUST PLAYED DRUNK THAT TIME.
AND SHE UNDERSTOOD WHEN I SAID I LIKED HER. THIS IS HER INDIRECT WAY OF BLOWING ME OFF!
ANYWAY...
I GUESS OUR JOB IS DONE.
WE CAN GO HOME NOW.
HEY...WAIT! GIVE ME A LITTLE MORE TIME TO FIND OUT WHAT YOU REALLY MEAN!
IORI...
ARE YOU STILL DRUNK?
HUH?

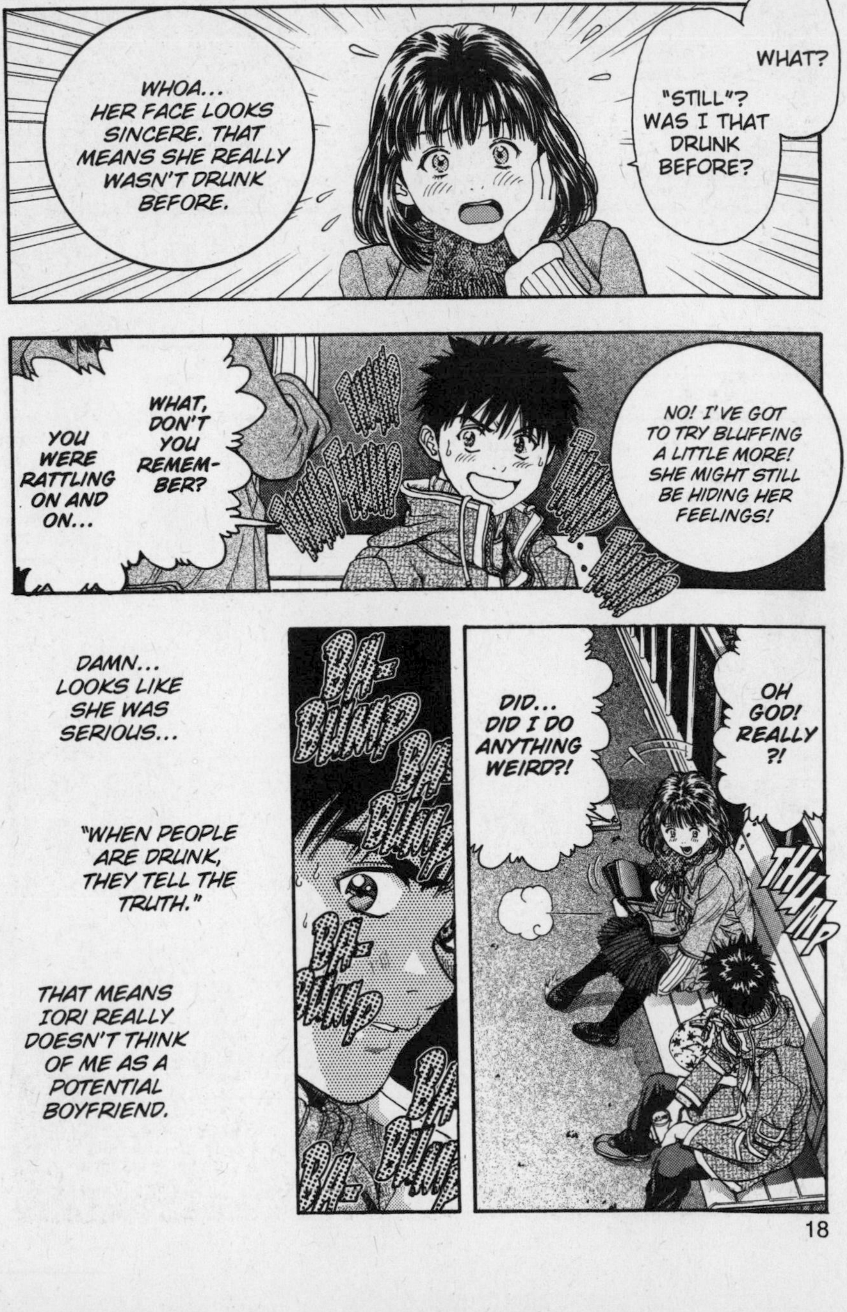
WHAT?
"STILL"? WAS I THAT DRUNK BEFORE?
WHOA... HER FACE LOOKS SINCERE. THAT MEANS SHE REALLY WASN'T DRUNK BEFORE.
NO! I'VE GOT TO TRY BLUFFING A LITTLE MORE! SHE MIGHT STILL BE HIDING HER FEELINGS!
WHAT, DON'T YOU REMEM-BER?
YOU WERE RATTLING ON AND ON...
OH GOD! REALLY ?!
DID... DID I DO ANYTHING WEIRD?!
THUMP
BA-DUMP
DAMN... LOOKS LIKE SHE WAS SERIOUS...
"WHEN PEOPLE ARE DRUNK, THEY TELL THE TRUTH."
THAT MEANS IORI REALLY DOESN'T THINK OF ME AS A POTENTIAL BOYFRIEND.

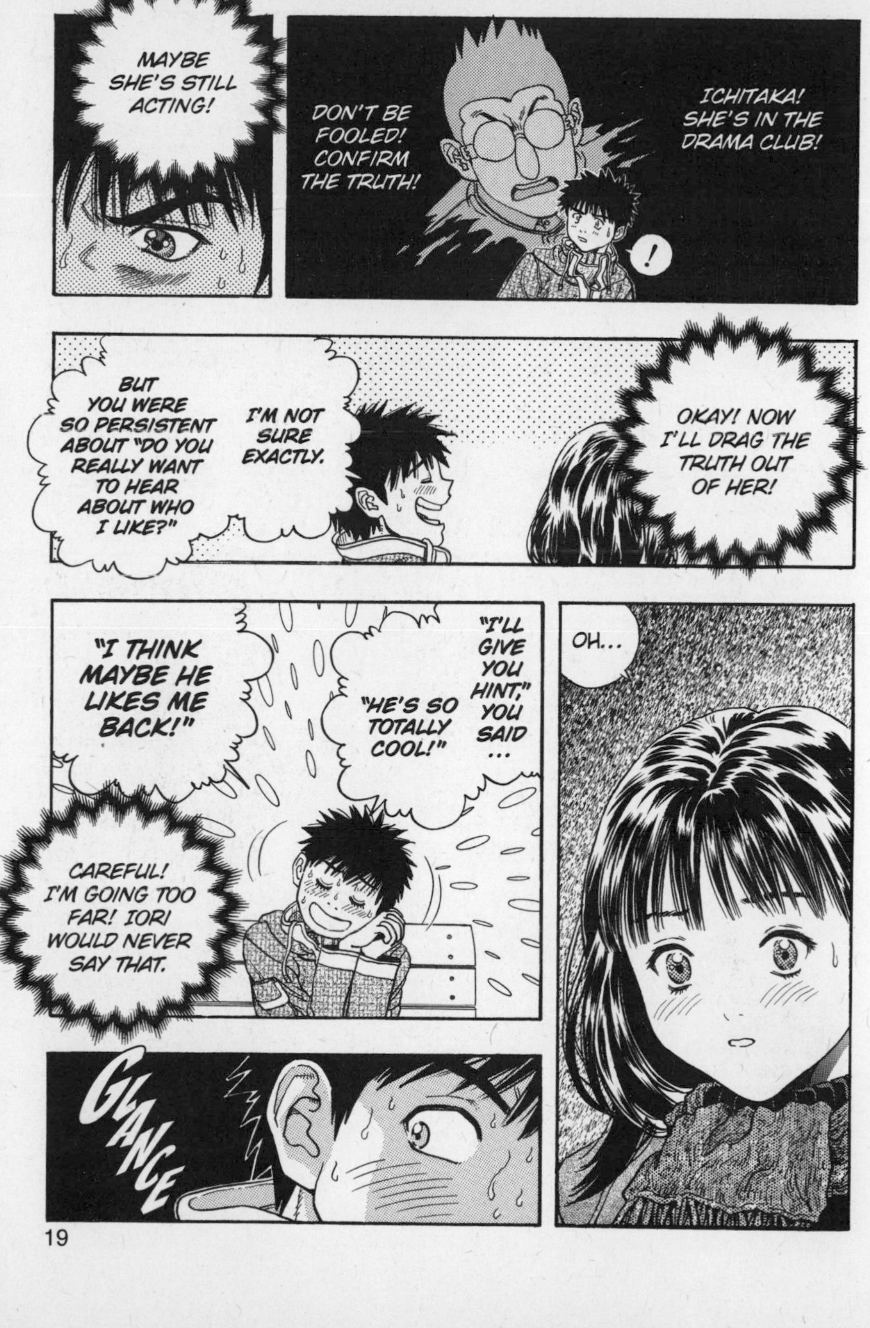
ICHITAKA! SHE'S IN THE DRAMA CLUB!
DON'T BE FOOLED! CONFIRM THE TRUTH!
!
MAYBE SHE'S STILL ACTING!
OKAY! NOW I'LL DRAG THE TRUTH OUT OF HER!
I'M NOT SURE EXACTLY.
BUT YOU WERE SO PERSISTENT ABOUT "DO YOU REALLY WANT TO HEAR ABOUT WHO I LIKE?"
OH...
"I'LL GIVE YOU HINT," YOU SAID...
"HE'S SO TOTALLY COOL!"
"I THINK MAYBE HE LIKES ME BACK!"
CAREFUL! I'M GOING TOO FAR! IORI WOULD NEVER SAY THAT.
GLANCE

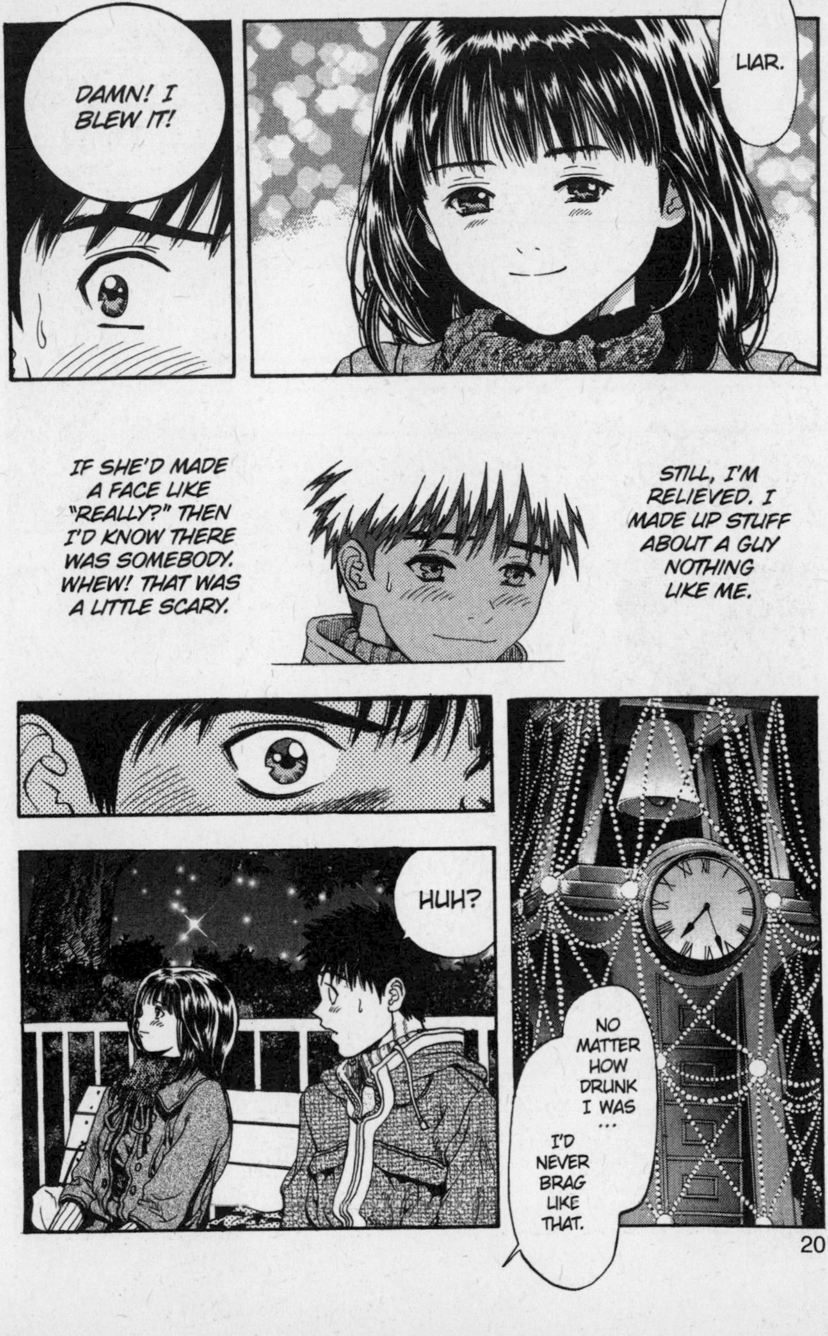
LIAR.
DAMN! I BLEW IT!
STILL, I'M RELIEVED. I MADE UP STUFF ABOUT A GUY NOTHING LIKE ME.
IF SHE'D MADE A FACE LIKE "REALLY?" THEN I'D KNOW THERE WAS SOMEBODY. WHEW! THAT WAS A LITTLE SCARY.
NO MATTER HOW DRUNK I WAS ...
I'D NEVER BRAG LIKE THAT.
HUH?

READ THIS WAY

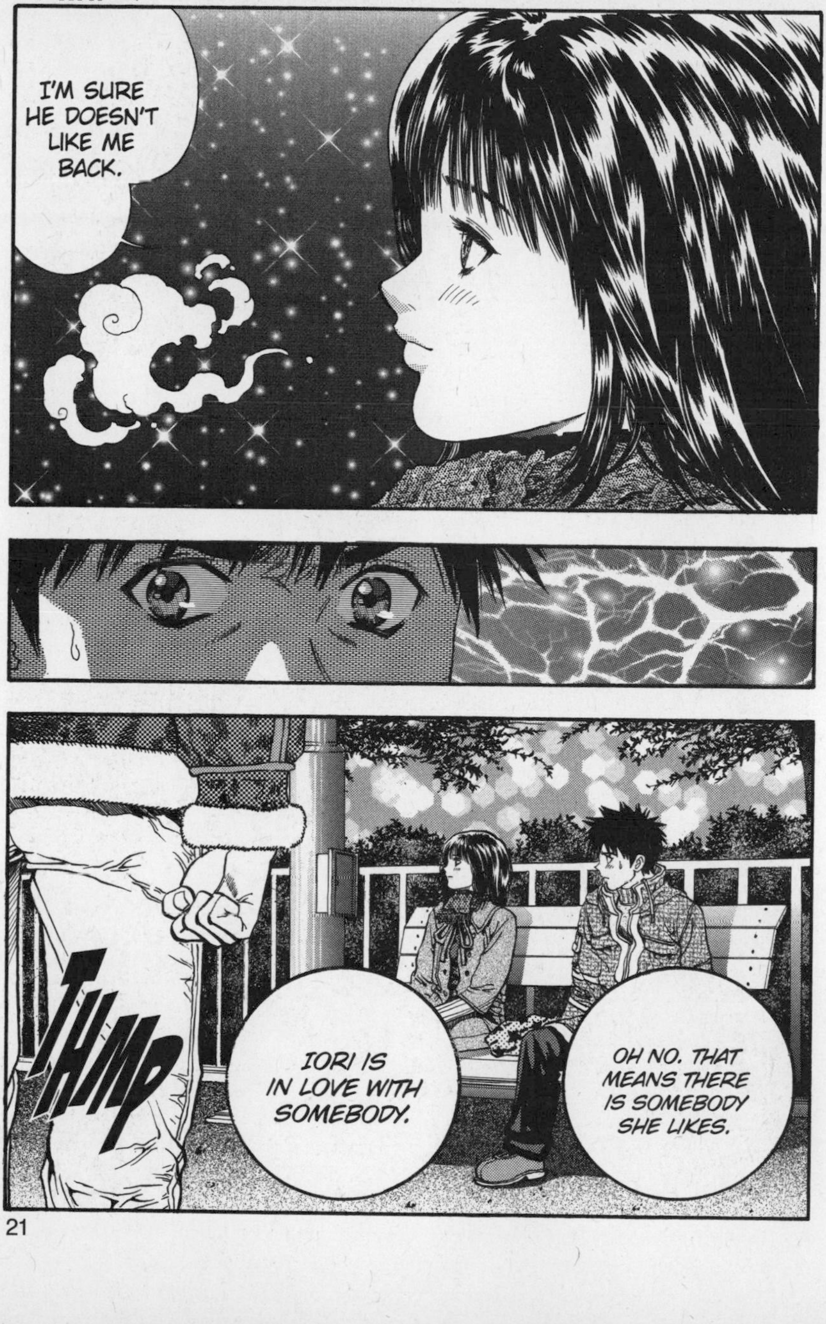

I'M SURE HE DOESN'T LIKE ME BACK.
OH NO. THAT MEANS THERE IS SOMEBODY SHE LIKES.
IORI IS IN LOVE WITH SOMEBODY.
THUMP

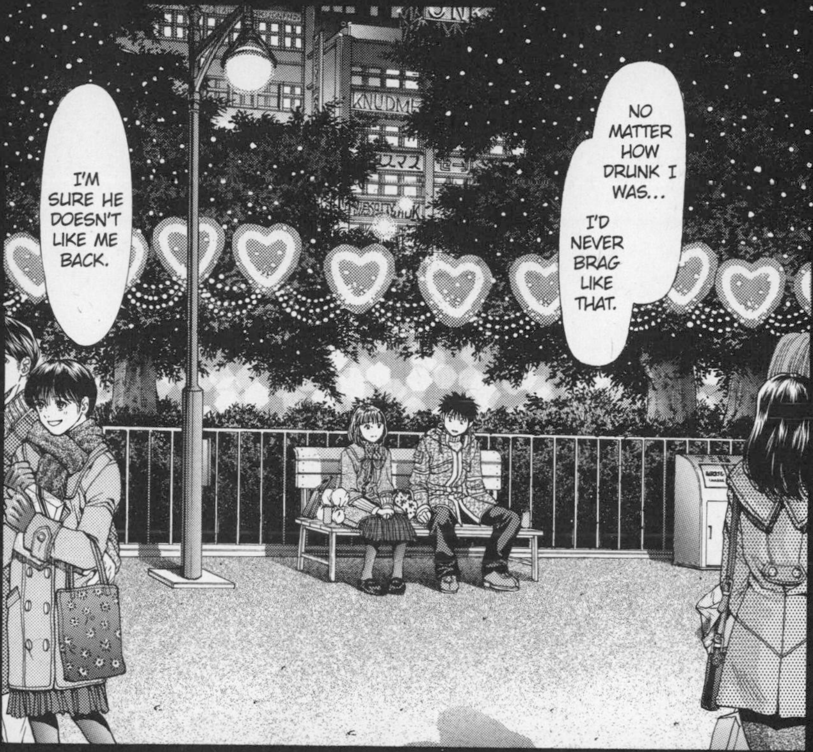
NO MATTER HOW DRUNK I WAS...
I'D NEVER BRAG LIKE THAT.
I'M SURE HE DOESN'T LIKE ME BACK.

Chapter 85: Too Late Now

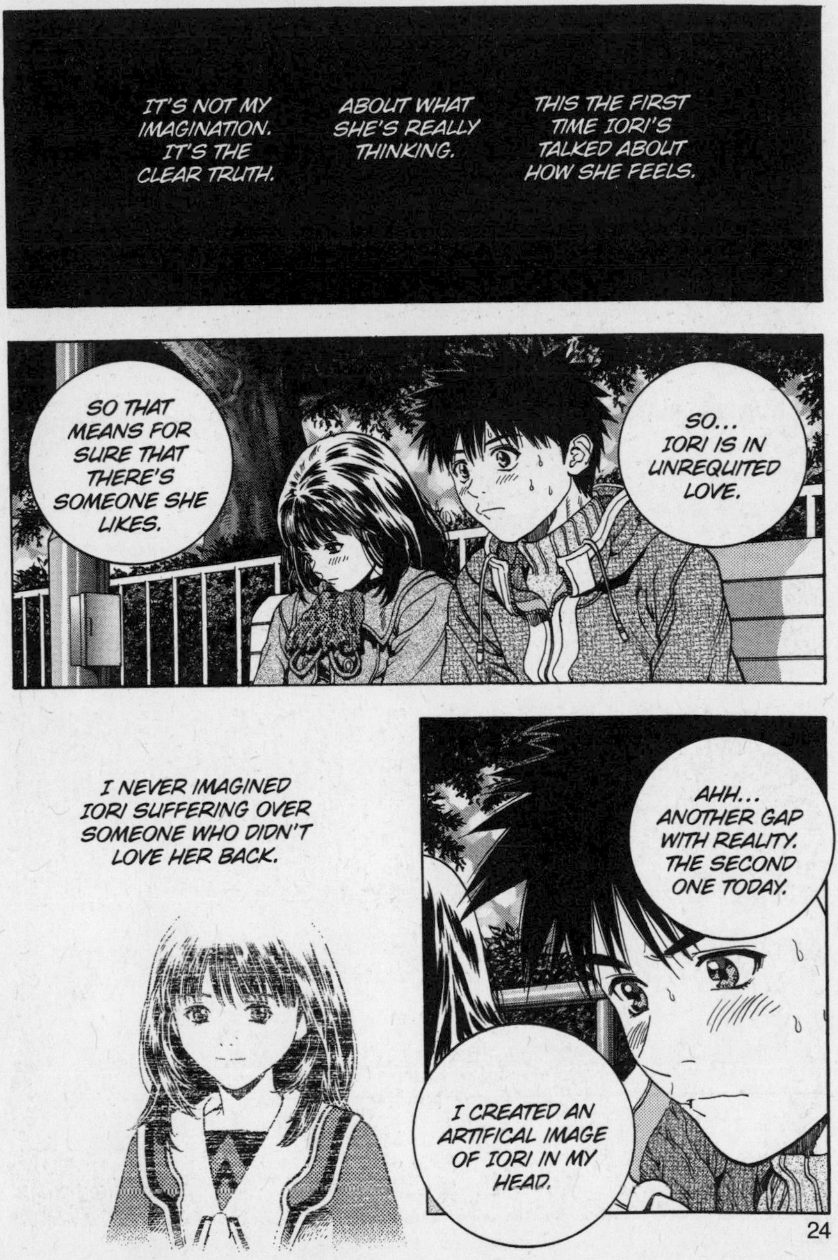
THIS THE FIRST TIME IORI'S TALKED ABOUT HOW SHE FEELS.
ABOUT WHAT SHE'S REALLY THINKING.
IT'S NOT MY IMAGINATION. IT'S THE CLEAR TRUTH.
SO... IORI IS IN UNREQUITED LOVE.
SO THAT MEANS FOR SURE THAT THERE'S SOMEONE SHE LIKES.
AHH... ANOTHER GAP WITH REALITY. THE SECOND ONE TODAY.
I CREATED AN ARTIFICAL IMAGE OF IORI IN MY HEAD.
I NEVER IMAGINED IORI SUFFERING OVER SOMEONE WHO DIDN'T LOVE HER BACK.

READ THIS WAY

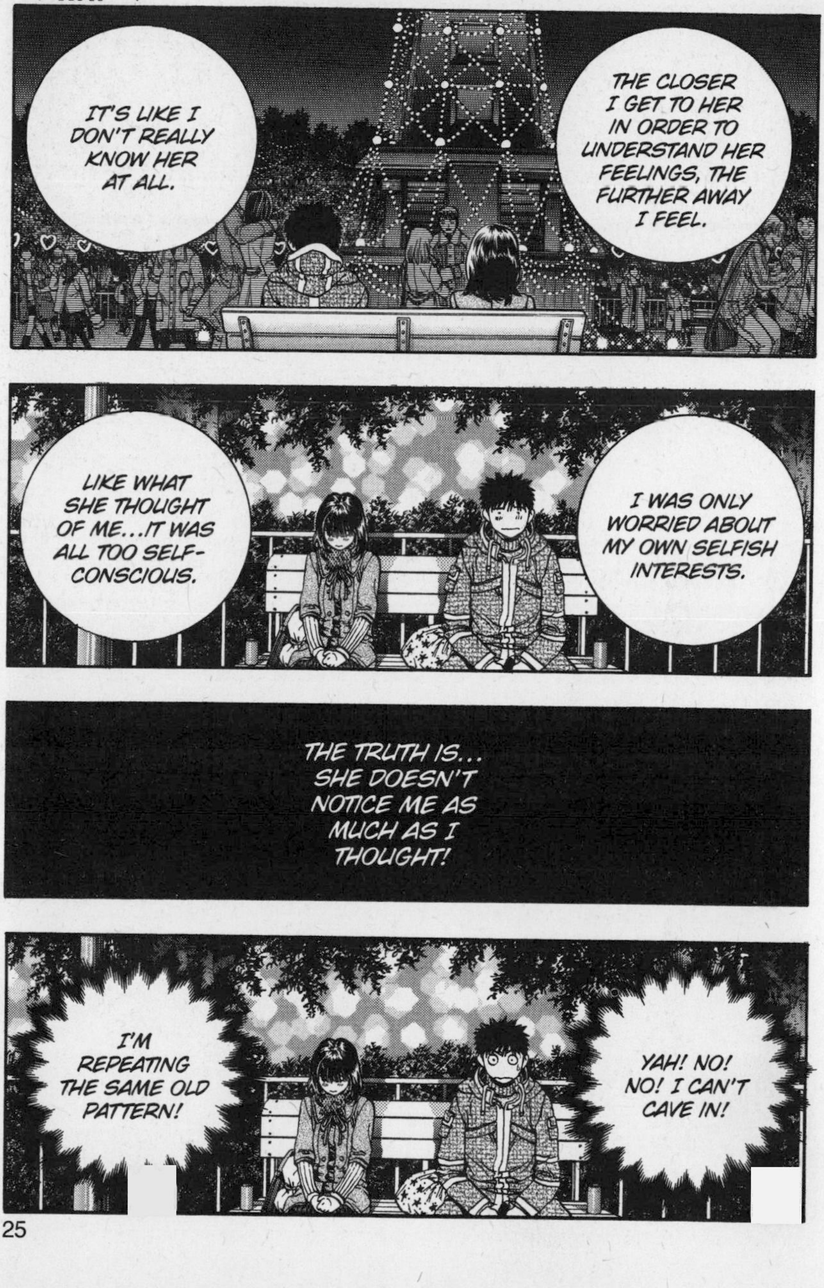
THE CLOSER I GET TO HER IN ORDER TO UNDERSTAND HER FEELINGS, THE FURTHER AWAY I FEEL.
IT'S LIKE I DON'T REALLY KNOW HER AT ALL.
I WAS ONLY WORRIED ABOUT MY OWN SELFISH INTERESTS.
LIKE WHAT SHE THOUGHT OF ME...IT WAS ALL TOO SELF-CONSCIOUS.
THE TRUTH IS... SHE DOESN'T NOTICE ME AS MUCH AS I THOUGHT!
YAH! NO! NO! I CAN'T CAVE IN!
I'M REPEATING THE SAME OLD PATTERN!

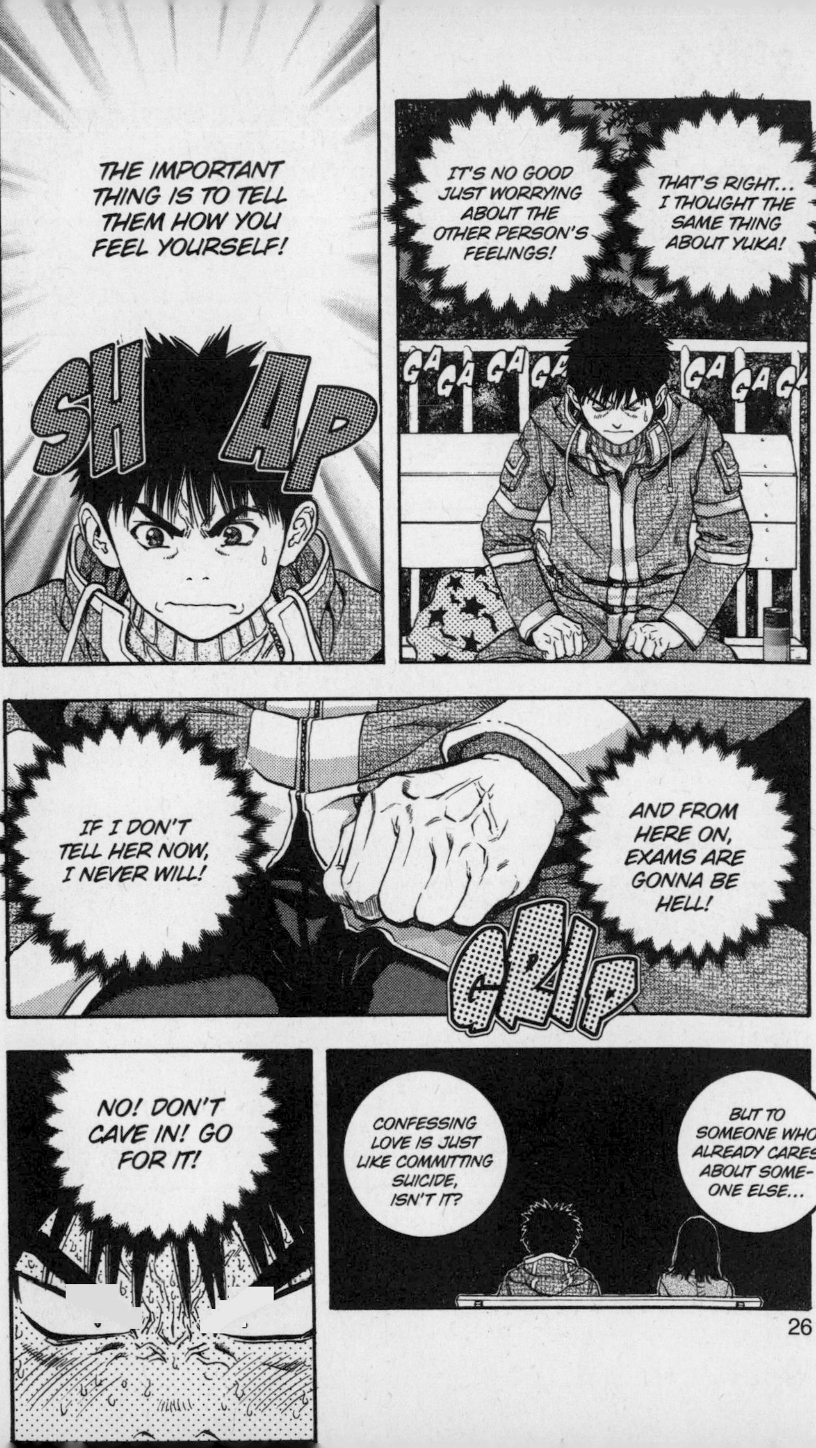
THAT'S RIGHT... I THOUGHT THE SAME THING ABOUT YUKA!
IT'S NO GOOD JUST WORRYING ABOUT THE OTHER PERSON'S FEELINGS!
GA GA GA GA GA GA GA GA GA
THE IMPORTANT THING IS TO TELL THEM HOW YOU FEEL YOURSELF!
SHAP
AND FROM HERE ON, EXAMS ARE GONNA BE HELL!
IF I DON'T TELL HER NOW, I NEVER WILL!
GRIP
BUT TO SOMEONE WHO ALREADY CARES ABOUT SOME-ONE ELSE...
CONFESSING LOVE IS JUST LIKE COMMITTING SUICIDE, ISN'T IT?
NO! DON'T CAVE IN! GO FOR IT!

READ THIS WAY

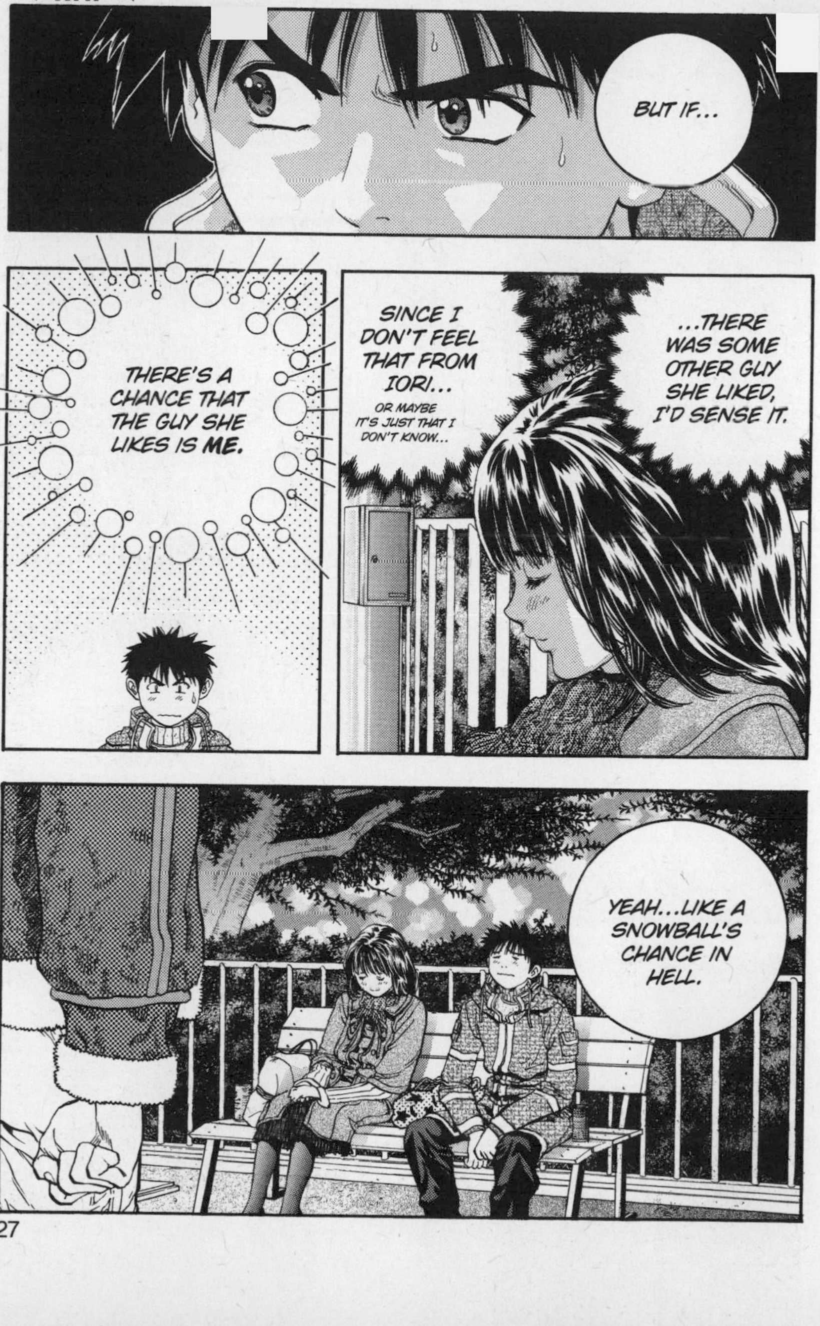
BUT IF...
...THERE WAS SOME OTHER GUY SHE LIKED, I'D SENSE IT.
SINCE I DON'T FEEL THAT FROM IORI...
OR MAYBE IT'S JUST THAT I DON'T KNOW...
THERE'S A CHANCE THAT THE GUY SHE LIKES IS ME.
YEAH...LIKE A SNOWBALL'S CHANCE IN HELL.

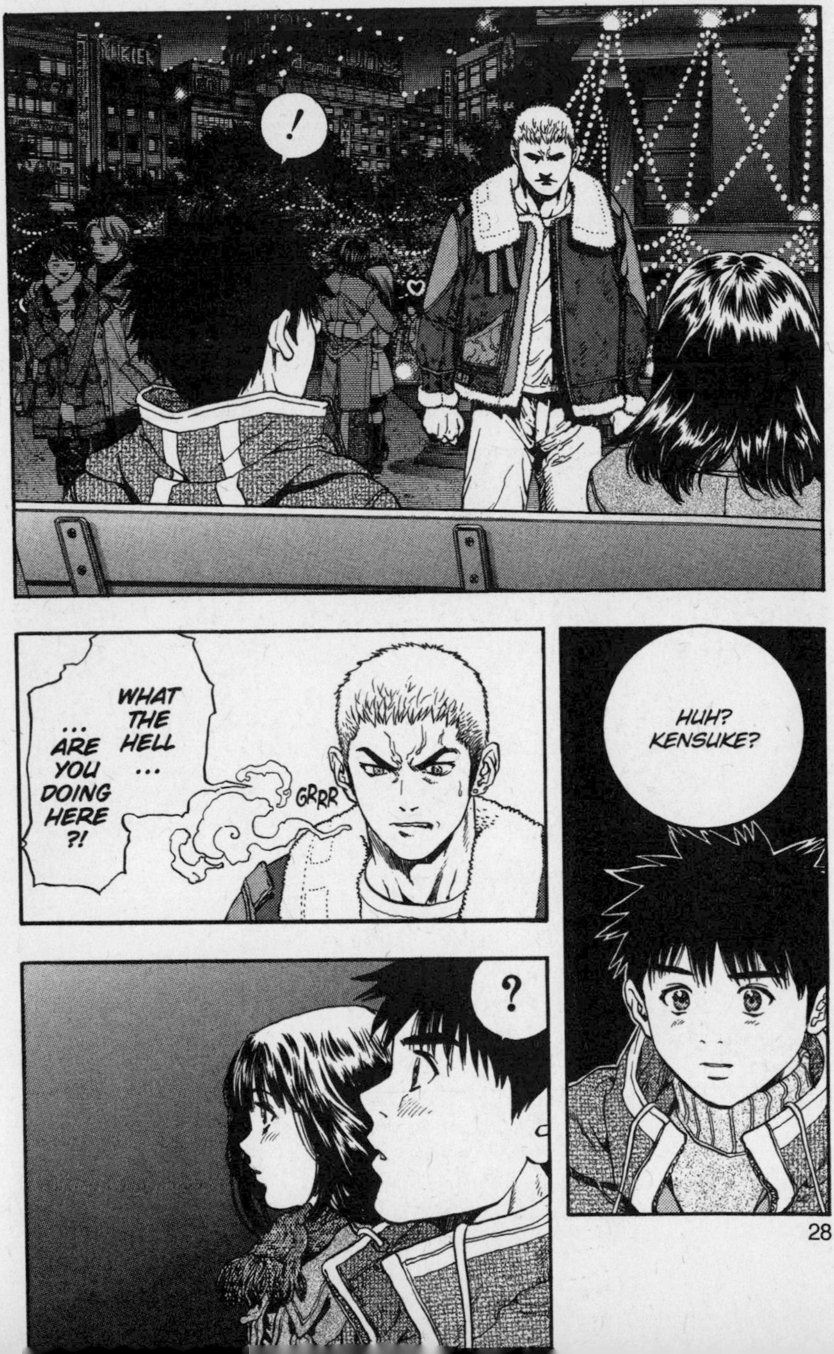
!
HUH? KENSUKE?
WHAT THE HELL ...
... ARE YOU DOING HERE ?!
GRRR
?

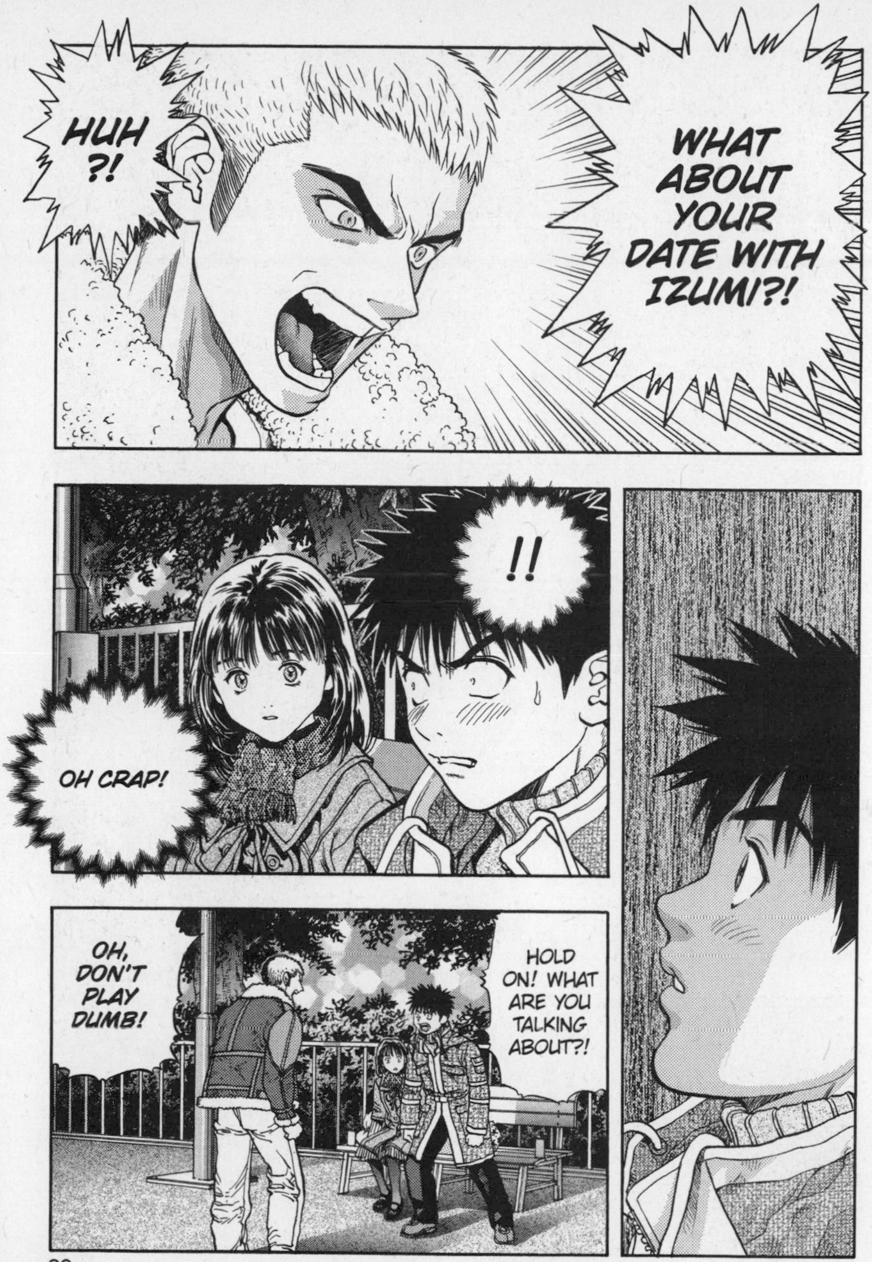
WHAT ABOUT YOUR DATE WITH IZUMI?!
HUH ?!
!!
OH CRAP!
HOLD ON! WHAT ARE YOU TALKING ABOUT?!
OH, DON'T PLAY DUMB!

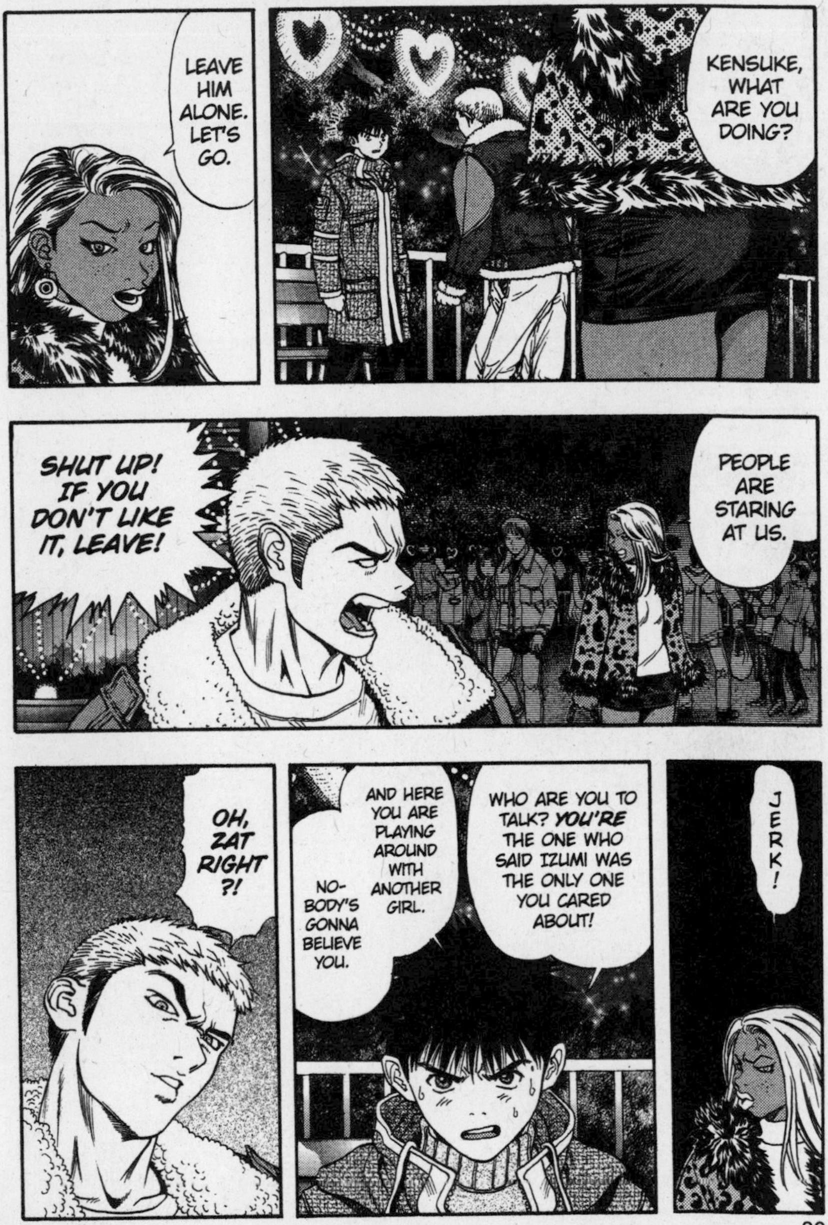
KENSUKE, WHAT ARE YOU DOING?
LEAVE HIM ALONE. LET'S GO.
PEOPLE ARE STARING AT US.
SHUT UP! IF YOU DON'T LIKE IT, LEAVE!
JERK!
WHO ARE YOU TO TALK? YOU'RE THE ONE WHO SAID IZUMI WAS THE ONLY ONE YOU CARED ABOUT!
AND HERE YOU ARE PLAYING AROUND WITH ANOTHER GIRL.
NO-BODY'S GONNA BELIEVE YOU.
OH, ZAT RIGHT?!

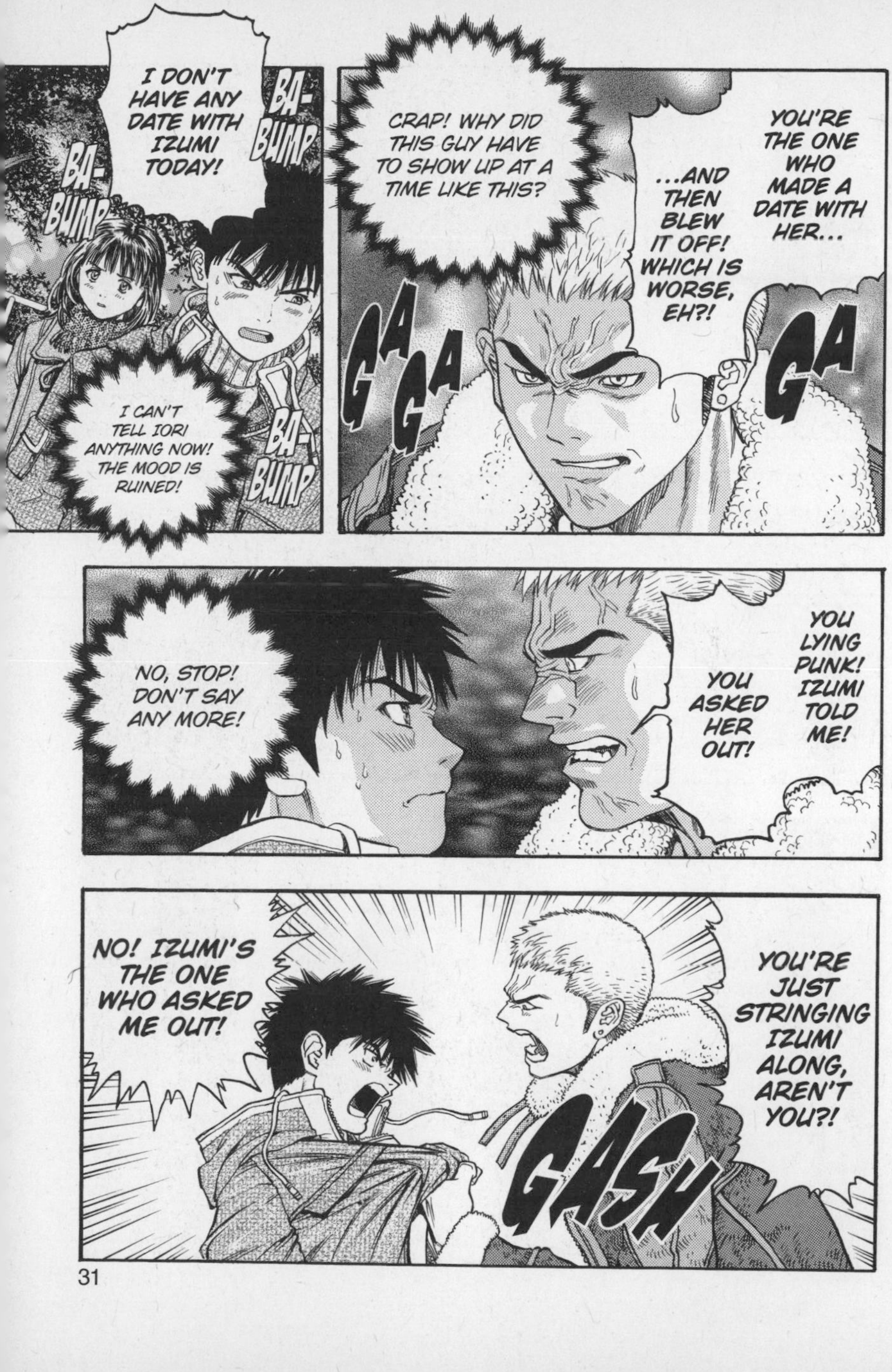
YOU'RE THE ONE WHO MADE A DATE WITH HER...
...AND THEN BLEW IT OFF! WHICH IS WORSE, EH?!
GA
CRAP! WHY DID THIS GUY HAVE TO SHOW UP AT A TIME LIKE THIS?
GAGA
I DON'T HAVE ANY DATE WITH IZUMI TODAY!
BA-BUMP
BA-BUMP
BA-BUMP
I CAN'T TELL IORI ANYTHING NOW! THE MOOD IS RUINED!
YOU LYING PUNK! IZUMI TOLD ME!
YOU ASKED HER OUT!
NO, STOP! DON'T SAY ANY MORE!
YOU'RE JUST STRINGING IZUMI ALONG, AREN'T YOU?!
GASH
NO! IZUMI'S THE ONE WHO ASKED ME OUT!

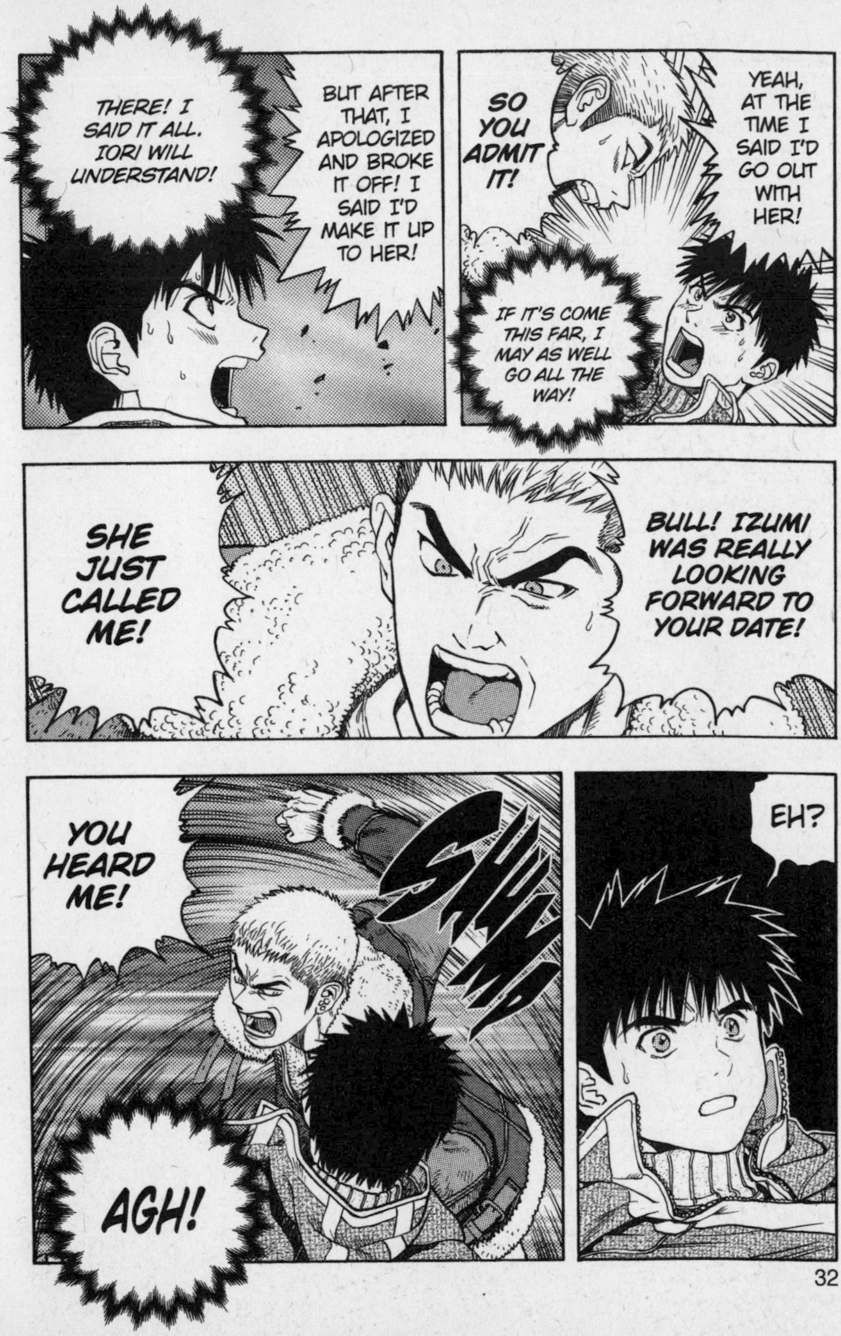
YEAH, AT THE TIME I SAID I'D GO OUT WITH HER!
SO YOU ADMIT IT!
IF IT'S COME THIS FAR, I MAY AS WELL GO ALL THE WAY!
BUT AFTER THAT, I APOLOGIZED AND BROKE IT OFF! I SAID I'D MAKE IT UP TO HER!
THERE! I SAID IT ALL. IORI WILL UNDERSTAND!
BULL! IZUMI WAS REALLY LOOKING FORWARD TO YOUR DATE!
SHE JUST CALLED ME!
EH?
YOU HEARD ME!
AGH!

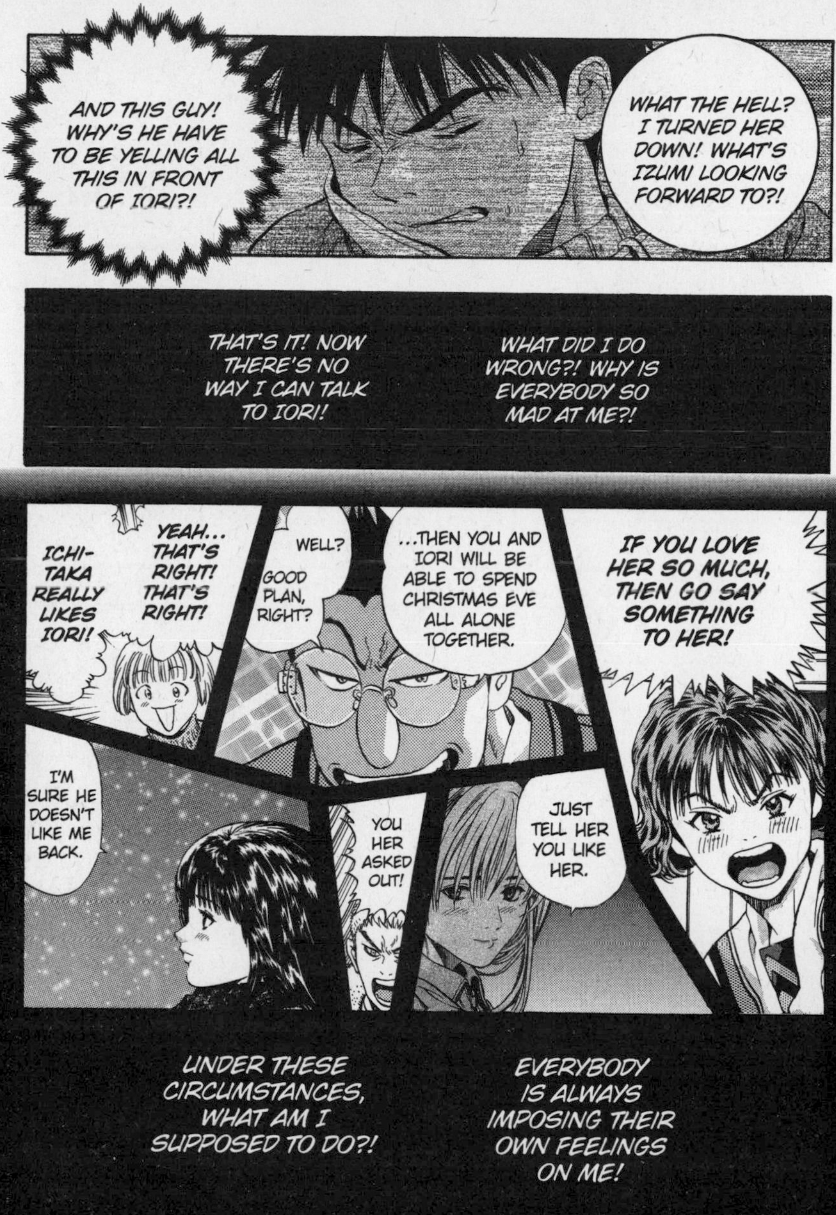
WHAT THE HELL? I TURNED HER DOWN! WHAT'S IZUMI LOOKING FORWARD TO?!
AND THIS GUY! WHY'S HE HAVE TO BE YELLING ALL THIS IN FRONT OF IORI?!
WHAT DID I DO WRONG?! WHY IS EVERYBODY SO MAD AT ME?!
THAT'S IT! NOW THERE'S NO WAY I CAN TALK TO IORI!
IF YOU LOVE HER SO MUCH, THEN GO SAY SOMETHING TO HER!
...THEN YOU AND IORI WILL BE ABLE TO SPEND CHRISTMAS EVE ALL ALONE TOGETHER.
WELL?
GOOD PLAN, RIGHT?
YEAH... THAT'S RIGHT! THAT'S RIGHT!
ICHI-TAKA REALLY LIKES IORI!
JUST TELL HER YOU LIKE HER.
YOU HER ASKED OUT!
I'M SURE HE DOESN'T LIKE ME BACK.
EVERYBODY IS ALWAYS IMPOSING THEIR OWN FEELINGS ON ME!
UNDER THESE CIRCUMSTANCES, WHAT AM I SUPPOSED TO DO?!

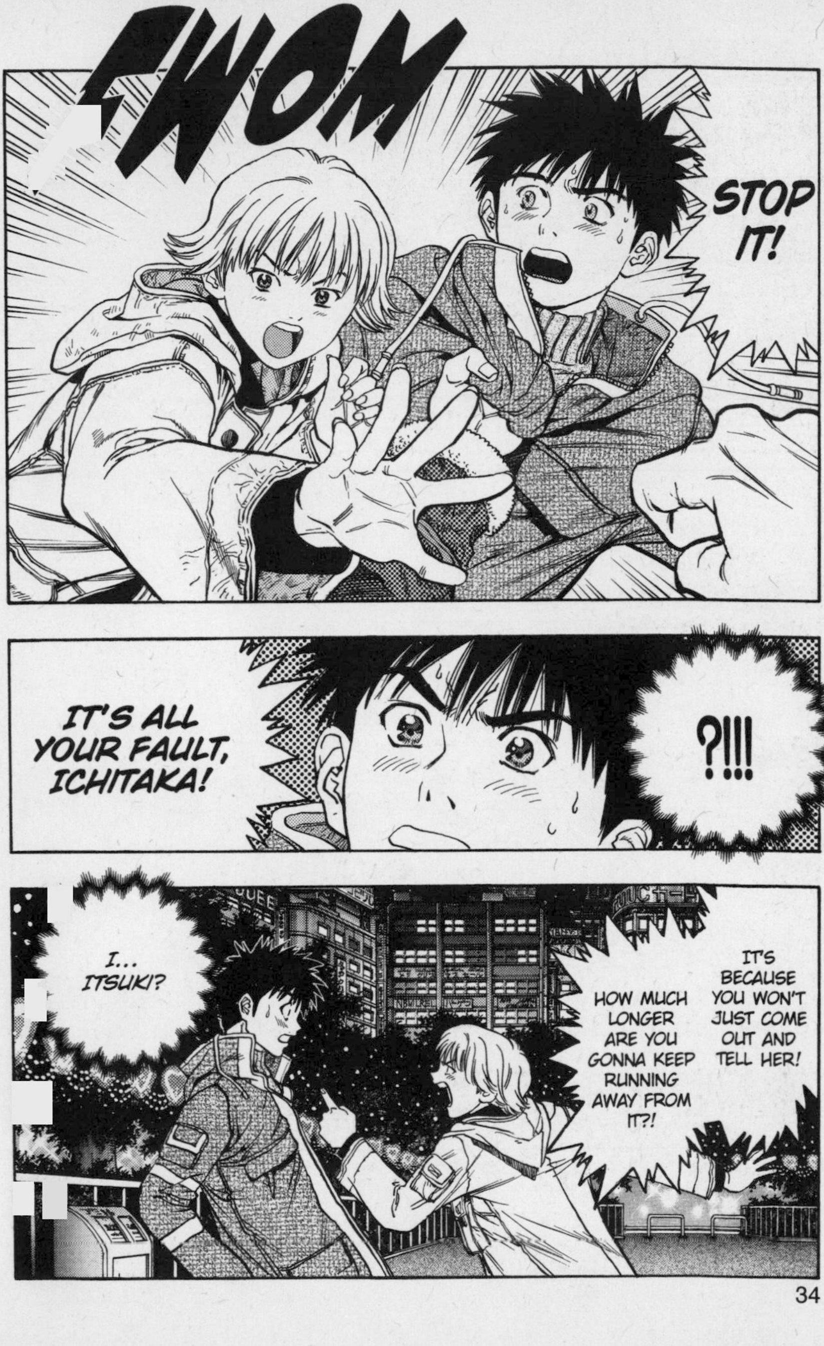
FWOM
STOP IT!
?!!!
IT'S ALL YOUR FAULT, ICHITAKA!
IT'S BECAUSE YOU WON'T JUST COME OUT AND TELL HER!
HOW MUCH LONGER ARE YOU GONNA KEEP RUNNING AWAY FROM IT?!
I... ITSUKI?

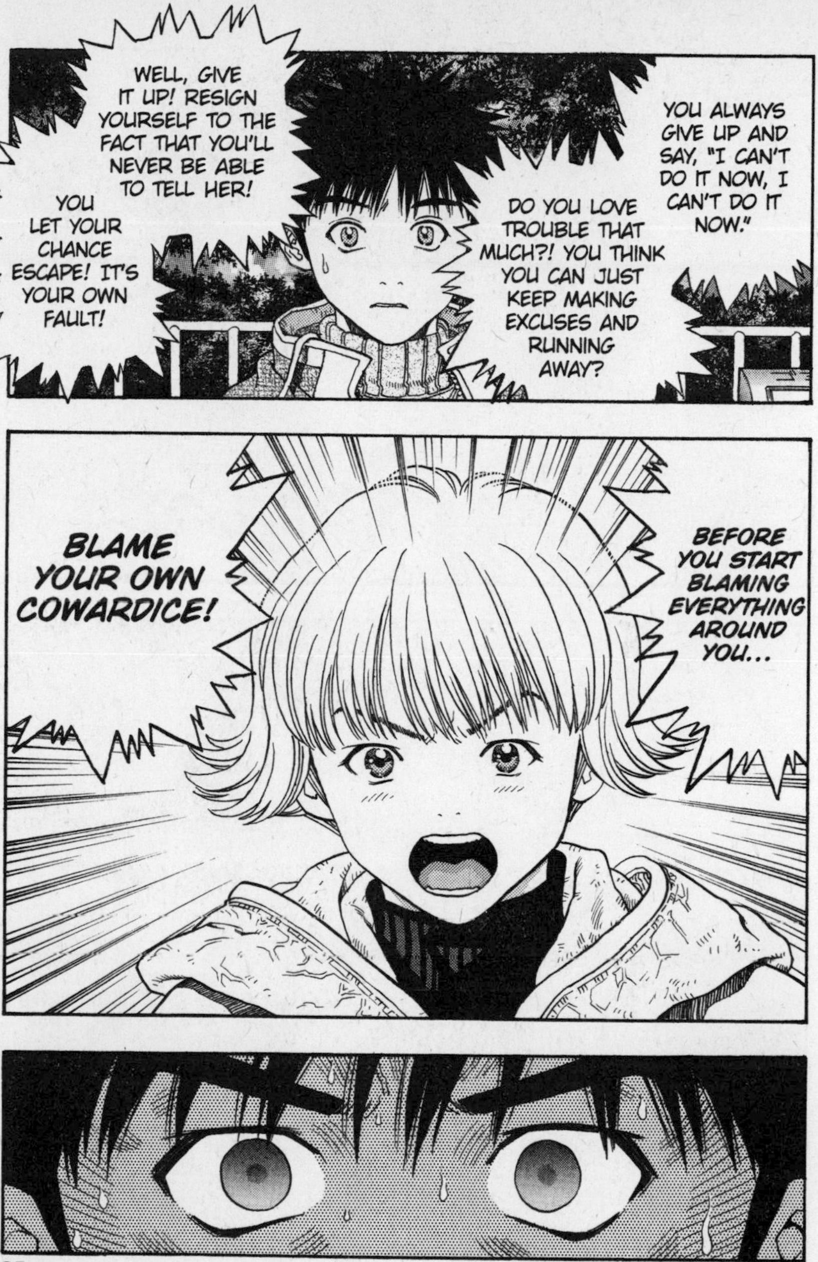
YOU ALWAYS GIVE UP AND SAY, "I CAN'T DO IT NOW, I CAN'T DO IT NOW."
DO YOU LOVE TROUBLE THAT MUCH?! YOU THINK YOU CAN JUST KEEP MAKING EXCUSES AND RUNNING AWAY?
WELL, GIVE IT UP! RESIGN YOURSELF TO THE FACT THAT YOU'LL NEVER BE ABLE TO TELL HER!
YOU LET YOUR CHANCE ESCAPE! IT'S YOUR OWN FAULT!
BEFORE YOU START BLAMING EVERYTHING AROUND YOU...
BLAME YOUR OWN COWARDICE!

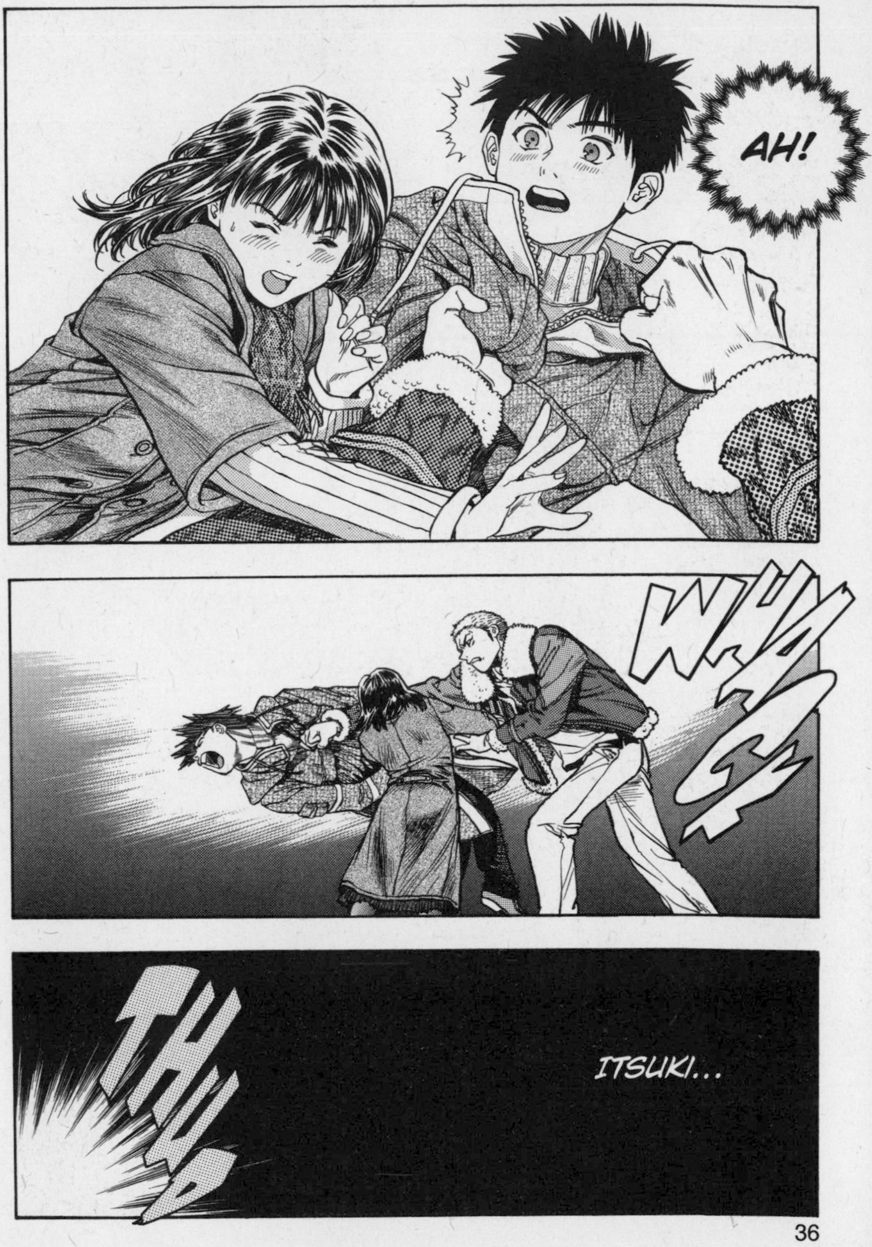
AH!
WHACK
ITSUKI...
THUD

READ THIS WAY

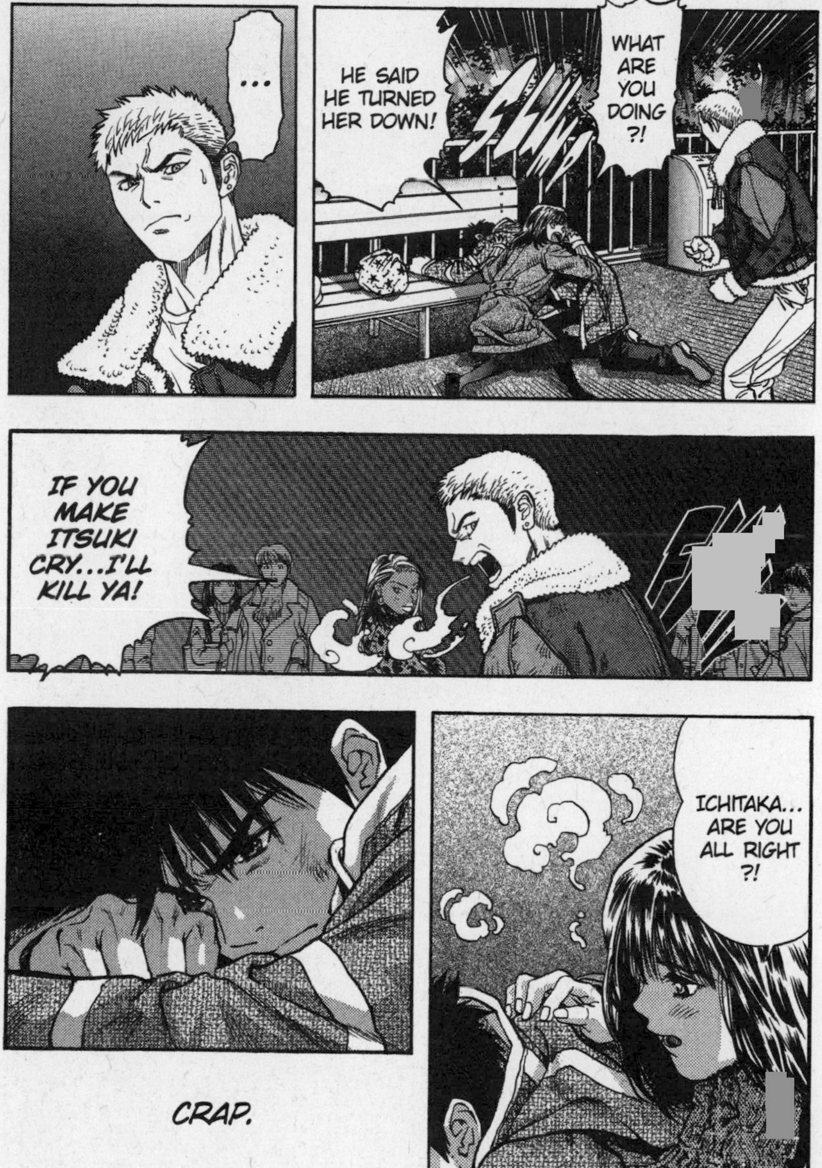
WHAT ARE YOU DOING ?!
HE SAID HE TURNED HER DOWN!
...
IF YOU MAKE ITSUKI CRY...I'LL KILL YA!
ICHITAKA... ARE YOU ALL RIGHT ?!
CRAP.

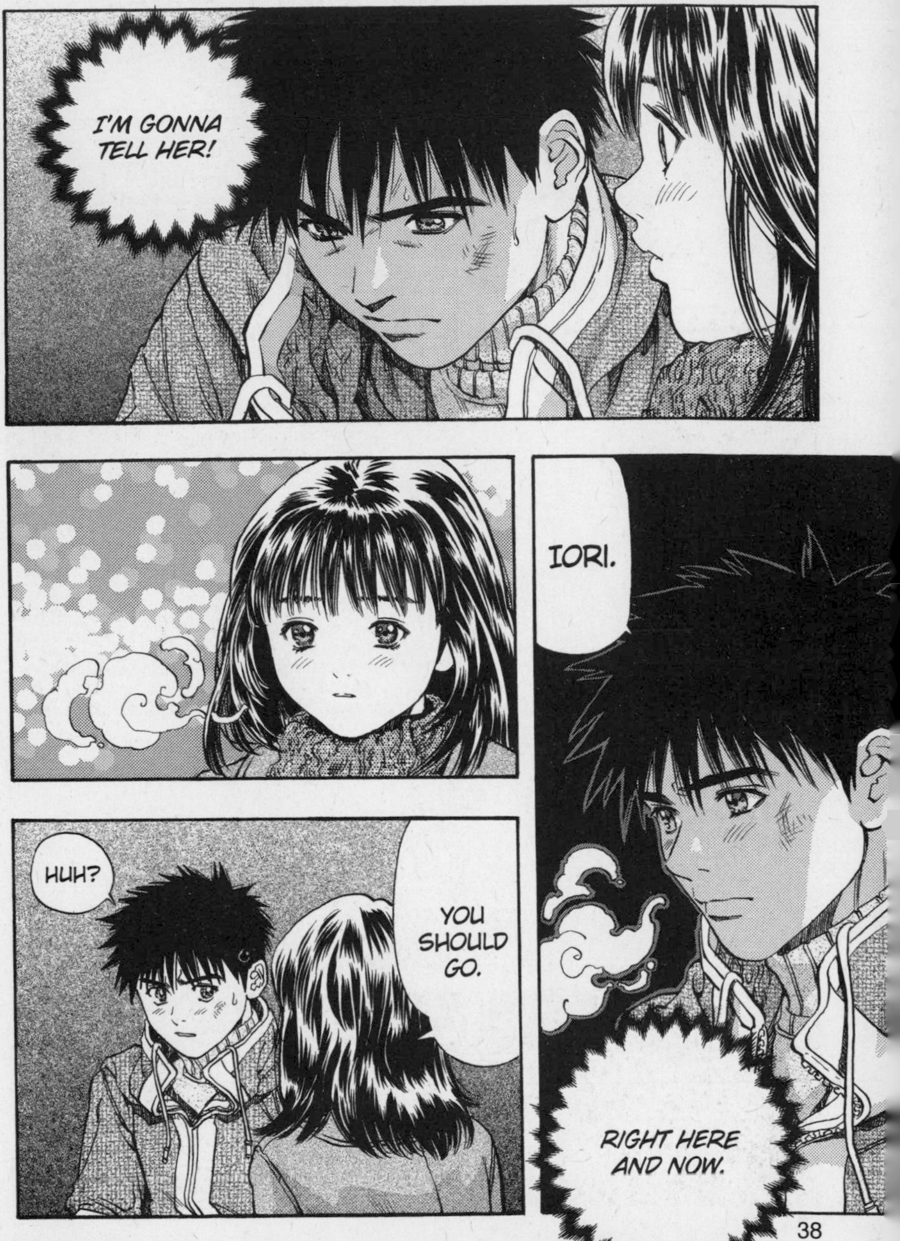
I'M GONNA TELL HER!
IORI.
RIGHT HERE AND NOW.
YOU SHOULD GO.
HUH?

READ THIS WAY

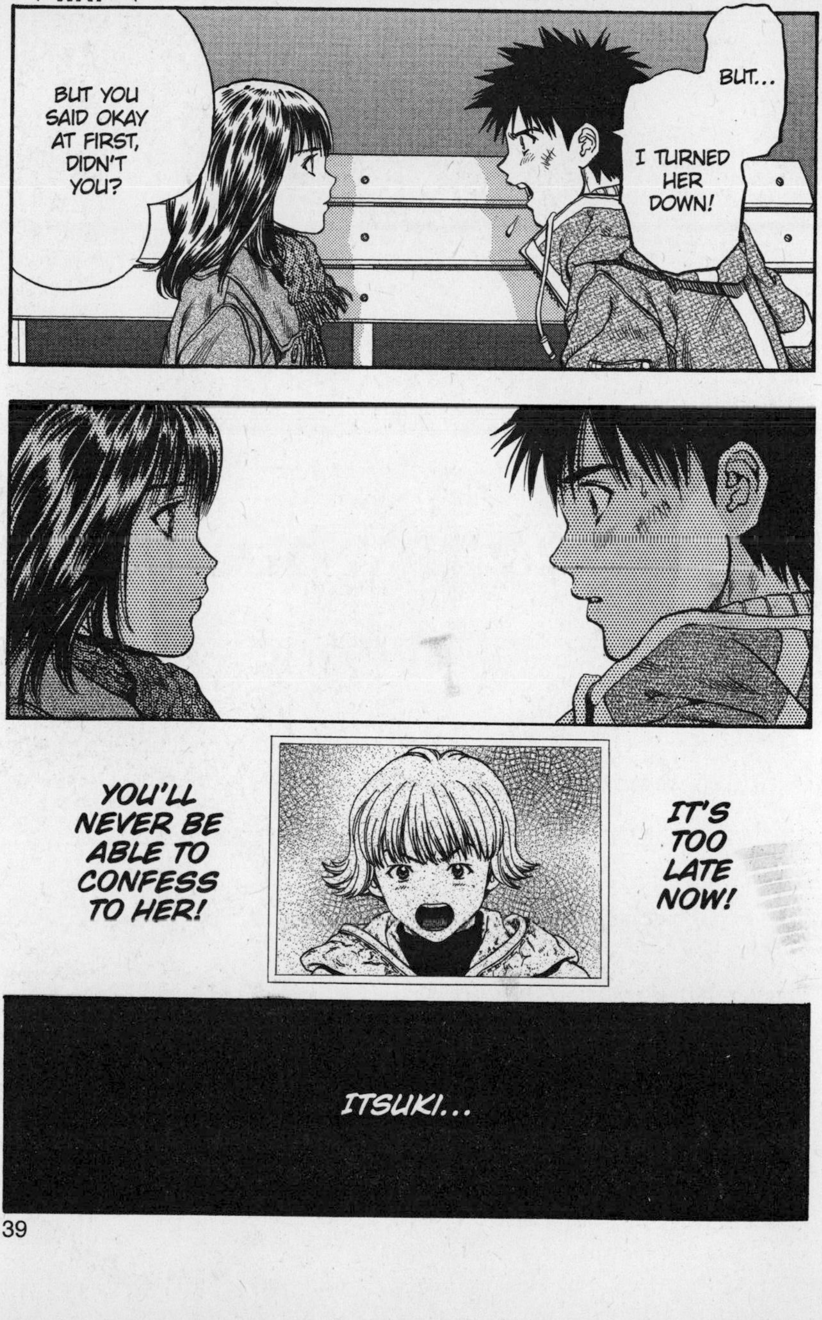
BUT...
I TURNED HER DOWN!
BUT YOU SAID OKAY AT FIRST, DIDN'T YOU?
IT'S TOO LATE NOW!
YOU'LL NEVER BE ABLE TO CONFESS TO HER!
ITSUKI...

Chapter 86:
I Win

READ THIS WAY

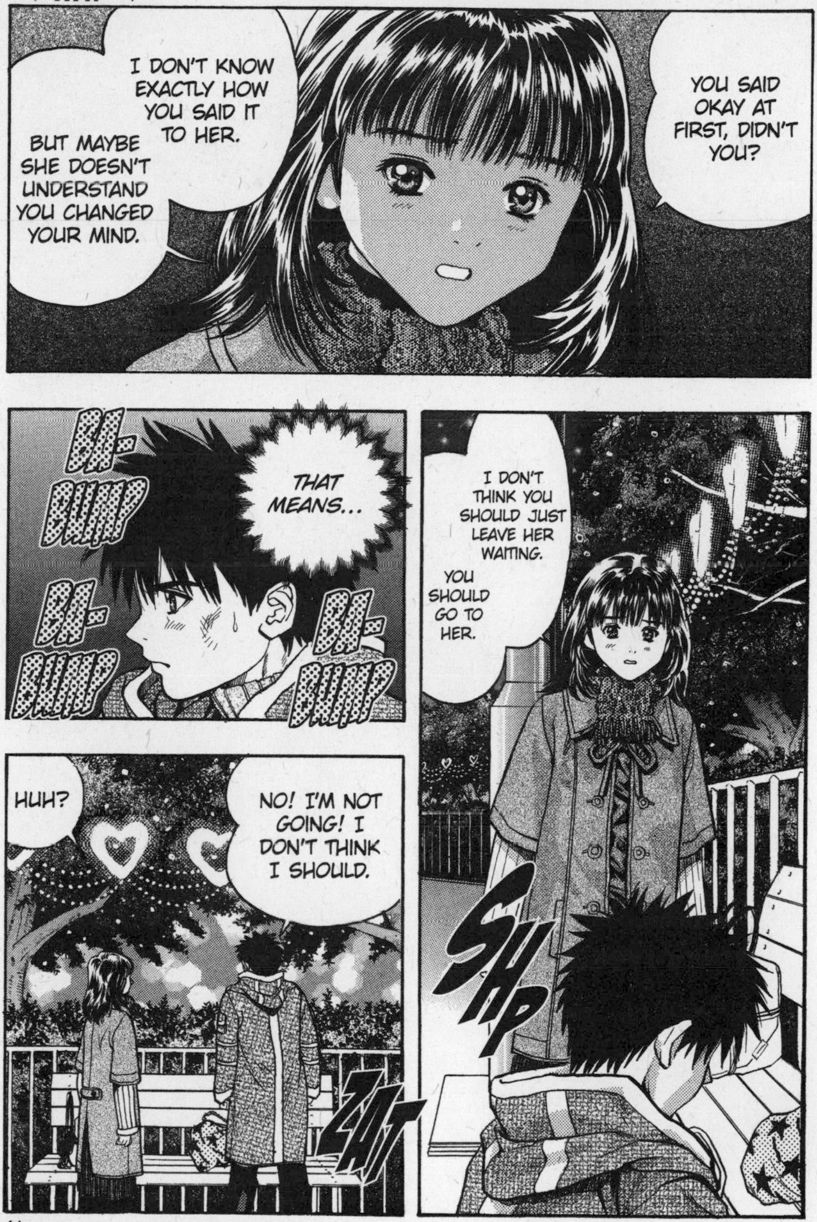
YOU SAID OKAY AT FIRST, DIDN'T YOU?
I DON'T KNOW EXACTLY HOW YOU SAID IT TO HER.
BUT MAYBE SHE DOESN'T UNDERSTAND YOU CHANGED YOUR MIND.
I DON'T THINK YOU SHOULD JUST LEAVE HER WAITING.
YOU SHOULD GO TO HER.
SHP
THAT MEANS...
BA-BUMP
BA-BUMP
BA-BUMP
NO! I'M NOT GOING! I DON'T THINK I SHOULD.
HUH?
ZAT

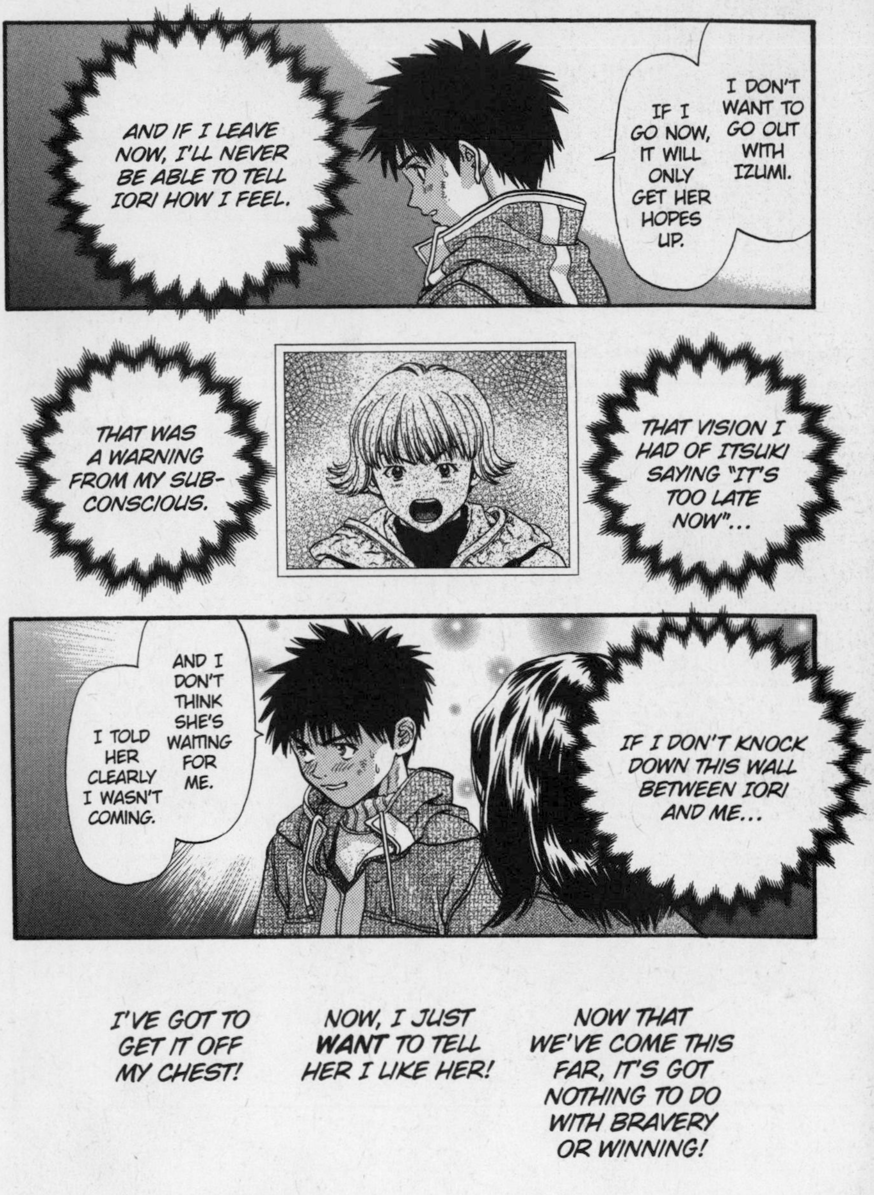
I DON'T WANT TO GO OUT WITH IZUMI.
IF I GO NOW, IT WILL ONLY GET HER HOPES UP.
AND IF I LEAVE NOW, I'LL NEVER BE ABLE TO TELL IORI HOW I FEEL.
THAT VISION I HAD OF ITSUKI SAYING "IT'S TOO LATE NOW"...
THAT WAS A WARNING FROM MY SUB-CONSCIOUS.
IF I DON'T KNOCK DOWN THIS WALL BETWEEN IORI AND ME...
AND I DON'T THINK SHE'S WAITING FOR ME.
I TOLD HER CLEARLY I WASN'T COMING.
NOW THAT WE'VE COME THIS FAR, IT'S GOT NOTHING TO DO WITH BRAVERY OR WINNING!
NOW, I JUST **WANT** TO TELL HER I LIKE HER!
I'VE GOT TO GET IT OFF MY CHEST!

READ THIS WAY

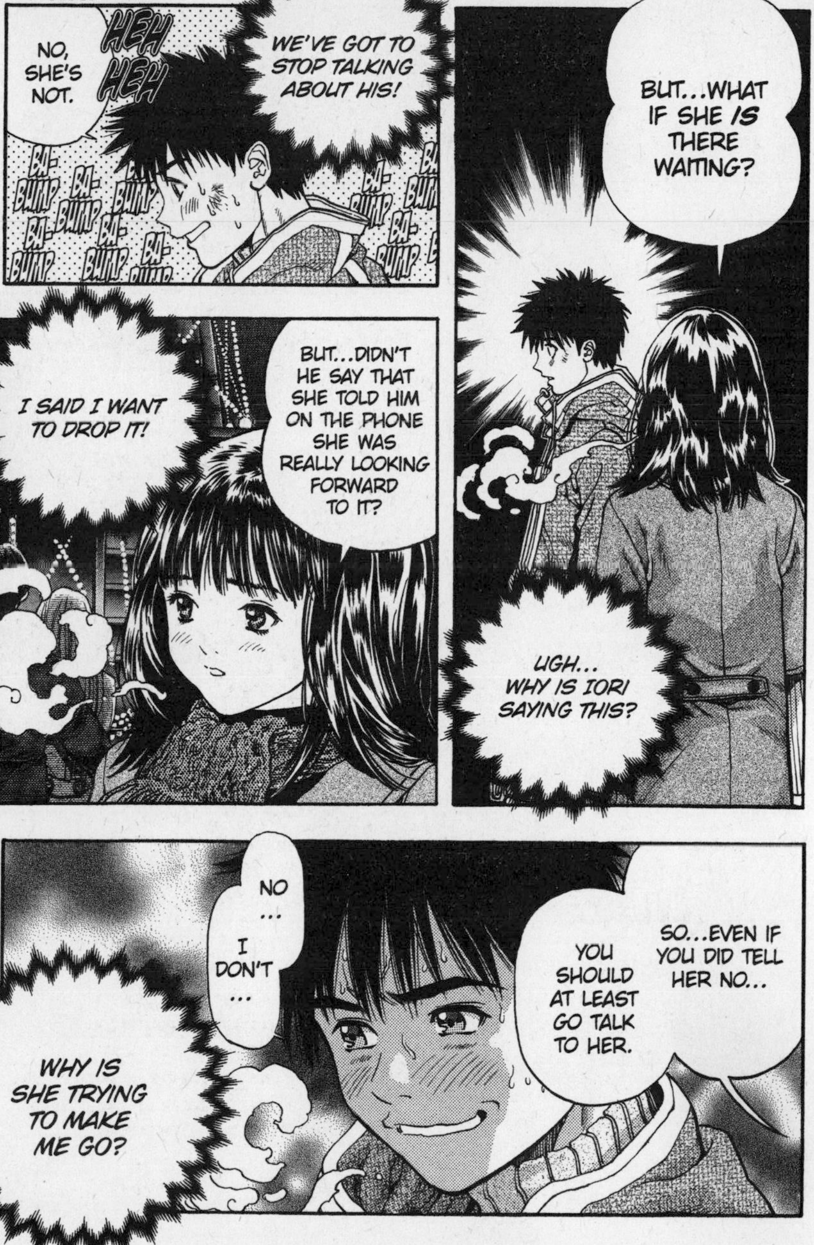
BUT...WHAT IF SHE *IS* THERE WAITING?
UGH... WHY IS IORI SAYING THIS?
WE'VE GOT TO STOP TALKING ABOUT HIS!
HEH HEH
NO, SHE'S NOT.
BA-BUMP BA-BUMP BA-BUMP BA-BUMP BA-BUMP BA-BUMP BA-BUMP BA-BUMP
BUT...DIDN'T HE SAY THAT SHE TOLD HIM ON THE PHONE SHE WAS REALLY LOOKING FORWARD TO IT?
I SAID I WANT TO DROP IT!
SO...EVEN IF YOU DID TELL HER NO...
YOU SHOULD AT LEAST GO TALK TO HER.
NO... I DON'T...
WHY IS SHE TRYING TO MAKE ME GO?

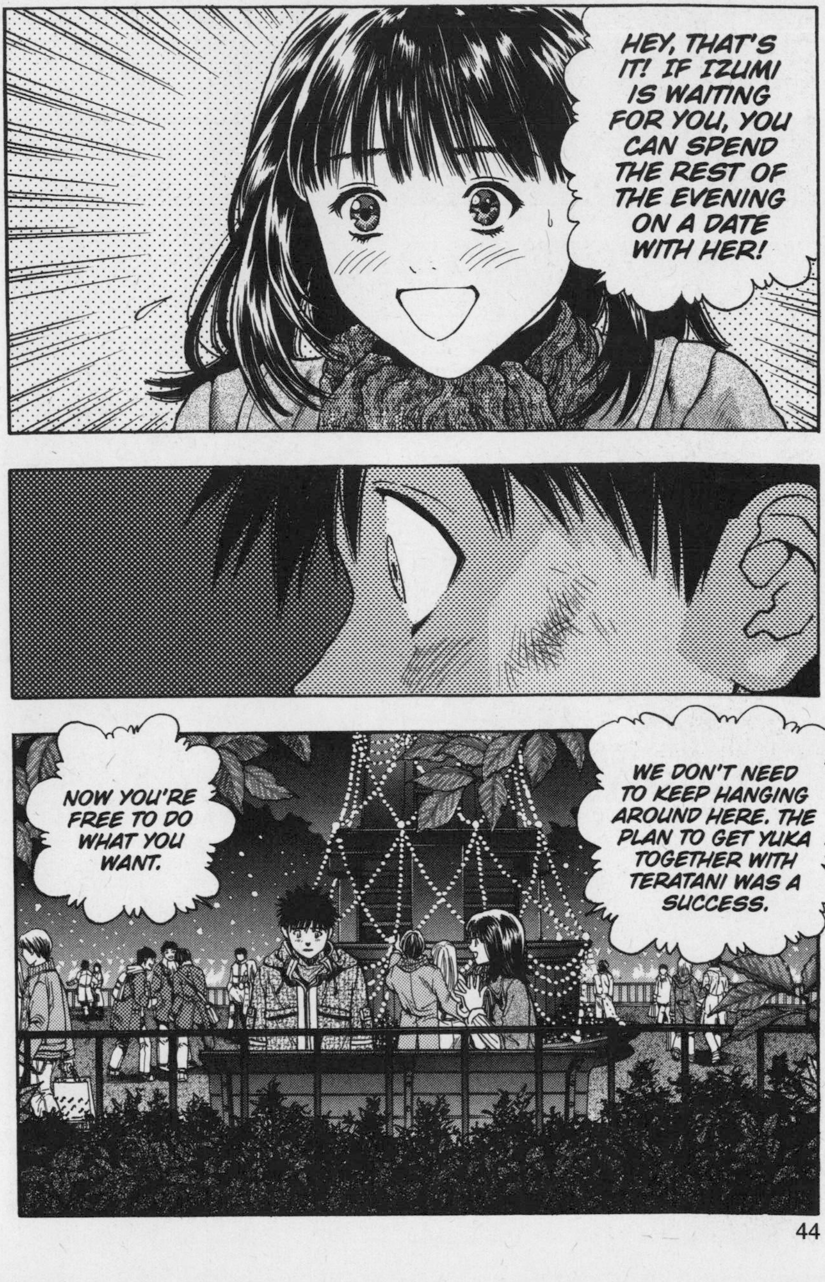
HEY, THAT'S IT! IF IZUMI IS WAITING FOR YOU, YOU CAN SPEND THE REST OF THE EVENING ON A DATE WITH HER!
WE DON'T NEED TO KEEP HANGING AROUND HERE. THE PLAN TO GET YUKA TOGETHER WITH TERATANI WAS A SUCCESS.
NOW YOU'RE FREE TO DO WHAT YOU WANT.

READ THIS WAY

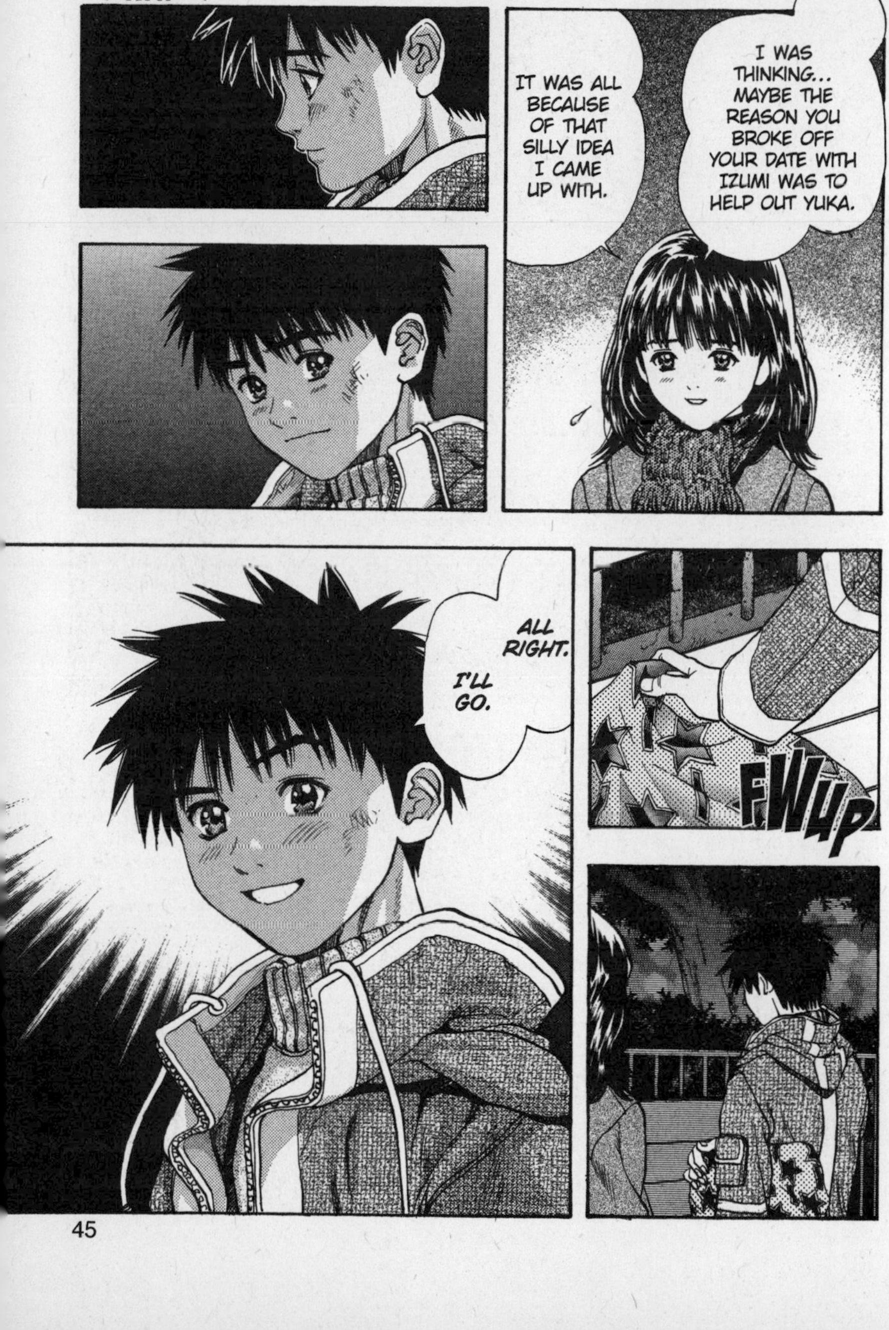

I WAS THINKING... MAYBE THE REASON YOU BROKE OFF YOUR DATE WITH IZUMI WAS TO HELP OUT YUKA.
IT WAS ALL BECAUSE OF THAT SILLY IDEA I CAME UP WITH.
FWUP
ALL RIGHT.
I'LL GO.

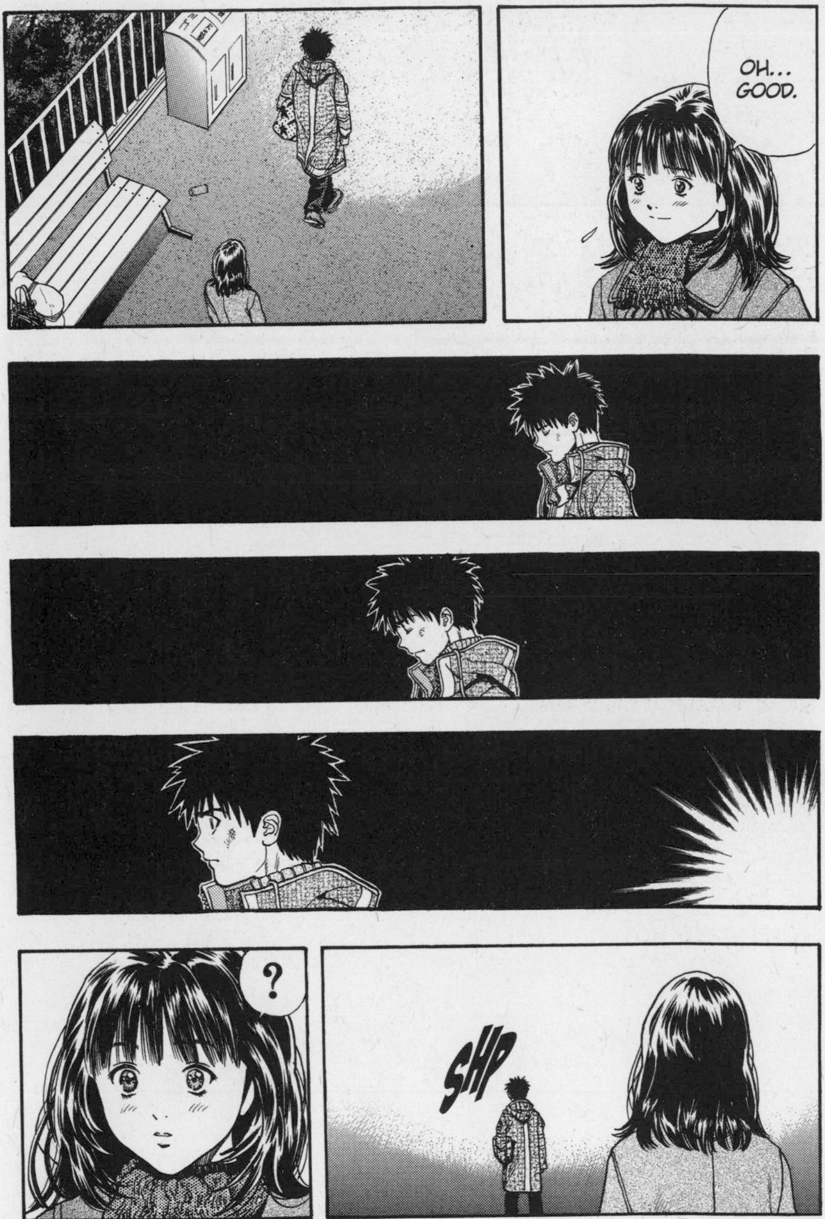
OH... GOOD.
SHP
?

READ THIS WAY

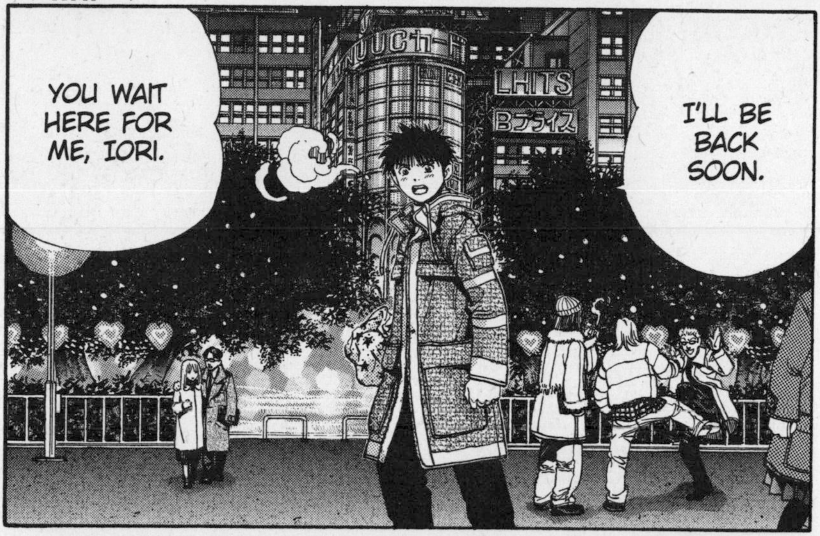
I'LL BE BACK SOON.
LHITS
YOU WAIT HERE FOR ME, IORI.

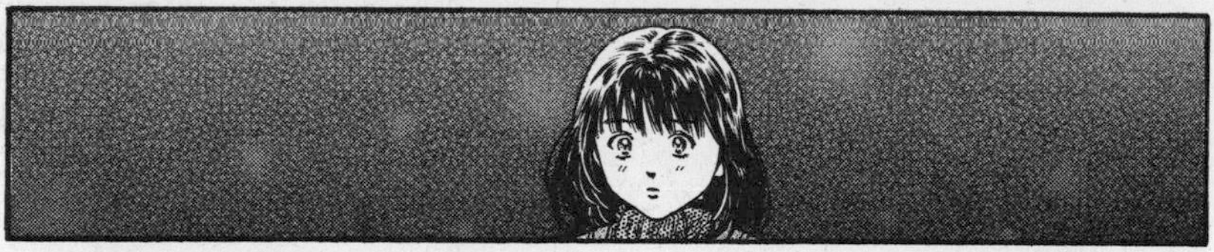

IT'S PROBABLY NO GOOD. "GO HAVE A DATE WITH IZUMI" IS WHAT SHE WAS SAYING. THERE'S A 99 PERCENT CHANCE SHE'S NOT INTERESTED IN ME. BUT I'LL GIVE IT ONE LAST SHOT!

IF IORI IS WAITING WHEN I GET BACK, I'LL BET ON THE ONE PERCENT CHANCE AND TELL HER I LIKE HER.

IF SHE'S NOT WAITING HERE... WELL...THEN I'LL GIVE UP ON HER FOREVER. EITHER WAY, I WANT TO FINISH THIS ONCE AND FOR ALL.

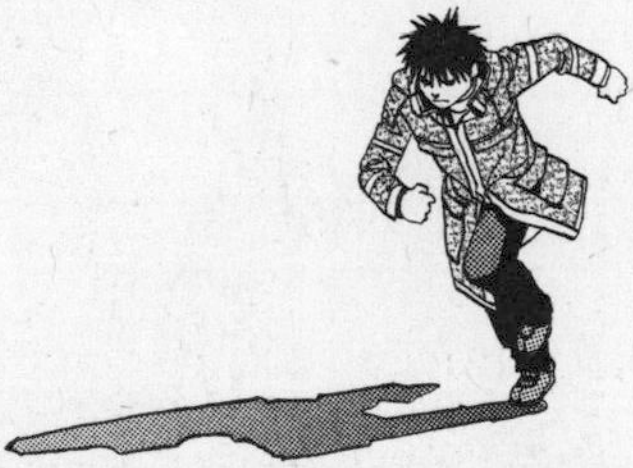

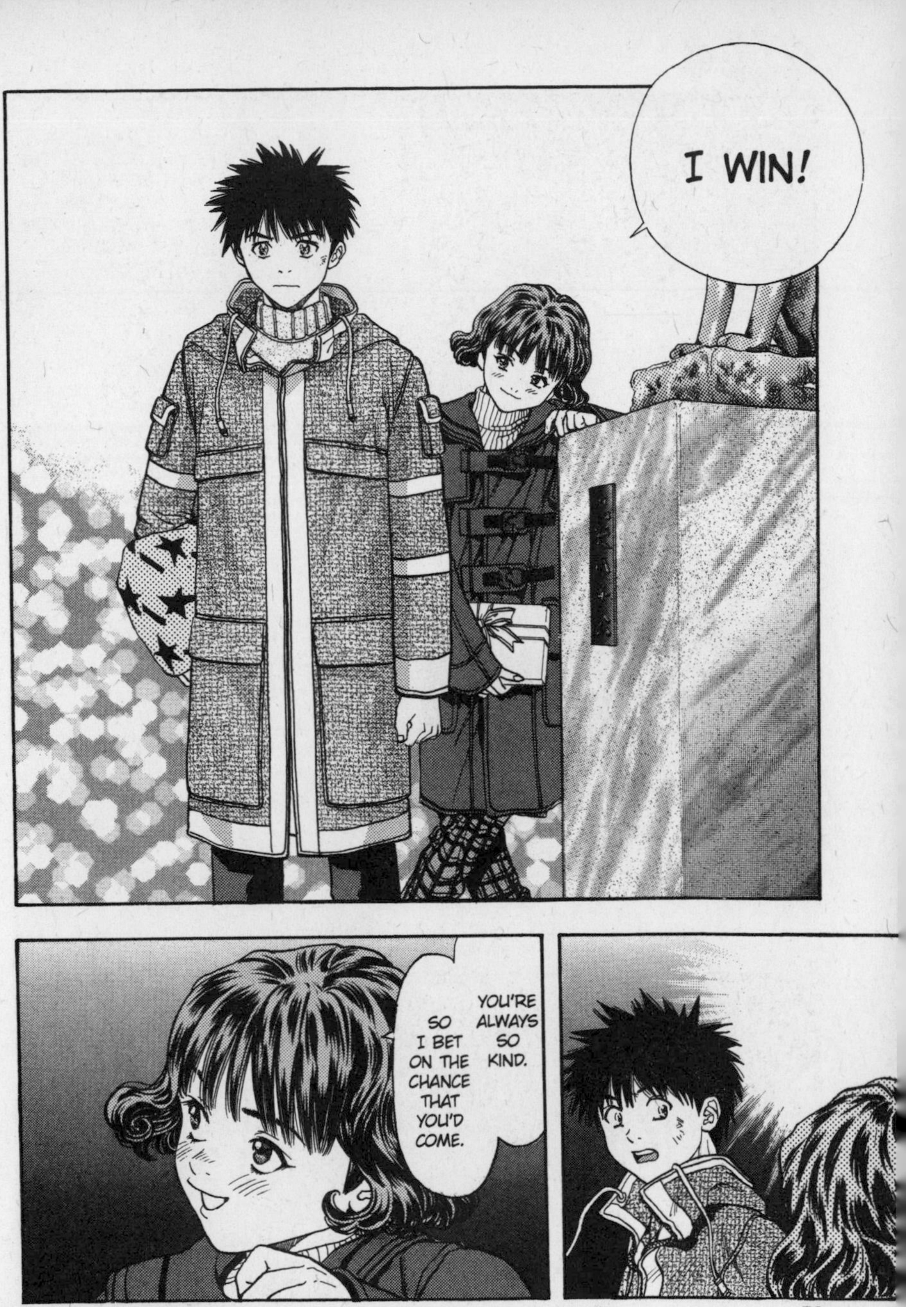
I WIN!
YOU'RE ALWAYS SO KIND.
SO I BET ON THE CHANCE THAT YOU'D COME.

READ THIS WAY

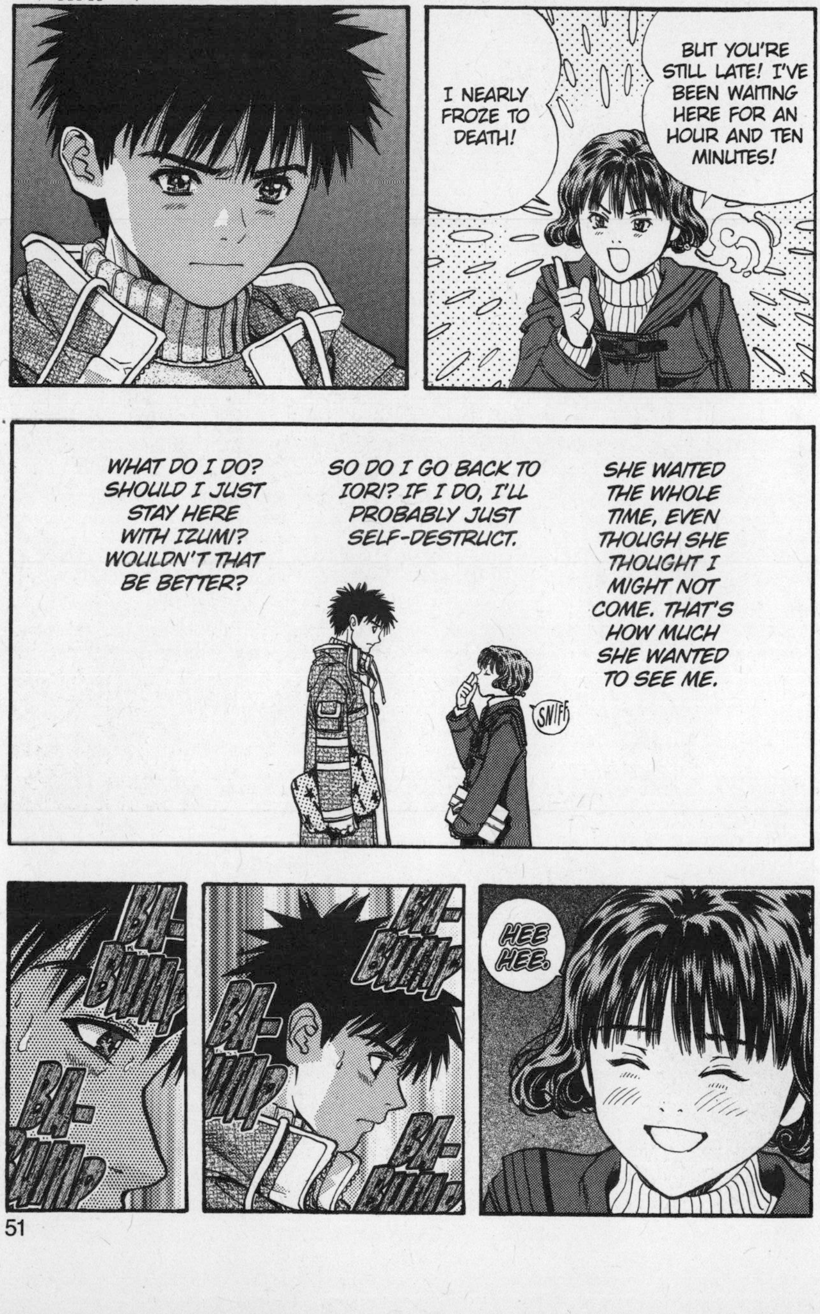

BUT YOU'RE STILL LATE! I'VE BEEN WAITING HERE FOR AN HOUR AND TEN MINUTES!
I NEARLY FROZE TO DEATH!
SHE WAITED THE WHOLE TIME, EVEN THOUGH SHE THOUGHT I MIGHT NOT COME. THAT'S HOW MUCH SHE WANTED TO SEE ME.
SO DO I GO BACK TO IORI? IF I DO, I'LL PROBABLY JUST SELF-DESTRUCT.
WHAT DO I DO? SHOULD I JUST STAY HERE WITH IZUMI? WOULDN'T THAT BE BETTER?
SNIFF
HEE HEE.
BA-BUMP
BA-BUMP
BA-BUMP
BA-BUMP
BA-BUMP

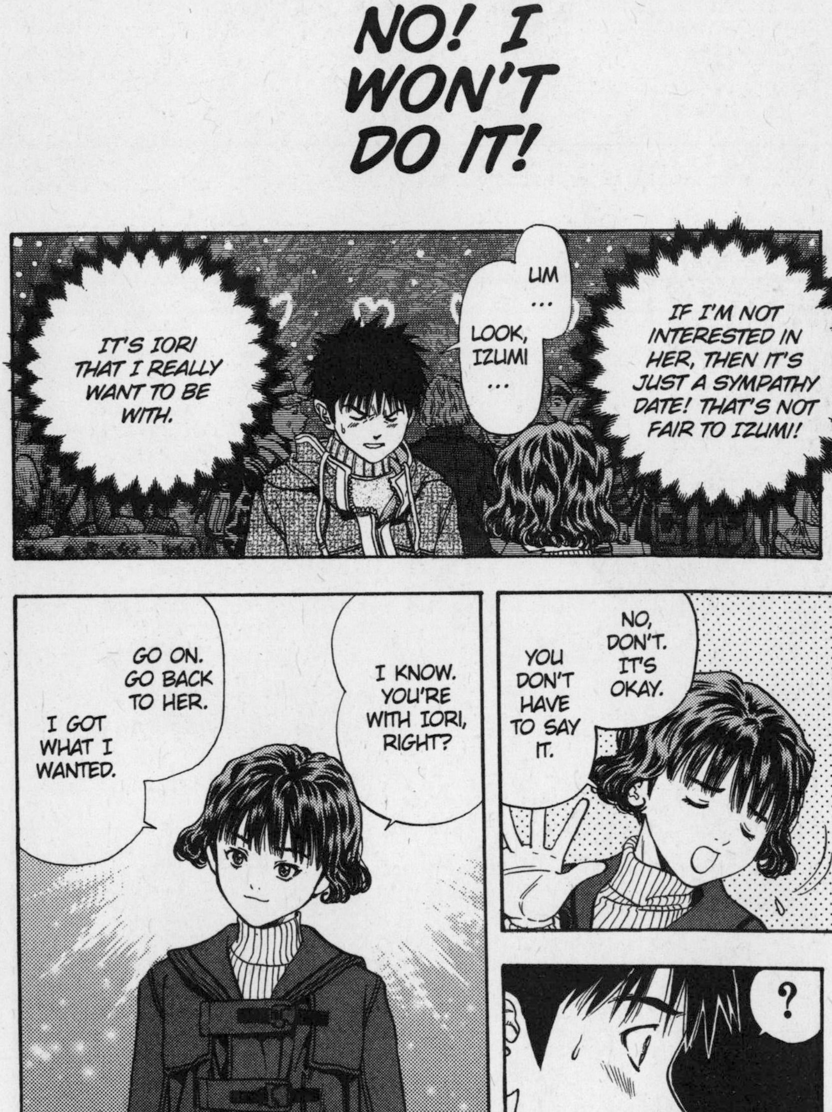
NO! I WON'T DO IT!
IF I'M NOT INTERESTED IN HER, THEN IT'S JUST A SYMPATHY DATE! THAT'S NOT FAIR TO IZUMI!
UM ... LOOK, IZUMI ...
IT'S IORI THAT I REALLY WANT TO BE WITH.
NO, DON'T. IT'S OKAY.
YOU DON'T HAVE TO SAY IT.
?
I KNOW. YOU'RE WITH IORI, RIGHT?
GO ON. GO BACK TO HER.
I GOT WHAT I WANTED.

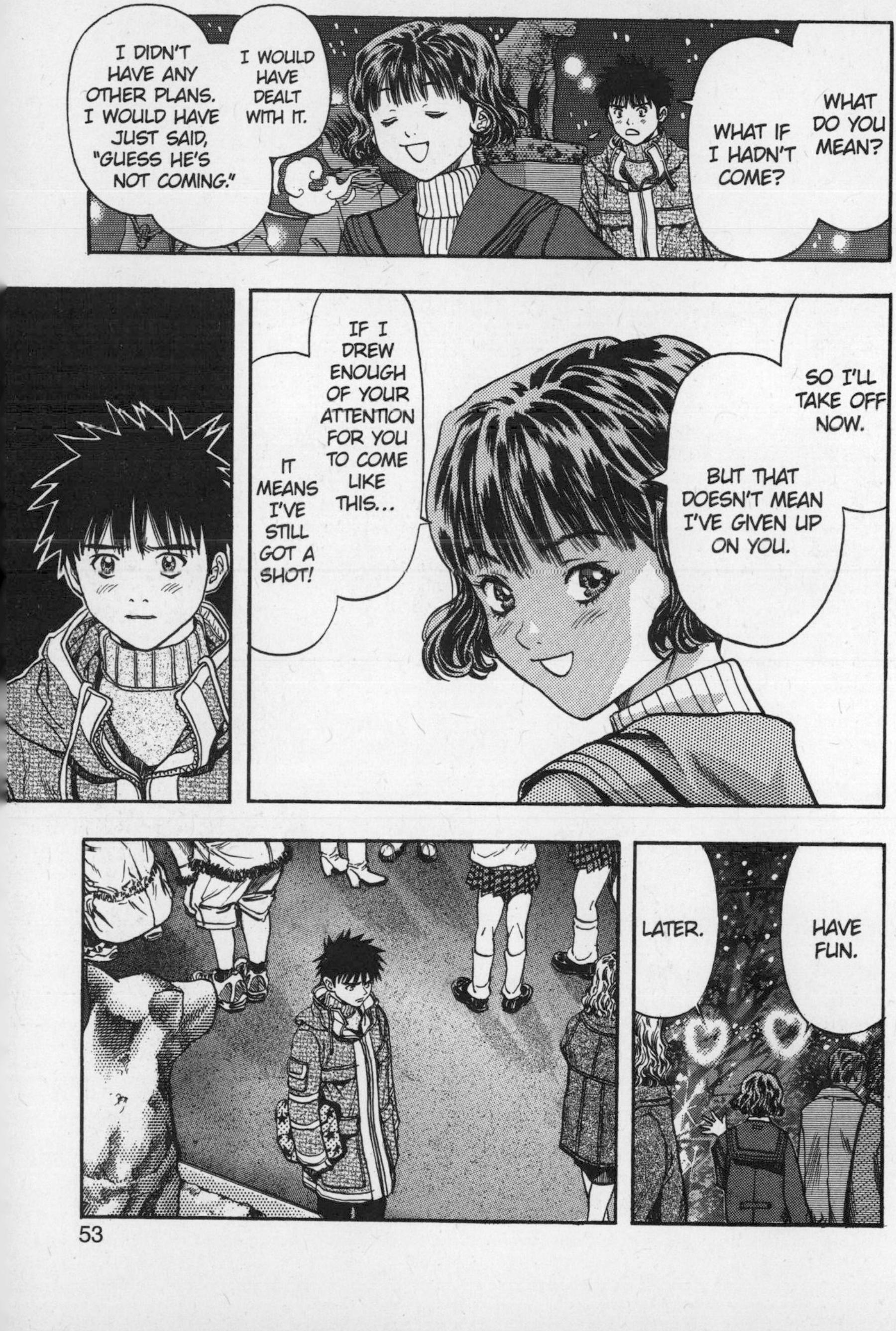
WHAT DO YOU MEAN?
WHAT IF I HADN'T COME?
I WOULD HAVE DEALT WITH IT.
I DIDN'T HAVE ANY OTHER PLANS. I WOULD HAVE JUST SAID, "GUESS HE'S NOT COMING."
SO I'LL TAKE OFF NOW.
BUT THAT DOESN'T MEAN I'VE GIVEN UP ON YOU.
IF I DREW ENOUGH OF YOUR ATTENTION FOR YOU TO COME LIKE THIS...
IT MEANS I'VE STILL GOT A SHOT!
HAVE FUN.
LATER.

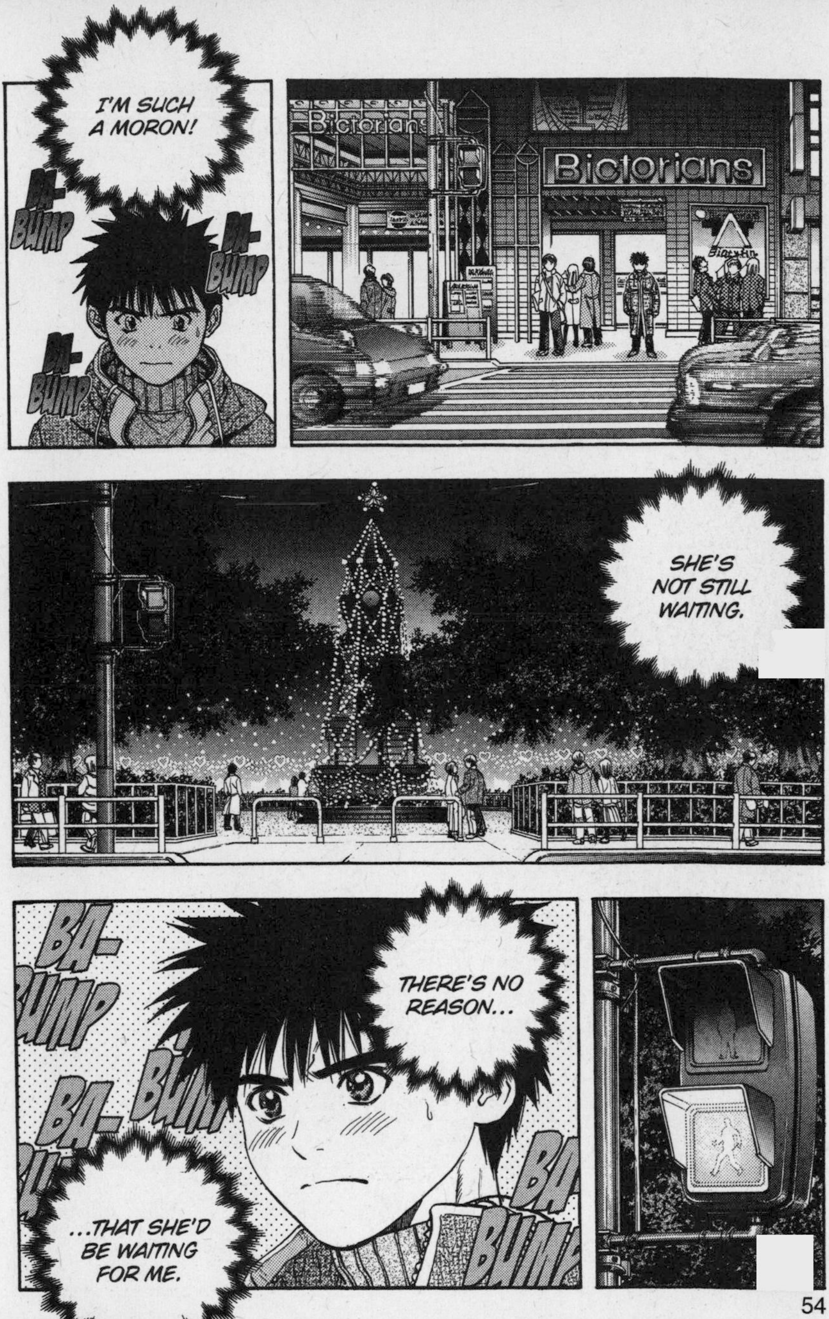
Bictorians
Bictorians
I'M SUCH A MORON!
BA-BUMP
BA-BUMP
BA-BUMP
SHE'S NOT STILL WAITING.
THERE'S NO REASON...
...THAT SHE'D BE WAITING FOR ME.

READ THIS WAY

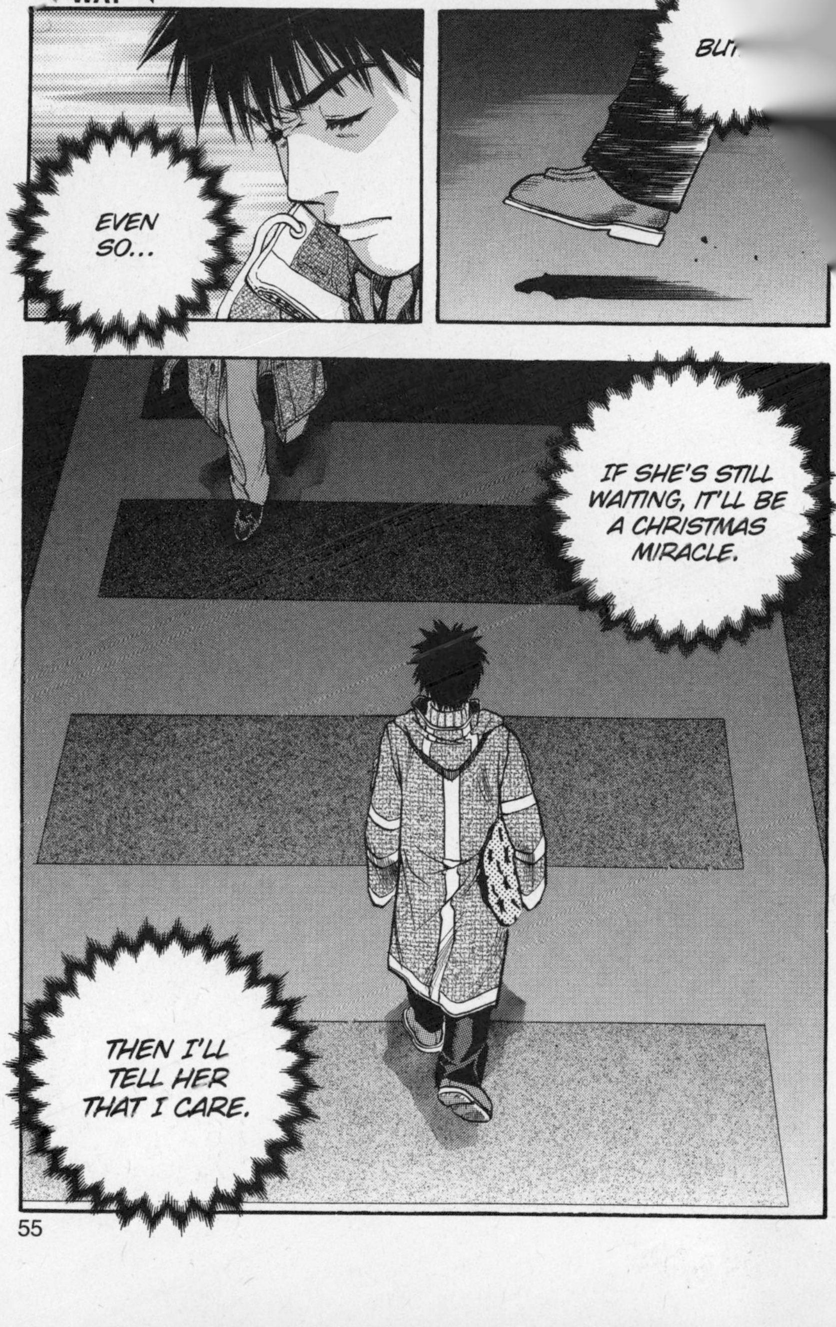
BUT
EVEN SO...
IF SHE'S STILL WAITING, IT'LL BE A CHRISTMAS MIRACLE.
THEN I'LL TELL HER THAT I CARE.

READ THIS WAY

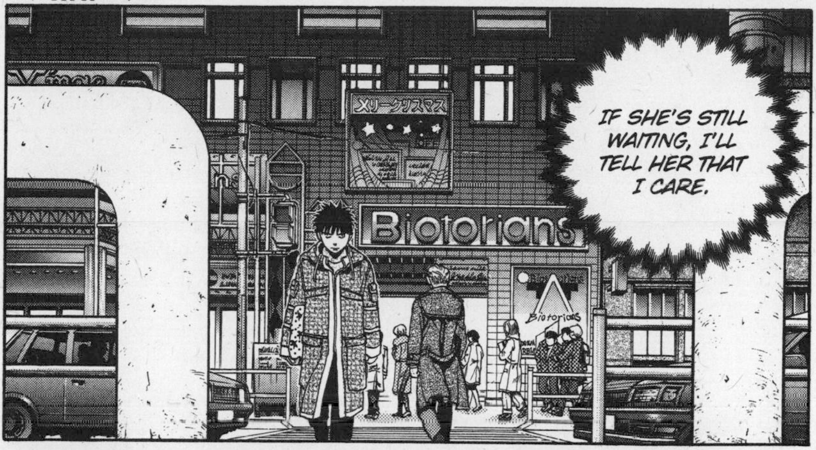
メリークリスマス
Biotorians
IF SHE'S STILL WAITING, I'LL TELL HER THAT I CARE.

Chapter 87: To You

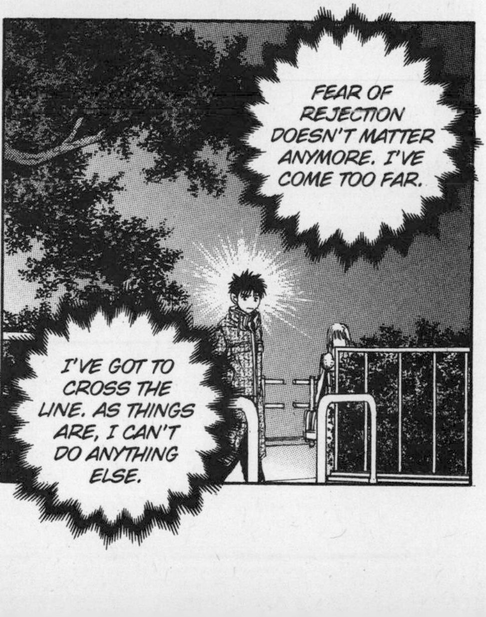
FEAR OF REJECTION DOESN'T MATTER ANYMORE. I'VE COME TOO FAR.
I'VE GOT TO CROSS THE LINE. AS THINGS ARE, I CAN'T DO ANYTHING ELSE.

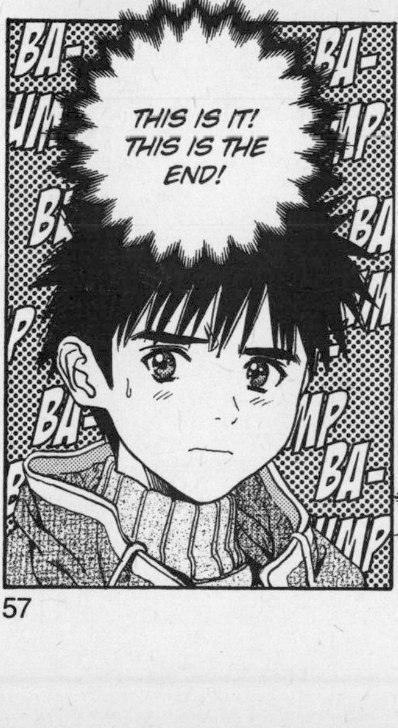
THIS IS IT! THIS IS THE END!
BA-BUMP

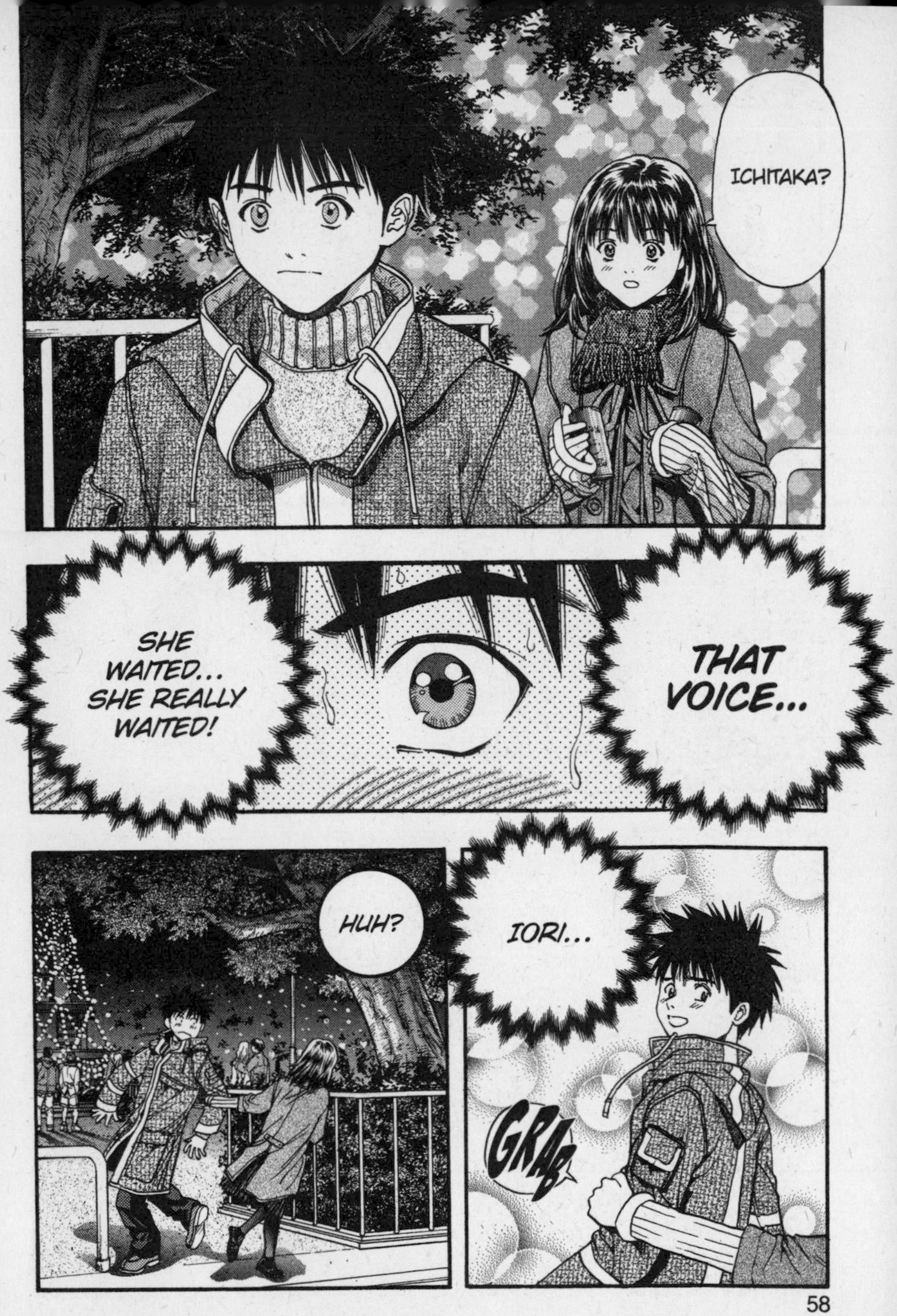
ICHITAKA?
THAT VOICE...
SHE WAITED... SHE REALLY WAITED!
IORI...
GRAB
HUH?

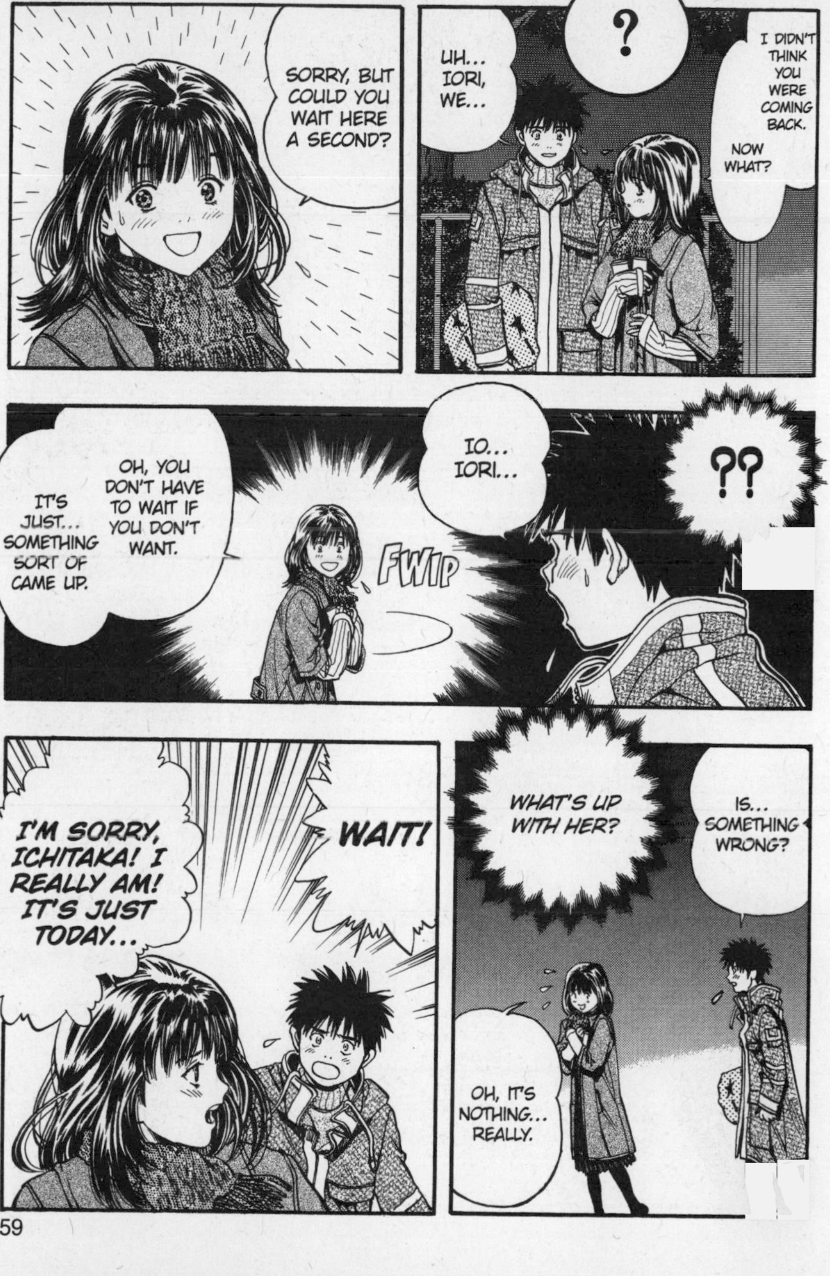
?
I DIDN'T THINK YOU WERE COMING BACK.
NOW WHAT?
UH... IORI, WE...
SORRY, BUT COULD YOU WAIT HERE A SECOND?
??
IO... IORI...
FWIP
OH, YOU DON'T HAVE TO WAIT IF YOU DON'T WANT.
IT'S JUST... SOMETHING SORT OF CAME UP.
IS... SOMETHING WRONG?
WHAT'S UP WITH HER?
OH, IT'S NOTHING... REALLY.
WAIT!
I'M SORRY, ICHITAKA! I REALLY AM! IT'S JUST TODAY...

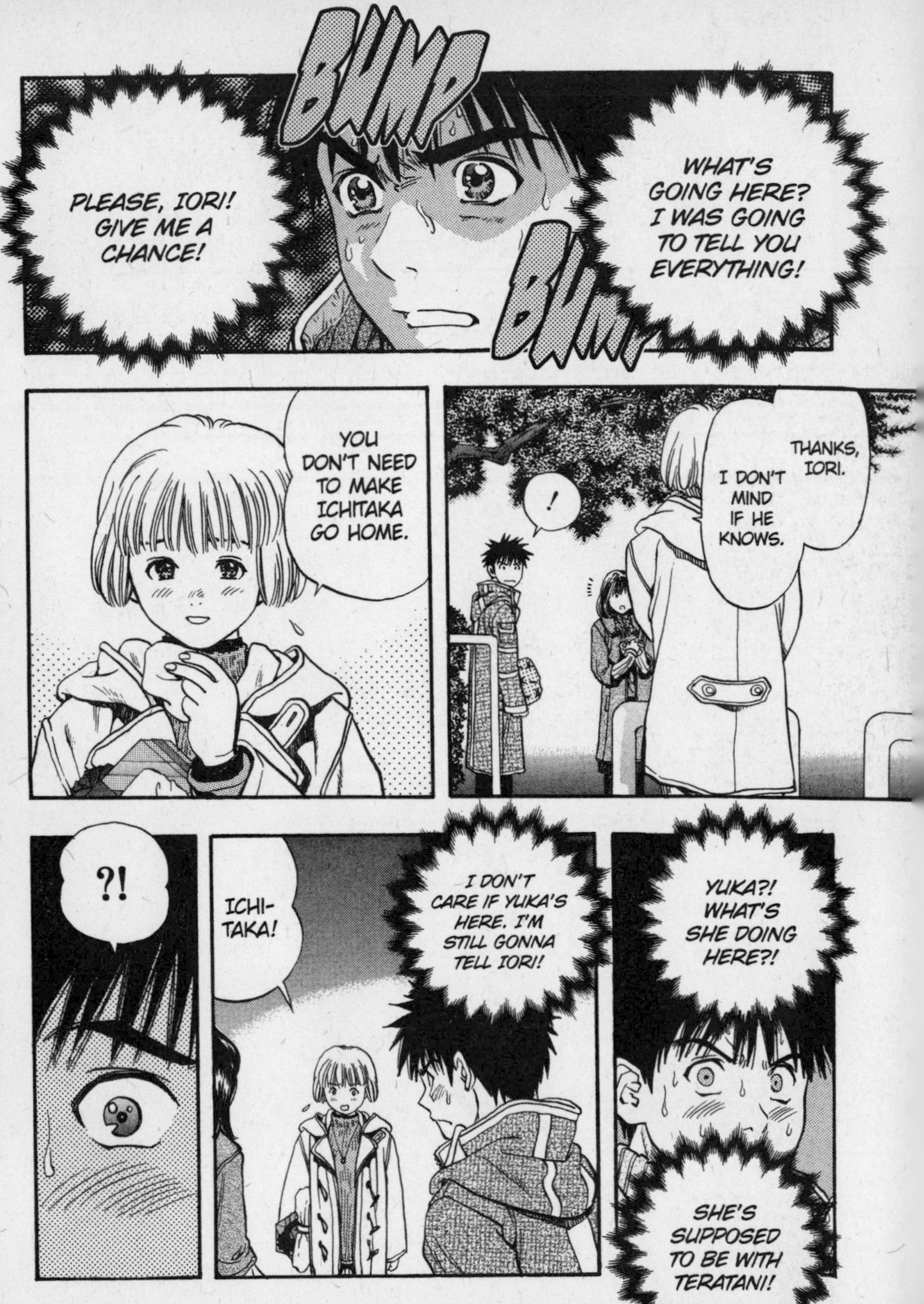
BUMP
WHAT'S GOING HERE? I WAS GOING TO TELL YOU EVERYTHING!
PLEASE, IORI! GIVE ME A CHANCE!
BUM
THANKS, IORI.
I DON'T MIND IF HE KNOWS.
!
YOU DON'T NEED TO MAKE ICHITAKA GO HOME.
YUKA?! WHAT'S SHE DOING HERE?!
SHE'S SUPPOSED TO BE WITH TERATANI!
I DON'T CARE IF YUKA'S HERE. I'M STILL GONNA TELL IORI!
ICHI-TAKA!
?!

READ THIS WAY

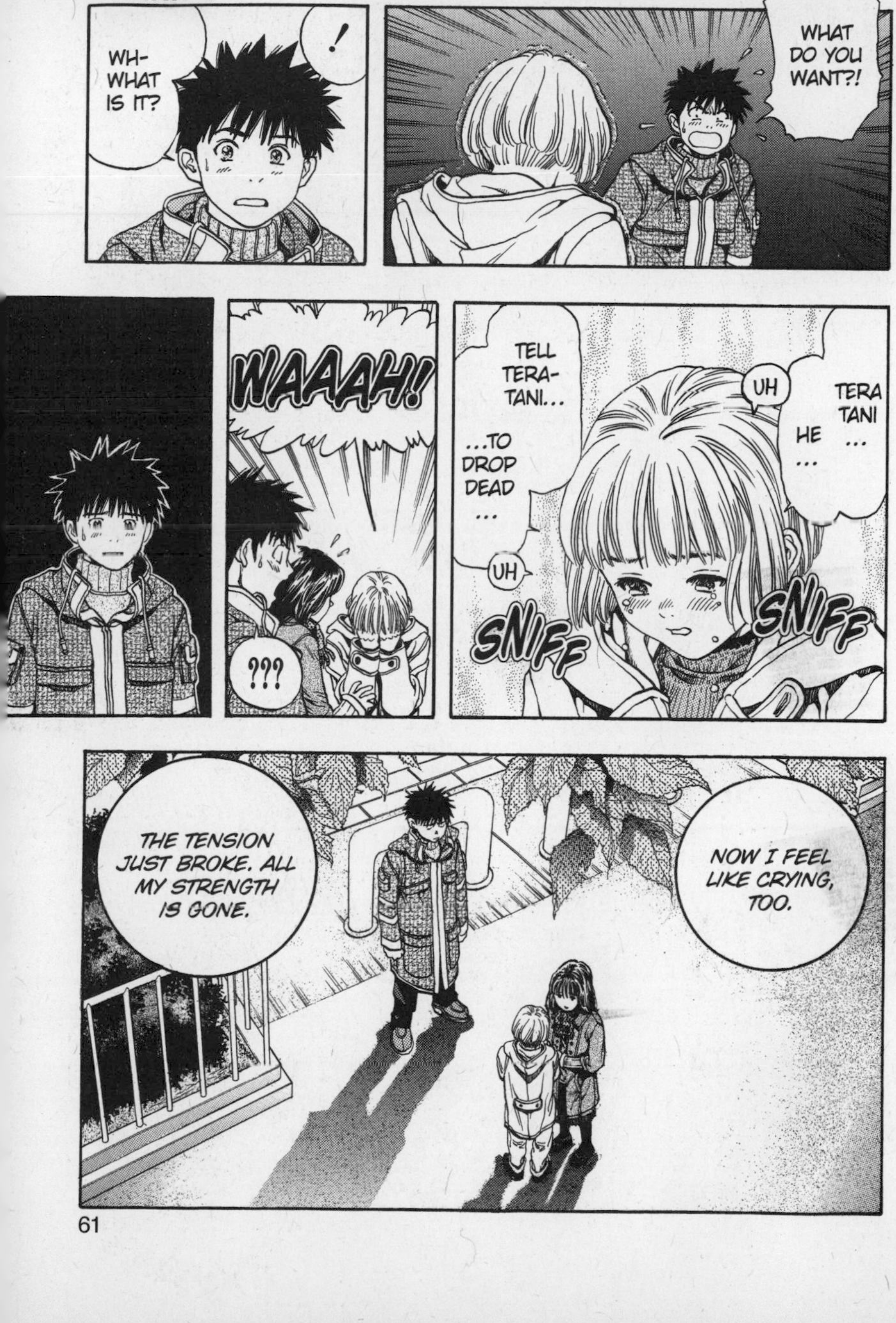

WHAT DO YOU WANT?!
!
WH- WHAT IS IT?
TERA TANI ...
HE ...
UH
TELL TERA-TANI...
...TO DROP DEAD ...
UH
SNIFF
SNIFF
WAAAH!
???
NOW I FEEL LIKE CRYING, TOO.
THE TENSION JUST BROKE. ALL MY STRENGTH IS GONE.

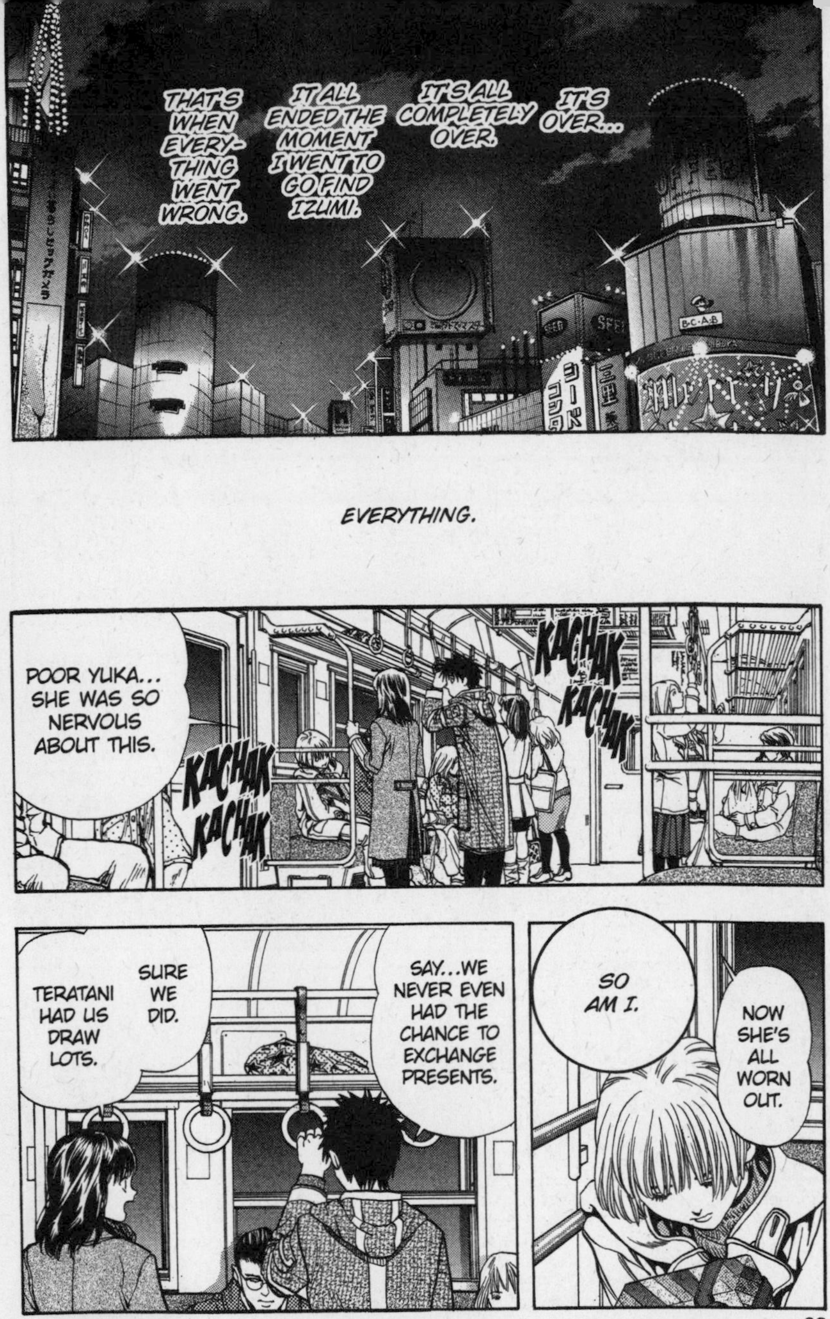
IT'S OVER...
IT'S ALL COMPLETELY OVER.
IT ALL ENDED THE MOMENT I WENT TO GO FIND IZUMI.
THAT'S WHEN EVERY-THING WENT WRONG.
EVERYTHING.
KACHAK KACHAK
POOR YUKA... SHE WAS SO NERVOUS ABOUT THIS.
KACHAK KACHAK
NOW SHE'S ALL WORN OUT.
SO AM I.
SAY...WE NEVER EVEN HAD THE CHANCE TO EXCHANGE PRESENTS.
SURE WE DID.
TERATANI HAD US DRAW LOTS.

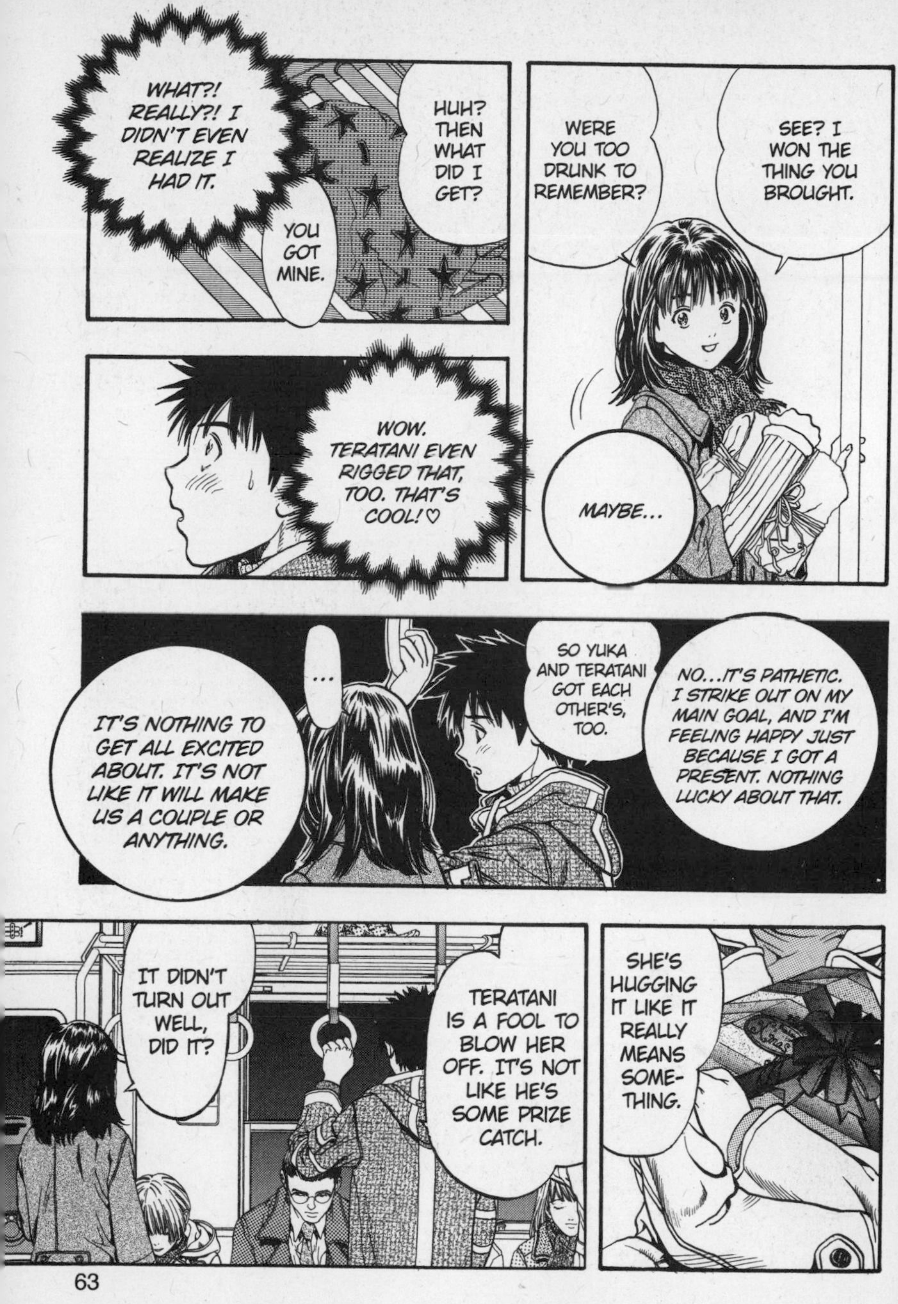
SEE? I WON THE THING YOU BROUGHT.
WERE YOU TOO DRUNK TO REMEMBER?
MAYBE...
HUH? THEN WHAT DID I GET?
YOU GOT MINE.
WHAT?! REALLY?! I DIDN'T EVEN REALIZE I HAD IT.
WOW. TERATANI EVEN RIGGED THAT, TOO. THAT'S COOL! ♡
NO...IT'S PATHETIC. I STRIKE OUT ON MY MAIN GOAL, AND I'M FEELING HAPPY JUST BECAUSE I GOT A PRESENT. NOTHING LUCKY ABOUT THAT.
SO YUKA AND TERATANI GOT EACH OTHER'S, TOO.
...
IT'S NOTHING TO GET ALL EXCITED ABOUT. IT'S NOT LIKE IT WILL MAKE US A COUPLE OR ANYTHING.
SHE'S HUGGING IT LIKE IT REALLY MEANS SOME-THING.
TERATANI IS A FOOL TO BLOW HER OFF. IT'S NOT LIKE HE'S SOME PRIZE CATCH.
IT DIDN'T TURN OUT WELL, DID IT?

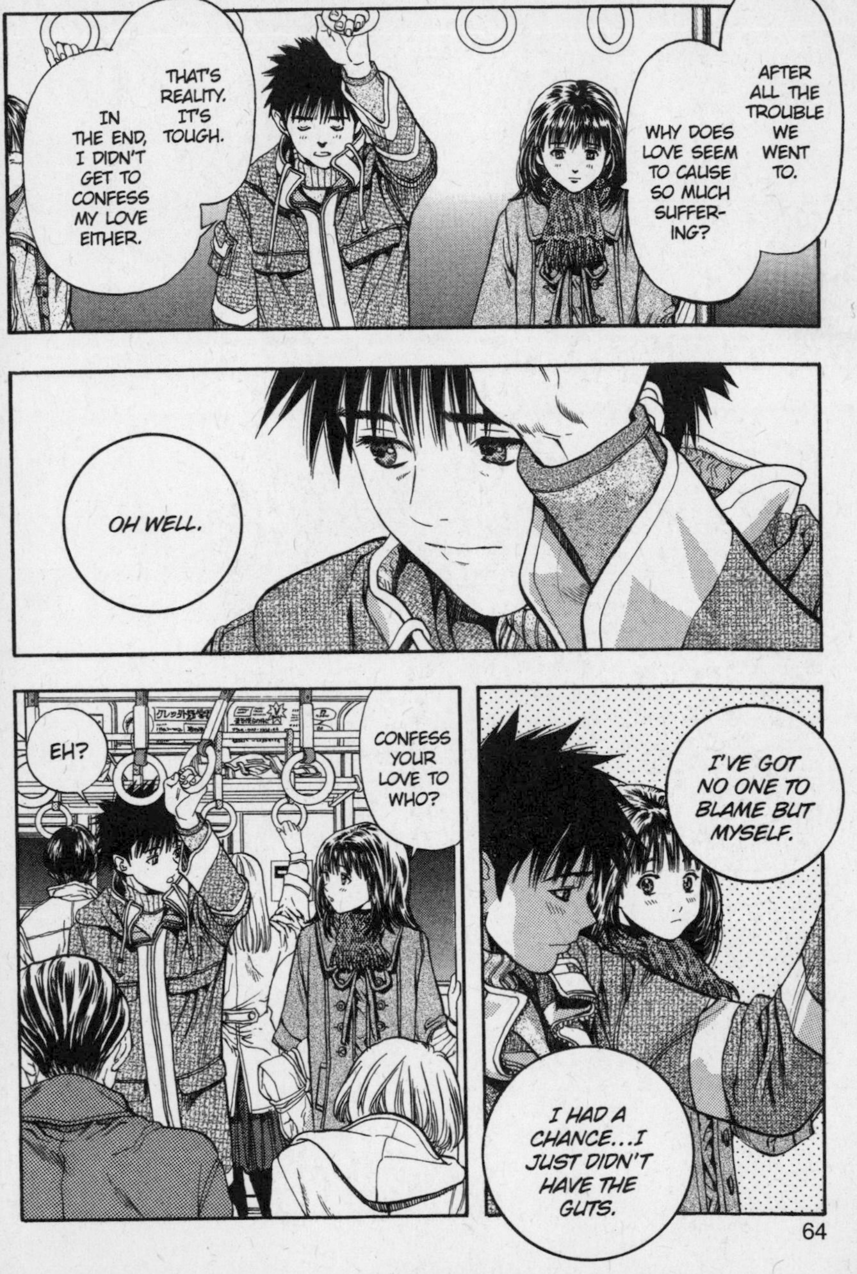
AFTER ALL THE TROUBLE WE WENT TO.
WHY DOES LOVE SEEM TO CAUSE SO MUCH SUFFER-ING?
THAT'S REALITY. IT'S TOUGH.
IN THE END, I DIDN'T GET TO CONFESS MY LOVE EITHER.
OH WELL.
I'VE GOT NO ONE TO BLAME BUT MYSELF.
I HAD A CHANCE...I JUST DIDN'T HAVE THE GUTS.
CONFESS YOUR LOVE TO WHO?
EH?

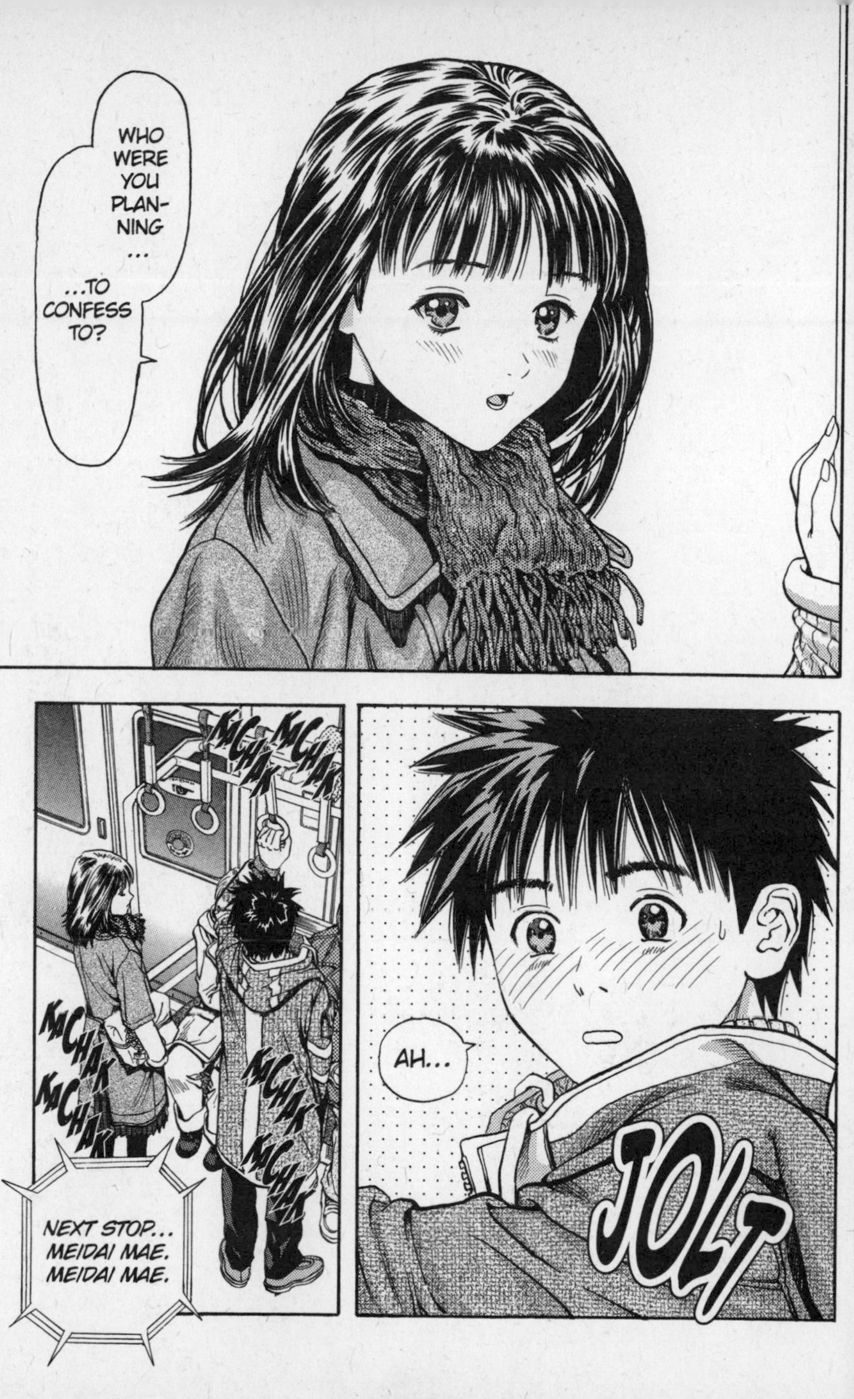
WHO WERE YOU PLAN-NING ...
...TO CONFESS TO?
AH...
JOLT
KACHAK KACHAK
KACHAK KACHAK
KACHAK KACHAK
NEXT STOP... MEIDAI MAE. MEIDAI MAE.

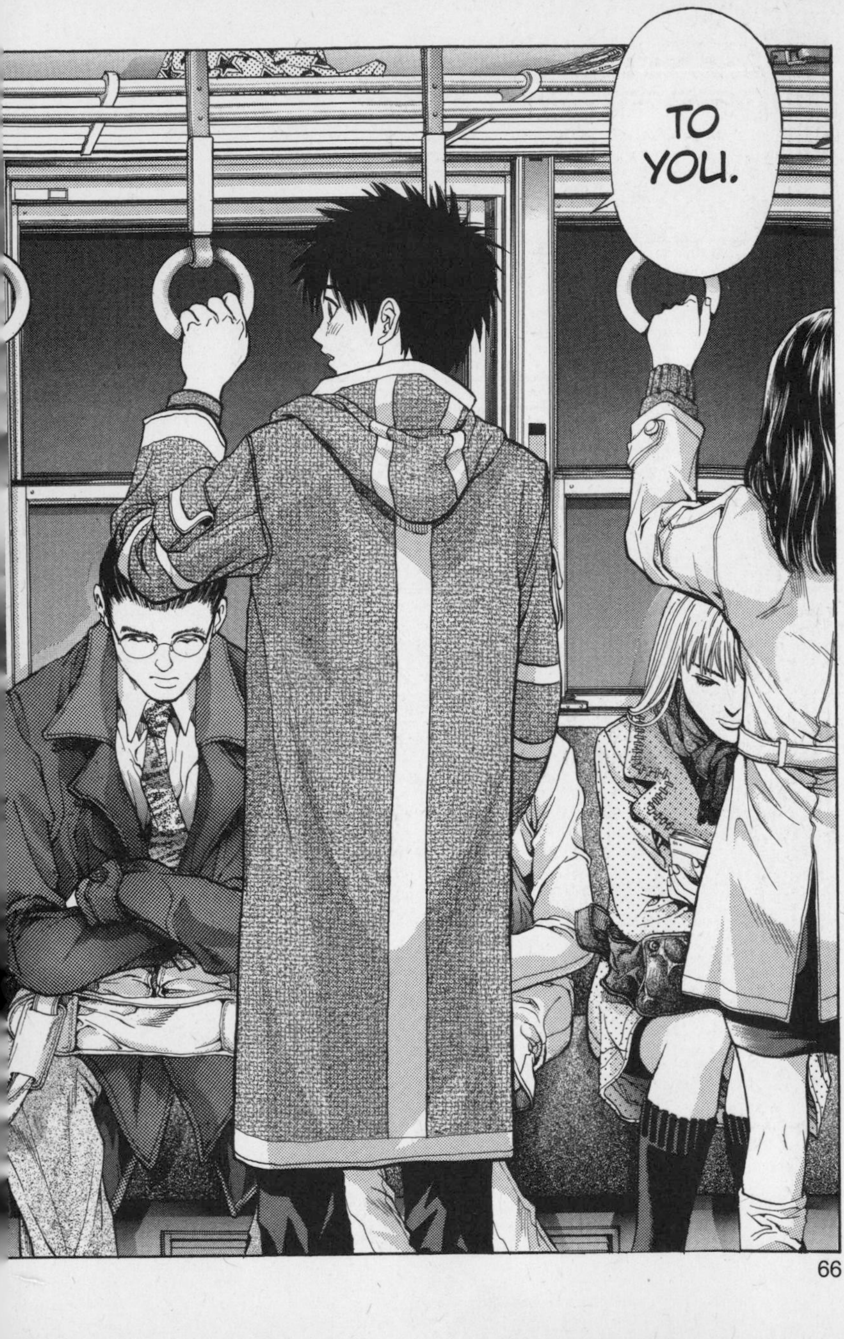
TO YOU.

READ THIS WAY

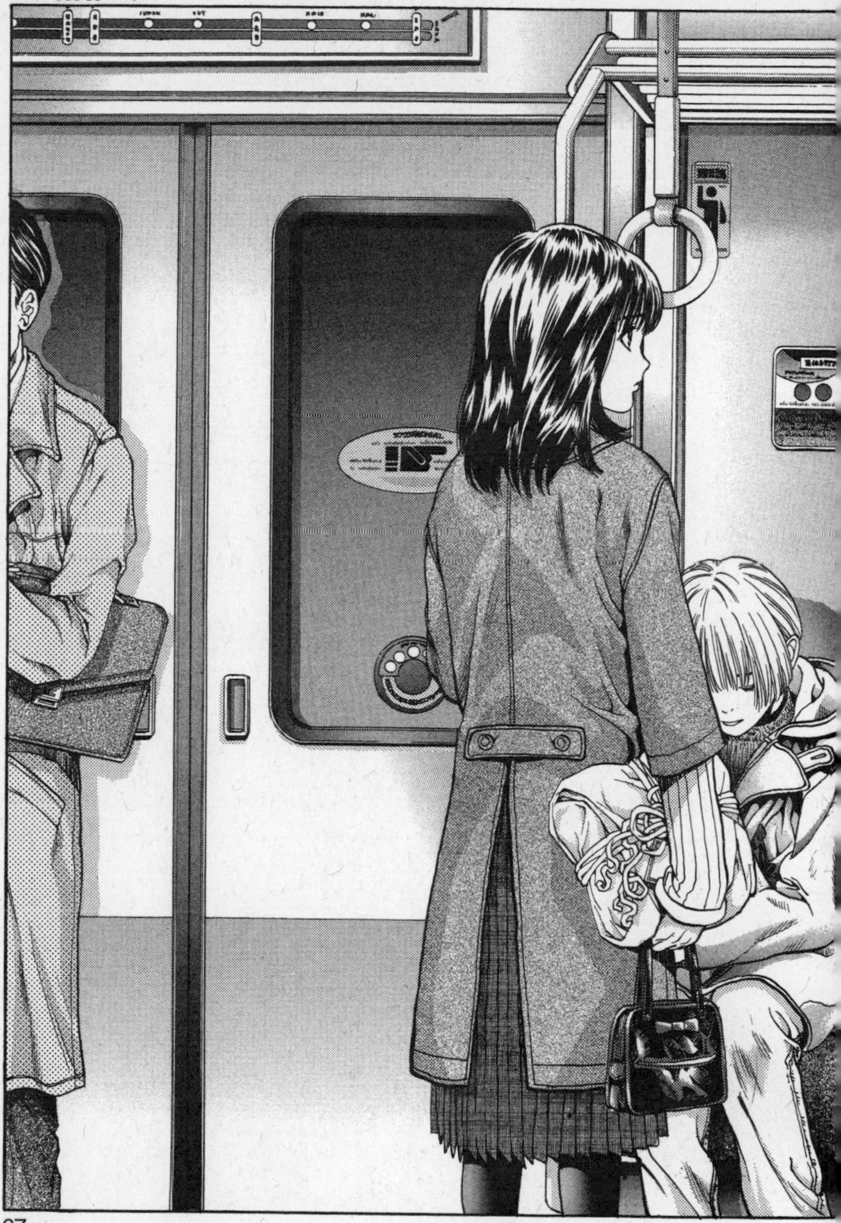

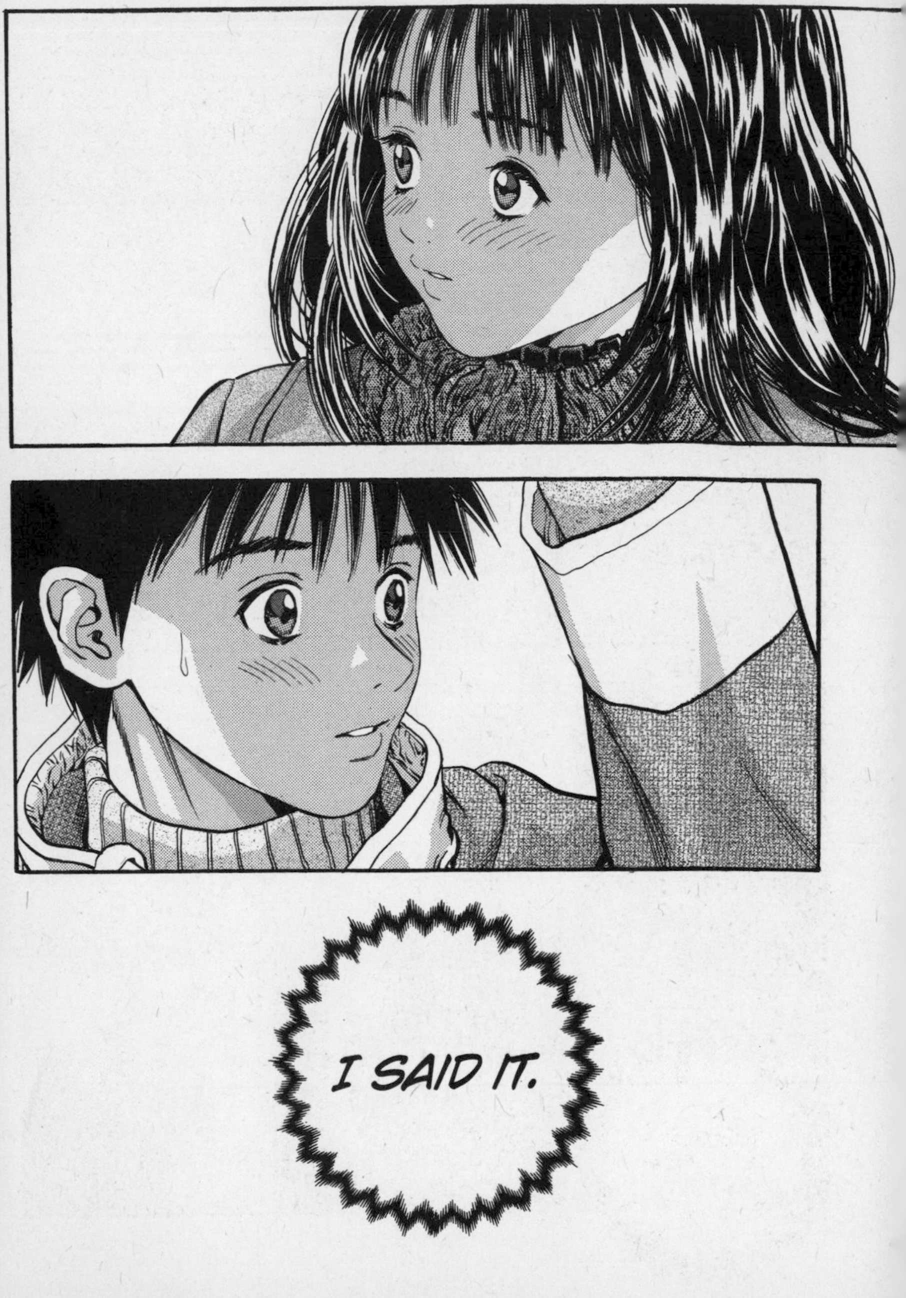
I SAID IT.

READ THIS WAY

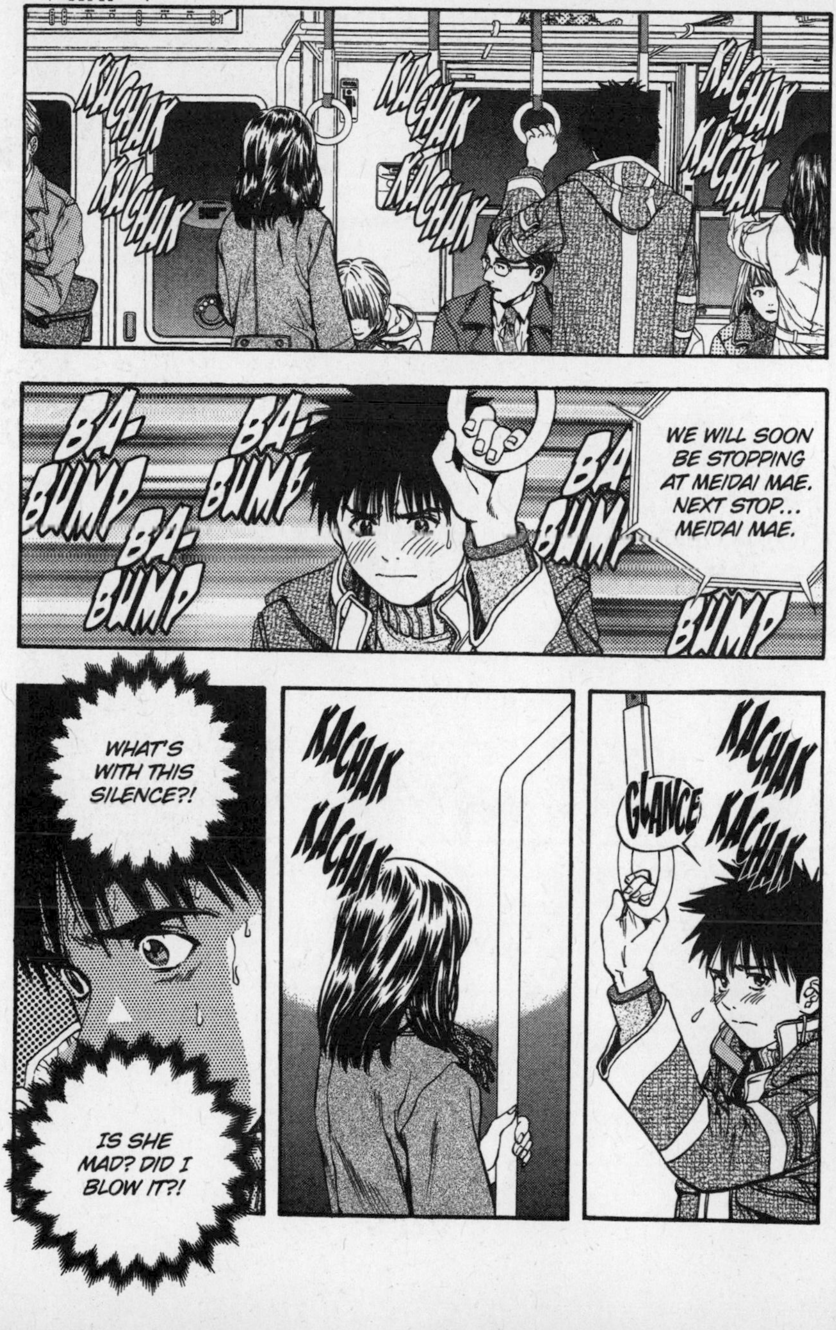

KACHAK KACHAK
KACHAK KACHAK
KACHAK KACHAK
WE WILL SOON BE STOPPING AT MEIDAI MAE. NEXT STOP... MEIDAI MAE.
BA-BUMP
BUMP
BA-BUMP
BA-BUMP
BA-BUMP
KACHAK KACHAK
GLANCE
KACHAK KACHAK
WHAT'S WITH THIS SILENCE?!
IS SHE MAD? DID I BLOW IT?!

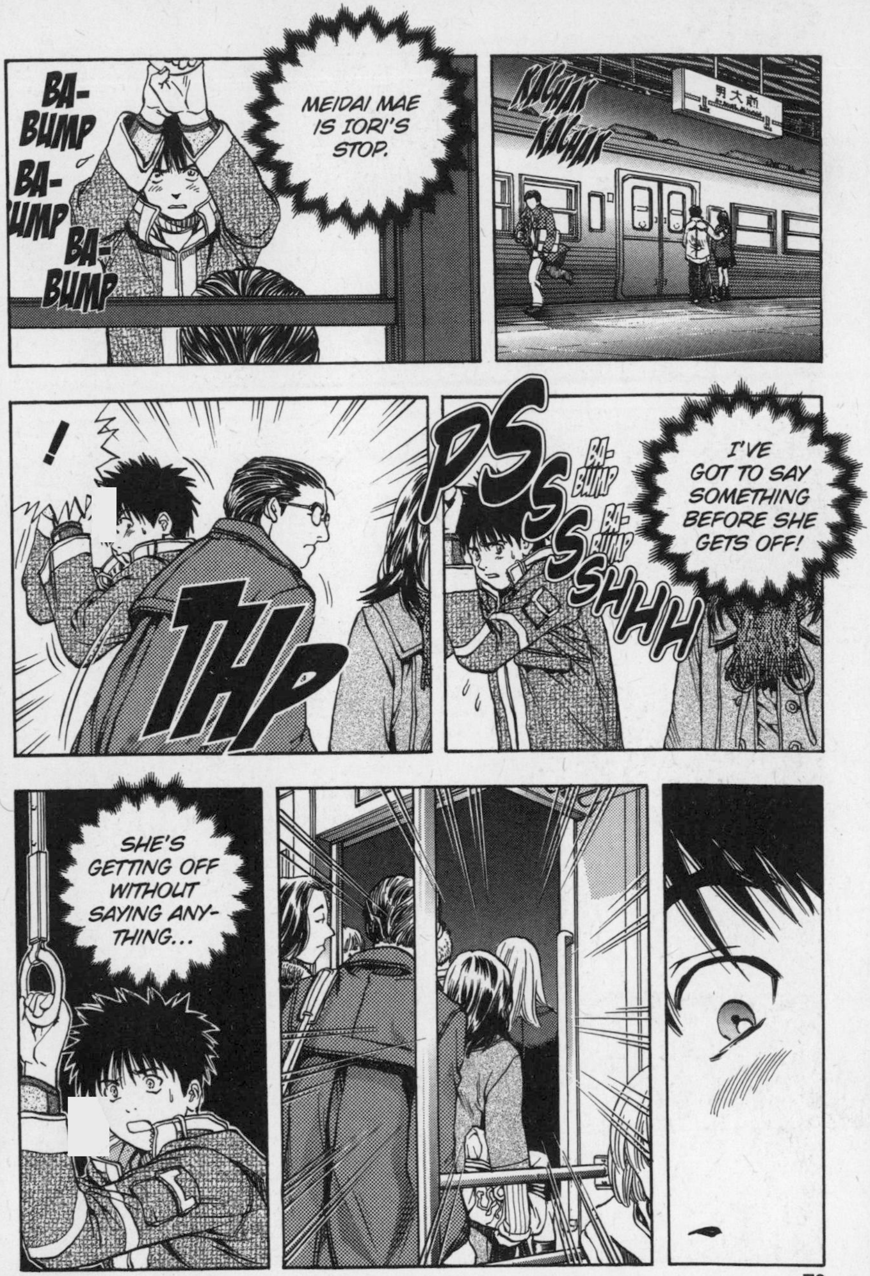
明大前
KACHAK KACHAK
MEIDAI MAE IS IORI'S STOP.
BA-BUMP BA-BUMP BA-BUMP
PSSSSHHHH
BA-BUMP BA-BUMP
I'VE GOT TO SAY SOMETHING BEFORE SHE GETS OFF!
!
THP
SHE'S GETTING OFF WITHOUT SAYING ANY-THING...

READ THIS WAY

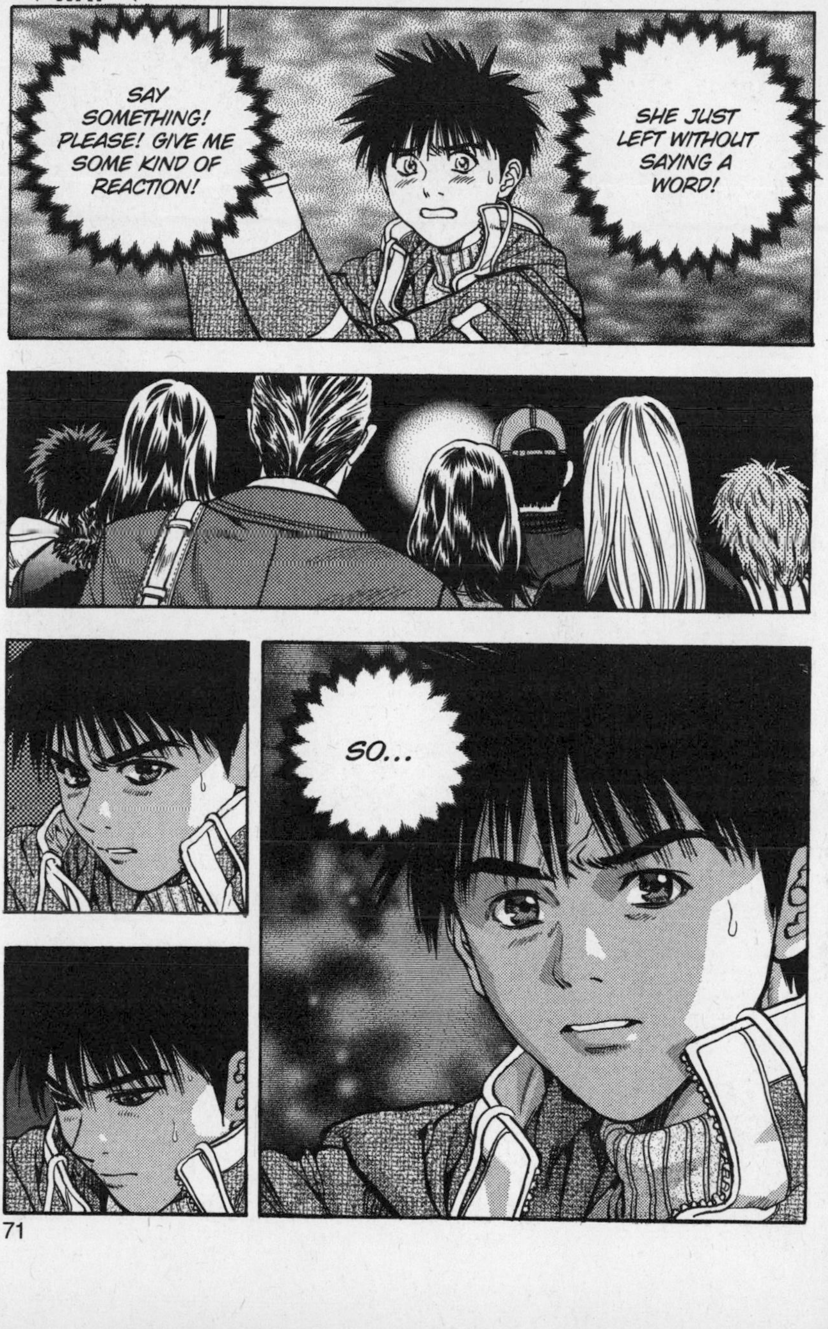
SHE JUST LEFT WITHOUT SAYING A WORD!
SAY SOMETHING! PLEASE! GIVE ME SOME KIND OF REACTION!
SO...

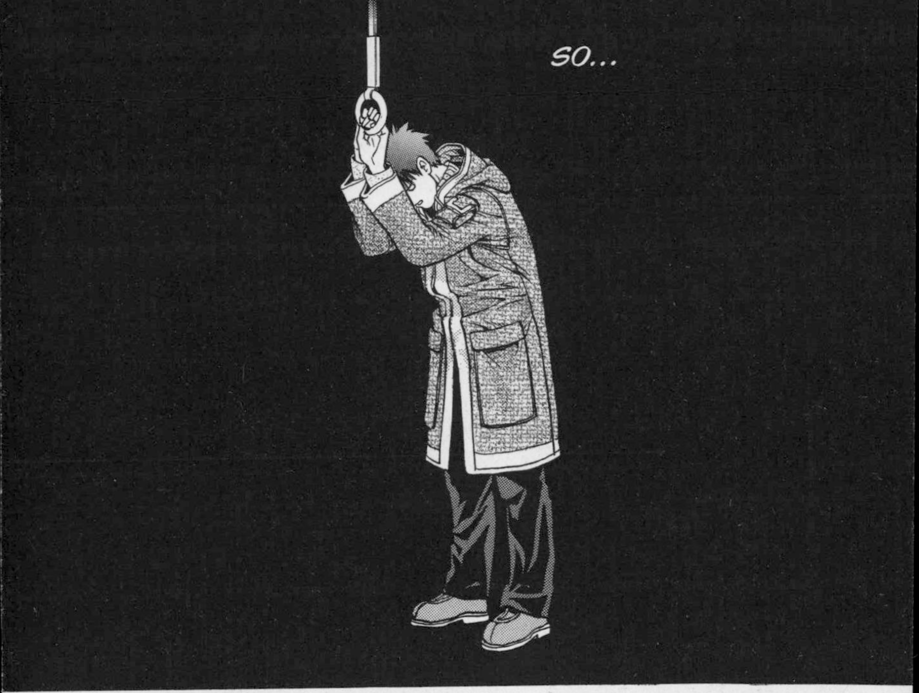
SO...

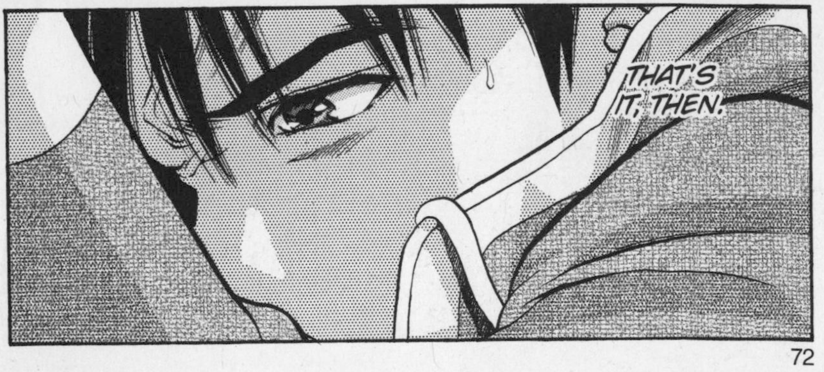
THAT'S IT, THEN.

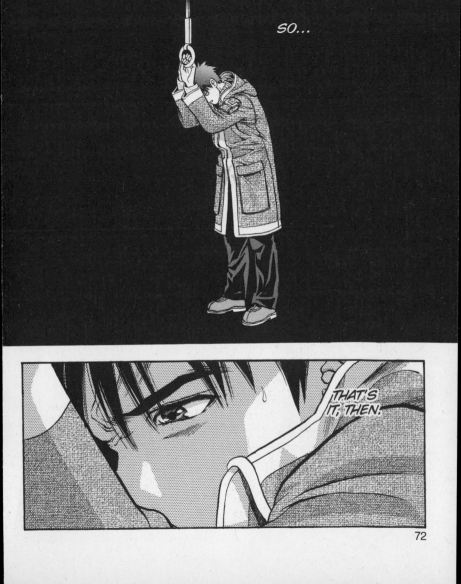

READ THIS WAY

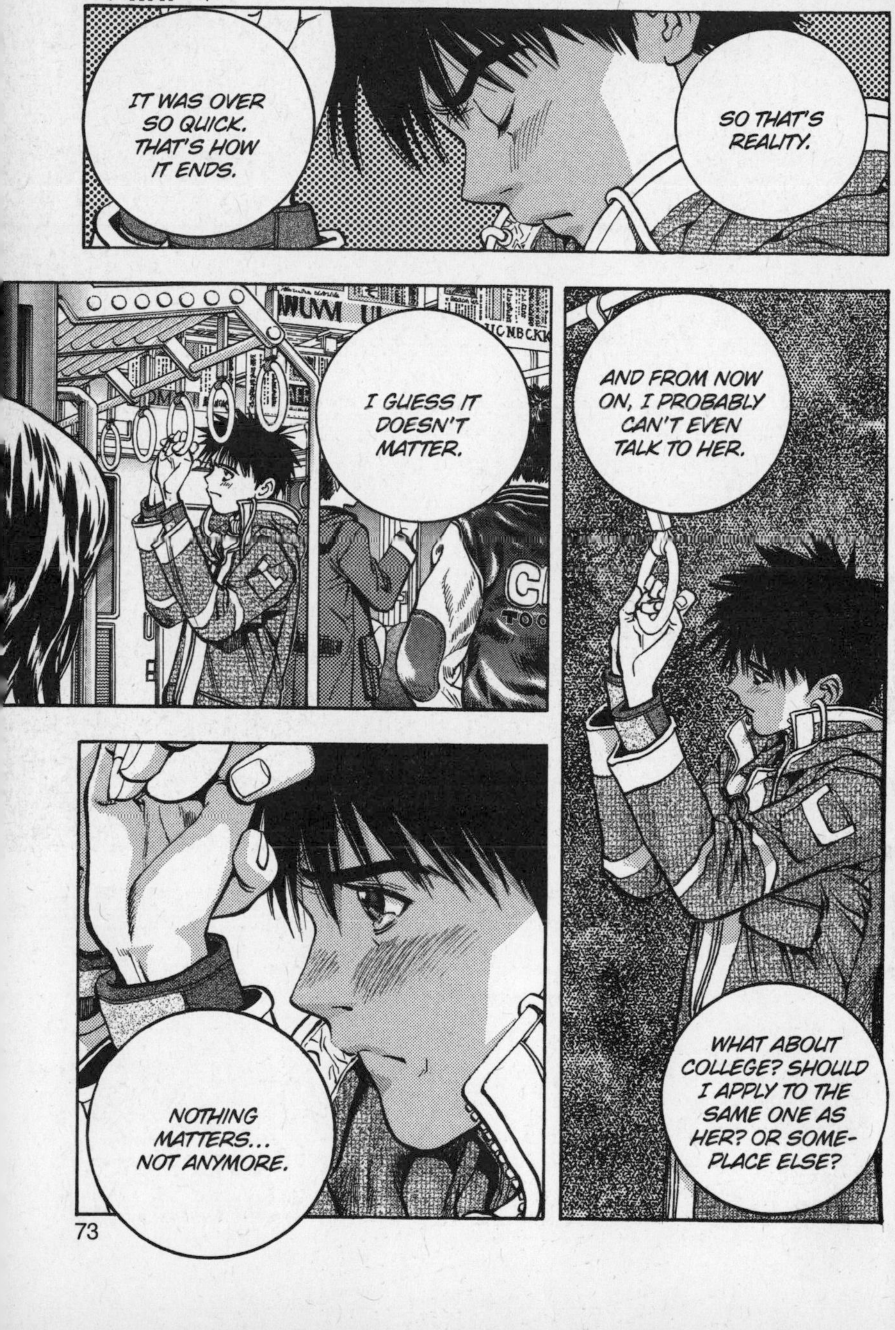

SO THAT'S REALITY.
IT WAS OVER SO QUICK. THAT'S HOW IT ENDS.
AND FROM NOW ON, I PROBABLY CAN'T EVEN TALK TO HER.
WHAT ABOUT COLLEGE? SHOULD I APPLY TO THE SAME ONE AS HER? OR SOME-PLACE ELSE?
I GUESS IT DOESN'T MATTER.
NOTHING MATTERS... NOT ANYMORE.

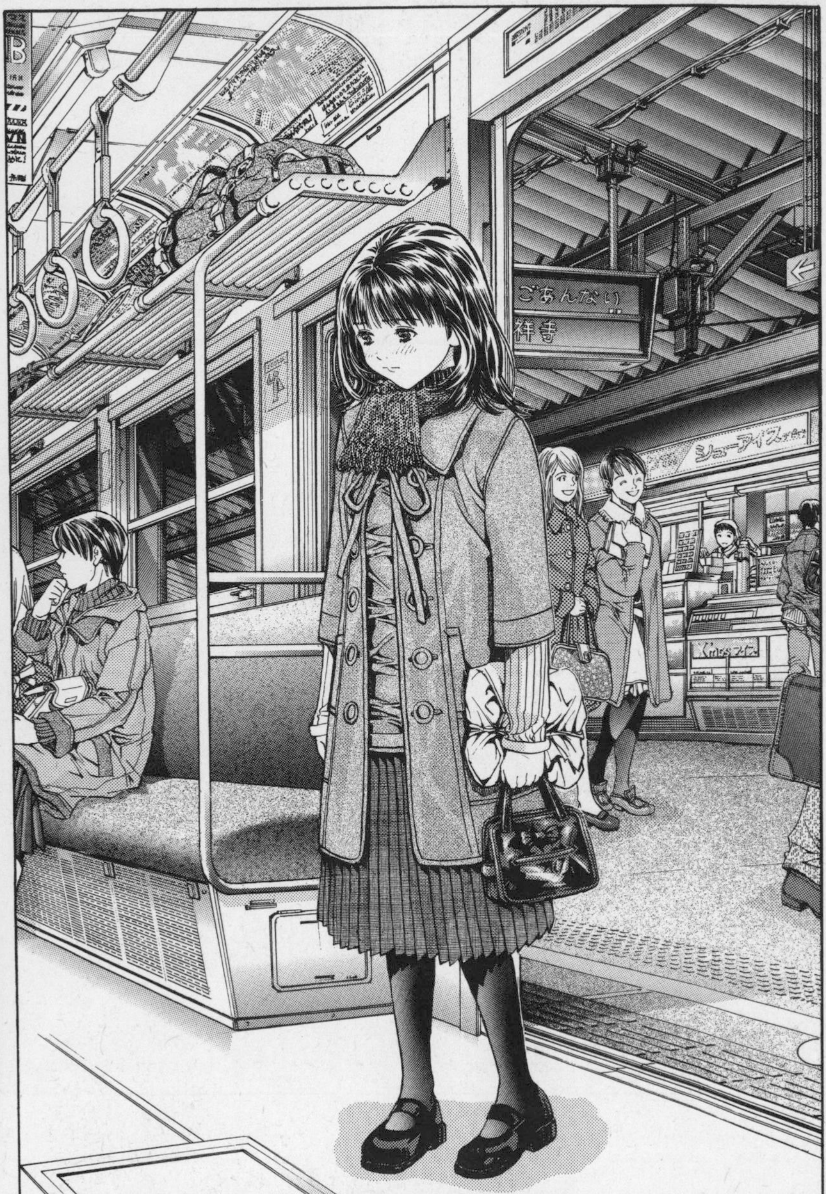
ごあんない
祥寺
シューアイス

READ THIS WAY

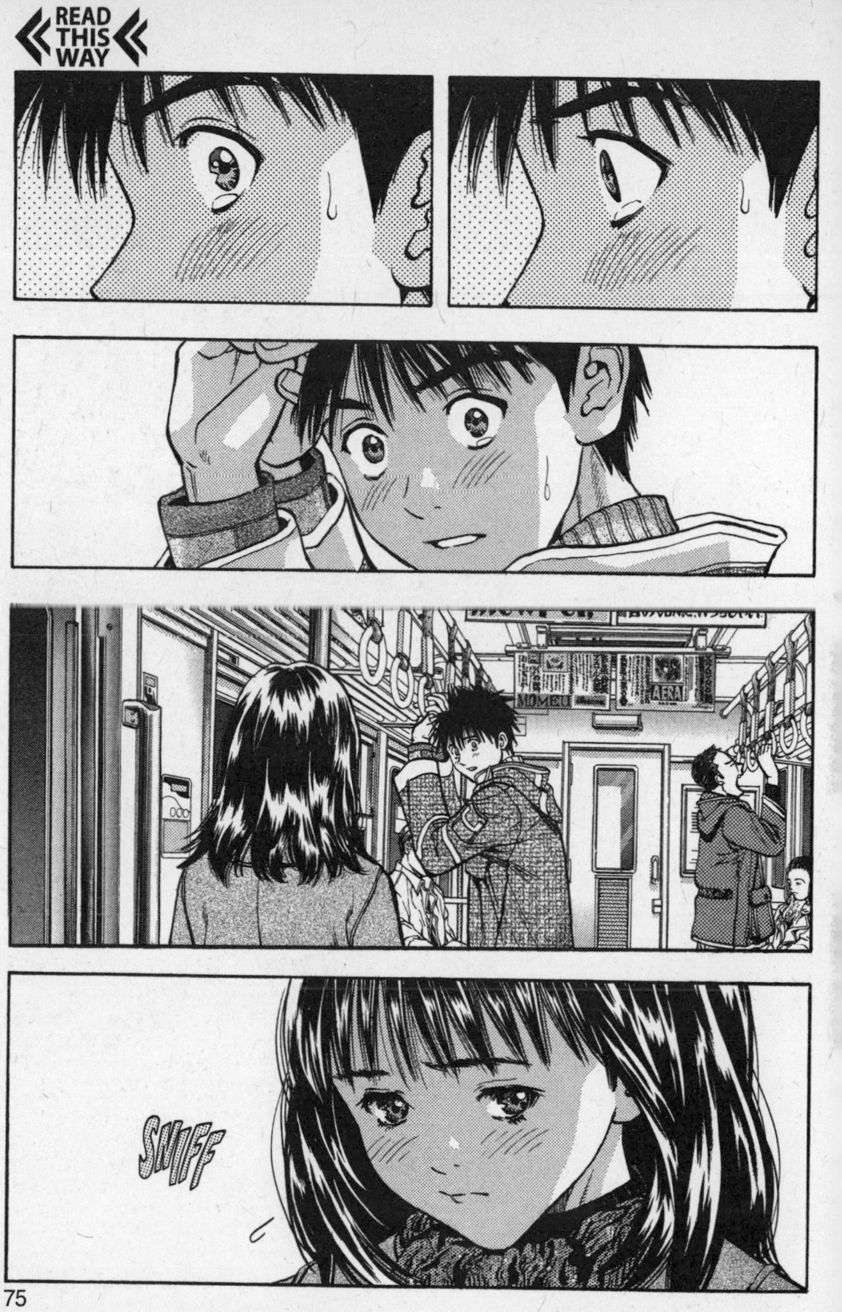
SNIFF

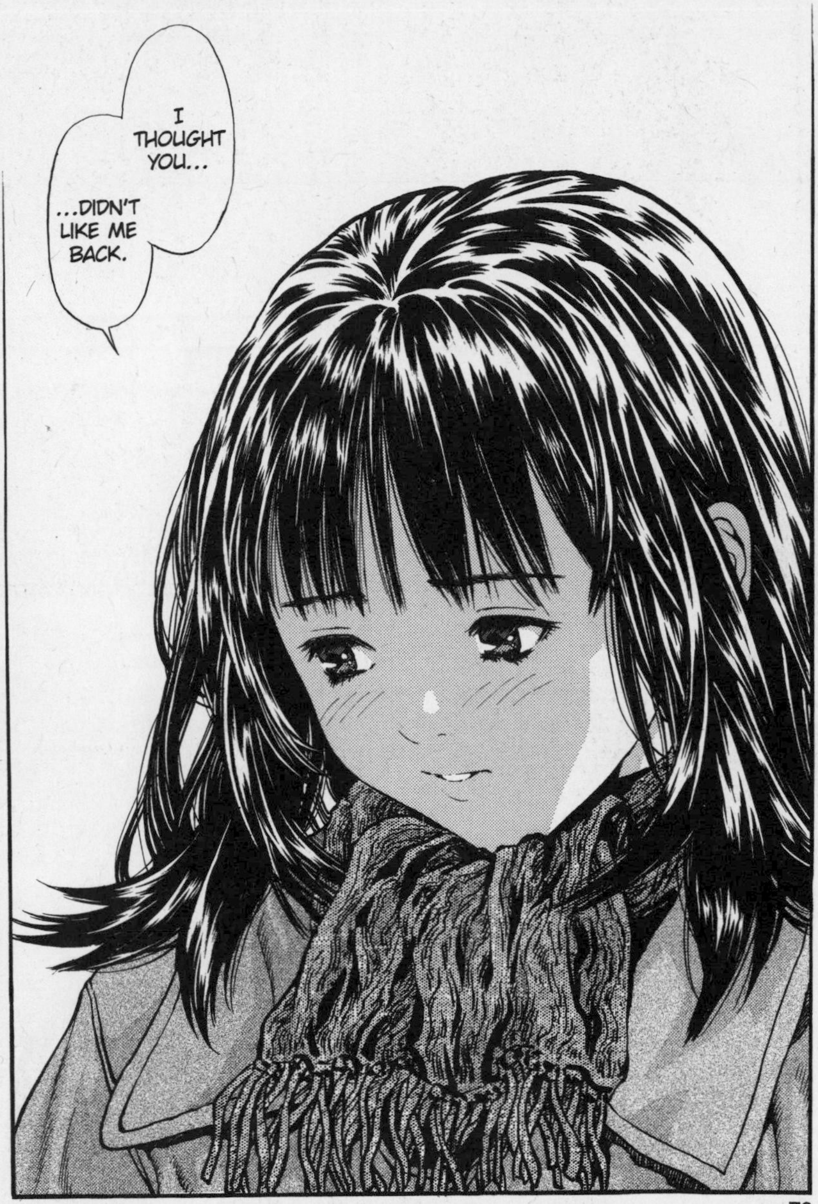
I THOUGHT YOU...
...DIDN'T LIKE ME BACK.

Chapter 88: Reminiscence, Part 1

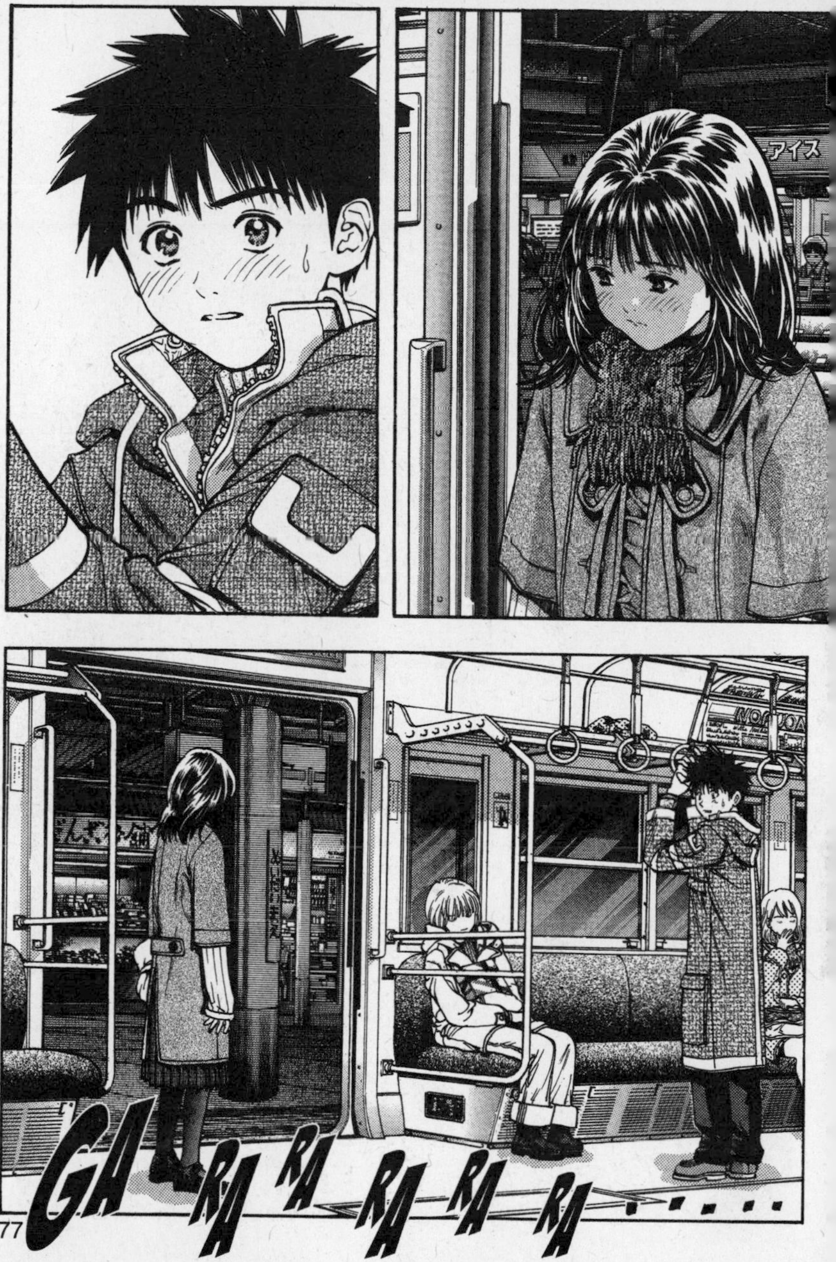
アイス
GARARARARARARARARARA.....

Chapter 88: Reminiscence, Part 1

READ THIS WAY

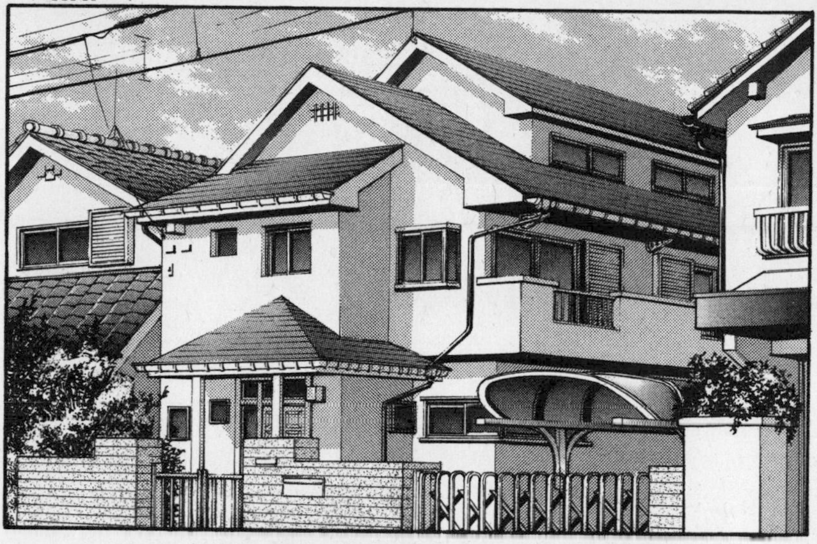

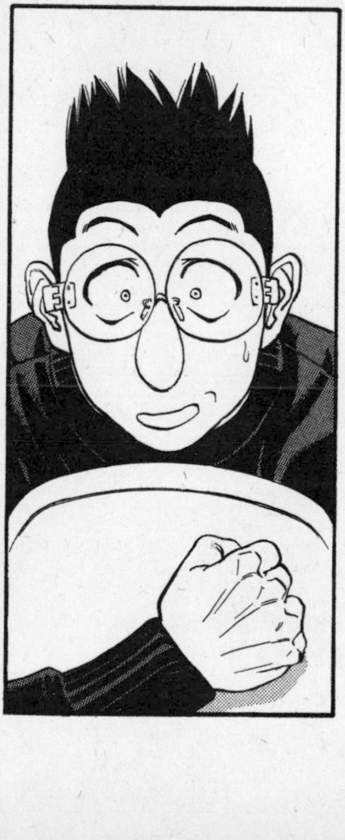

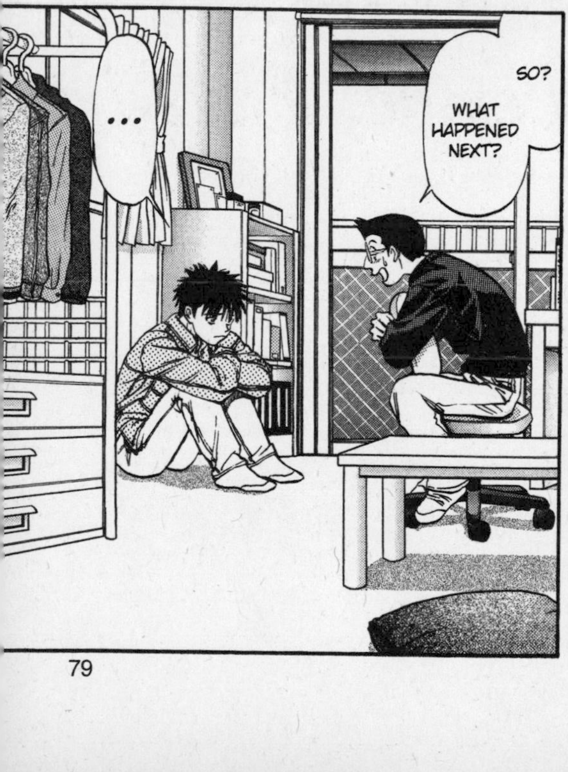
SO? WHAT HAPPENED NEXT?
...

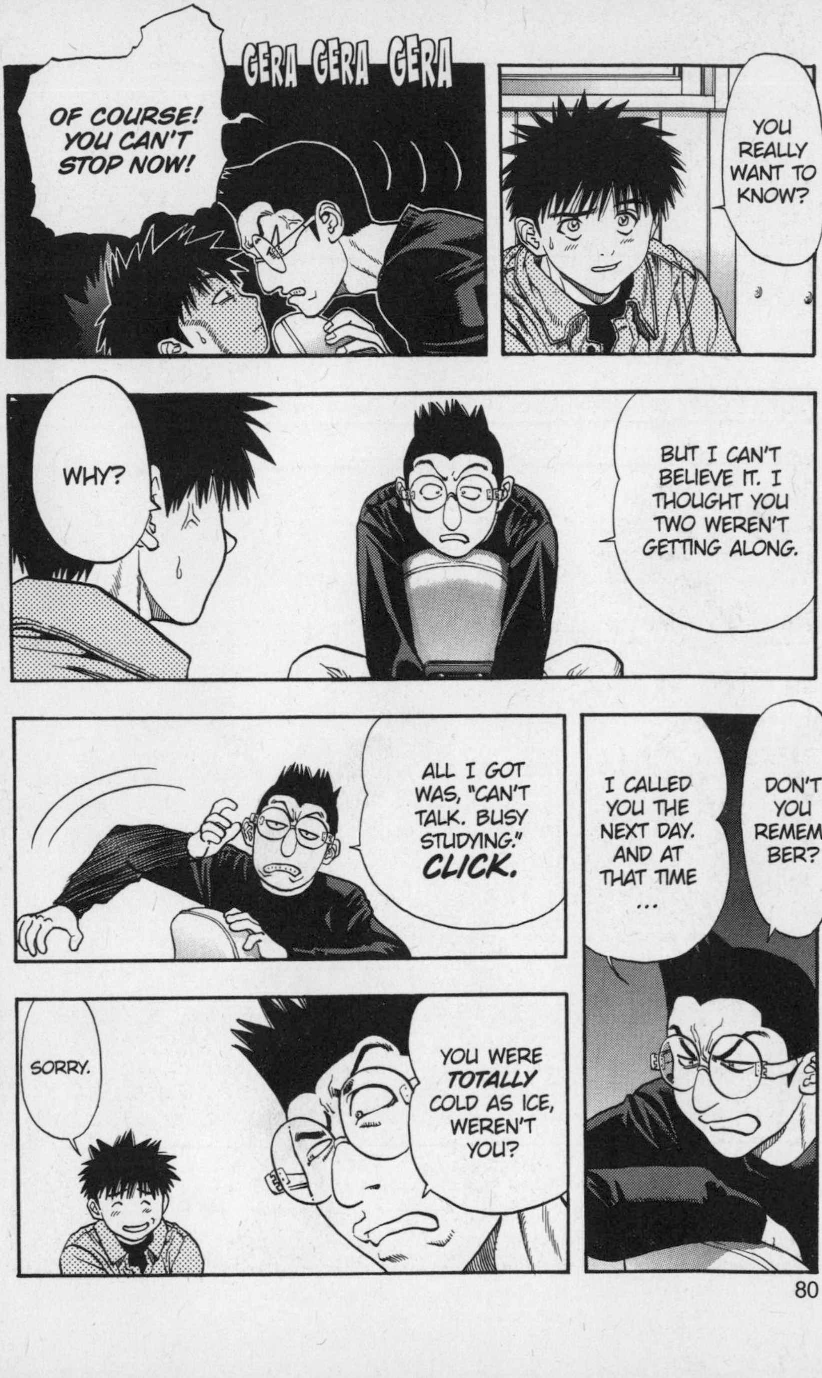
YOU REALLY WANT TO KNOW?
GERA GERA GERA
OF COURSE! YOU CAN'T STOP NOW!
BUT I CAN'T BELIEVE IT. I THOUGHT YOU TWO WEREN'T GETTING ALONG.
WHY?
DON'T YOU REMEMBER?
I CALLED YOU THE NEXT DAY. AND AT THAT TIME ...
ALL I GOT WAS, "CAN'T TALK. BUSY STUDYING." CLICK.
YOU WERE TOTALLY COLD AS ICE, WEREN'T YOU?
SORRY.

READ THIS WAY

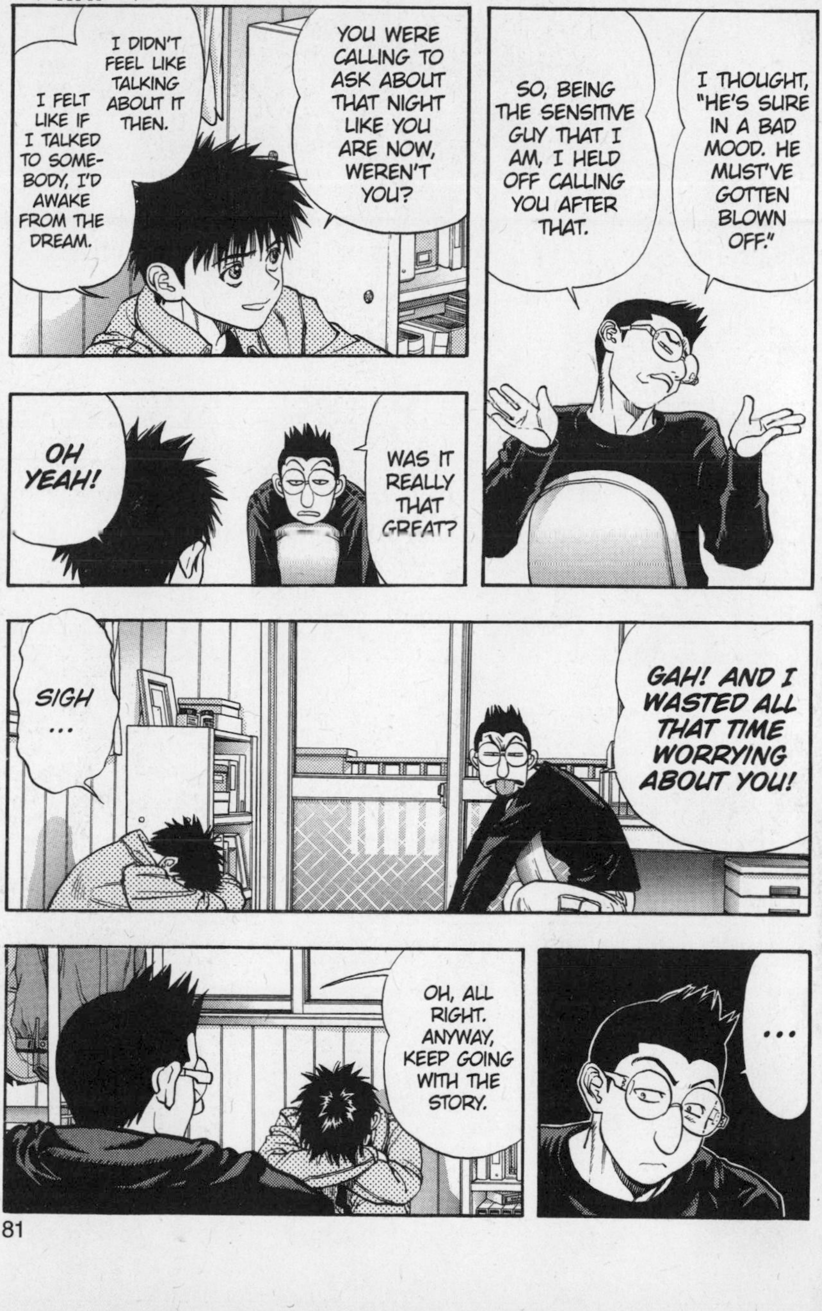
I THOUGHT, "HE'S SURE IN A BAD MOOD. HE MUST'VE GOTTEN BLOWN OFF."
SO, BEING THE SENSITIVE GUY THAT I AM, I HELD OFF CALLING YOU AFTER THAT.
YOU WERE CALLING TO ASK ABOUT THAT NIGHT LIKE YOU ARE NOW, WEREN'T YOU?
I DIDN'T FEEL LIKE TALKING ABOUT IT THEN.
I FELT LIKE IF I TALKED TO SOMEBODY, I'D AWAKE FROM THE DREAM.
WAS IT REALLY THAT GREAT?
OH YEAH!
GAH! AND I WASTED ALL THAT TIME WORRYING ABOUT YOU!
SIGH ...
...
OH, ALL RIGHT. ANYWAY, KEEP GOING WITH THE STORY.

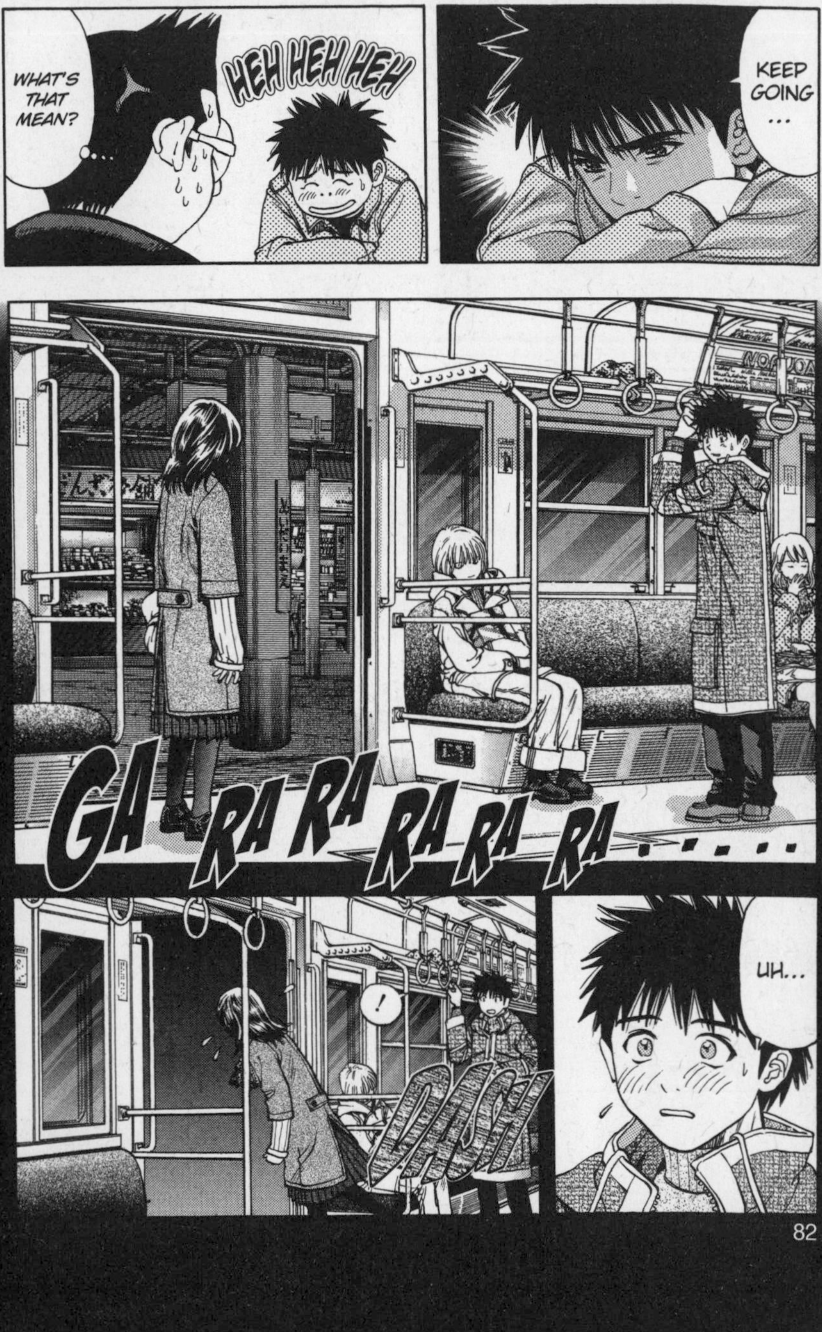
KEEP GOING ...
HEH HEH HEH
WHAT'S THAT MEAN?
GA RA RA RA RA RA.....
UH...
!
DASH

READ THIS WAY

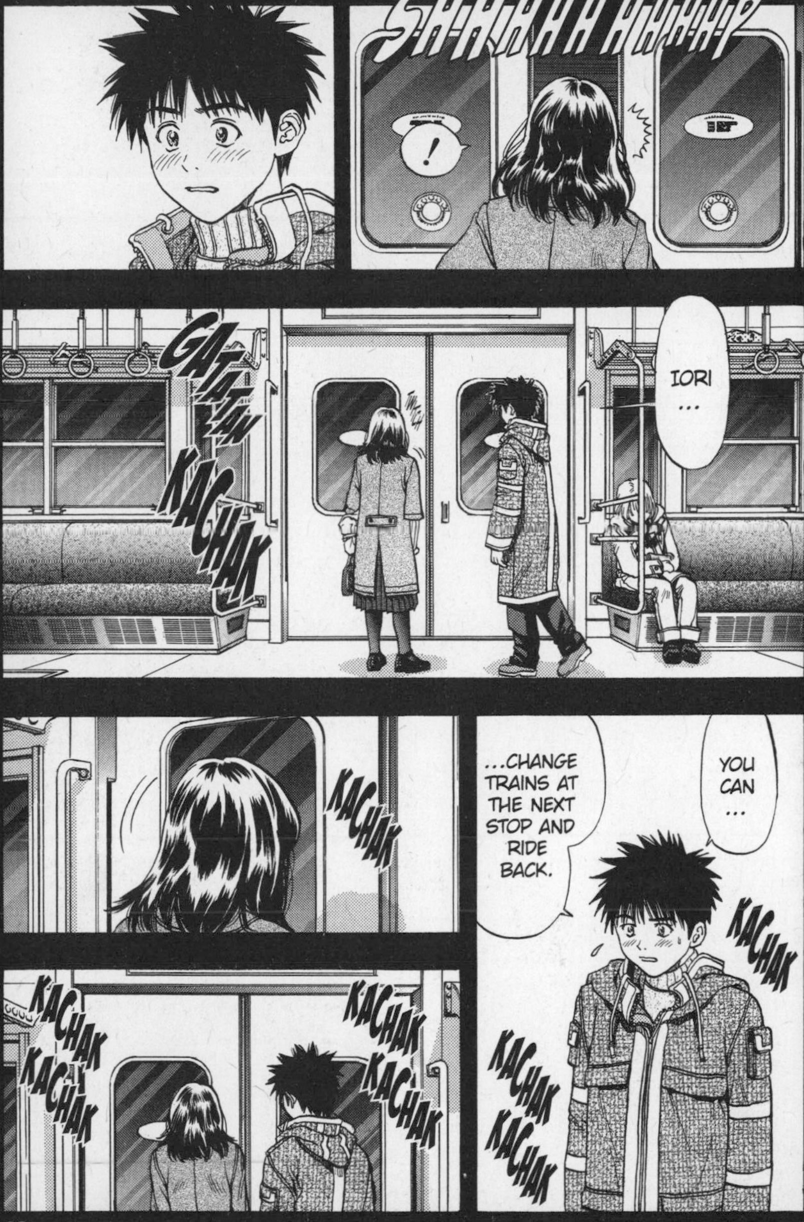

!
GATATAN
KACHAK
IORI ...
YOU CAN ...
...CHANGE TRAINS AT THE NEXT STOP AND RIDE BACK.
KACHAK
KACHAK KACHAK
KACHAK
KACHAK KACHAK
KACHAK KACHAK

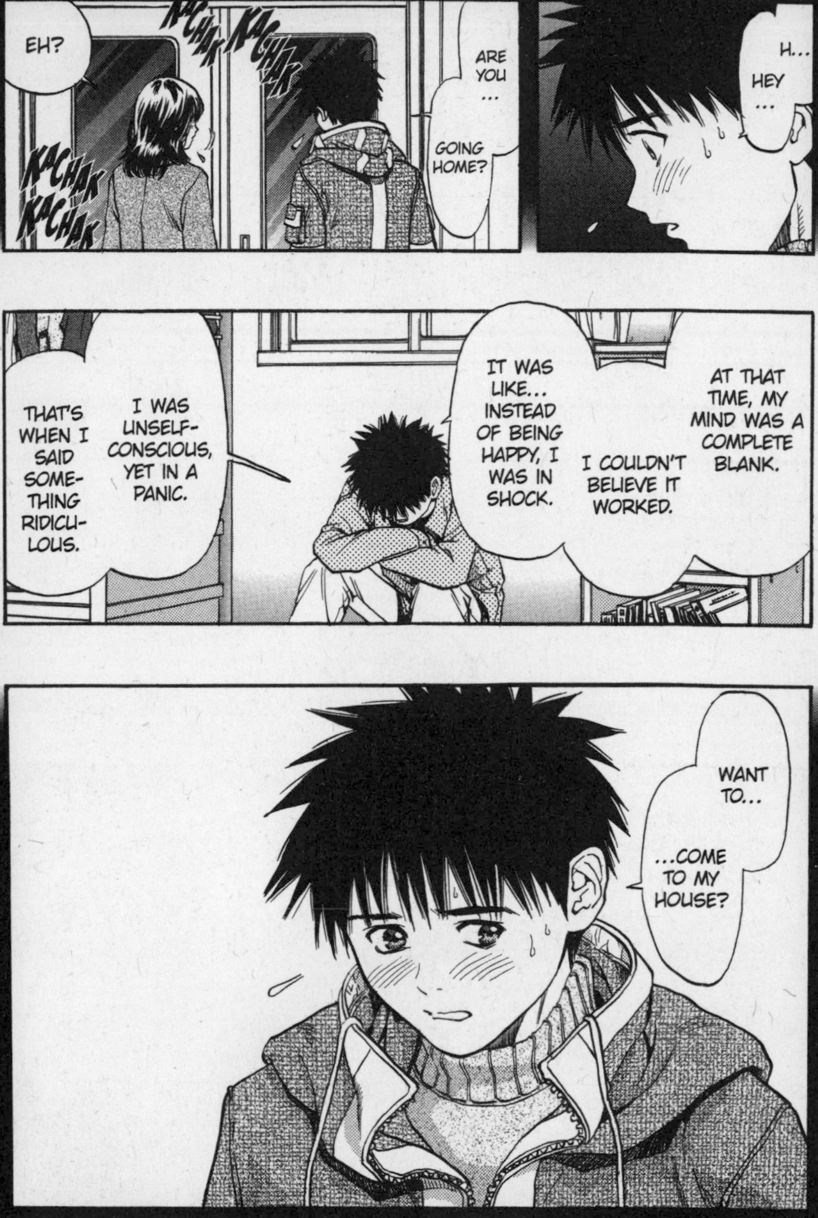
H... HEY ...
KACHAK KACHAK
ARE YOU ... GOING HOME?
EH?
KACHAK KACHAK
AT THAT TIME, MY MIND WAS A COMPLETE BLANK.
I COULDN'T BELIEVE IT WORKED.
IT WAS LIKE... INSTEAD OF BEING HAPPY, I WAS IN SHOCK.
I WAS UNSELF-CONSCIOUS, YET IN A PANIC.
THAT'S WHEN I SAID SOMETHING RIDICULOUS.
WANT TO...
...COME TO MY HOUSE?

READ THIS WAY

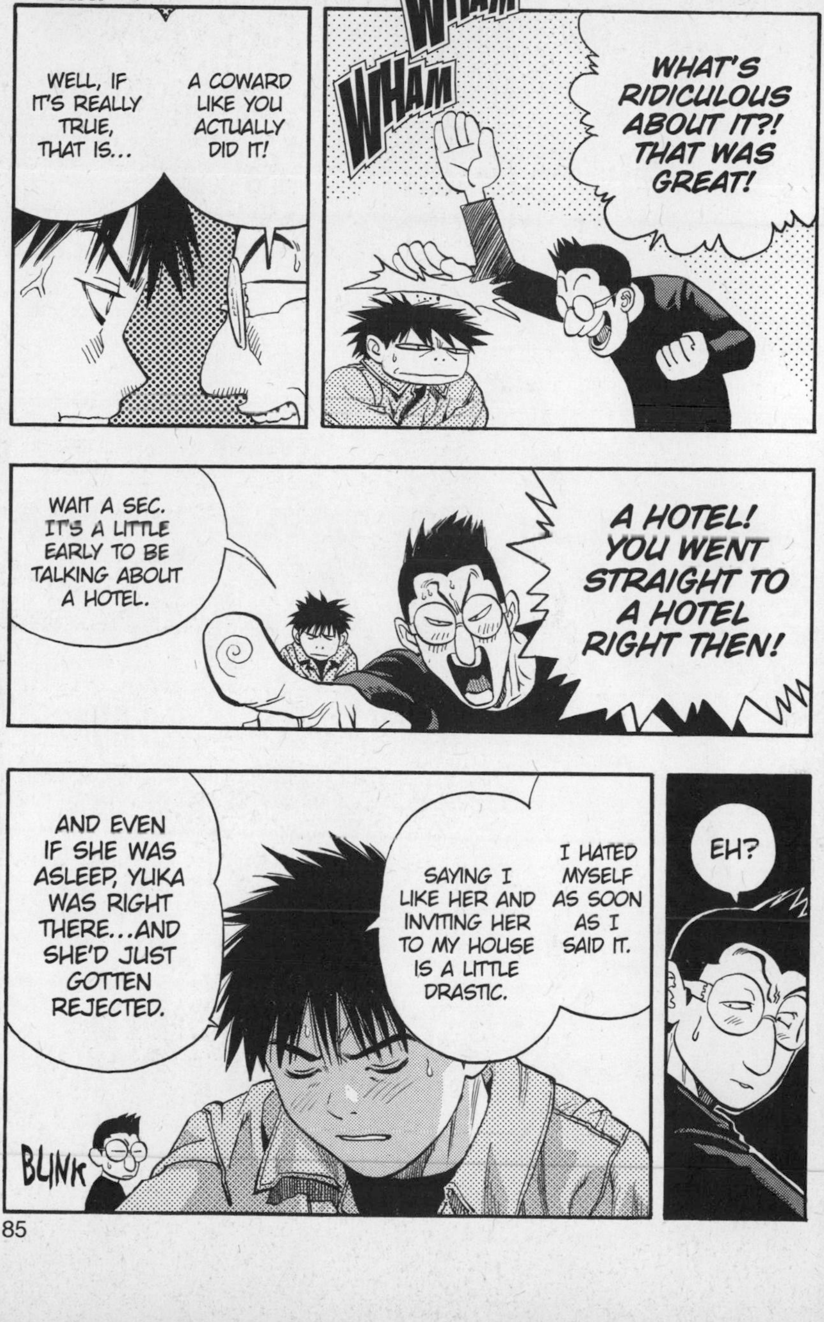
WHAM
WHAM
WHAT'S RIDICULOUS ABOUT IT?! THAT WAS GREAT!
A COWARD LIKE YOU ACTUALLY DID IT!
WELL, IF IT'S REALLY TRUE, THAT IS...
A HOTEL! YOU WENT STRAIGHT TO A HOTEL RIGHT THEN!
WAIT A SEC. IT'S A LITTLE EARLY TO BE TALKING ABOUT A HOTEL.
EH?
I HATED MYSELF AS SOON AS I SAID IT.
SAYING I LIKE HER AND INVITING HER TO MY HOUSE IS A LITTLE DRASTIC.
AND EVEN IF SHE WAS ASLEEP, YUKA WAS RIGHT THERE...AND SHE'D JUST GOTTEN REJECTED.
BLINK

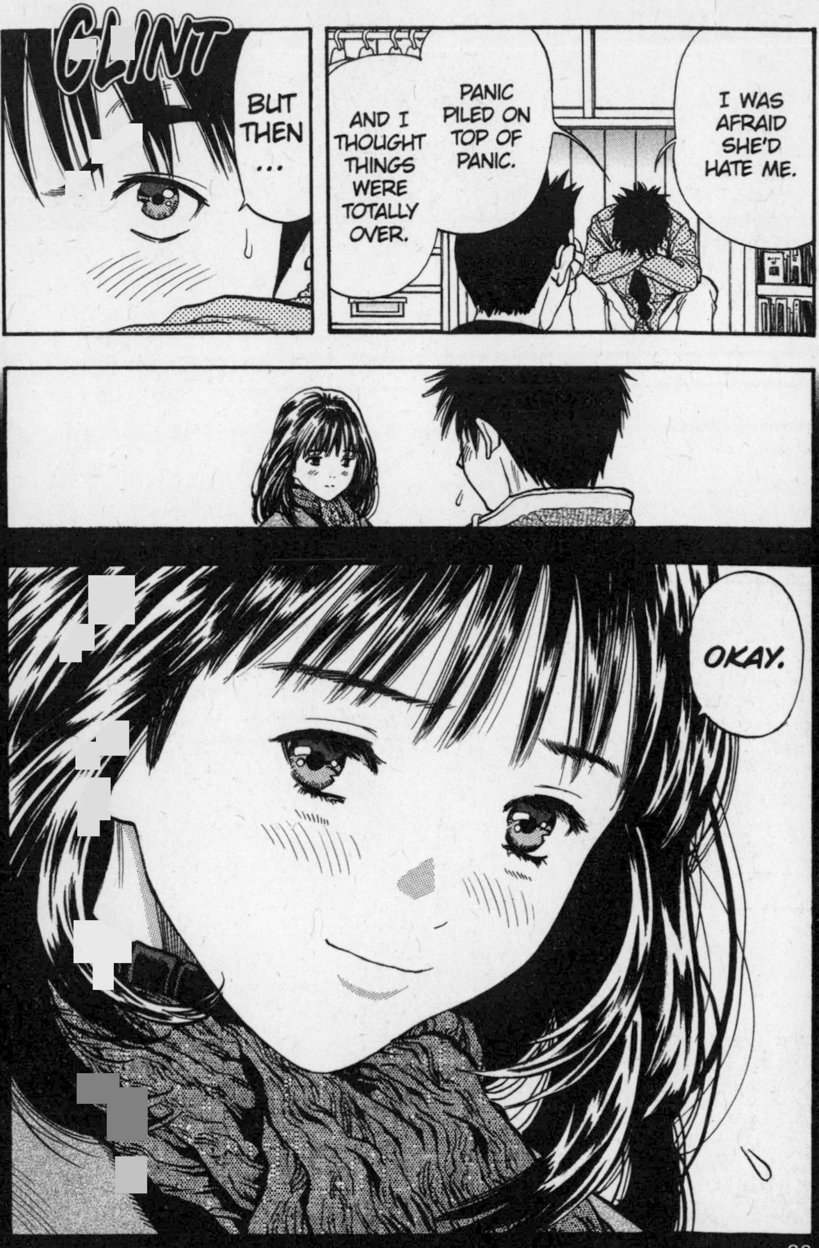
I WAS AFRAID SHE'D HATE ME.
PANIC PILED ON TOP OF PANIC.
AND I THOUGHT THINGS WERE TOTALLY OVER.
CLINT
BUT THEN ...
OKAY.

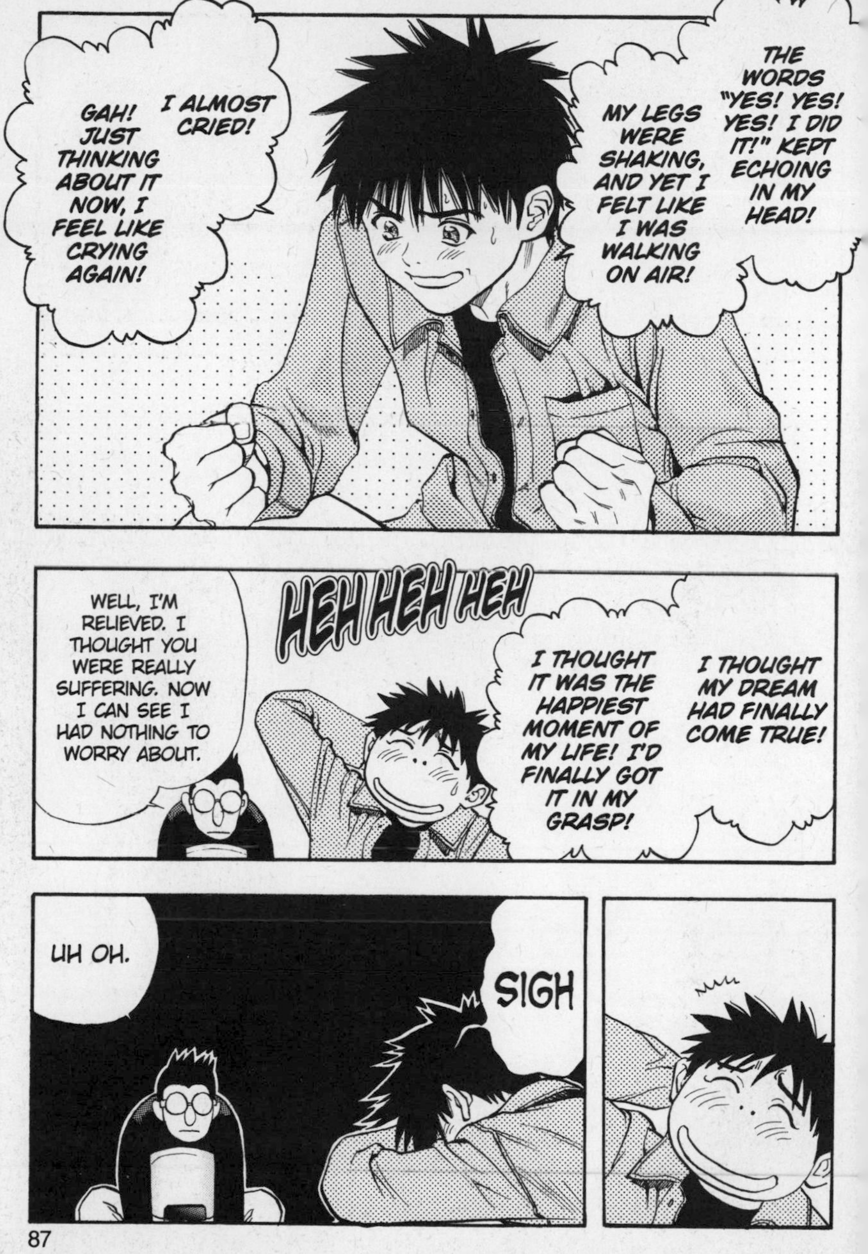
THE WORDS "YES! YES! YES! I DID IT!" KEPT ECHOING IN MY HEAD!
MY LEGS WERE SHAKING, AND YET I FELT LIKE I WAS WALKING ON AIR!
I ALMOST CRIED!
GAH! JUST THINKING ABOUT IT NOW, I FEEL LIKE CRYING AGAIN!
I THOUGHT MY DREAM HAD FINALLY COME TRUE!
I THOUGHT IT WAS THE HAPPIEST MOMENT OF MY LIFE! I'D FINALLY GOT IT IN MY GRASP!
HEH HEH HEH
WELL, I'M RELIEVED. I THOUGHT YOU WERE REALLY SUFFERING. NOW I CAN SEE I HAD NOTHING TO WORRY ABOUT.
SIGH
UH OH.

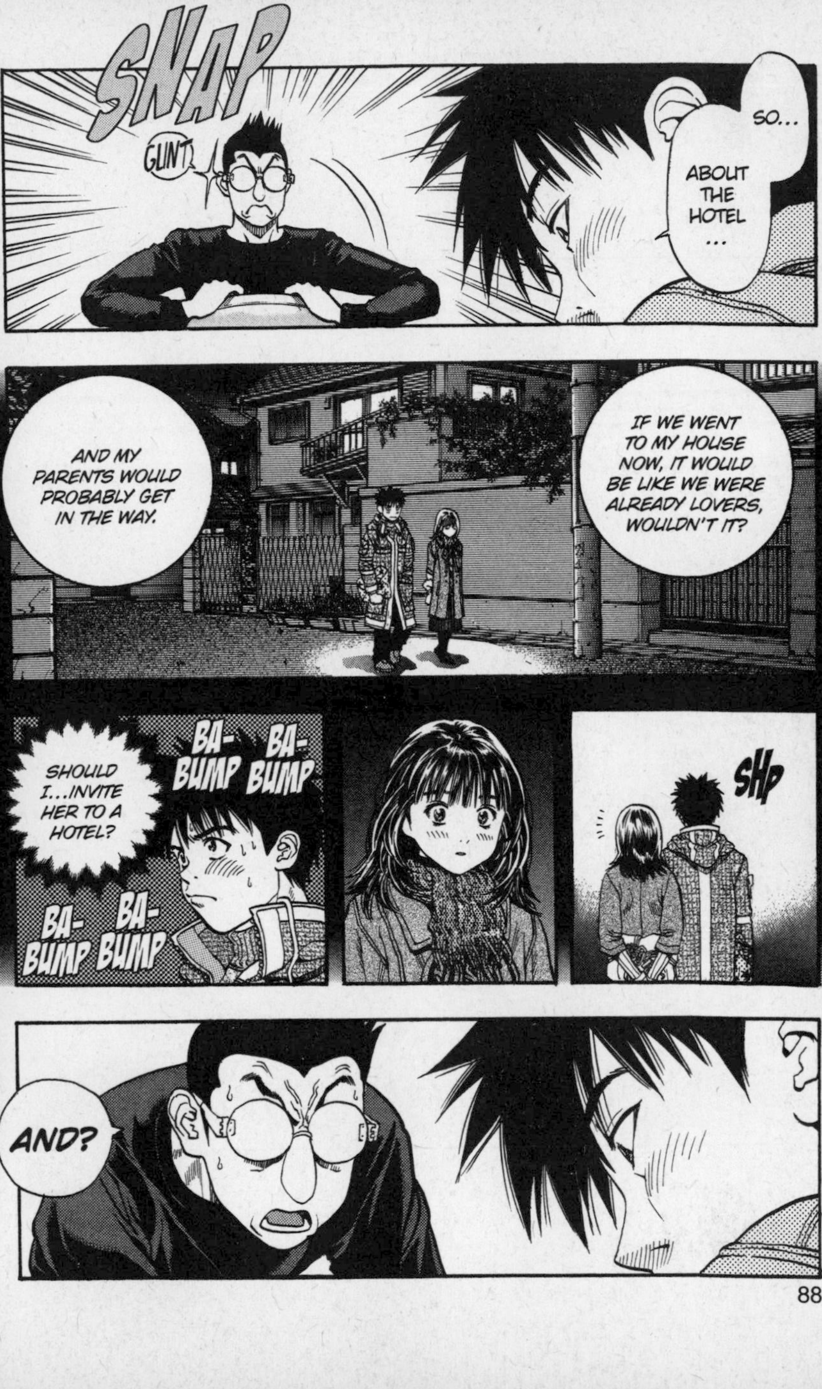
SO...
ABOUT THE HOTEL ...
SNAP
GLINT
IF WE WENT TO MY HOUSE NOW, IT WOULD BE LIKE WE WERE ALREADY LOVERS, WOULDN'T IT?
AND MY PARENTS WOULD PROBABLY GET IN THE WAY.
SHP
BA-BUMP BA-BUMP
SHOULD I...INVITE HER TO A HOTEL?
BA-BUMP BA-BUMP
AND?

READ THIS WAY

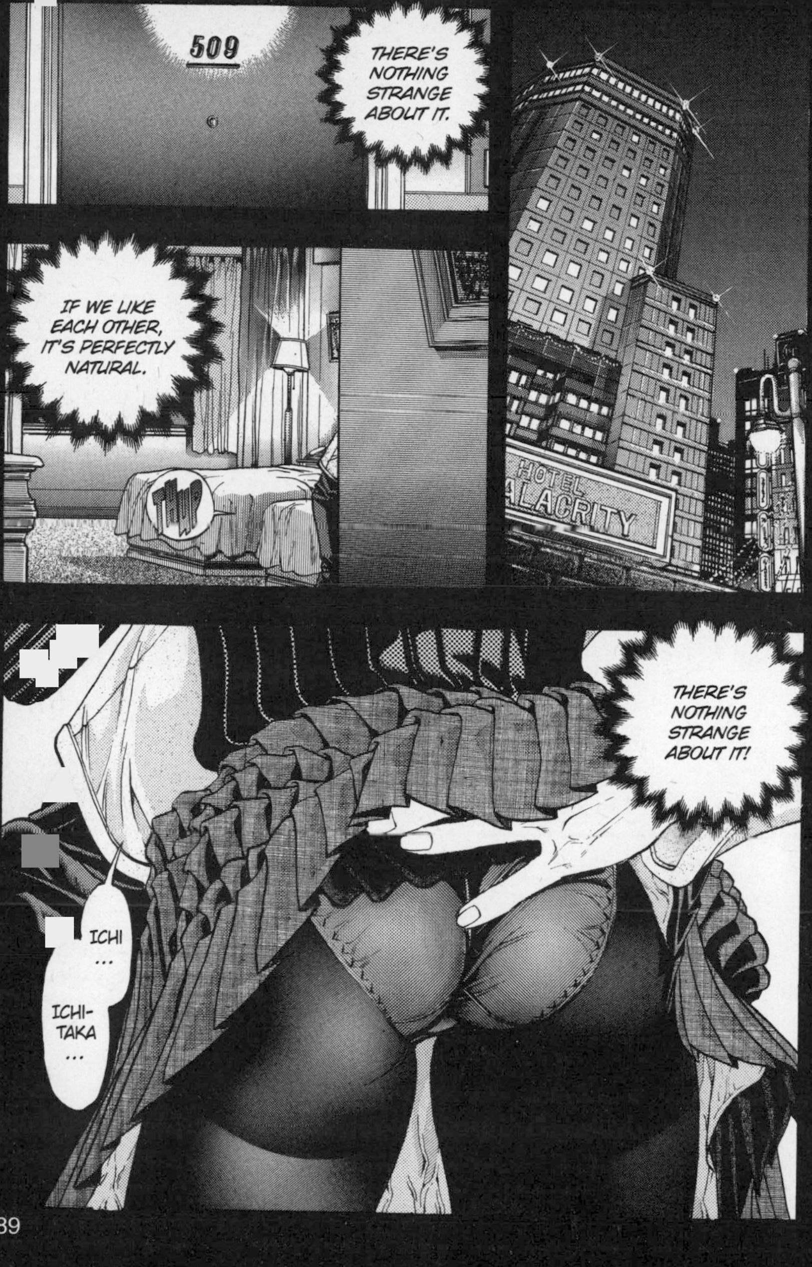
HOTEL ALACRITY
509
THERE'S NOTHING STRANGE ABOUT IT.
IF WE LIKE EACH OTHER, IT'S PERFECTLY NATURAL.
THUP
THERE'S NOTHING STRANGE ABOUT IT!
ICHI ... ICHI-TAKA ...

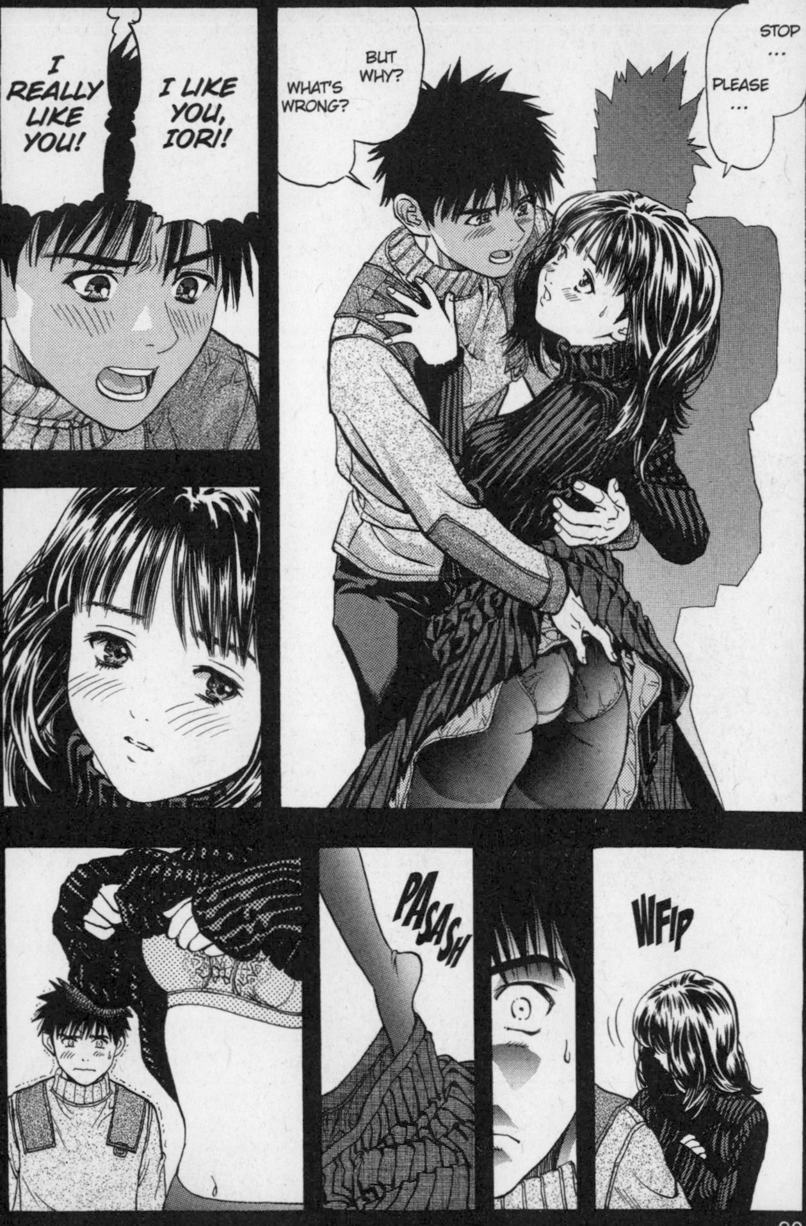
STOP ... PLEASE ...
BUT WHY?
WHAT'S WRONG?
I LIKE YOU, IORI!
I REALLY LIKE YOU!
WFIP
PASASH

READ THIS WAY

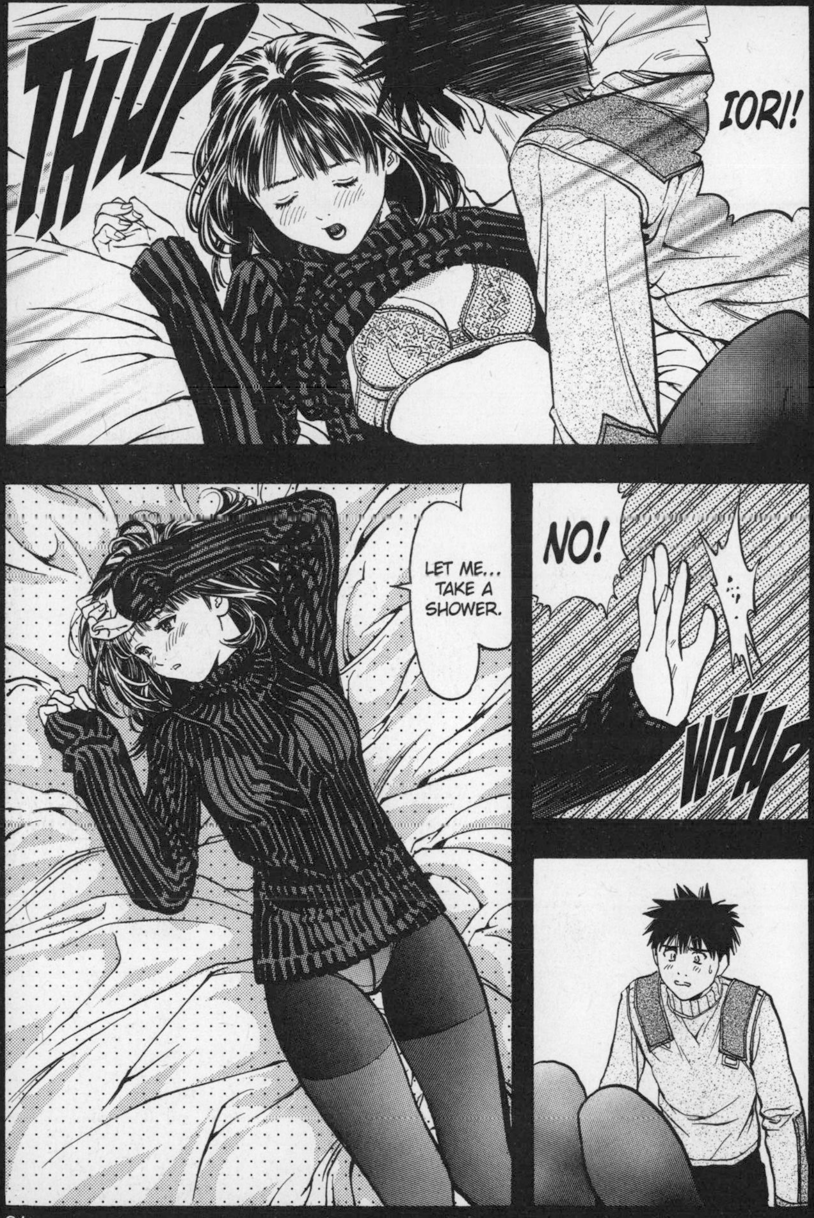
IORI!
THUD
NO!
WHAP
LET ME... TAKE A SHOWER.

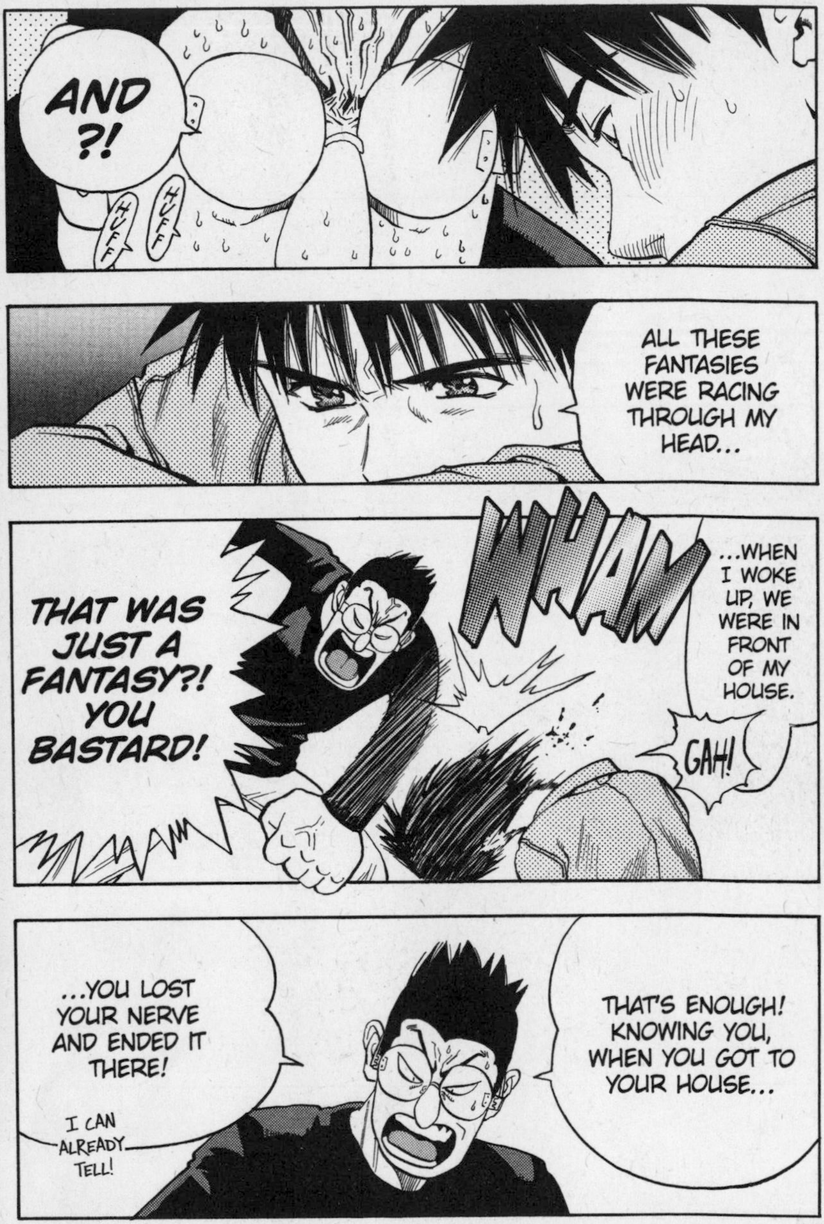
AND ?!
HUFF
HUFF
ALL THESE FANTASIES WERE RACING THROUGH MY HEAD...
...WHEN I WOKE UP, WE WERE IN FRONT OF MY HOUSE.
WHAM
GAH!
THAT WAS JUST A FANTASY?! YOU BASTARD!
THAT'S ENOUGH! KNOWING YOU, WHEN YOU GOT TO YOUR HOUSE...
...YOU LOST YOUR NERVE AND ENDED IT THERE!
I CAN ALREADY TELL!

READ THIS WAY

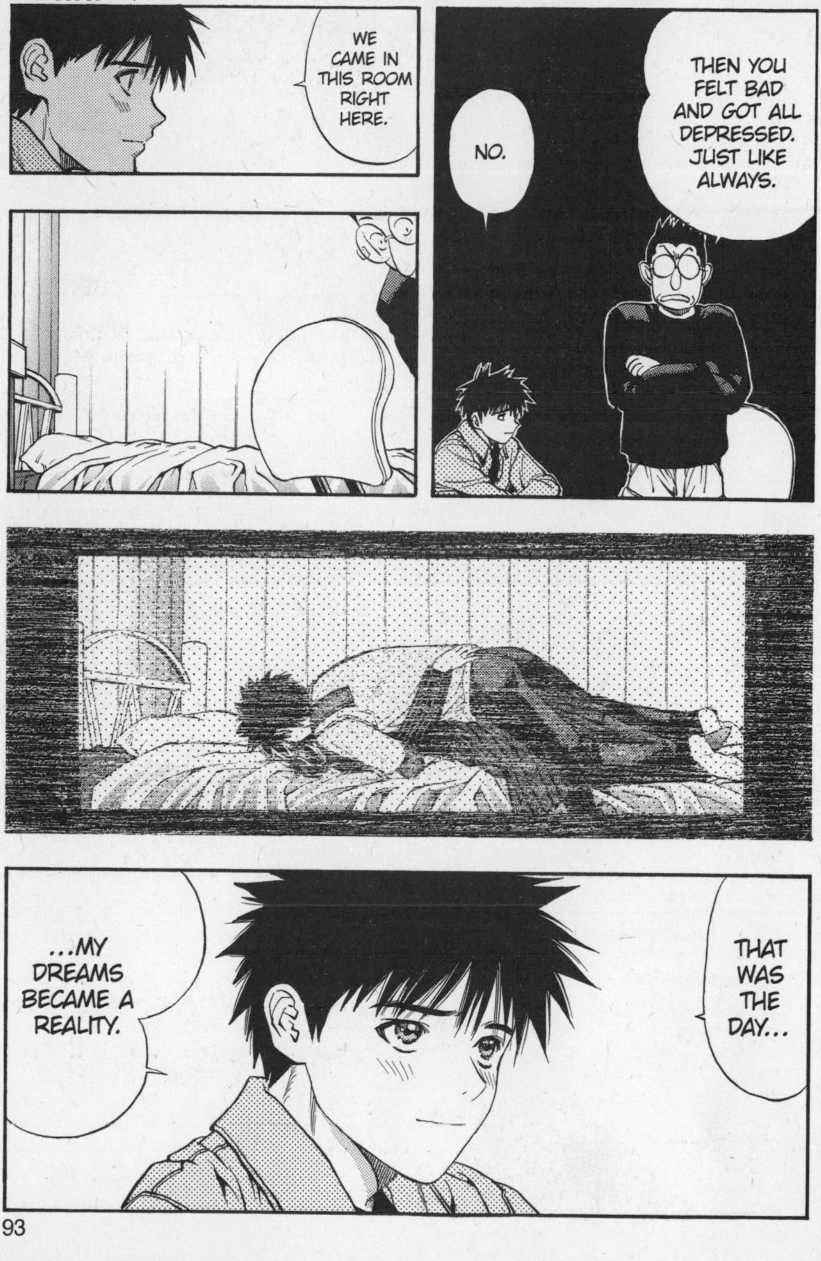
THEN YOU FELT BAD AND GOT ALL DEPRESSED. JUST LIKE ALWAYS.
NO.
WE CAME IN THIS ROOM RIGHT HERE.
THAT WAS THE DAY...
...MY DREAMS BECAME A REALITY.

Chapter 89:
Reminiscence, Part 2

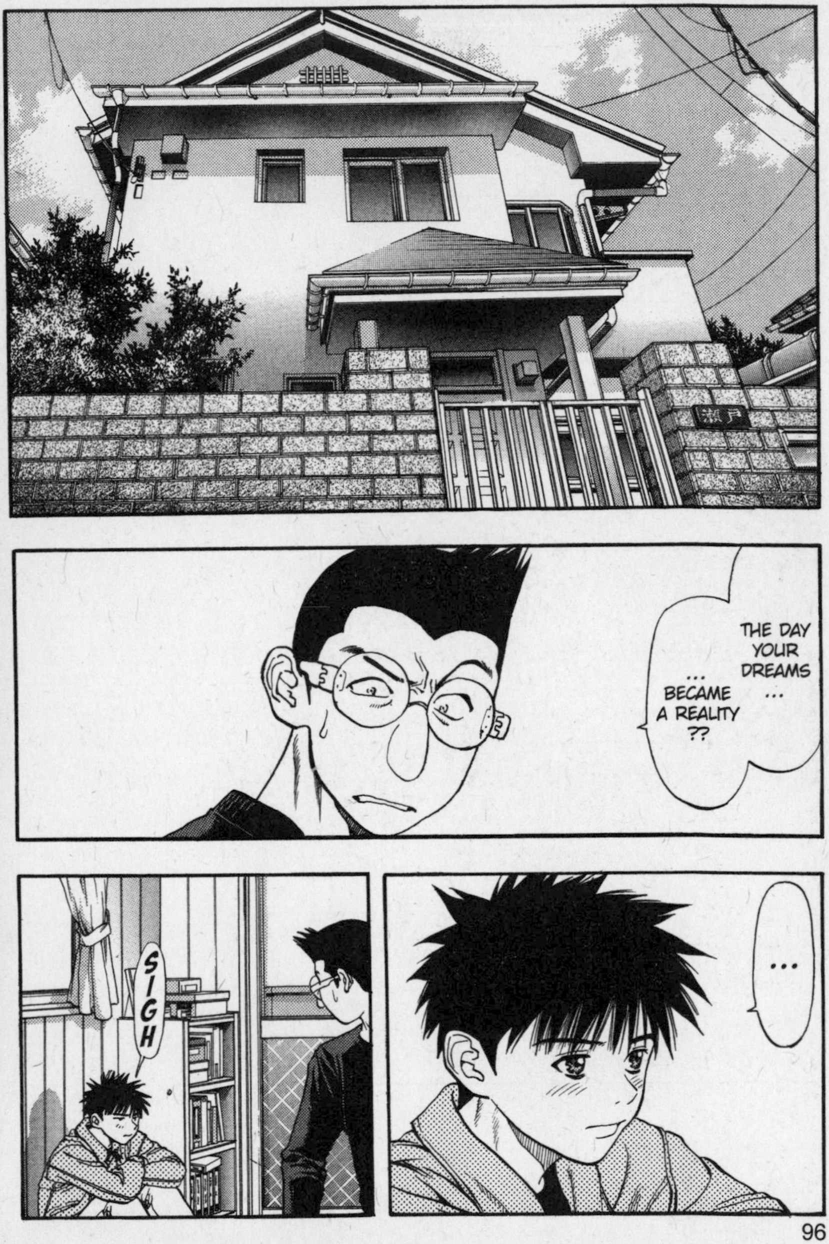

瀬戸
THE DAY YOUR DREAMS ...
... BECAME A REALITY ??
...
SIGH

READ THIS WAY

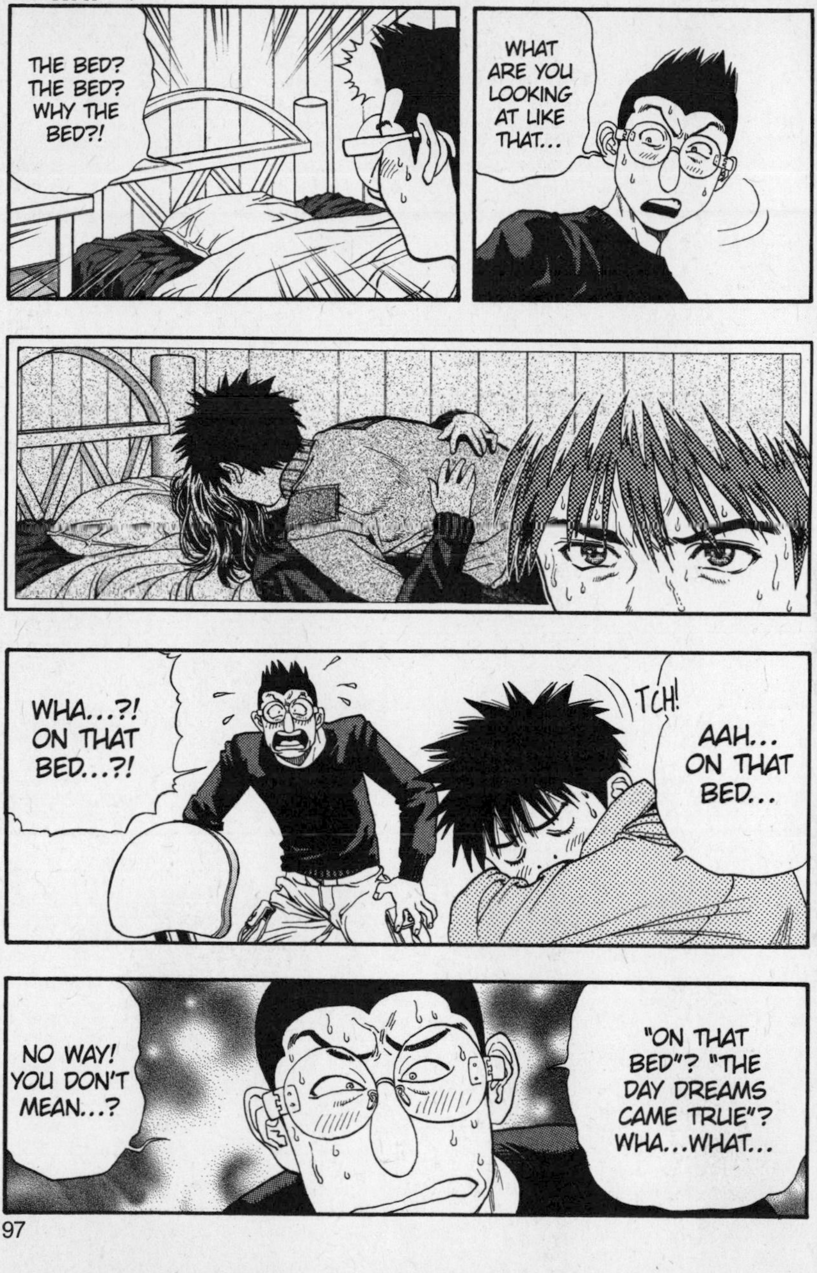

WHAT ARE YOU LOOKING AT LIKE THAT...
THE BED? THE BED? WHY THE BED?!
AAH... ON THAT BED...
TCH!
WHA...?! ON THAT BED...?!
"ON THAT BED"? "THE DAY DREAMS CAME TRUE"? WHA...WHAT...
NO WAY! YOU DON'T MEAN...?

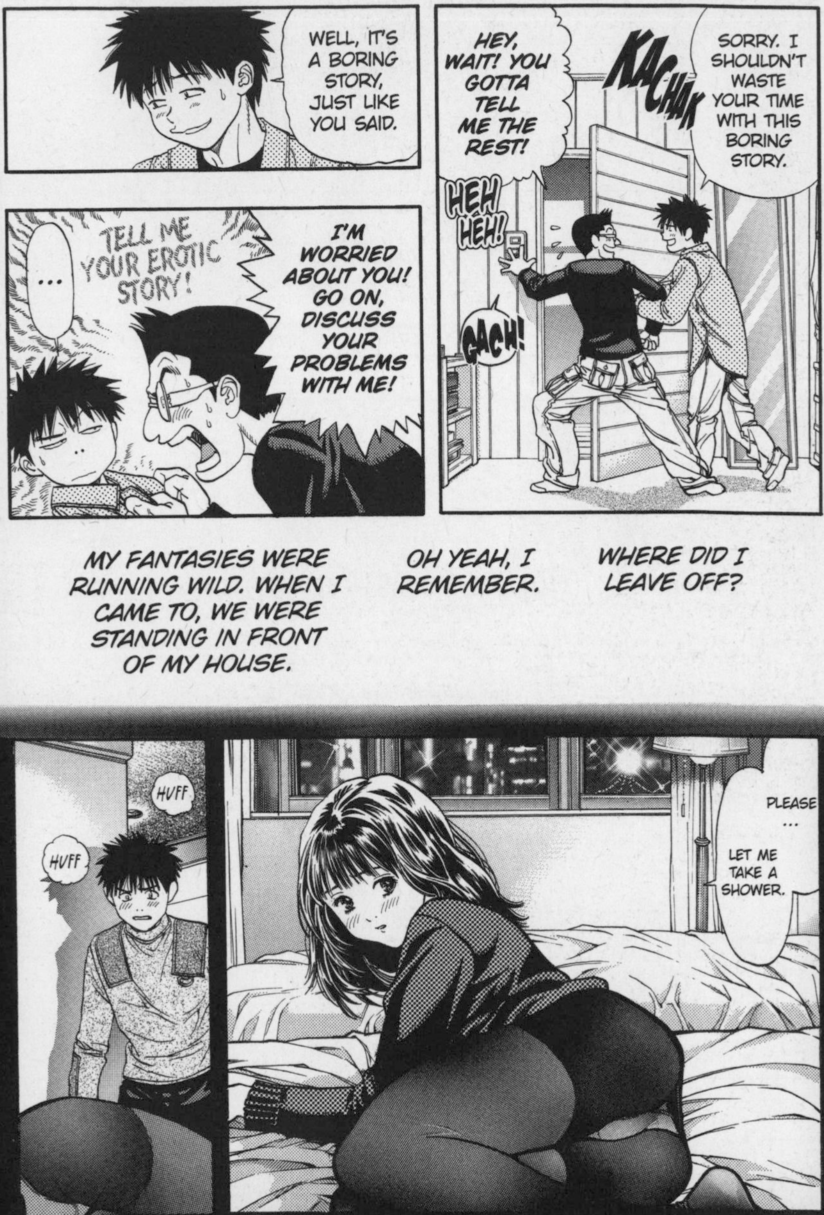
SORRY. I SHOULDN'T WASTE YOUR TIME WITH THIS BORING STORY.
KACHAK
HEY, WAIT! YOU GOTTA TELL ME THE REST!
HEH HEH!
GACH!
WELL, IT'S A BORING STORY, JUST LIKE YOU SAID.
I'M WORRIED ABOUT YOU! GO ON, DISCUSS YOUR PROBLEMS WITH ME!
TELL ME YOUR EROTIC STORY!
...
WHERE DID I LEAVE OFF?
OH YEAH, I REMEMBER.
MY FANTASIES WERE RUNNING WILD. WHEN I CAME TO, WE WERE STANDING IN FRONT OF MY HOUSE.
PLEASE ... LET ME TAKE A SHOWER.
HUFF
HUFF

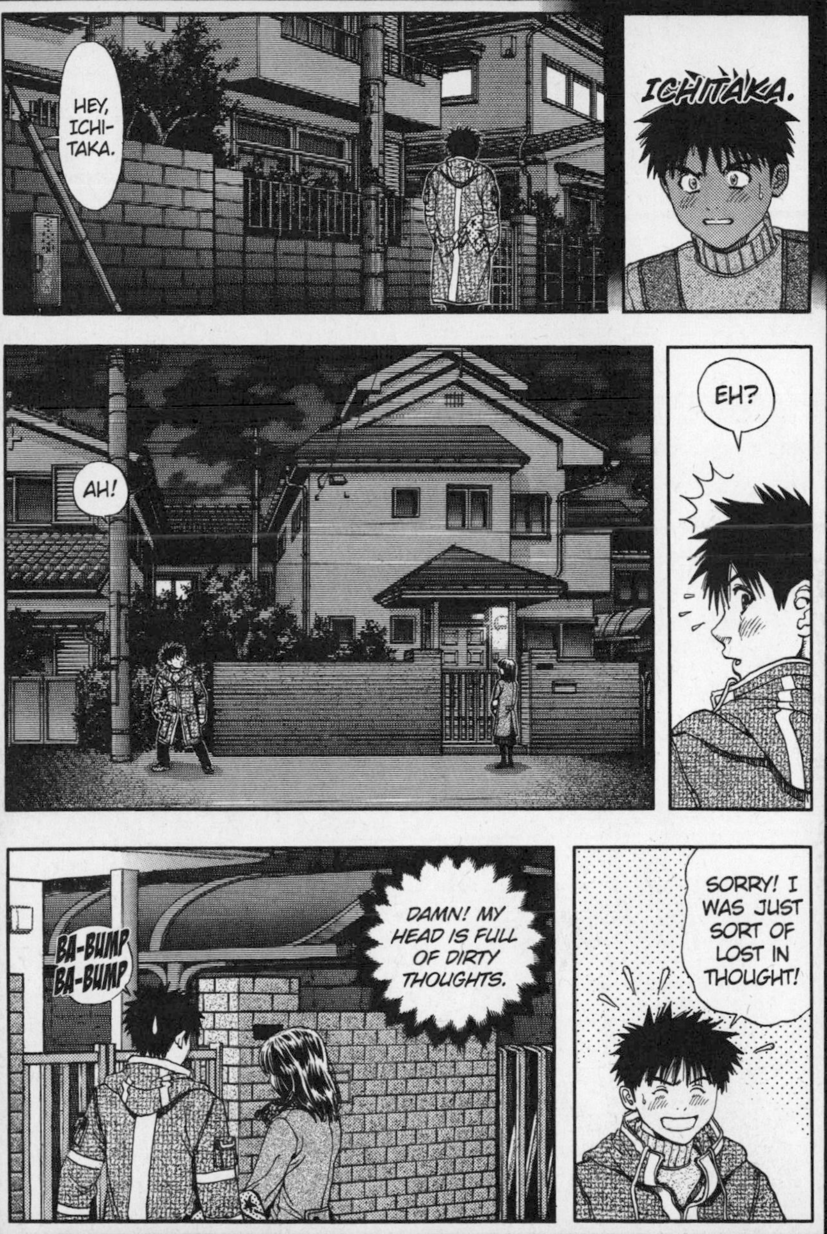
ICHITAKA.
HEY, ICHI-TAKA.
EH?
AH!
SORRY! I WAS JUST SORT OF LOST IN THOUGHT!
DAMN! MY HEAD IS FULL OF DIRTY THOUGHTS.
BA-BUMP BA-BUMP

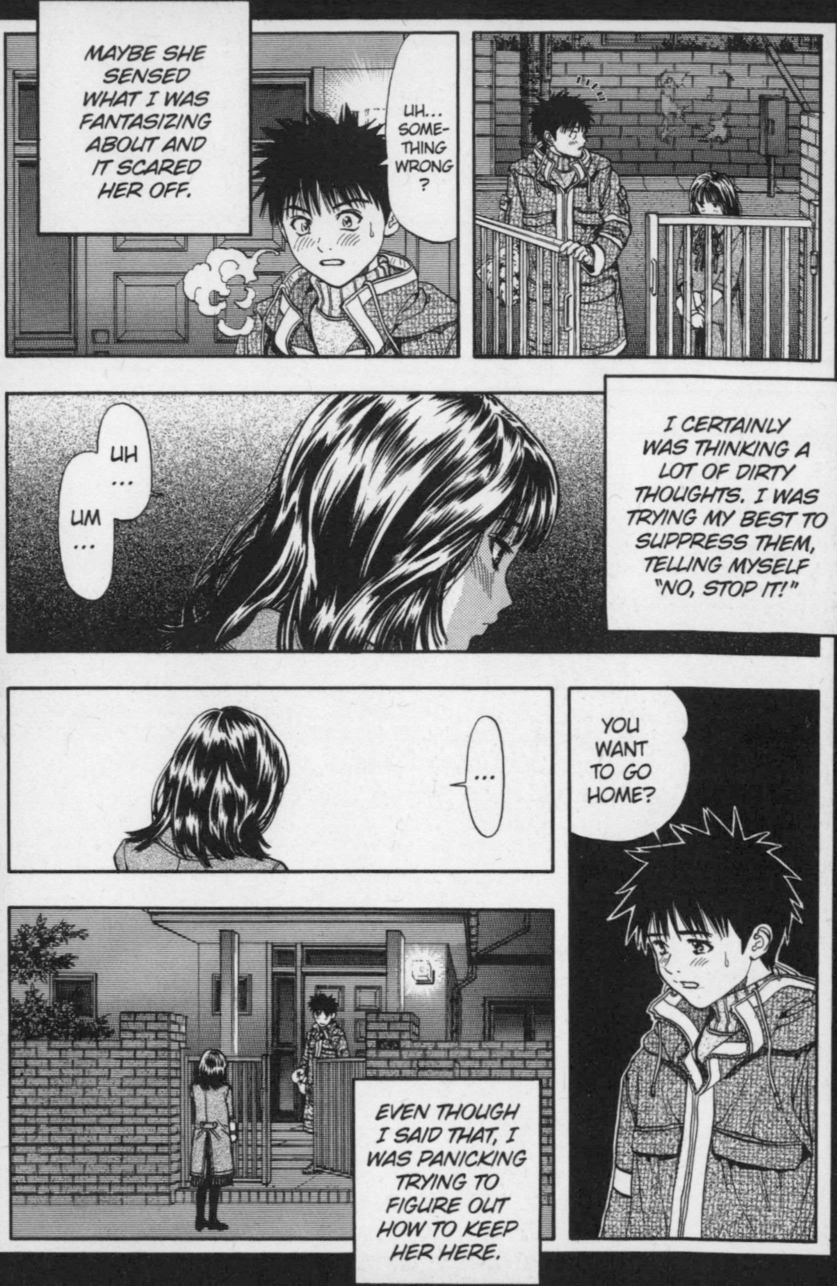
UH... SOMETHING WRONG?
MAYBE SHE SENSED WHAT I WAS FANTASIZING ABOUT AND IT SCARED HER OFF.
I CERTAINLY WAS THINKING A LOT OF DIRTY THOUGHTS. I WAS TRYING MY BEST TO SUPPRESS THEM, TELLING MYSELF "NO, STOP IT!"
UH ... UM ...
YOU WANT TO GO HOME?
...
EVEN THOUGH I SAID THAT, I WAS PANICKING TRYING TO FIGURE OUT HOW TO KEEP HER HERE.

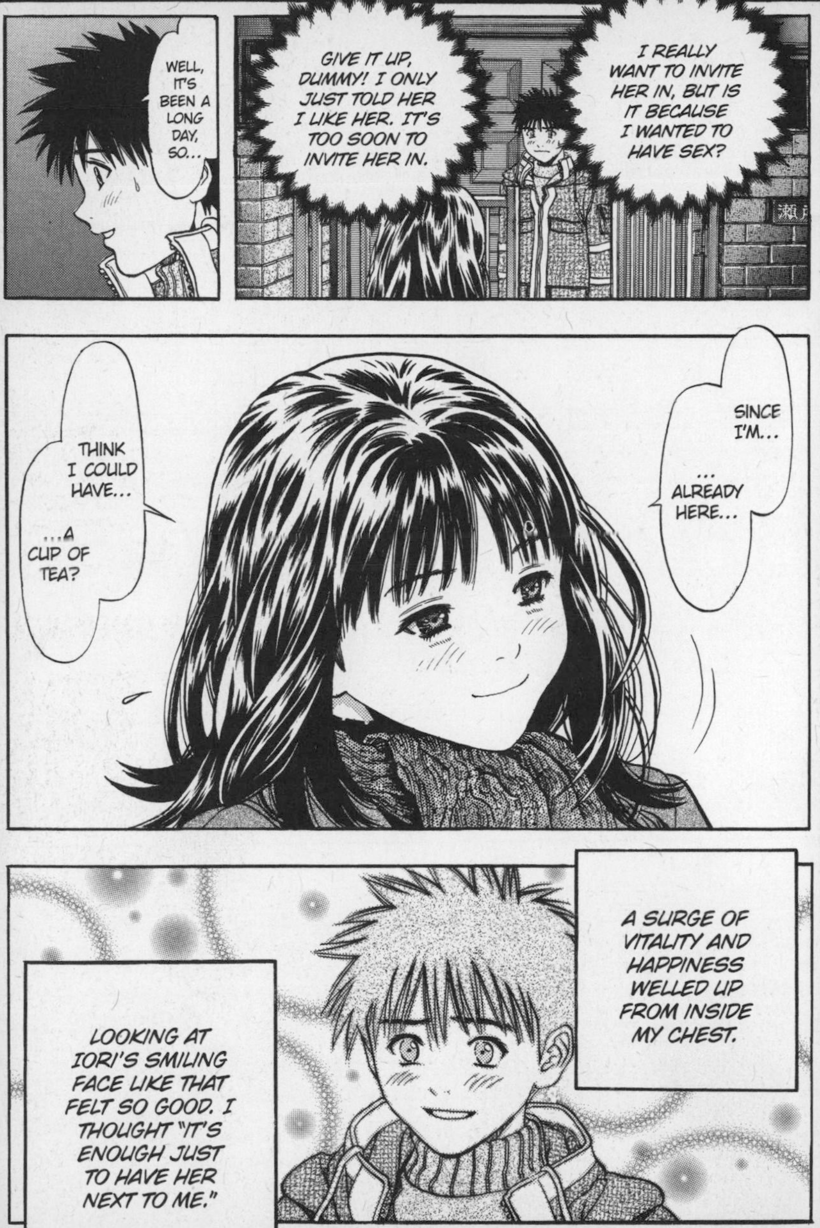
I REALLY WANT TO INVITE HER IN, BUT IS IT BECAUSE I WANTED TO HAVE SEX?
GIVE IT UP, DUMMY! I ONLY JUST TOLD HER I LIKE HER. IT'S TOO SOON TO INVITE HER IN.
WELL, IT'S BEEN A LONG DAY, SO...
SINCE I'M...
... ALREADY HERE...
THINK I COULD HAVE...
...A CUP OF TEA?
A SURGE OF VITALITY AND HAPPINESS WELLED UP FROM INSIDE MY CHEST.
LOOKING AT IORI'S SMILING FACE LIKE THAT FELT SO GOOD. I THOUGHT "IT'S ENOUGH JUST TO HAVE HER NEXT TO ME."

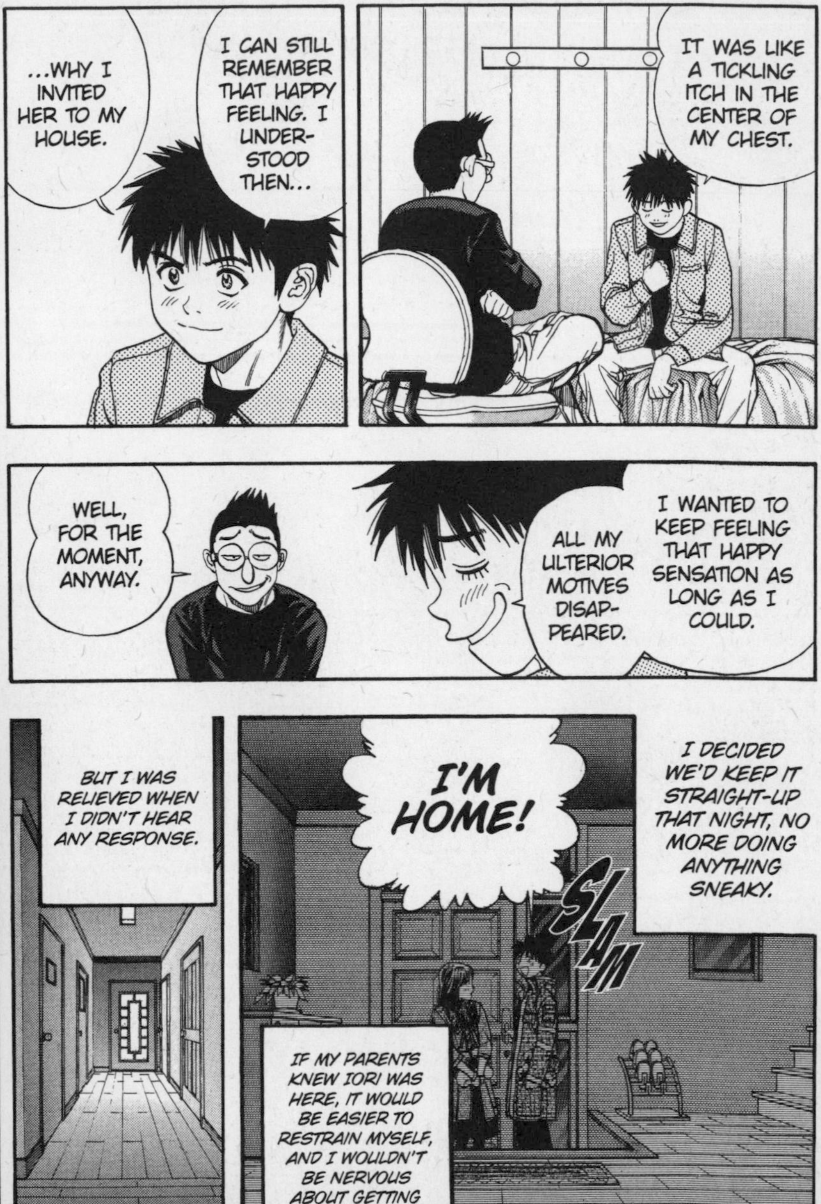
IT WAS LIKE A TICKLING ITCH IN THE CENTER OF MY CHEST.
I CAN STILL REMEMBER THAT HAPPY FEELING. I UNDERSTOOD THEN...
...WHY I INVITED HER TO MY HOUSE.
I WANTED TO KEEP FEELING THAT HAPPY SENSATION AS LONG AS I COULD.
ALL MY ULTERIOR MOTIVES DISAPPEARED.
WELL, FOR THE MOMENT, ANYWAY.
I DECIDED WE'D KEEP IT STRAIGHT-UP THAT NIGHT, NO MORE DOING ANYTHING SNEAKY.
I'M HOME!
SLAM
IF MY PARENTS KNEW IORI WAS HERE, IT WOULD BE EASIER TO RESTRAIN MYSELF, AND I WOULDN'T BE NERVOUS ABOUT GETTING CAUGHT.
BUT I WAS RELIEVED WHEN I DIDN'T HEAR ANY RESPONSE.

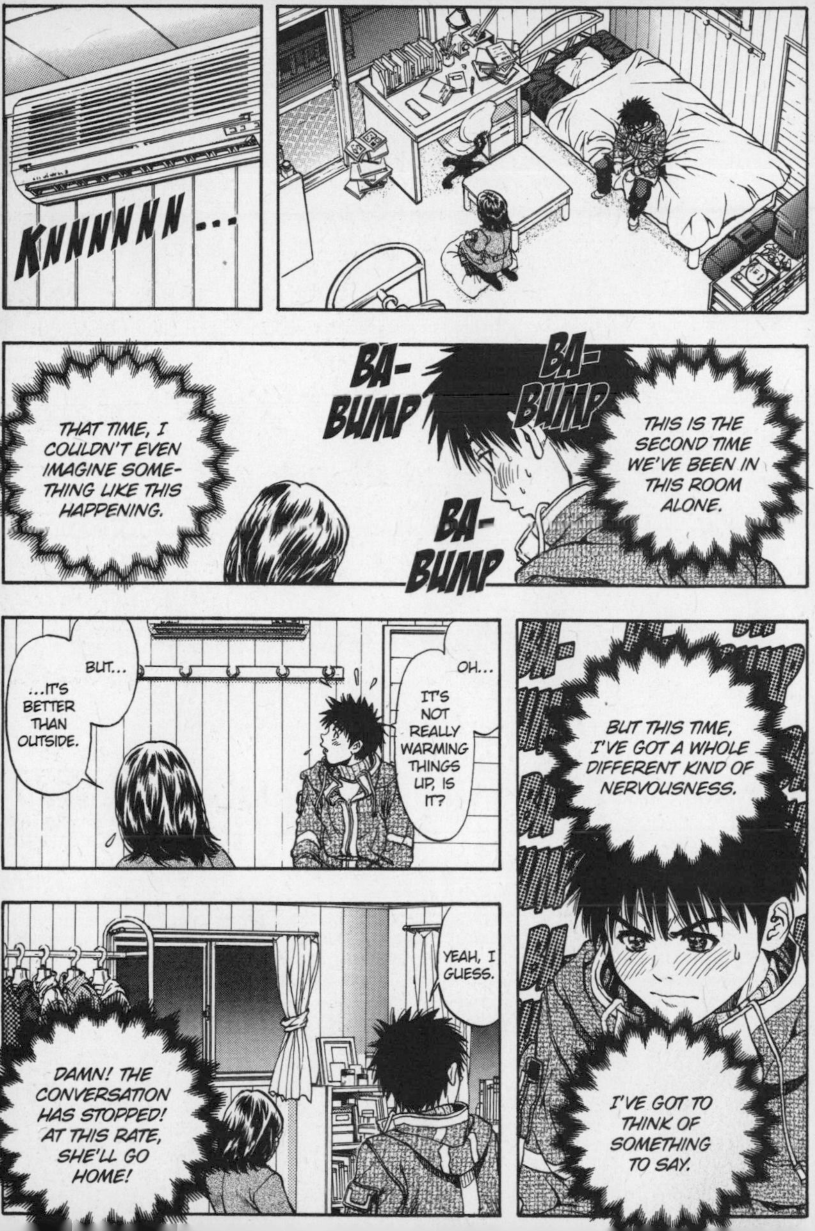
KNNNNNN...
BA-BUMP BA-BUMP BA-BUMP
THIS IS THE SECOND TIME WE'VE BEEN IN THIS ROOM ALONE.
THAT TIME, I COULDN'T EVEN IMAGINE SOME-THING LIKE THIS HAPPENING.
BUT THIS TIME, I'VE GOT A WHOLE DIFFERENT KIND OF NERVOUSNESS.
I'VE GOT TO THINK OF SOMETHING TO SAY.
OH... IT'S NOT REALLY WARMING THINGS UP, IS IT?
BUT... ...IT'S BETTER THAN OUTSIDE.
YEAH, I GUESS.
DAMN! THE CONVERSATION HAS STOPPED! AT THIS RATE, SHE'LL GO HOME!

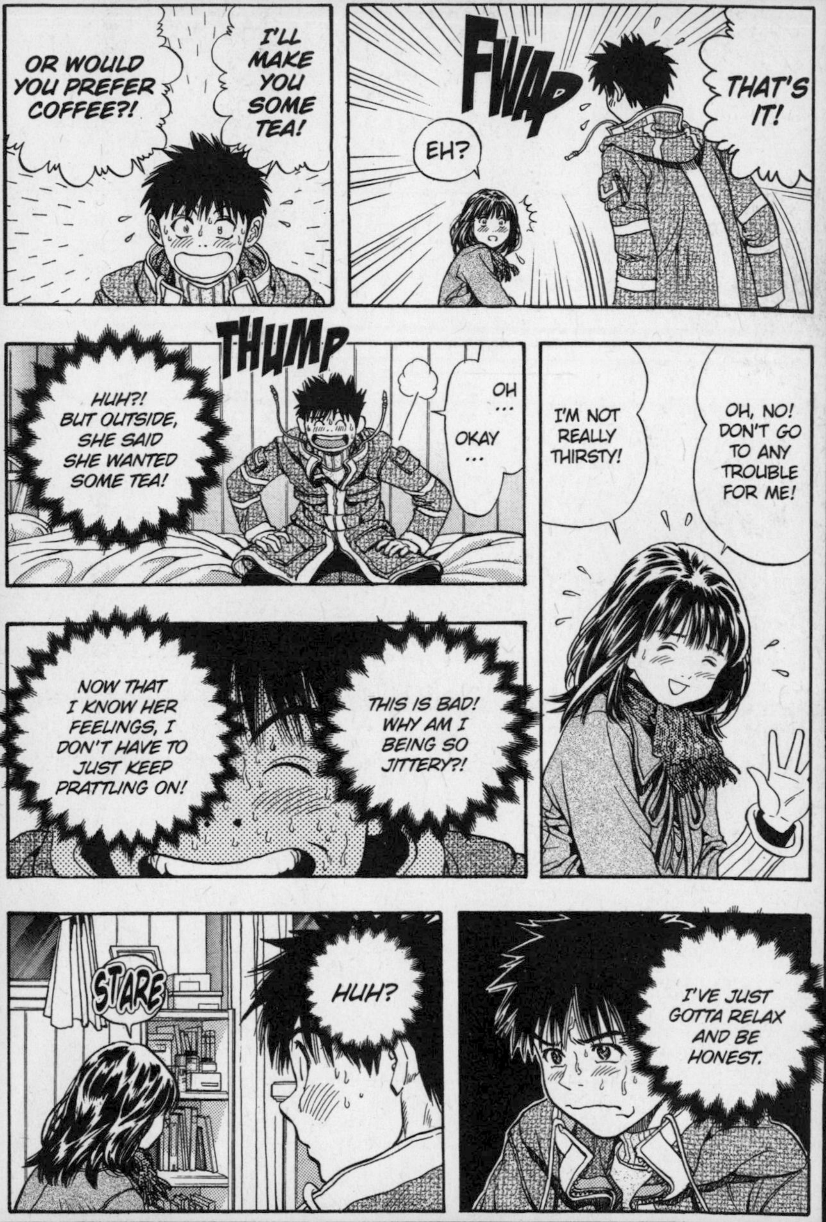
FWAP
THAT'S IT!
EH?
I'LL MAKE YOU SOME TEA!
OR WOULD YOU PREFER COFFEE?!
OH, NO! DON'T GO TO ANY TROUBLE FOR ME!
I'M NOT REALLY THIRSTY!
THUMP
OH ... OKAY ...
HUH?! BUT OUTSIDE, SHE SAID SHE WANTED SOME TEA!
THIS IS BAD! WHY AM I BEING SO JITTERY?!
NOW THAT I KNOW HER FEELINGS, I DON'T HAVE TO JUST KEEP PRATTLING ON!
I'VE JUST GOTTA RELAX AND BE HONEST.
HUH?
STARE

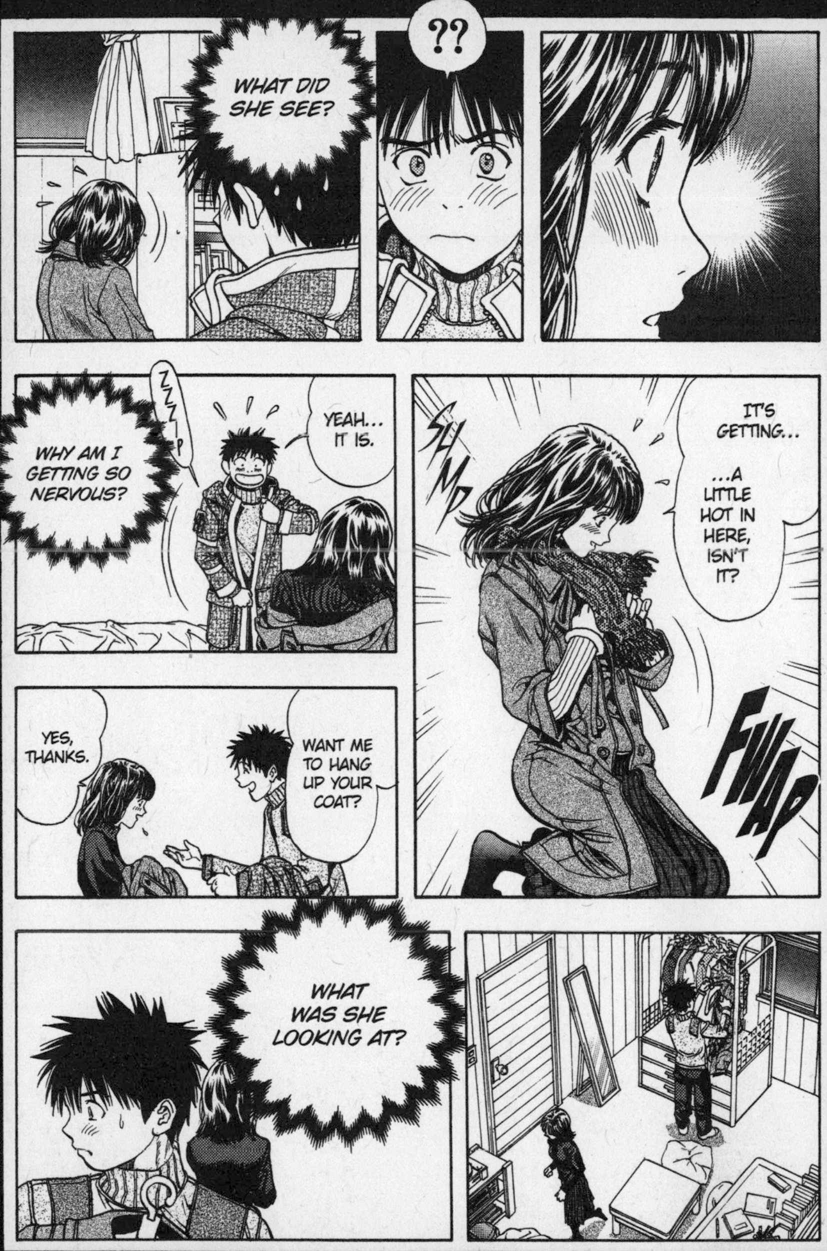
??
WHAT DID SHE SEE?
IT'S GETTING...
...A LITTLE HOT IN HERE, ISN'T IT?
FWAP
ZZZIP
YEAH... IT IS.
WHY AM I GETTING SO NERVOUS?
WANT ME TO HANG UP YOUR COAT?
YES, THANKS.
WHAT WAS SHE LOOKING AT?

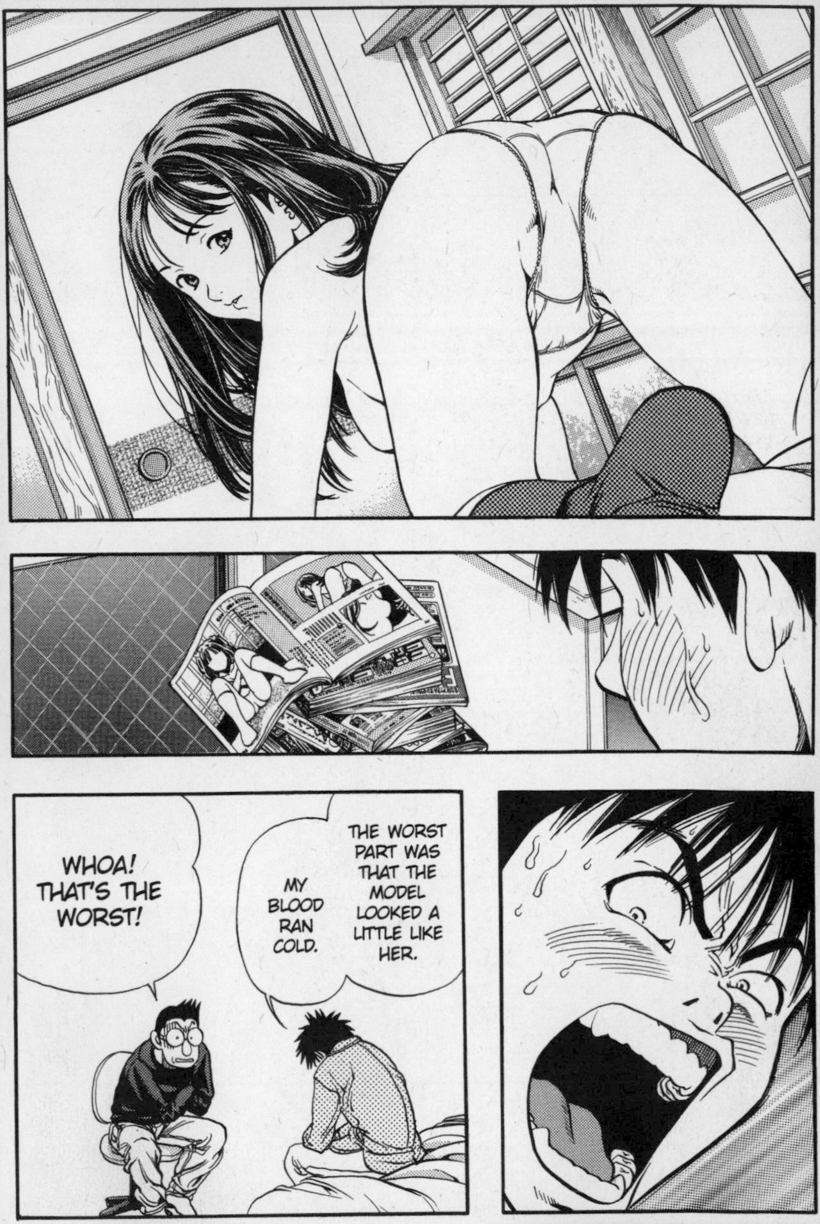
THE WORST PART WAS THAT THE MODEL LOOKED A LITTLE LIKE HER.
MY BLOOD RAN COLD.
WHOA! THAT'S THE WORST!

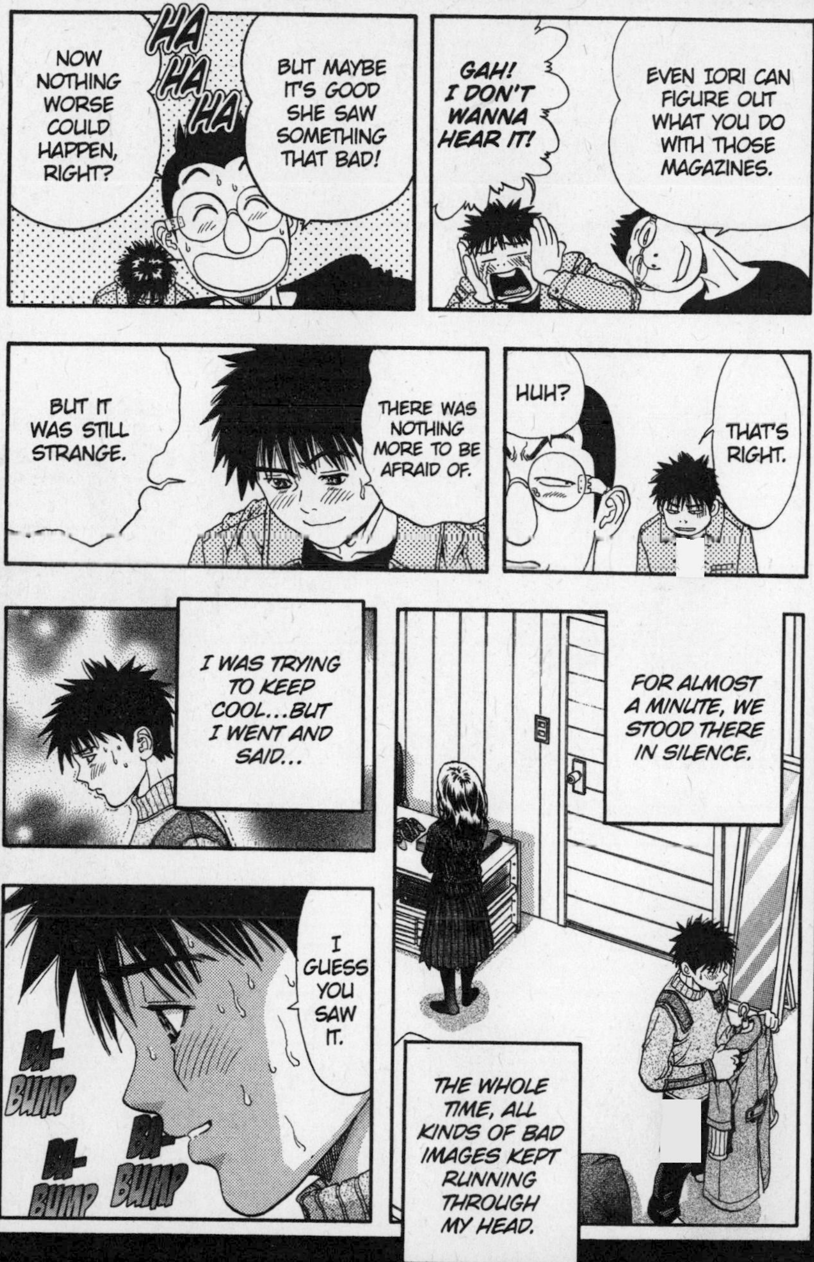
EVEN IORI CAN FIGURE OUT WHAT YOU DO WITH THOSE MAGAZINES.
GAH! I DON'T WANNA HEAR IT!
BUT MAYBE IT'S GOOD SHE SAW SOMETHING THAT BAD!
HA HA HA
NOW NOTHING WORSE COULD HAPPEN, RIGHT?
THAT'S RIGHT.
HUH?
THERE WAS NOTHING MORE TO BE AFRAID OF.
BUT IT WAS STILL STRANGE.
FOR ALMOST A MINUTE, WE STOOD THERE IN SILENCE.
THE WHOLE TIME, ALL KINDS OF BAD IMAGES KEPT RUNNING THROUGH MY HEAD.
I WAS TRYING TO KEEP COOL...BUT I WENT AND SAID...
I GUESS YOU SAW IT.
BA-BUMP
BA-BUMP
BA-BUMP

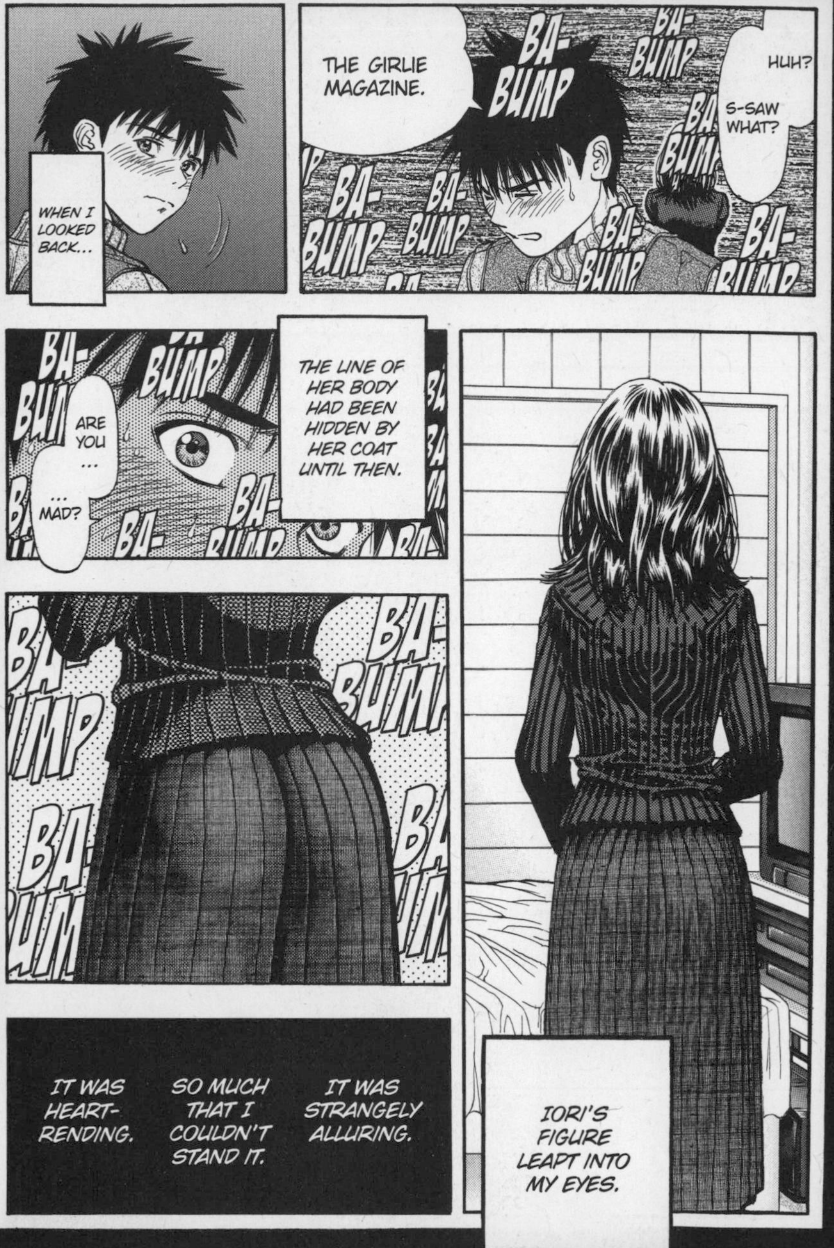
HUH?
S-SAW WHAT?
BA-BUMP
THE GIRLIE MAGAZINE.
BA-BUMP
BA-BUMP
BA-BUMP
BA-BUMP
BA-BUMP
WHEN I LOOKED BACK...
IORI'S FIGURE LEAPT INTO MY EYES.
THE LINE OF HER BODY HAD BEEN HIDDEN BY HER COAT UNTIL THEN.
BA-BUMP
ARE YOU ...
... MAD?
BA-BUMP
BA-BUMP
BA-BUMP
IT WAS STRANGELY ALLURING.
SO MUCH THAT I COULDN'T STAND IT.
IT WAS HEART-RENDING.

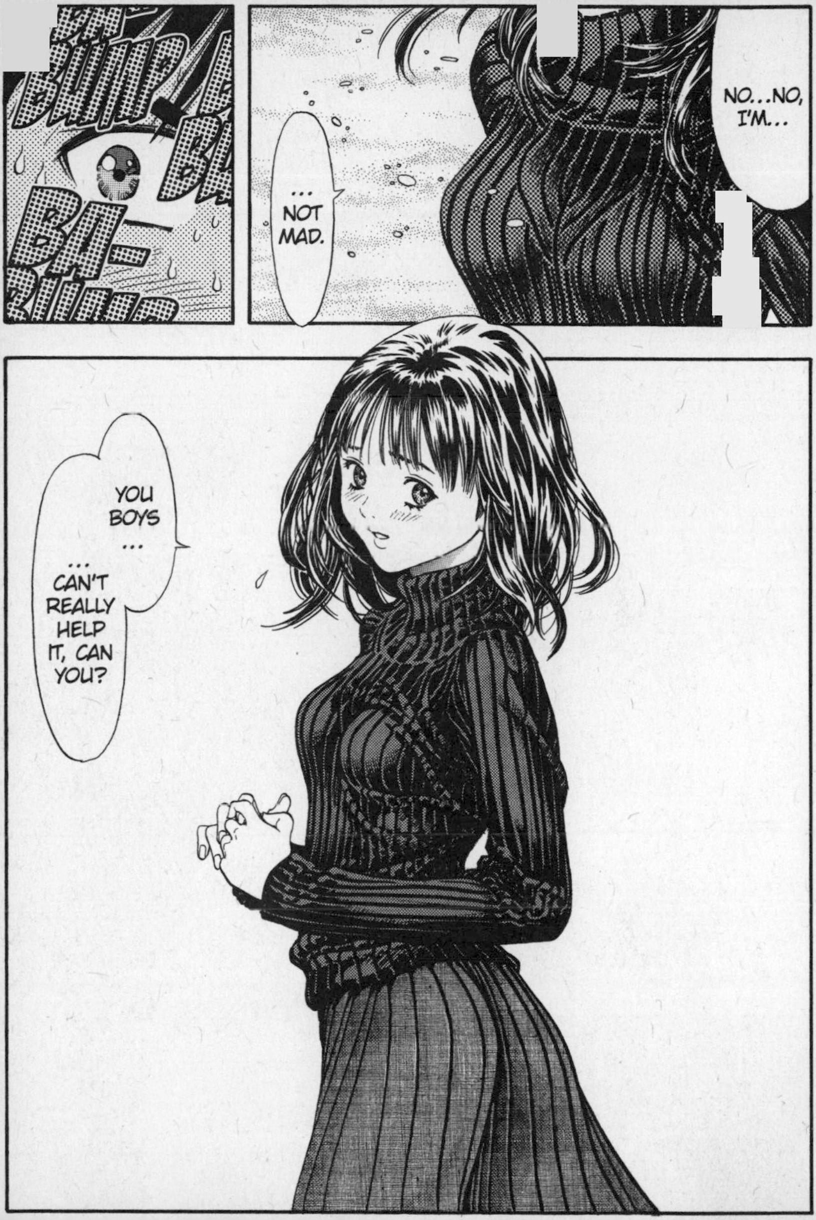
NO...NO, I'M...
...NOT MAD.
BUMP
BA-
YOU BOYS ...
...CAN'T REALLY HELP IT, CAN YOU?

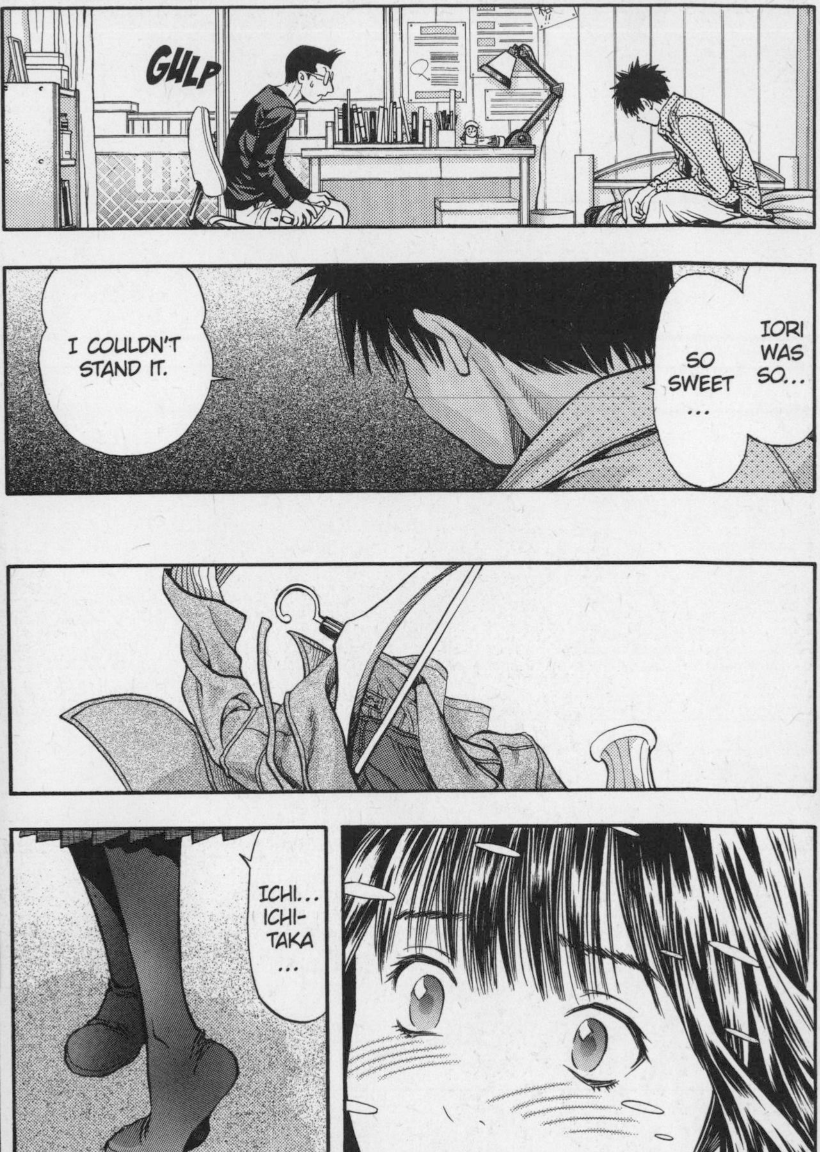
GULP
IORI WAS SO... SO SWEET...
I COULDN'T STAND IT.
ICHI... ICHI-TAKA...

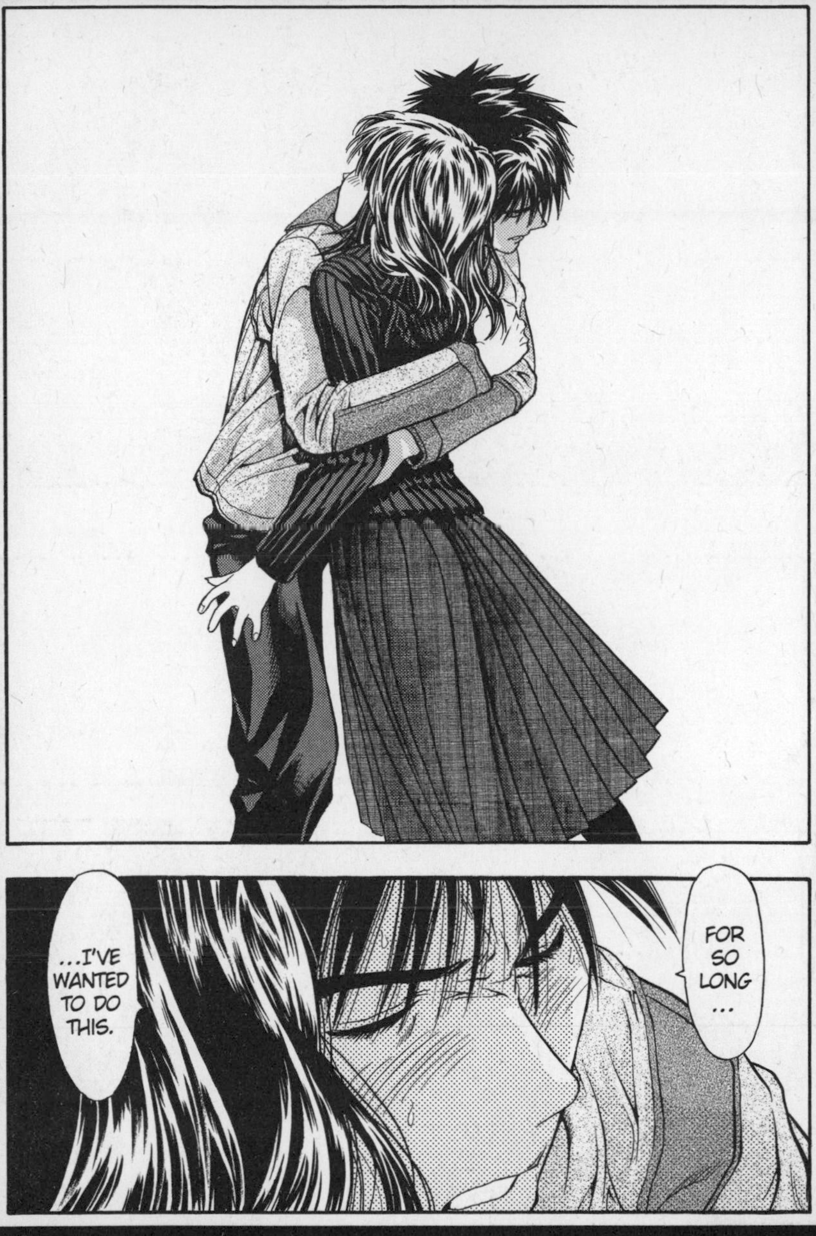
FOR SO LONG...
...I'VE WANTED TO DO THIS.

Chapter 90:
Reminiscence, Part 3

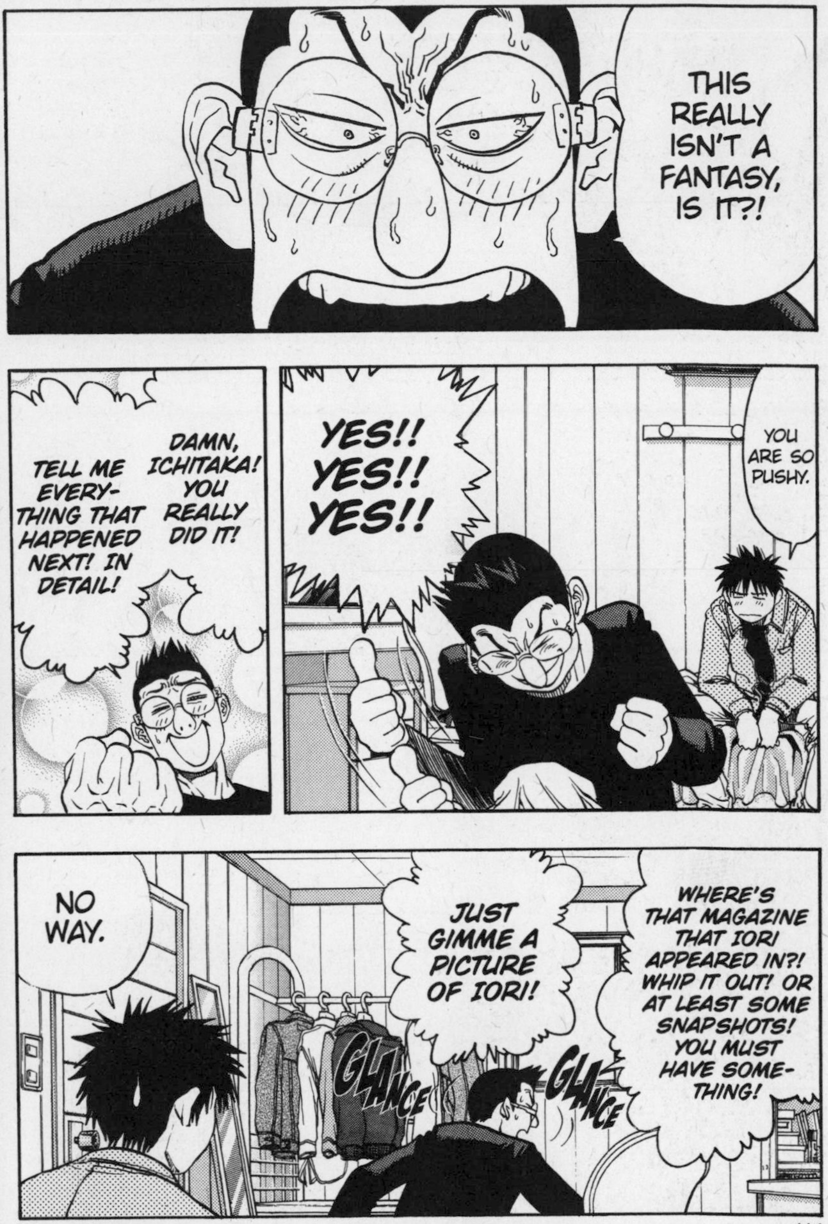
THIS REALLY ISN'T A FANTASY, IS IT?!
YOU ARE SO PUSHY.
YES!! YES!! YES!!
DAMN, ICHITAKA! YOU REALLY DID IT!
TELL ME EVERY-THING THAT HAPPENED NEXT! IN DETAIL!
WHERE'S THAT MAGAZINE THAT IORI APPEARED IN?! WHIP IT OUT! OR AT LEAST SOME SNAPSHOTS! YOU MUST HAVE SOME-THING!
GLANCE
GLANCE
JUST GIMME A PICTURE OF IORI!
NO WAY.

READ THIS WAY

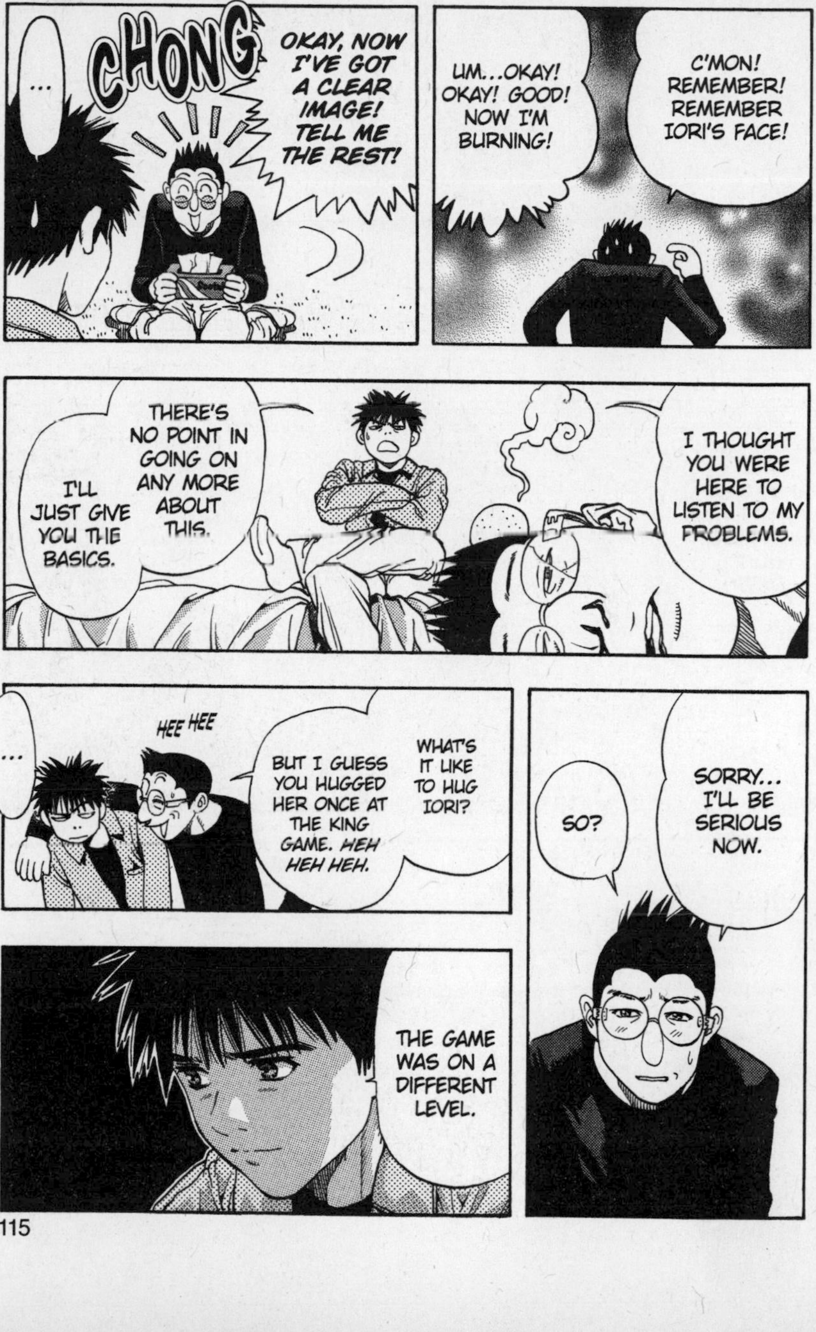
C'MON! REMEMBER! REMEMBER IORI'S FACE!
UM...OKAY! OKAY! GOOD! NOW I'M BURNING!
OKAY, NOW I'VE GOT A CLEAR IMAGE! TELL ME THE REST!
CHONG
...
I THOUGHT YOU WERE HERE TO LISTEN TO MY PROBLEMS.
THERE'S NO POINT IN GOING ON ANY MORE ABOUT THIS.
I'LL JUST GIVE YOU THE BASICS.
SORRY... I'LL BE SERIOUS NOW.
SO?
WHAT'S IT LIKE TO HUG IORI?
BUT I GUESS YOU HUGGED HER ONCE AT THE KING GAME. HEH HEH HEH.
HEE HEE
...
THE GAME WAS ON A DIFFERENT LEVEL.

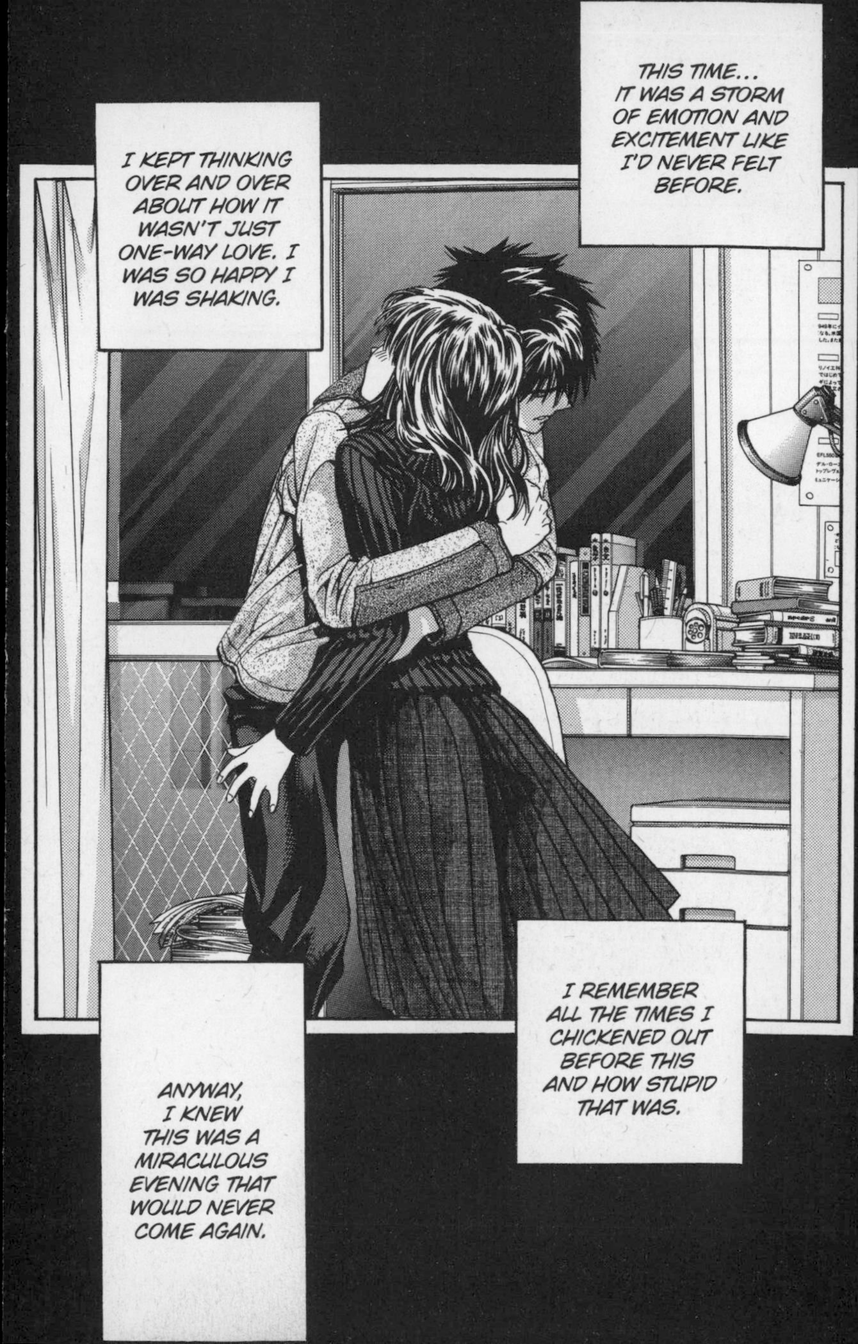
THIS TIME... IT WAS A STORM OF EMOTION AND EXCITEMENT LIKE I'D NEVER FELT BEFORE.
I KEPT THINKING OVER AND OVER ABOUT HOW IT WASN'T JUST ONE-WAY LOVE. I WAS SO HAPPY I WAS SHAKING.
I REMEMBER ALL THE TIMES I CHICKENED OUT BEFORE THIS AND HOW STUPID THAT WAS.
ANYWAY, I KNEW THIS WAS A MIRACULOUS EVENING THAT WOULD NEVER COME AGAIN.

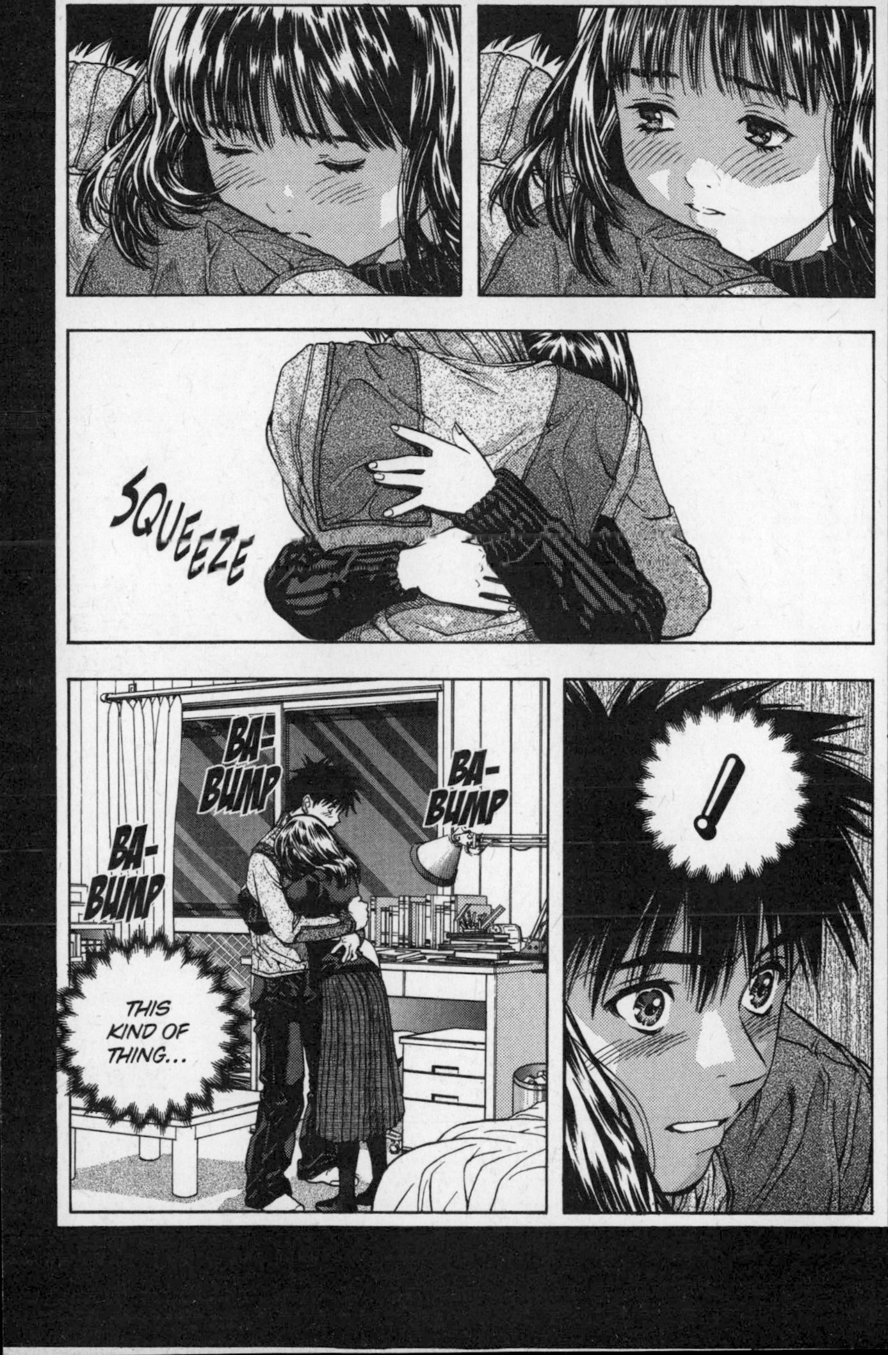
SQUEEZE
!
BA-BUMP
BA-BUMP
BA-BUMP
THIS KIND OF THING...

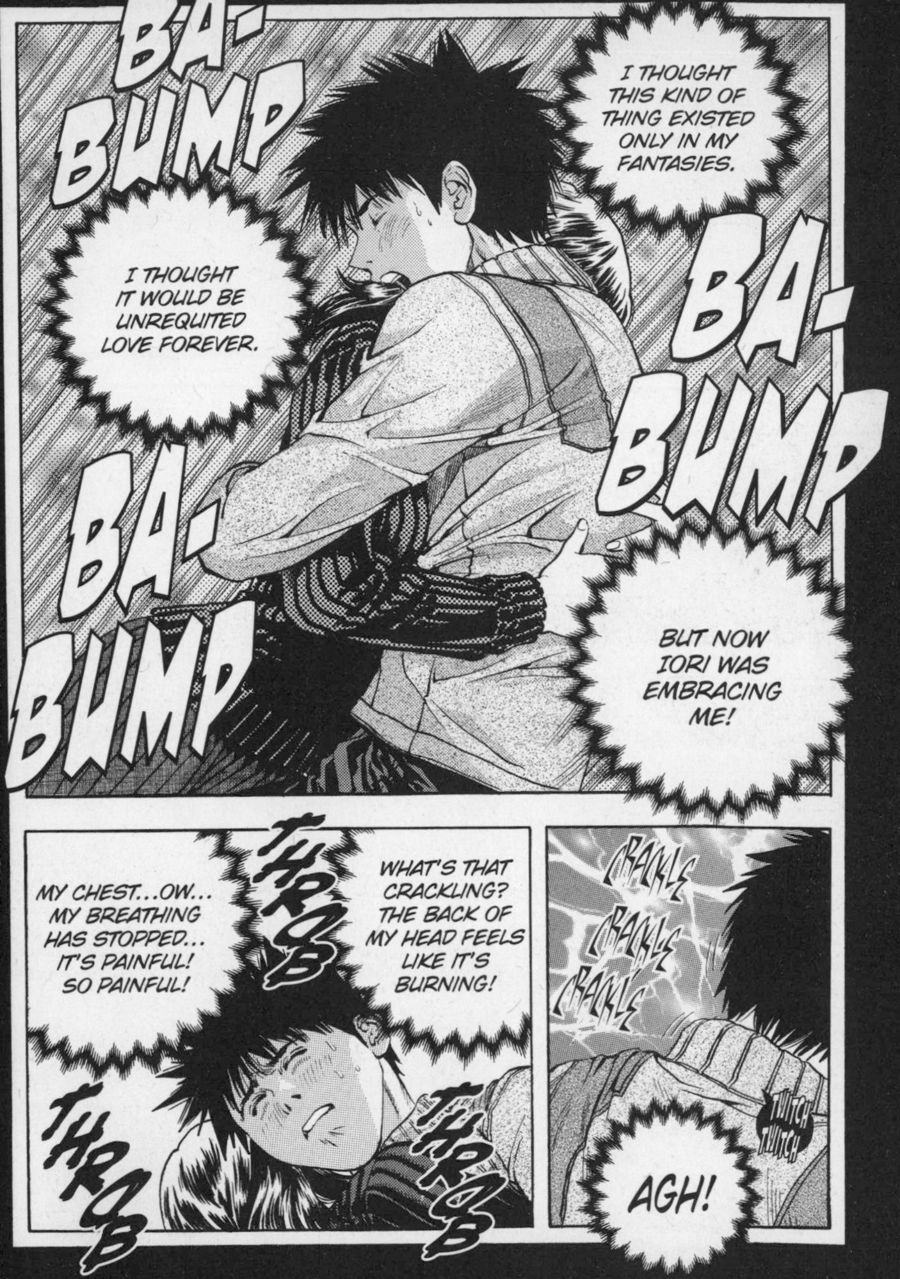
I THOUGHT THIS KIND OF THING EXISTED ONLY IN MY FANTASIES.
BA-BUMP
I THOUGHT IT WOULD BE UNREQUITED LOVE FOREVER.
BA-BUMP
BA-BUMP
BUT NOW IORI WAS EMBRACING ME!
CRACKLE
CRACKLE
CRACKLE
TWITCH TWITCH
AGH!
WHAT'S THAT CRACKLING? THE BACK OF MY HEAD FEELS LIKE IT'S BURNING!
THROB
MY CHEST...OW... MY BREATHING HAS STOPPED... IT'S PAINFUL! SO PAINFUL!
THROB
THROB

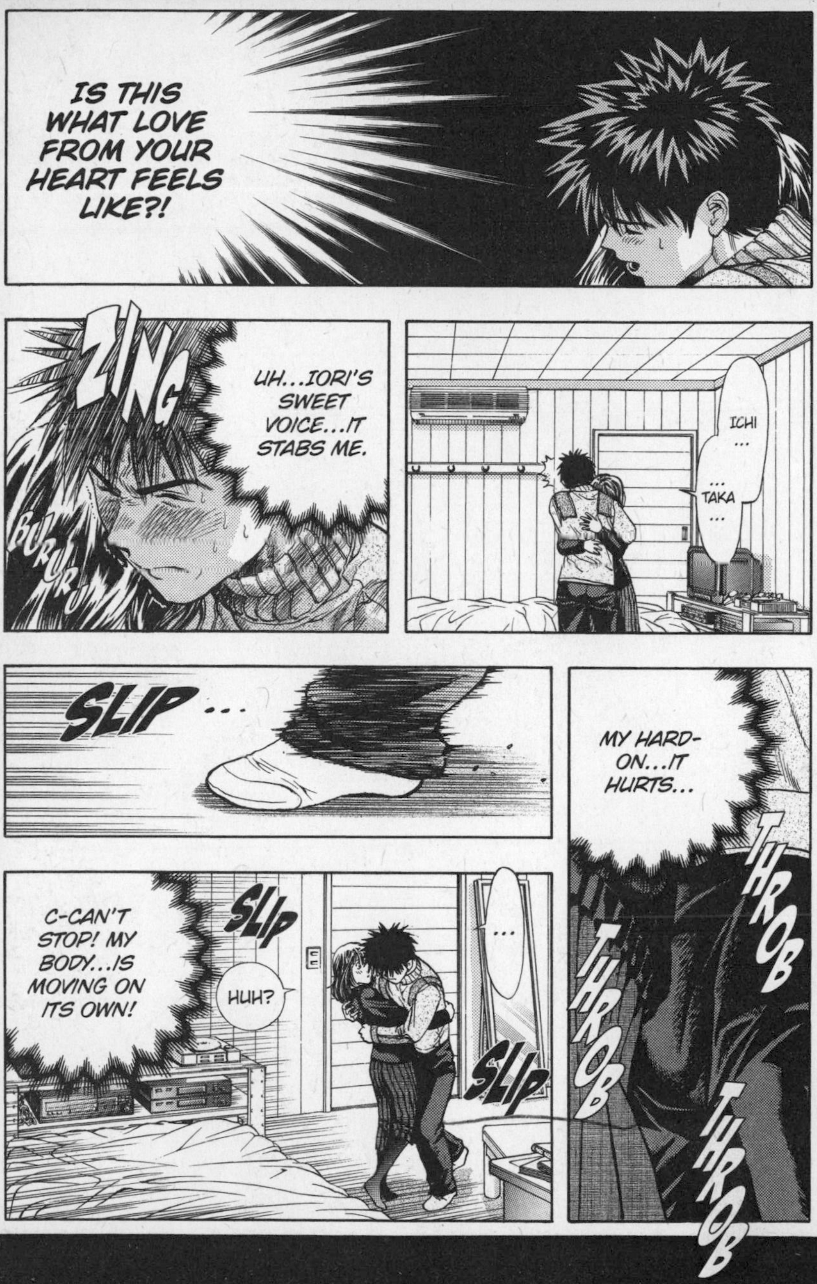
IS THIS WHAT LOVE FROM YOUR HEART FEELS LIKE?!
ICHI ...
... TAKA ...
ZING
UH...IORI'S SWEET VOICE...IT STABS ME.
BURURURU
MY HARD-ON...IT HURTS...
THROB
THROB
THROB
THROB
SLIP ...
...
SLIP
HUH?
C-CAN'T STOP! MY BODY...IS MOVING ON ITS OWN!
SLIP

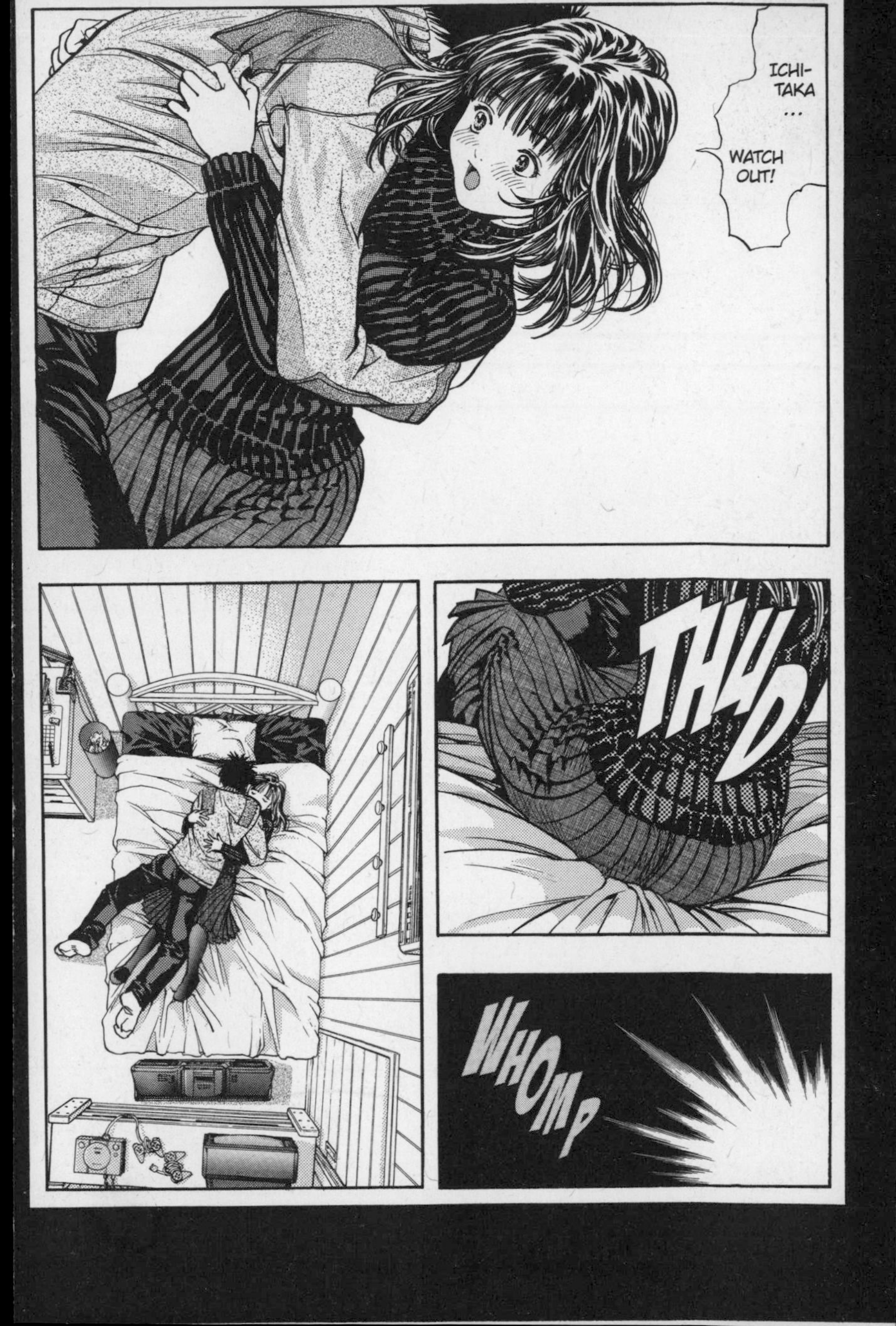
ICHI-TAKA ... WATCH OUT!
THUD
WHOMP

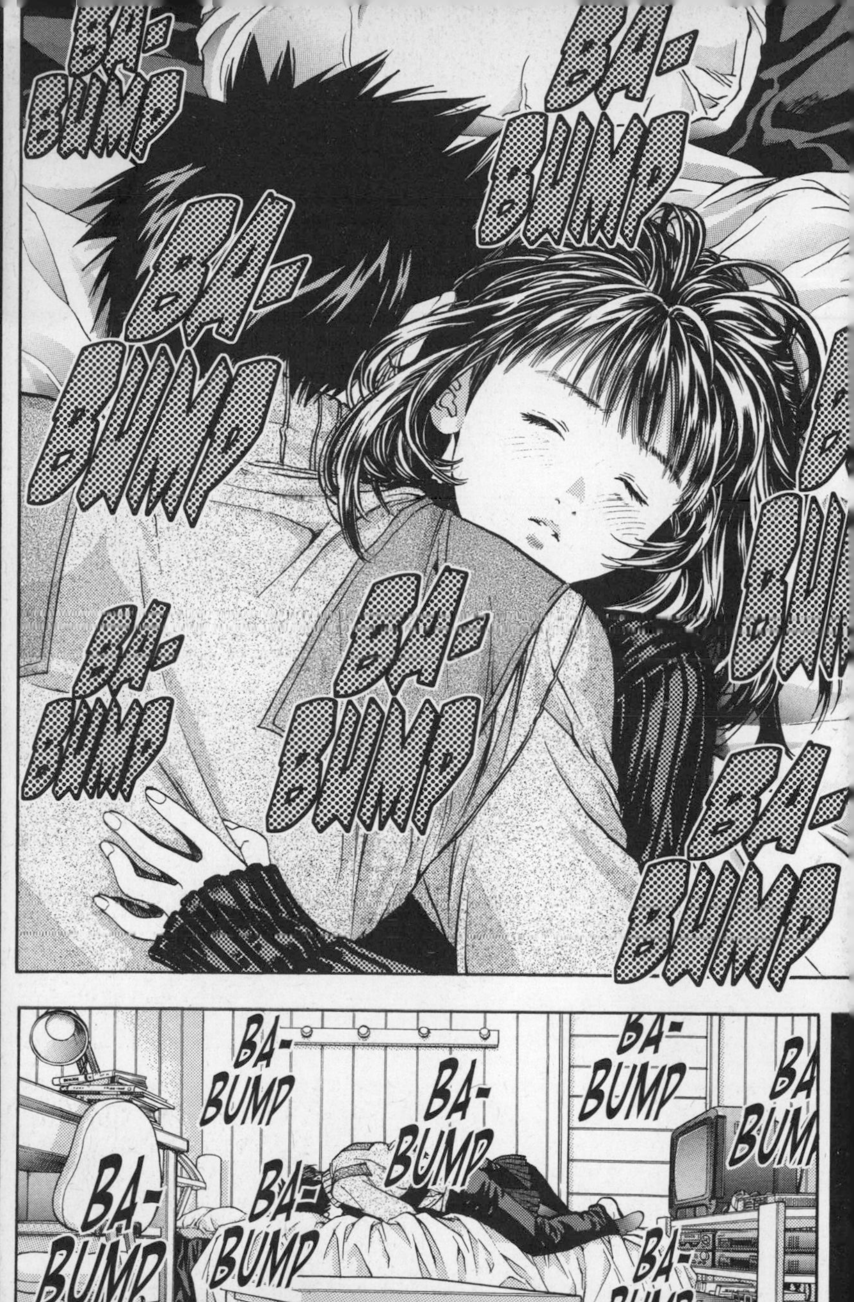

BA-BUMP
BA-BUMP
BA-BUMP
BA-BUMP
BA-BUMP
BA-BUMP
BA-BUMP
BA-BUMP
BA-BUMP
BA-BUMP
BA-BUMP
BA-BUMP
BA-

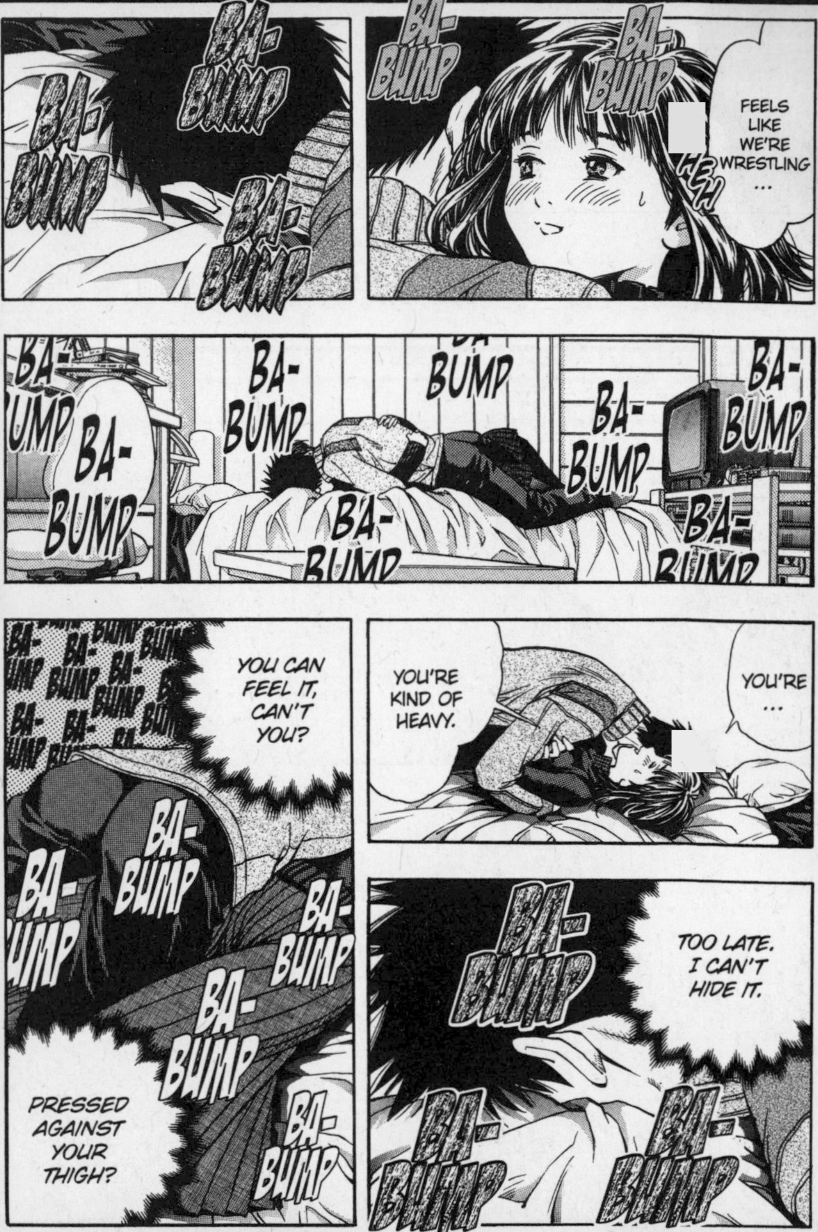

BA-BUMP
BA-BUMP
FEELS LIKE WE'RE WRESTLING ...
HEH
BA-BUMP
BA-BUMP
BA-BUMP
BA-BUMP
BA-BUMP
BA-BUMP
BA-BUMP
BA-BUMP
BA-BUMP
BA-BUMP
BA-BUMP
YOU'RE ...
YOU'RE KIND OF HEAVY.
TOO LATE. I CAN'T HIDE IT.
BA-BUMP
BA-BUMP
BA-BUMP
YOU CAN FEEL IT, CAN'T YOU?
BA-BUMP
BA-BUMP
BA-BUMP
BA-BUMP
BA-BUMP
PRESSED AGAINST YOUR THIGH?

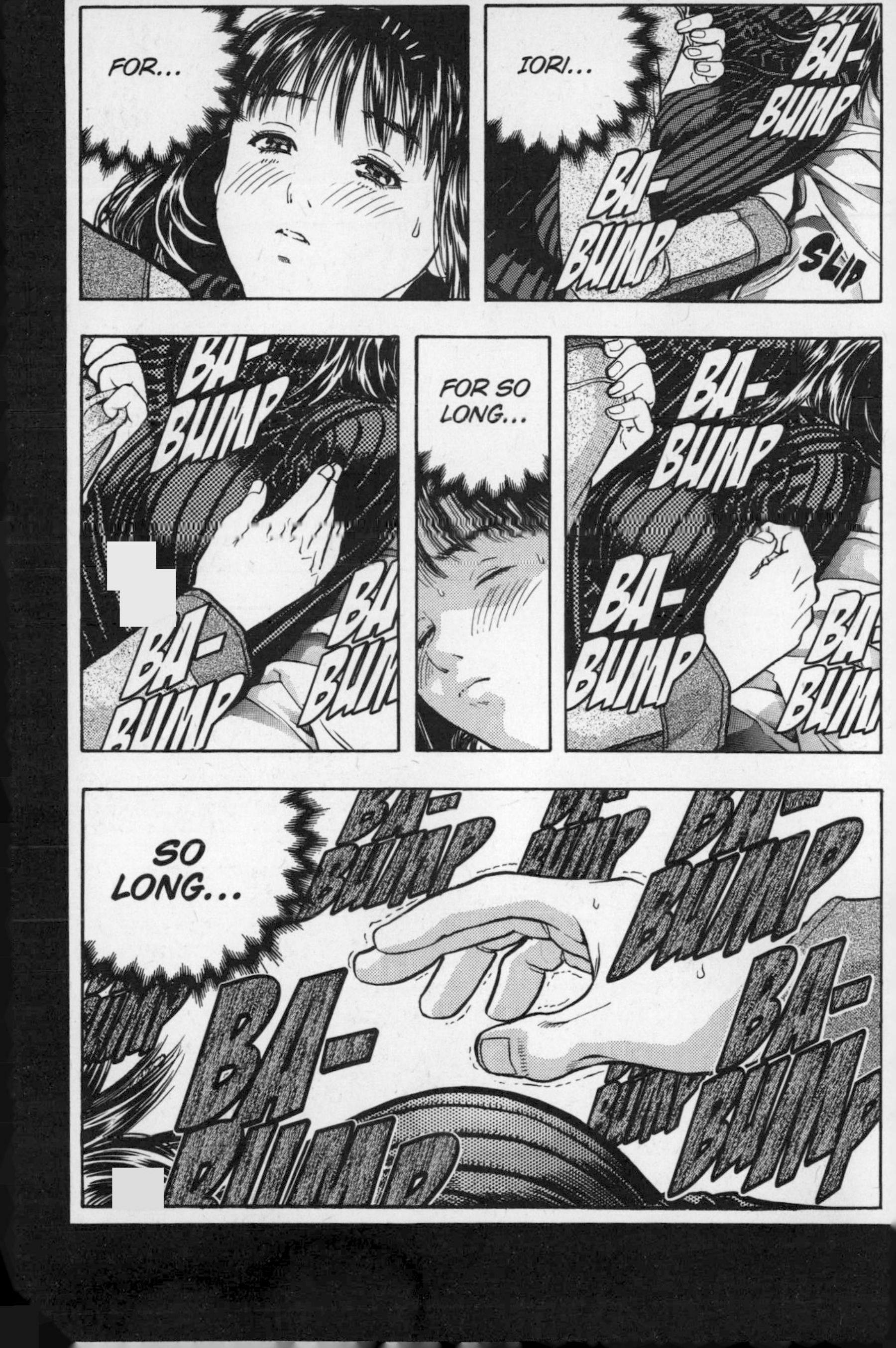
IORI...
BA-BUMP
BA-BUMP
SLIP
FOR...
BA-BUMP
BA-BUMP
BA-BUMP
FOR SO LONG...
BA-BUMP
BA-BUMP
BA-BUMP
SO LONG...
BA-BUMP
BA-BUMP
BA-BUMP
BA-BUMP
BA-BUMP

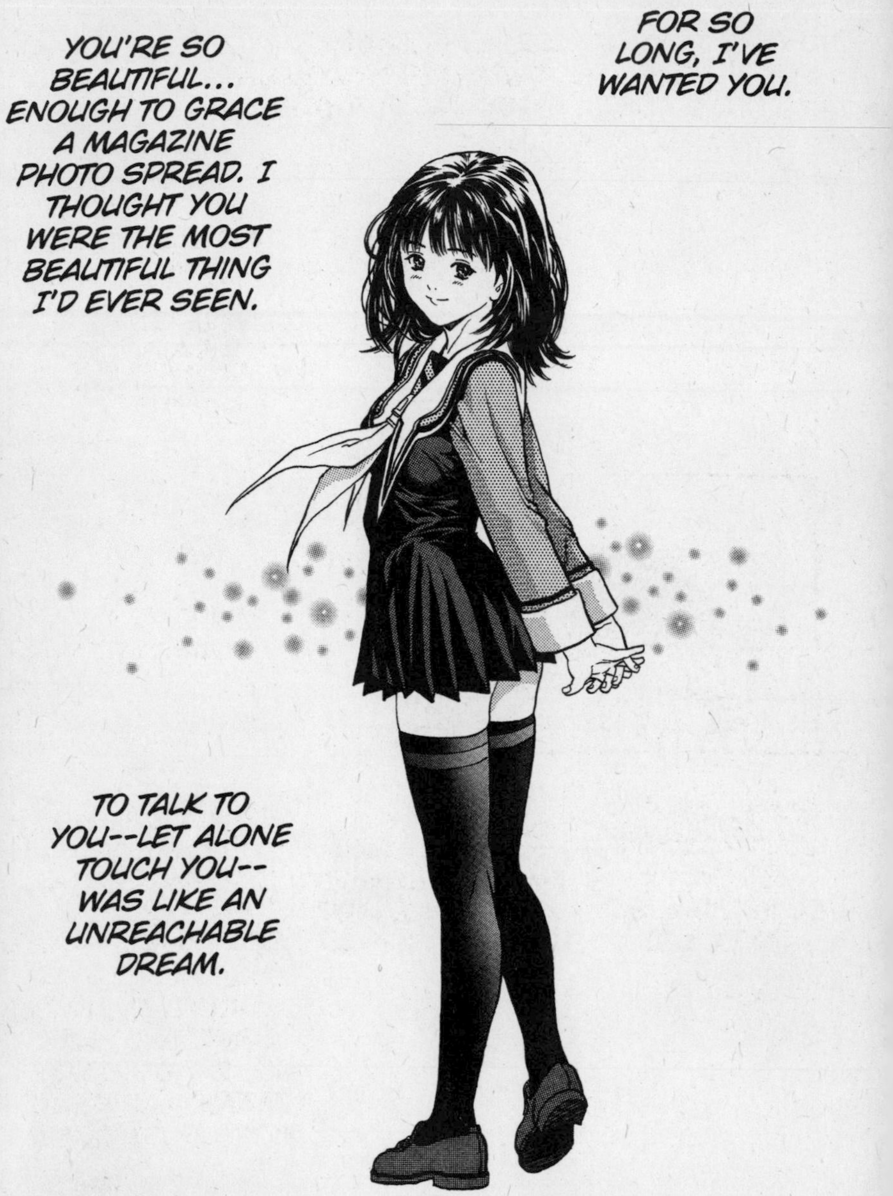
FOR SO LONG, I'VE WANTED YOU.
YOU'RE SO BEAUTIFUL... ENOUGH TO GRACE A MAGAZINE PHOTO SPREAD. I THOUGHT YOU WERE THE MOST BEAUTIFUL THING I'D EVER SEEN.
TO TALK TO YOU--LET ALONE TOUCH YOU--WAS LIKE AN UNREACHABLE DREAM.

LOOKING BACK ON IT,
I KNOW I GOT CLOSE TO
YOU MANY TIMES.

THE COMEDY SKIT...

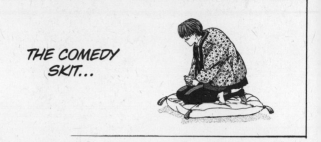

THE KING GAME...

OF COURSE, EACH TIME I WAS OUTRAGEOUSLY HAPPY. BUT... EACH TIME, THERE WAS SOME INVISIBLE WALL THAT WOULDN'T LET ME GET CLOSER... THERE WAS SOME KIND OF DISTANCE.

YOU WERE SO BEAUTIFUL, THERE WAS EVEN A FAN CLUB FOR YOU AT SCHOOL.

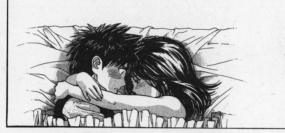

I THOUGHT I COULD NEVER GET NEAR SOMETHING SO PRECIOUS.

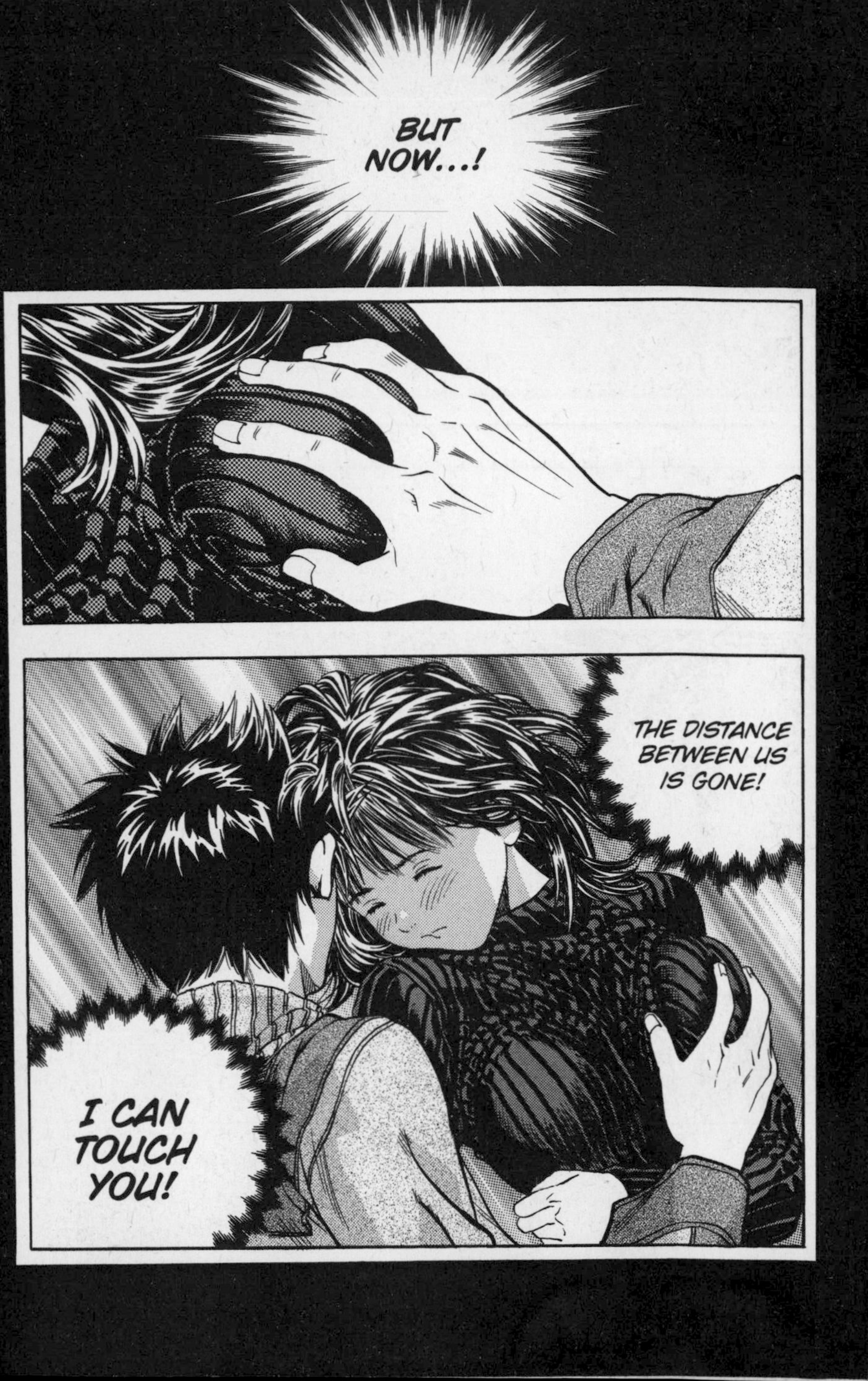
BUT NOW...!
THE DISTANCE BETWEEN US IS GONE!
I CAN TOUCH YOU!

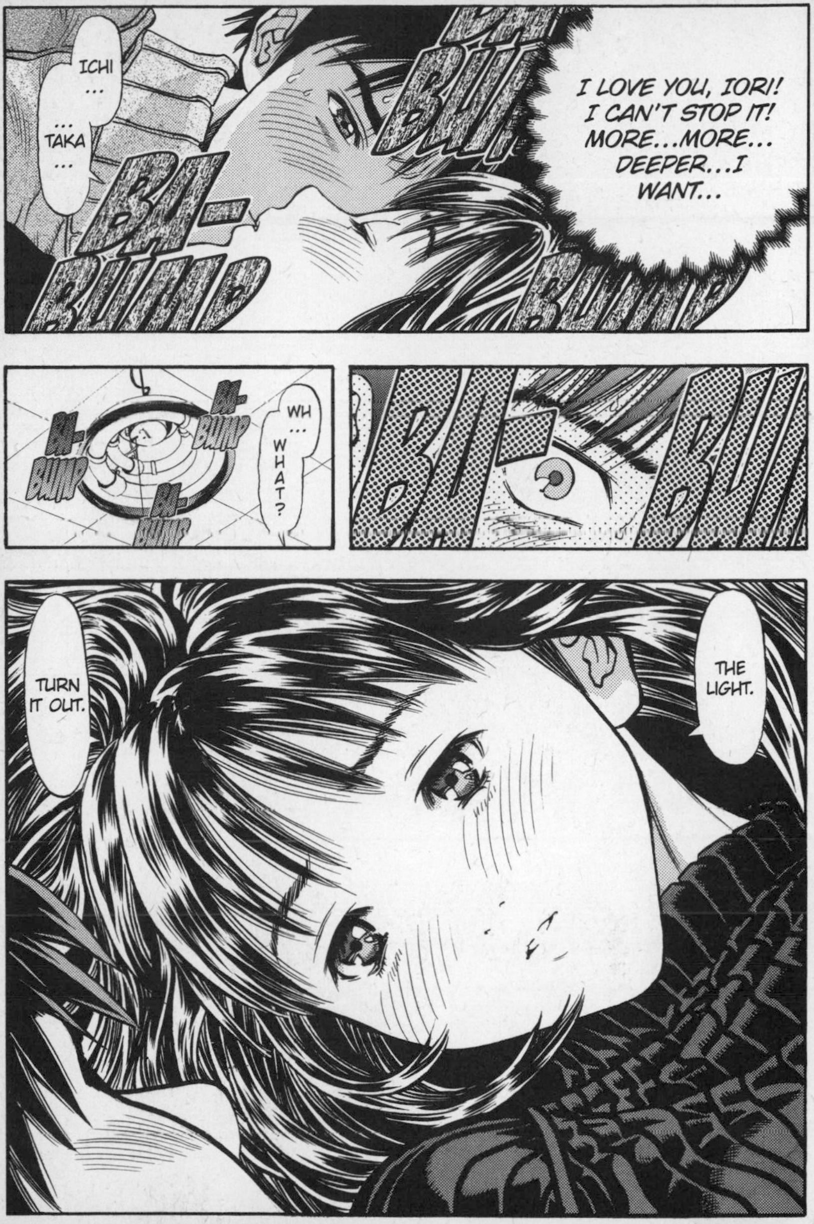
I LOVE YOU, IORI! I CAN'T STOP IT! MORE...MORE... DEEPER...I WANT...
BUMP
BA-BUMP
ICHI ...
... TAKA ...
BA-BU
WH ... WHAT?
BA-BUMP
BA-BUMP
BA-BUMP
THE LIGHT.
TURN IT OUT.

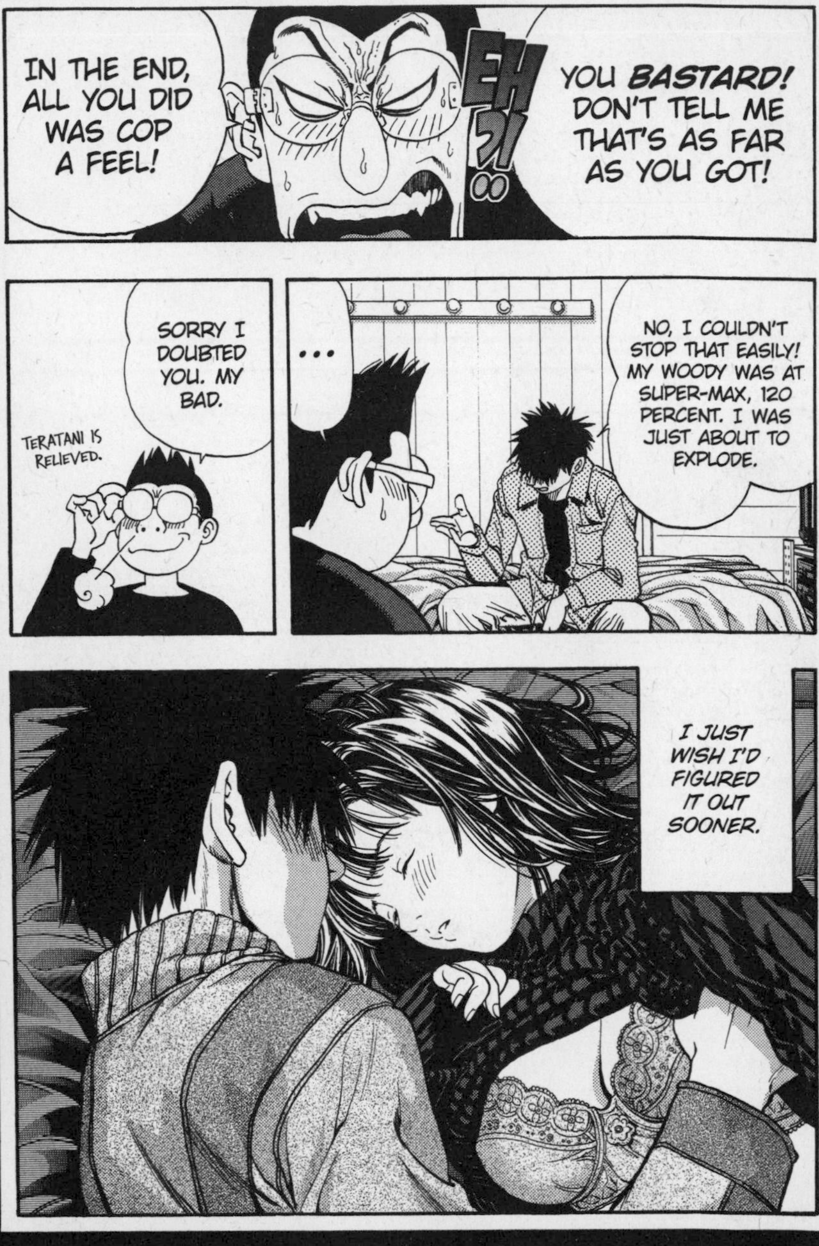
YOU BASTARD! DON'T TELL ME THAT'S AS FAR AS YOU GOT!
EH?!
IN THE END, ALL YOU DID WAS COP A FEEL!
NO, I COULDN'T STOP THAT EASILY! MY WOODY WAS AT SUPER-MAX, 120 PERCENT. I WAS JUST ABOUT TO EXPLODE.
...
SORRY I DOUBTED YOU. MY BAD.
TERATANI IS RELIEVED.
I JUST WISH I'D FIGURED IT OUT SOONER.

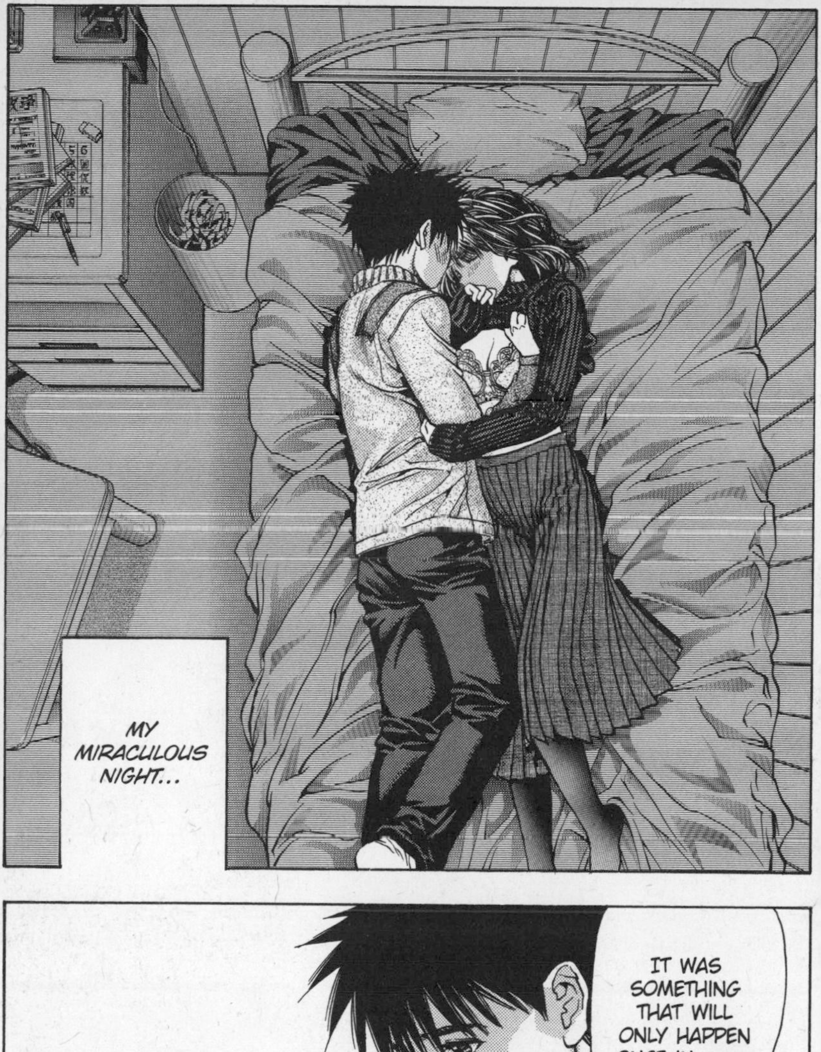
MY MIRACULOUS NIGHT...
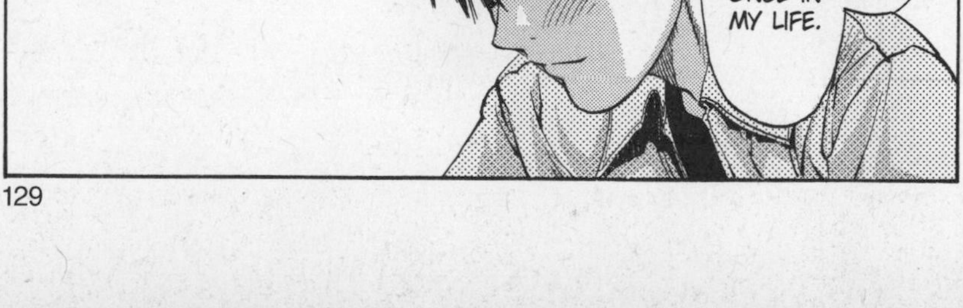
IT WAS SOMETHING THAT WILL ONLY HAPPEN ONCE IN MY LIFE.

Chapter 91:
The Telephone Call

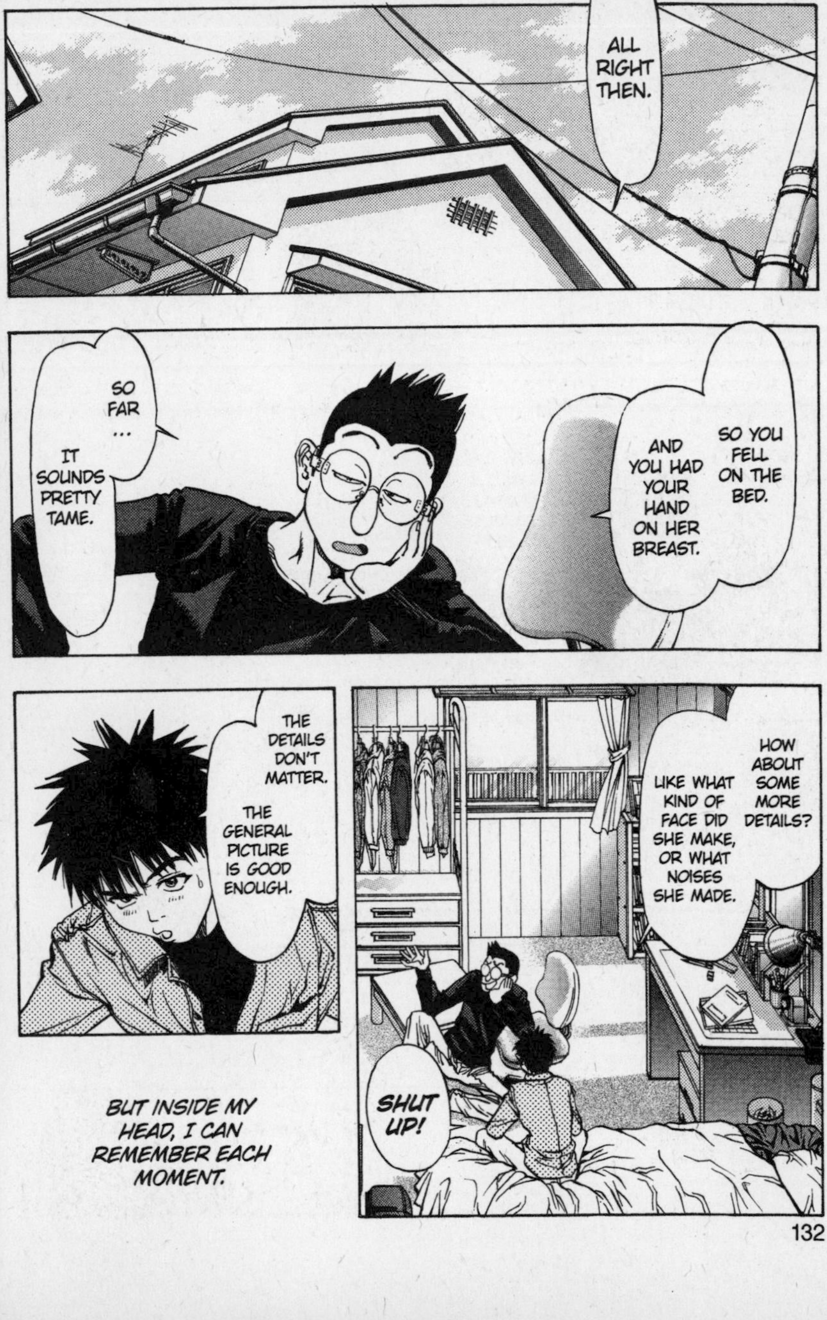
ALL RIGHT THEN.
SO YOU FELL ON THE BED.
AND YOU HAD YOUR HAND ON HER BREAST.
SO FAR ...
IT SOUNDS PRETTY TAME.
HOW ABOUT SOME MORE DETAILS?
LIKE WHAT KIND OF FACE DID SHE MAKE, OR WHAT NOISES SHE MADE.
SHUT UP!
THE DETAILS DON'T MATTER.
THE GENERAL PICTURE IS GOOD ENOUGH.
BUT INSIDE MY HEAD, I CAN REMEMBER EACH MOMENT.

READ THIS WAY

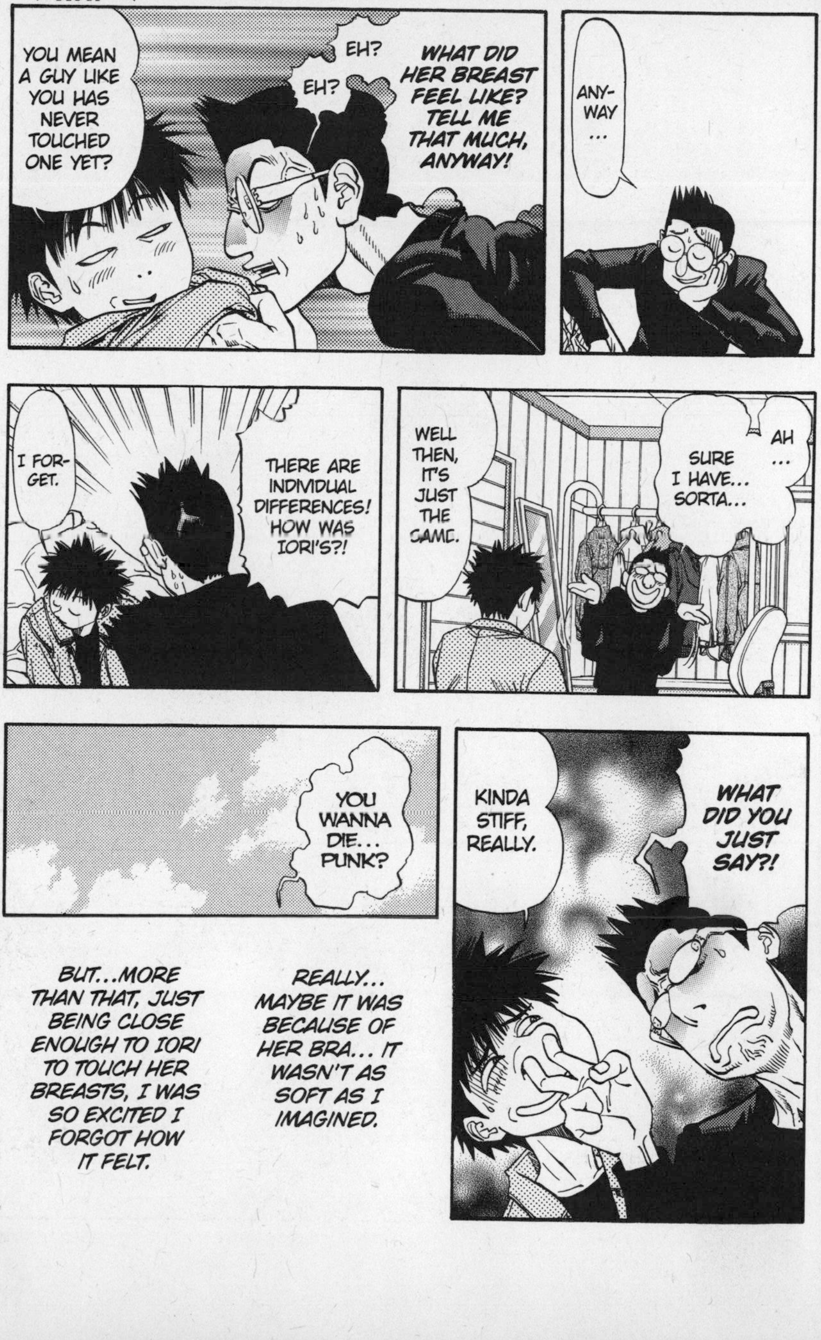
ANY-WAY ...
WHAT DID HER BREAST FEEL LIKE? TELL ME THAT MUCH, ANYWAY!
EH?
EH?
YOU MEAN A GUY LIKE YOU HAS NEVER TOUCHED ONE YET?
AH ...
SURE I HAVE... SORTA...
WELL THEN, IT'S JUST THE SAME.
THERE ARE INDIVIDUAL DIFFERENCES! HOW WAS IORI'S?!
I FOR-GET.
WHAT DID YOU JUST SAY?!
KINDA STIFF, REALLY.
YOU WANNA DIE... PUNK?
REALLY... MAYBE IT WAS BECAUSE OF HER BRA... IT WASN'T AS SOFT AS I IMAGINED.
BUT...MORE THAN THAT, JUST BEING CLOSE ENOUGH TO IORI TO TOUCH HER BREASTS, I WAS SO EXCITED I FORGOT HOW IT FELT.

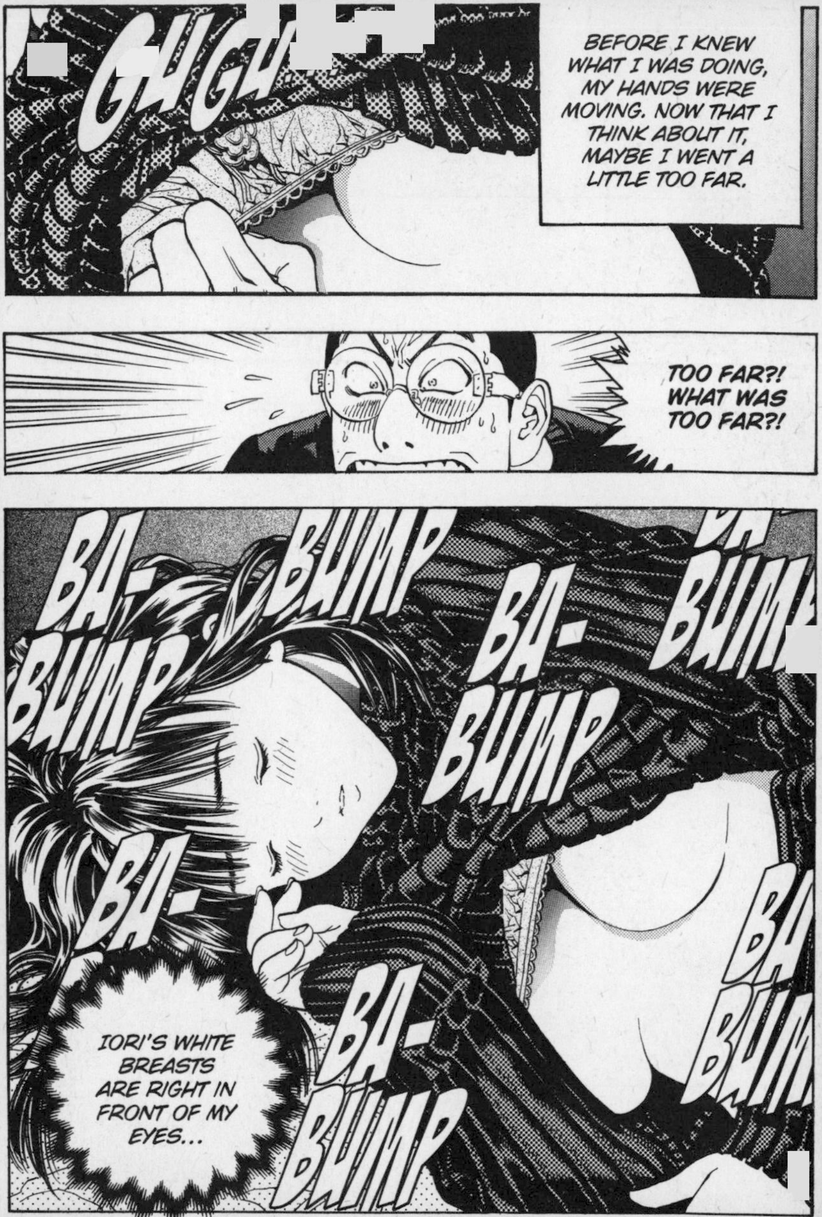
BEFORE I KNEW WHAT I WAS DOING, MY HANDS WERE MOVING. NOW THAT I THINK ABOUT IT, MAYBE I WENT A LITTLE TOO FAR.
TOO FAR?! WHAT WAS TOO FAR?!
BA-BUMP
BA-BUMP
BA-BUMP
BA-BUMP
IORI'S WHITE BREASTS ARE RIGHT IN FRONT OF MY EYES...

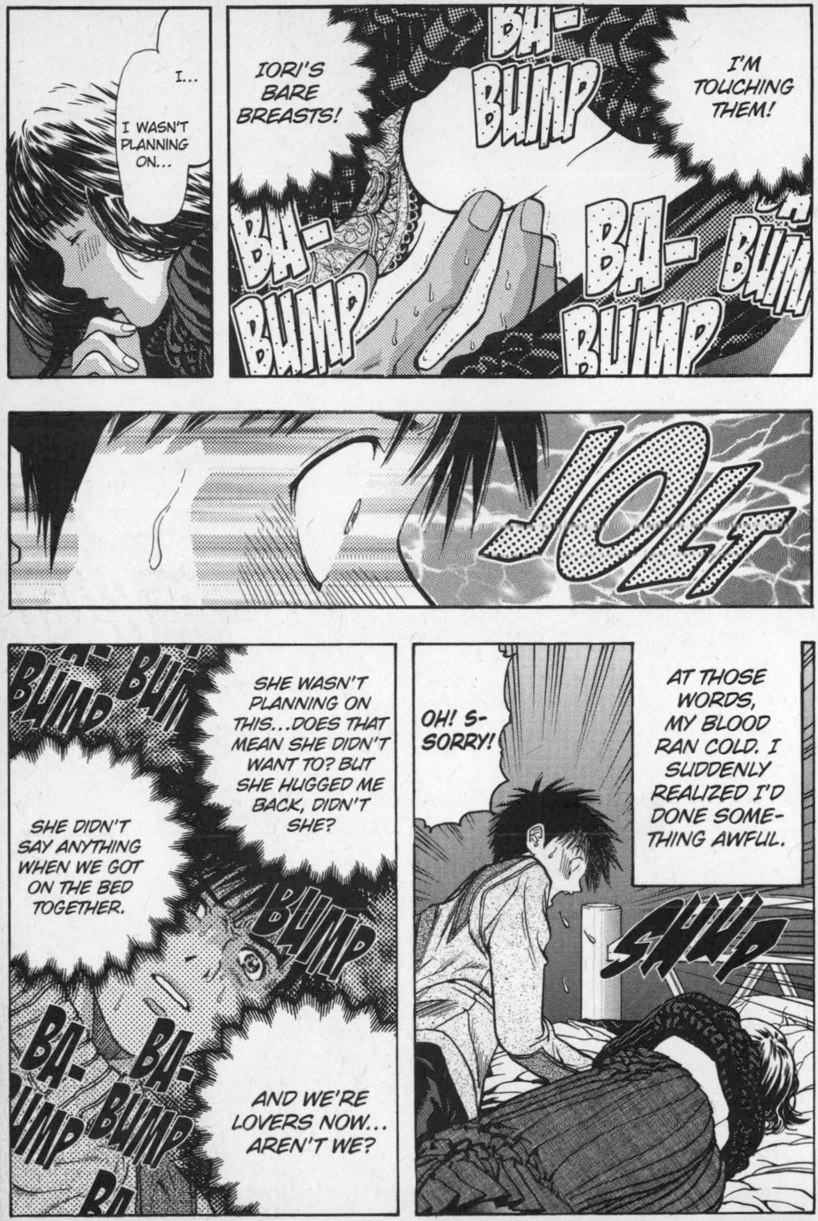
BA-BUMP
I'M TOUCHING THEM!
IORI'S BARE BREASTS!
BA-BUMP
BA-BUMP
BA-BUMP
I...
I WASN'T PLANNING ON...
JOLT
AT THOSE WORDS, MY BLOOD RAN COLD. I SUDDENLY REALIZED I'D DONE SOME-THING AWFUL.
OH! S-SORRY!
SHUD
SHE WASN'T PLANNING ON THIS...DOES THAT MEAN SHE DIDN'T WANT TO? BUT SHE HUGGED ME BACK, DIDN'T SHE?
BUMP
SHE DIDN'T SAY ANYTHING WHEN WE GOT ON THE BED TOGETHER.
BUMP
BA-BUMP
BA-BUMP
AND WE'RE LOVERS NOW... AREN'T WE?

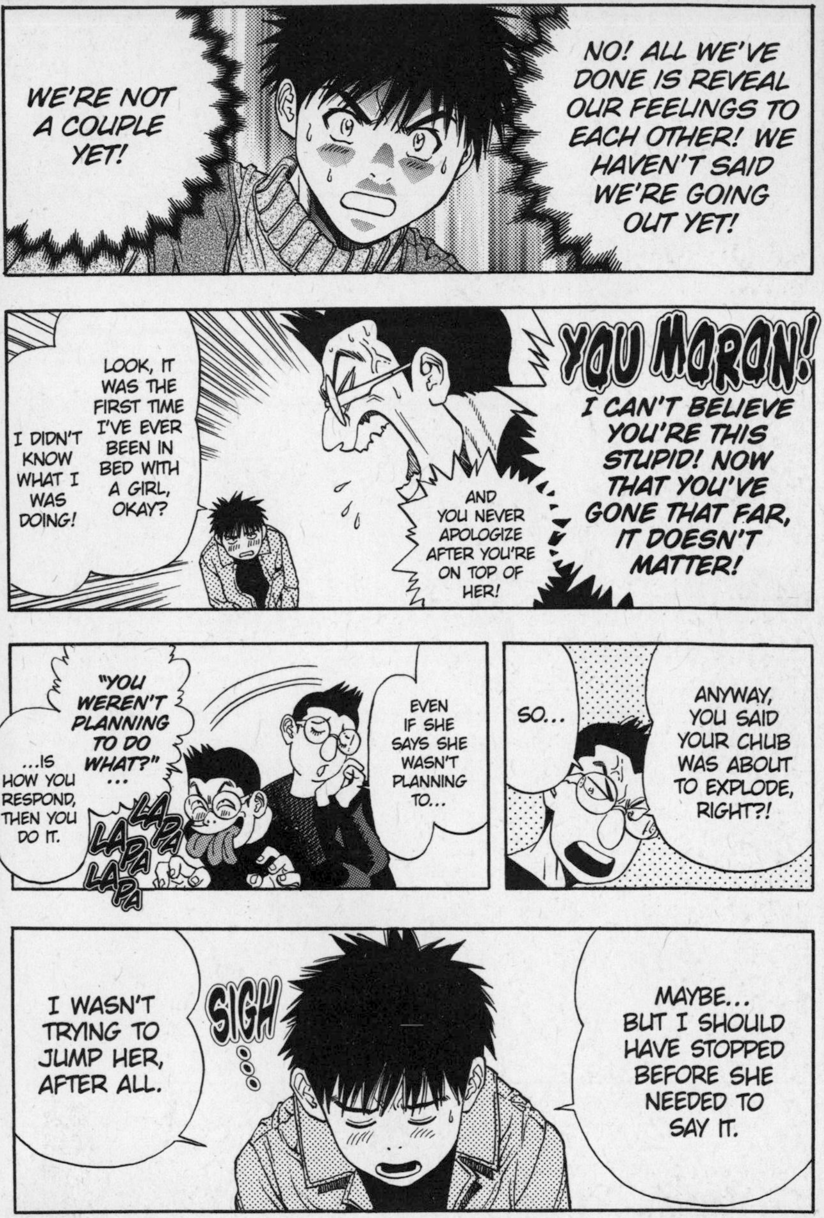
NO! ALL WE'VE DONE IS REVEAL OUR FEELINGS TO EACH OTHER! WE HAVEN'T SAID WE'RE GOING OUT YET!
WE'RE NOT A COUPLE YET!
YOU MORON!
I CAN'T BELIEVE YOU'RE THIS STUPID! NOW THAT YOU'VE GONE THAT FAR, IT DOESN'T MATTER!
AND YOU NEVER APOLOGIZE AFTER YOU'RE ON TOP OF HER!
LOOK, IT WAS THE FIRST TIME I'VE EVER BEEN IN BED WITH A GIRL, OKAY?
I DIDN'T KNOW WHAT I WAS DOING!
ANYWAY, YOU SAID YOUR CHUB WAS ABOUT TO EXPLODE, RIGHT?!
SO...
EVEN IF SHE SAYS SHE WASN'T PLANNING TO...
"YOU WEREN'T PLANNING TO DO WHAT?" ...
...IS HOW YOU RESPOND, THEN YOU DO IT.
LAPA LAPA LAPA LAPA
MAYBE... BUT I SHOULD HAVE STOPPED BEFORE SHE NEEDED TO SAY IT.
SIGH...
I WASN'T TRYING TO JUMP HER, AFTER ALL.

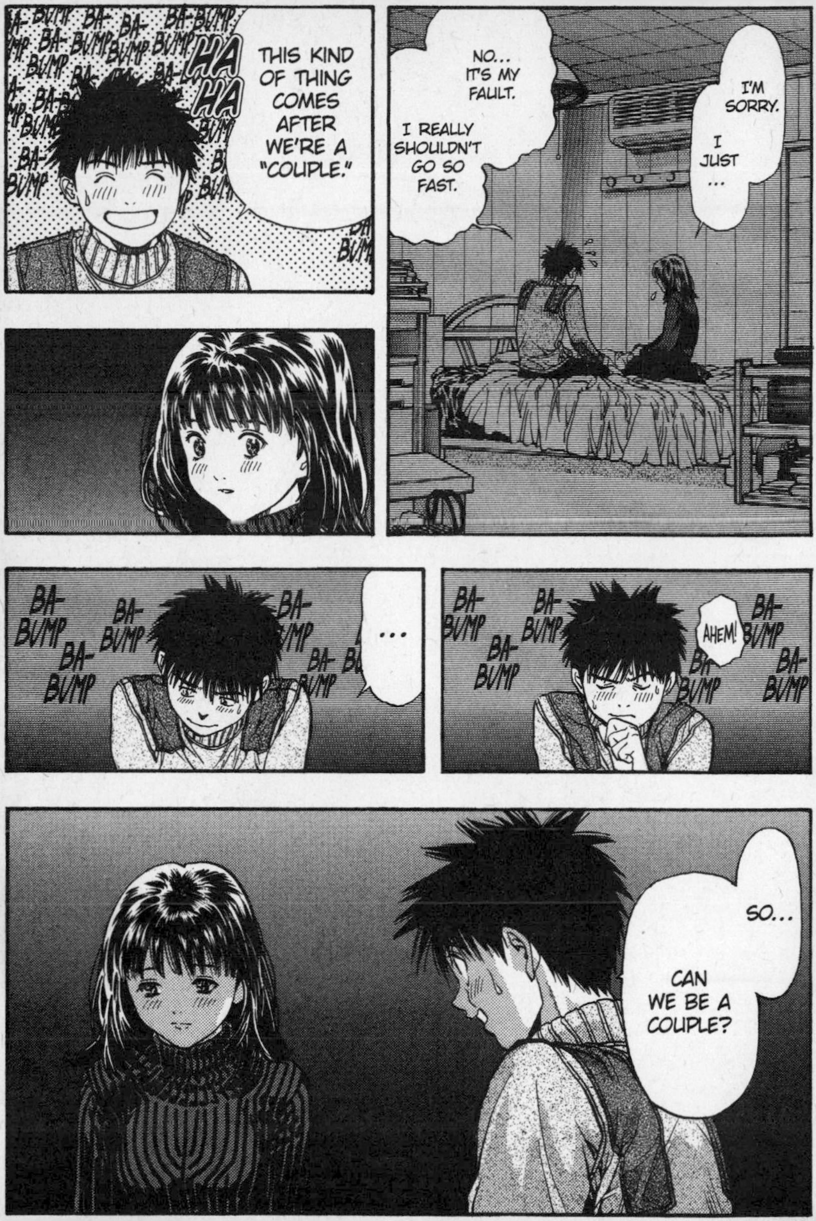
I'M SORRY.
I JUST ...
NO... IT'S MY FAULT.
I REALLY SHOULDN'T GO SO FAST.
BA-BUMP BA-BUMP BA-BUMP BA-BUMP BA-BUMP
HA HA
THIS KIND OF THING COMES AFTER WE'RE A "COUPLE."
BA-BUMP
BA-BUMP BA-BUMP BA-BUMP BA-BUMP BA-BUMP
AHEM!
BA-BUMP BA-BUMP BA-BUMP BA-BUMP BA-BUMP
...
SO...
CAN WE BE A COUPLE?

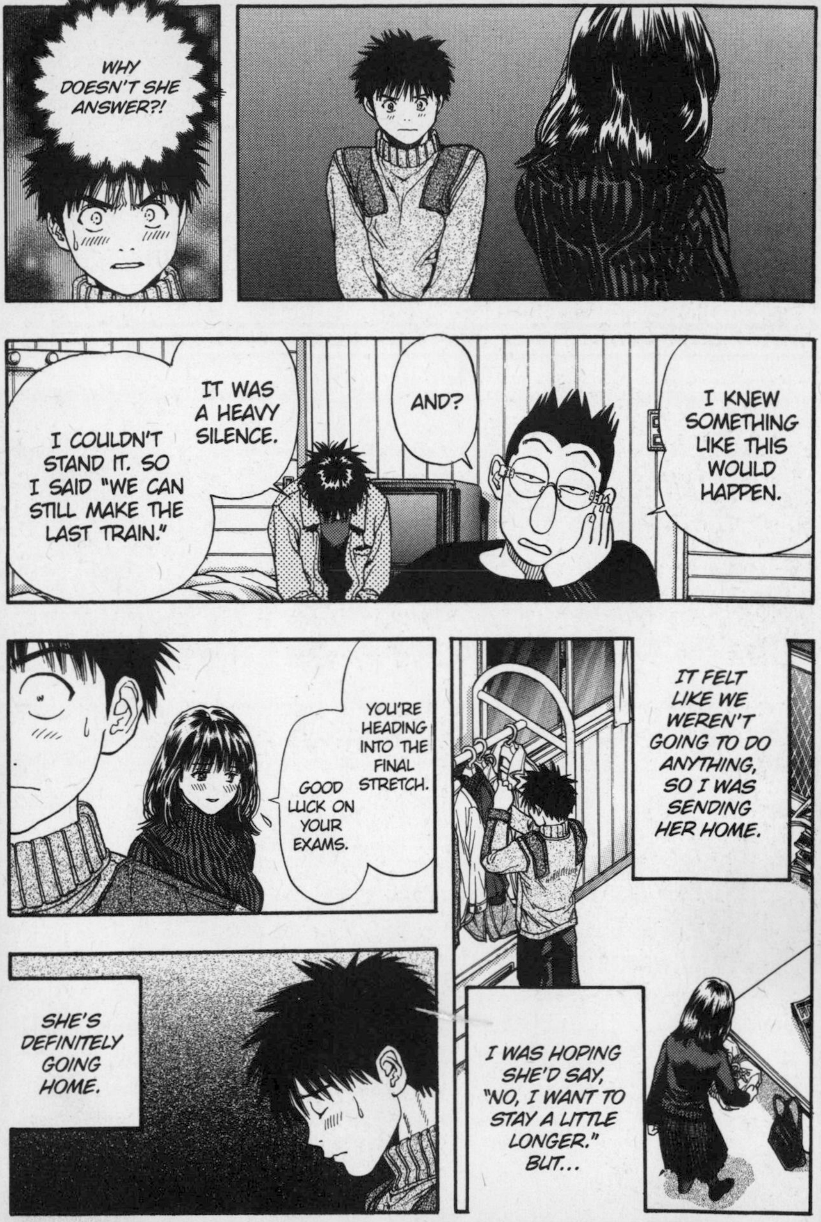
WHY DOESN'T SHE ANSWER?!
I KNEW SOMETHING LIKE THIS WOULD HAPPEN.
AND?
IT WAS A HEAVY SILENCE.
I COULDN'T STAND IT. SO I SAID "WE CAN STILL MAKE THE LAST TRAIN."
IT FELT LIKE WE WEREN'T GOING TO DO ANYTHING, SO I WAS SENDING HER HOME.
I WAS HOPING SHE'D SAY, "NO, I WANT TO STAY A LITTLE LONGER." BUT...
YOU'RE HEADING INTO THE FINAL STRETCH.
GOOD LUCK ON YOUR EXAMS.
SHE'S DEFINITELY GOING HOME.

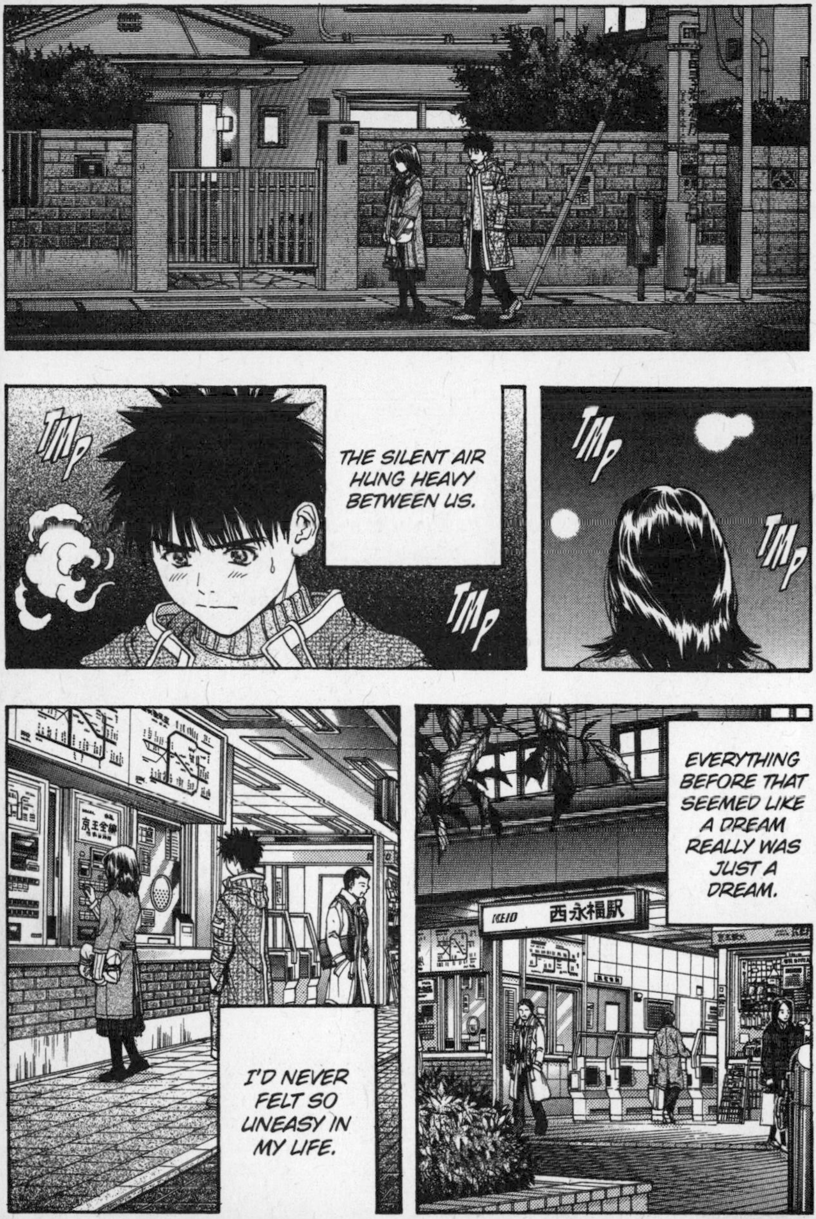
TMP
TMP
THE SILENT AIR HUNG HEAVY BETWEEN US.
TMP
TMP
EVERYTHING BEFORE THAT SEEMED LIKE A DREAM REALLY WAS JUST A DREAM.
KEIO 西永福駅
I'D NEVER FELT SO UNEASY IN MY LIFE.

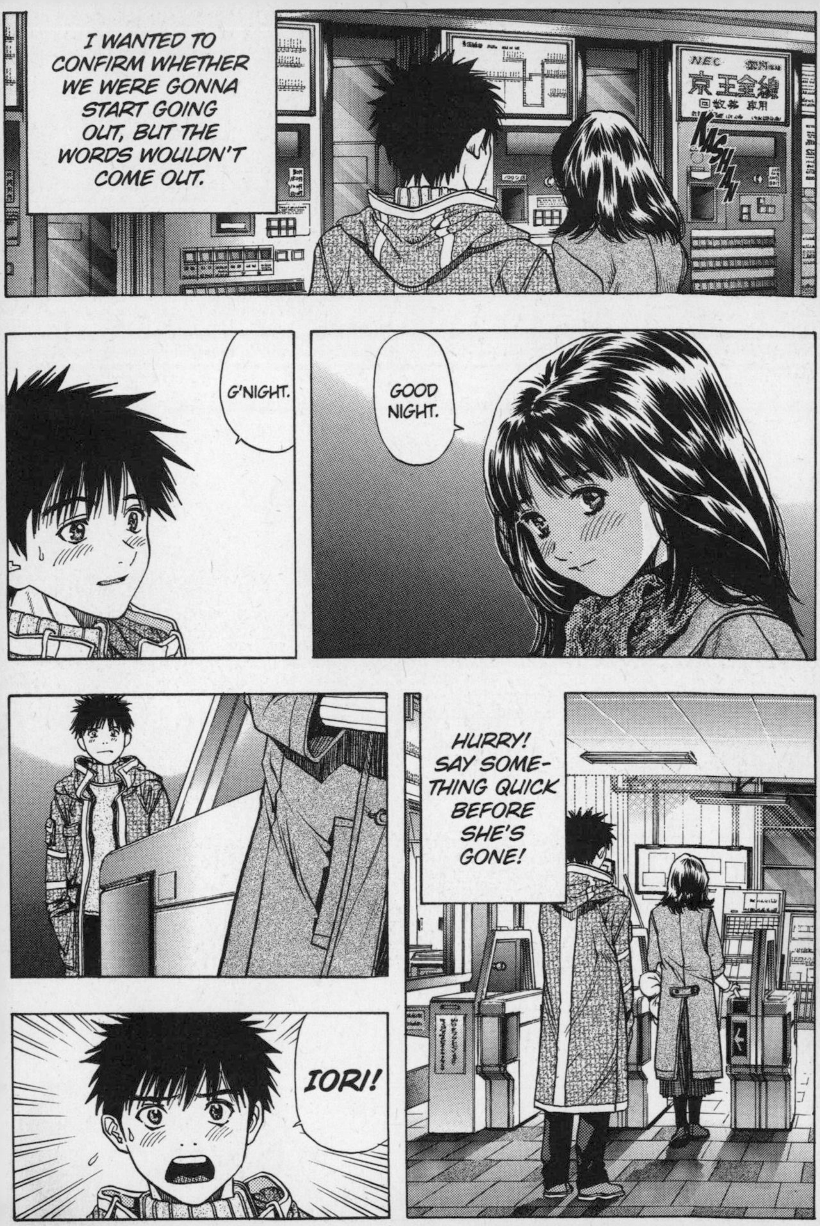
NEC
京王全線
回数券 専用
KASHAN
I WANTED TO CONFIRM WHETHER WE WERE GONNA START GOING OUT, BUT THE WORDS WOULDN'T COME OUT.
GOOD NIGHT.
G'NIGHT.
HURRY! SAY SOME-THING QUICK BEFORE SHE'S GONE!
IORI!

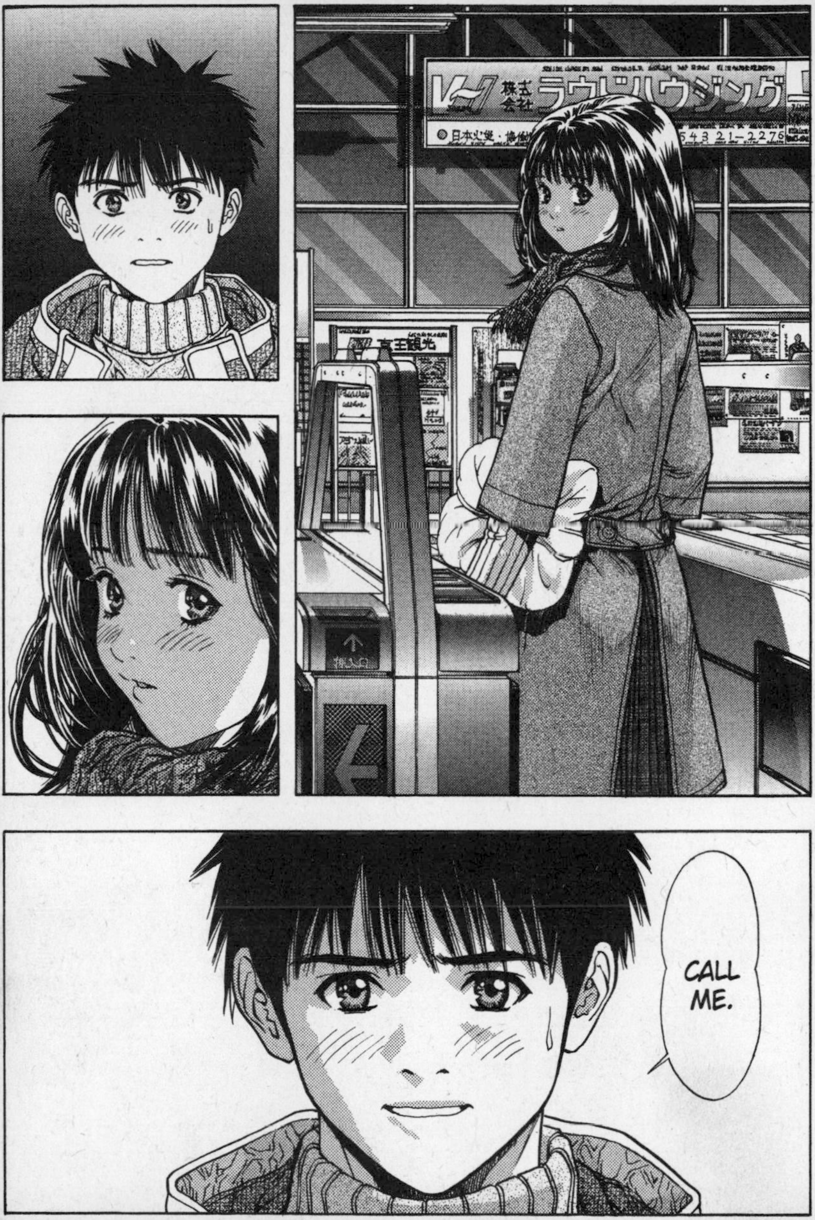
CALL ME.

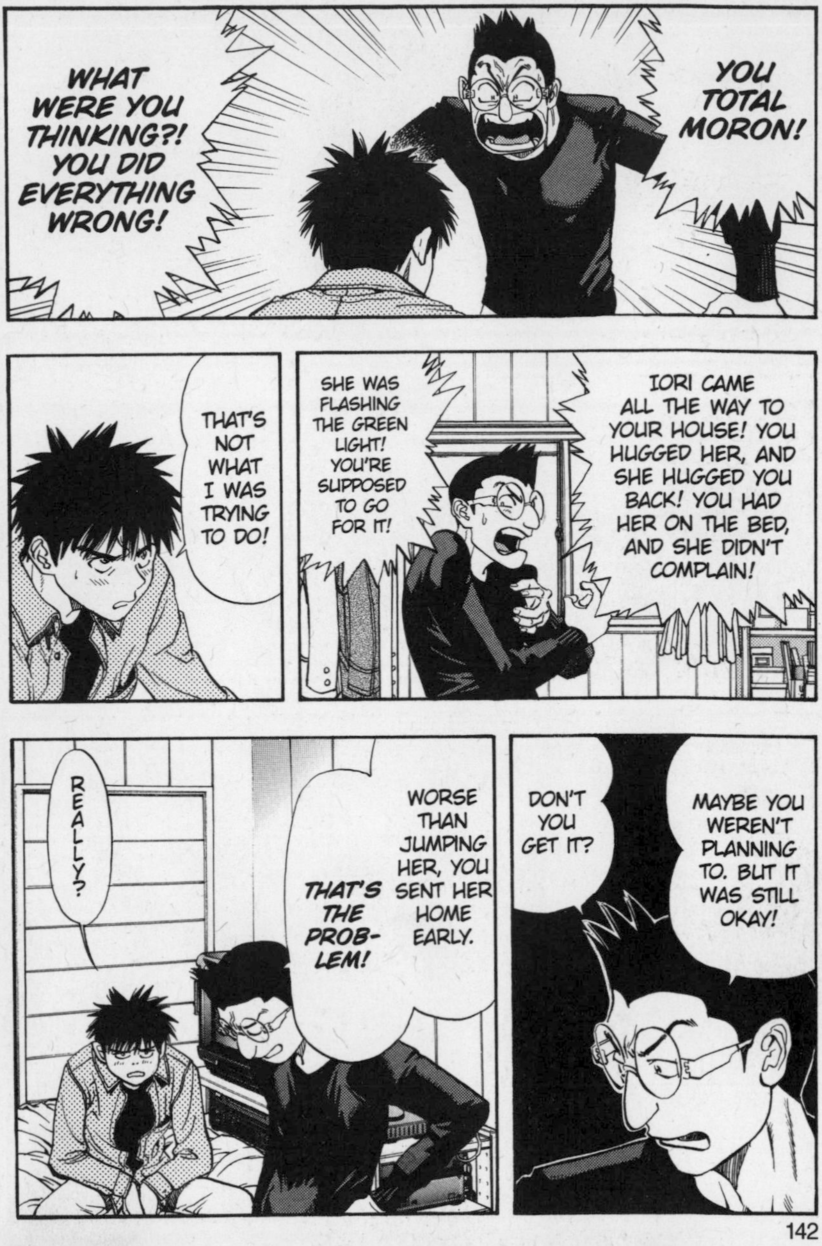
YOU TOTAL MORON!
WHAT WERE YOU THINKING?! YOU DID EVERYTHING WRONG!
IORI CAME ALL THE WAY TO YOUR HOUSE! YOU HUGGED HER, AND SHE HUGGED YOU BACK! YOU HAD HER ON THE BED, AND SHE DIDN'T COMPLAIN!
SHE WAS FLASHING THE GREEN LIGHT! YOU'RE SUPPOSED TO GO FOR IT!
THAT'S NOT WHAT I WAS TRYING TO DO!
MAYBE YOU WEREN'T PLANNING TO. BUT IT WAS STILL OKAY!
DON'T YOU GET IT?
WORSE THAN JUMPING HER, YOU SENT HER HOME EARLY.
THAT'S THE PROB-LEM!
REALLY?

READ THIS WAY

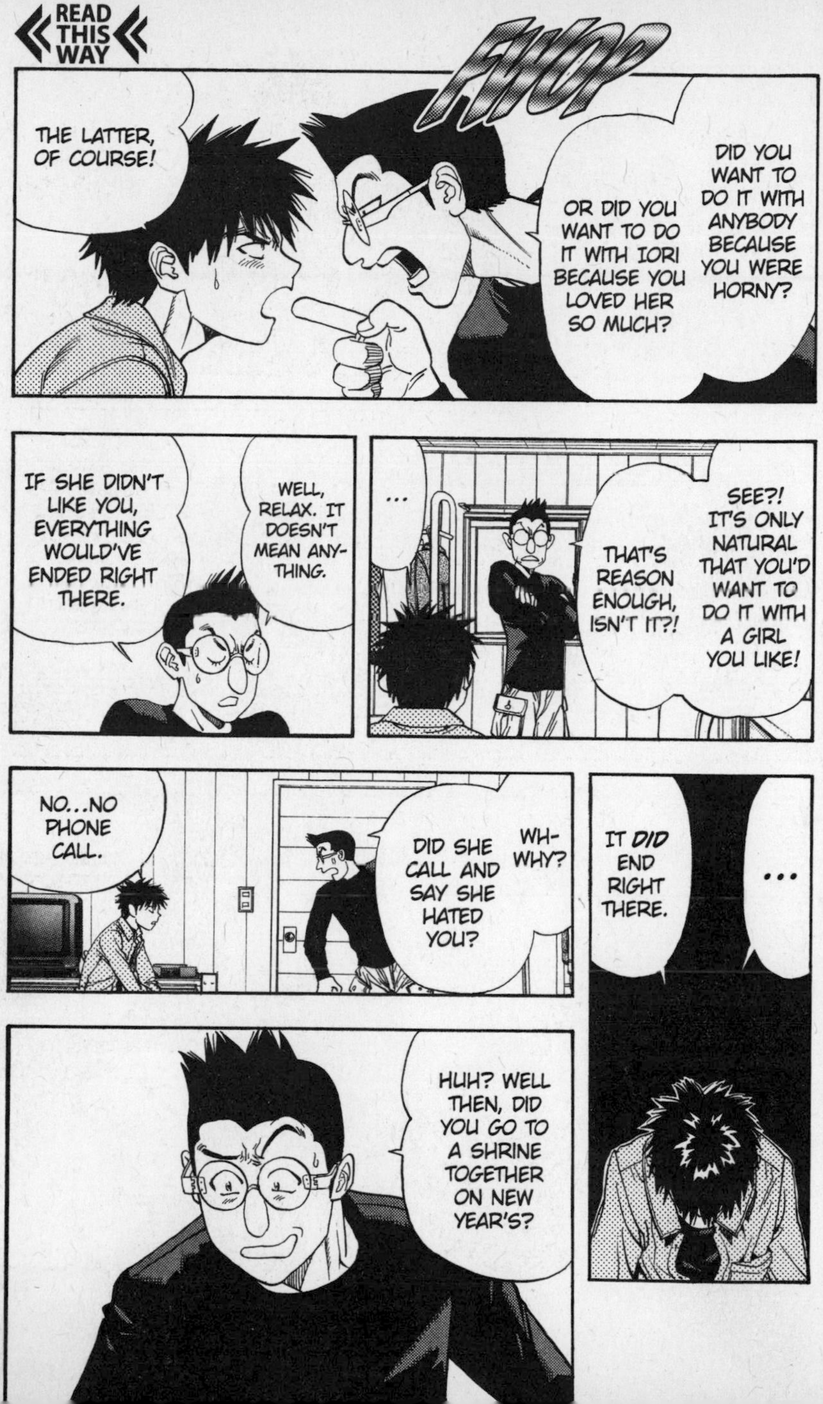
DID YOU WANT TO DO IT WITH ANYBODY BECAUSE YOU WERE HORNY?
OR DID YOU WANT TO DO IT WITH IORI BECAUSE YOU LOVED HER SO MUCH?
FWOP
THE LATTER, OF COURSE!
SEE?! IT'S ONLY NATURAL THAT YOU'D WANT TO DO IT WITH A GIRL YOU LIKE!
THAT'S REASON ENOUGH, ISN'T IT?!
...
WELL, RELAX. IT DOESN'T MEAN ANY-THING.
IF SHE DIDN'T LIKE YOU, EVERYTHING WOULD'VE ENDED RIGHT THERE.
...
IT *DID* END RIGHT THERE.
WH-WHY?
DID SHE CALL AND SAY SHE HATED YOU?
NO...NO PHONE CALL.
HUH? WELL THEN, DID YOU GO TO A SHRINE TOGETHER ON NEW YEAR'S?

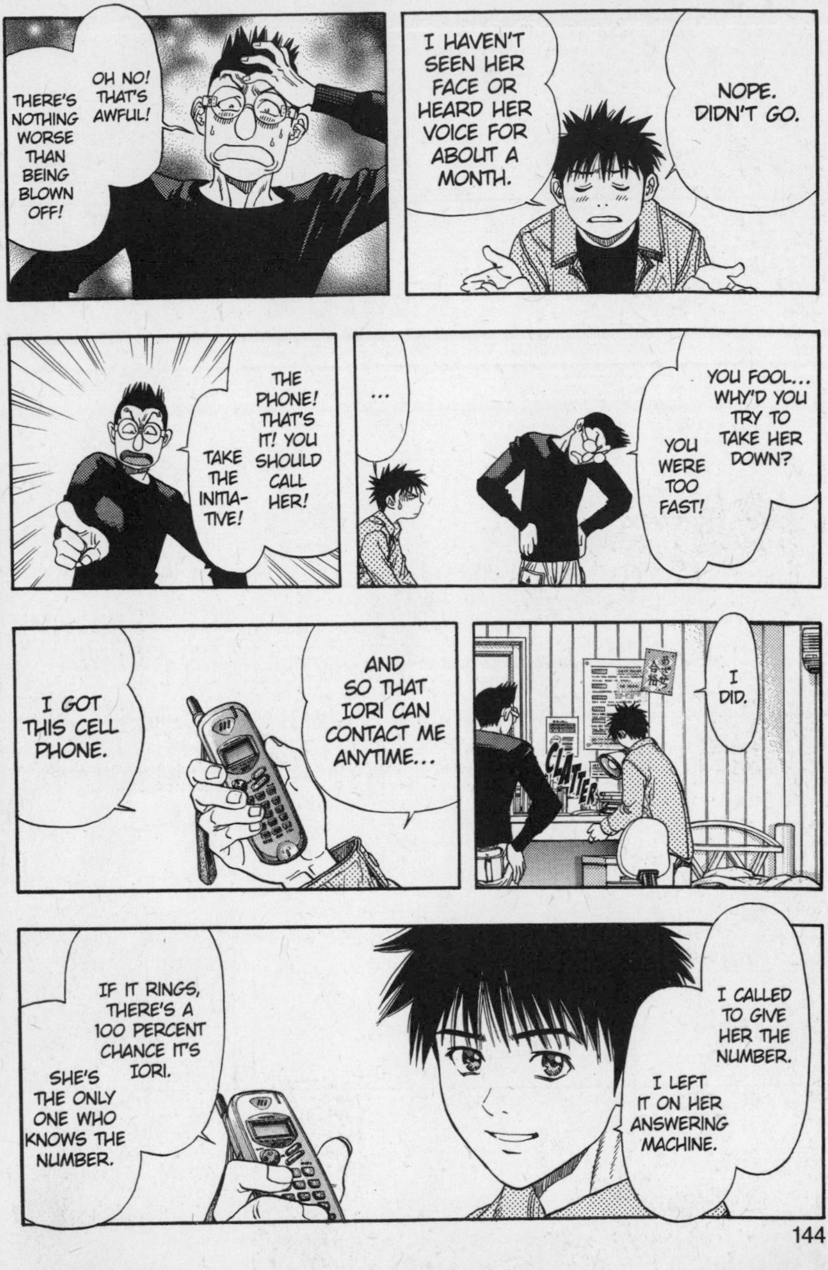
NOPE. DIDN'T GO.
I HAVEN'T SEEN HER FACE OR HEARD HER VOICE FOR ABOUT A MONTH.
OH NO! THAT'S AWFUL!
THERE'S NOTHING WORSE THAN BEING BLOWN OFF!
YOU FOOL... WHY'D YOU TRY TO TAKE HER DOWN?
YOU WERE TOO FAST!
...
THE PHONE! THAT'S IT! YOU SHOULD CALL HER!
TAKE THE INITIA-TIVE!
I DID.
CLATTER
AND SO THAT IORI CAN CONTACT ME ANYTIME...
I GOT THIS CELL PHONE.
I CALLED TO GIVE HER THE NUMBER.
I LEFT IT ON HER ANSWERING MACHINE.
IF IT RINGS, THERE'S A 100 PERCENT CHANCE IT'S IORI.
SHE'S THE ONLY ONE WHO KNOWS THE NUMBER.

READ THIS WAY

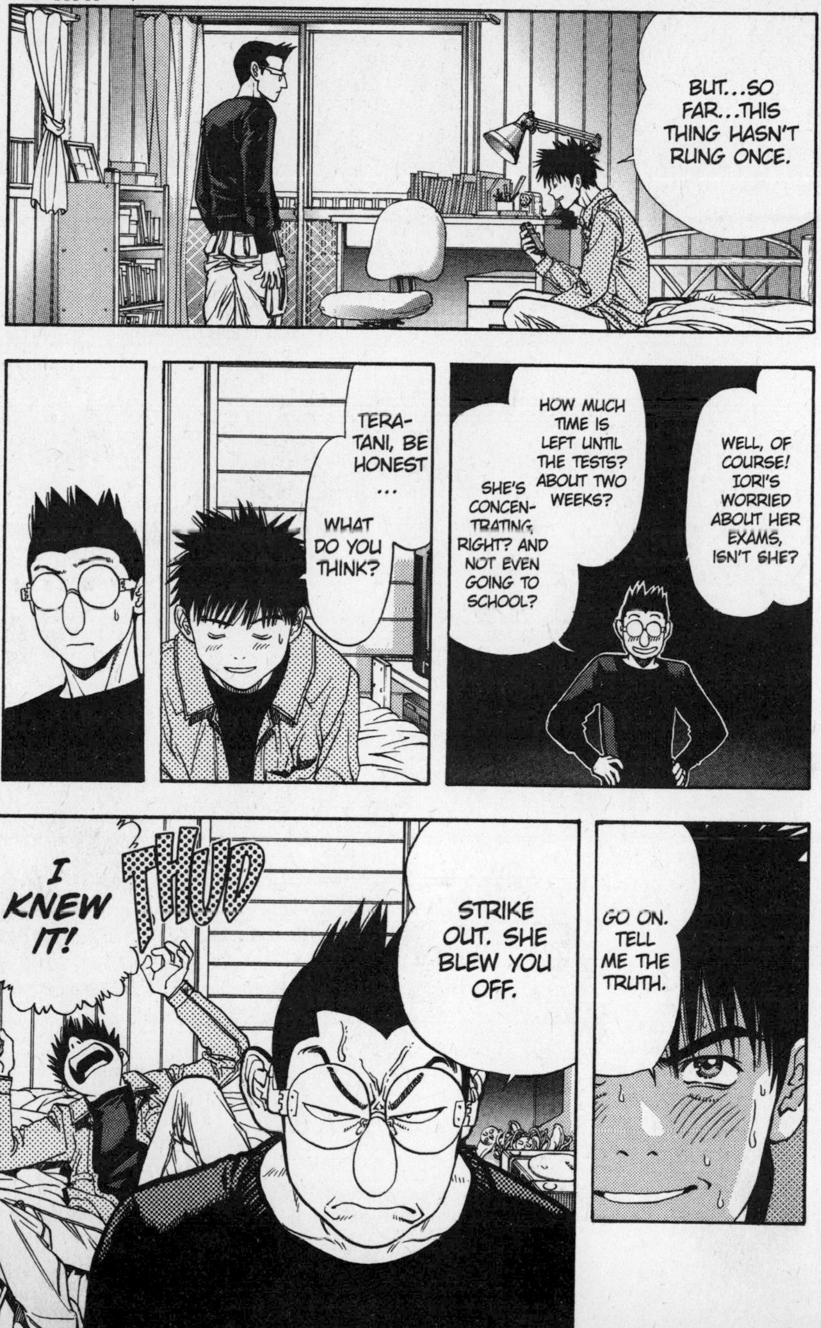
BUT...SO FAR...THIS THING HASN'T RUNG ONCE.
WELL, OF COURSE! IORI'S WORRIED ABOUT HER EXAMS, ISN'T SHE?
HOW MUCH TIME IS LEFT UNTIL THE TESTS? ABOUT TWO WEEKS?
SHE'S CONCEN-TRATING, RIGHT? AND NOT EVEN GOING TO SCHOOL?
TERA-TANI, BE HONEST ...
WHAT DO YOU THINK?
GO ON. TELL ME THE TRUTH.
STRIKE OUT. SHE BLEW YOU OFF.
THUD
I KNEW IT!

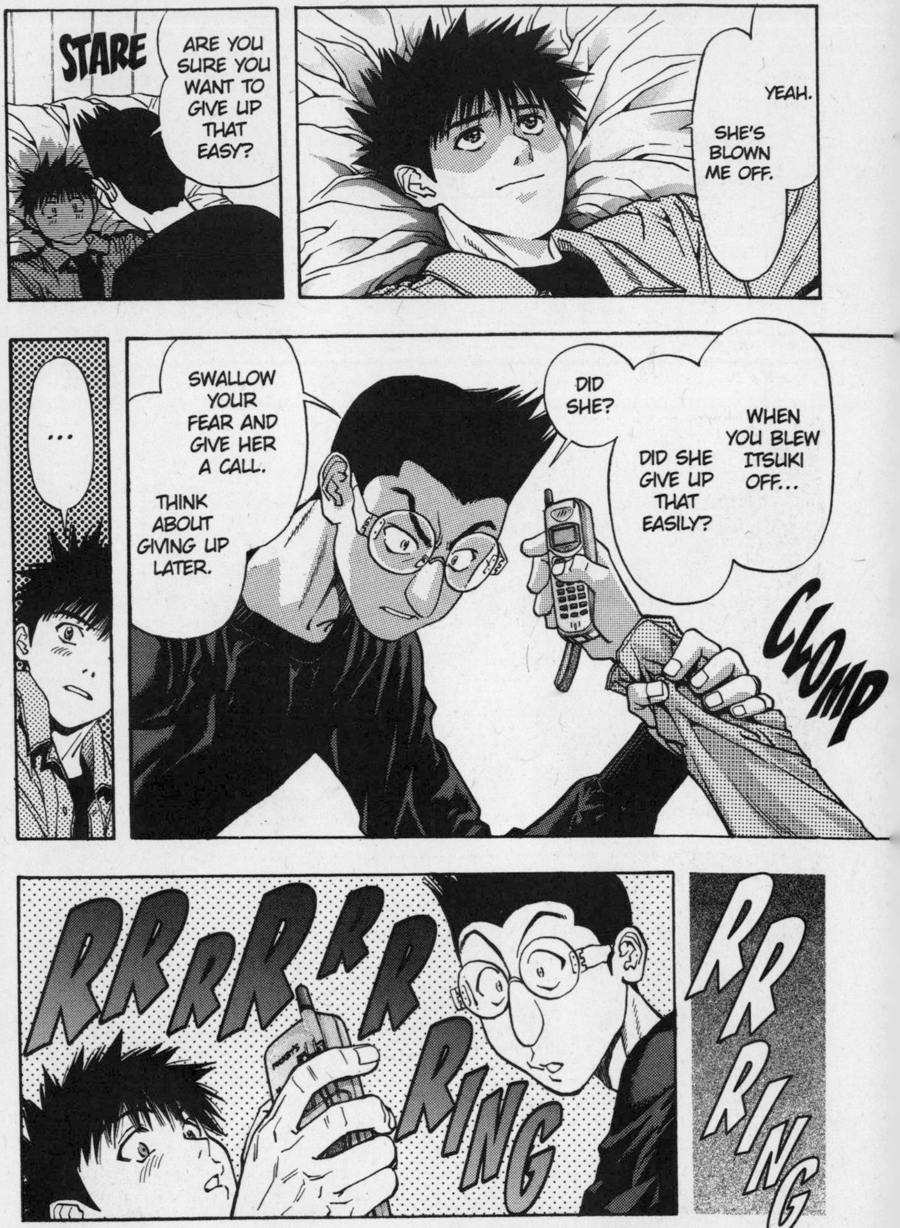
YEAH.
SHE'S BLOWN ME OFF.
STARE
ARE YOU SURE YOU WANT TO GIVE UP THAT EASY?
DID SHE?
WHEN YOU BLEW ITSUKI OFF...
DID SHE GIVE UP THAT EASILY?
SWALLOW YOUR FEAR AND GIVE HER A CALL.
THINK ABOUT GIVING UP LATER.
CLOMP
...
RRRRING
RRRRRRRING

READ THIS WAY

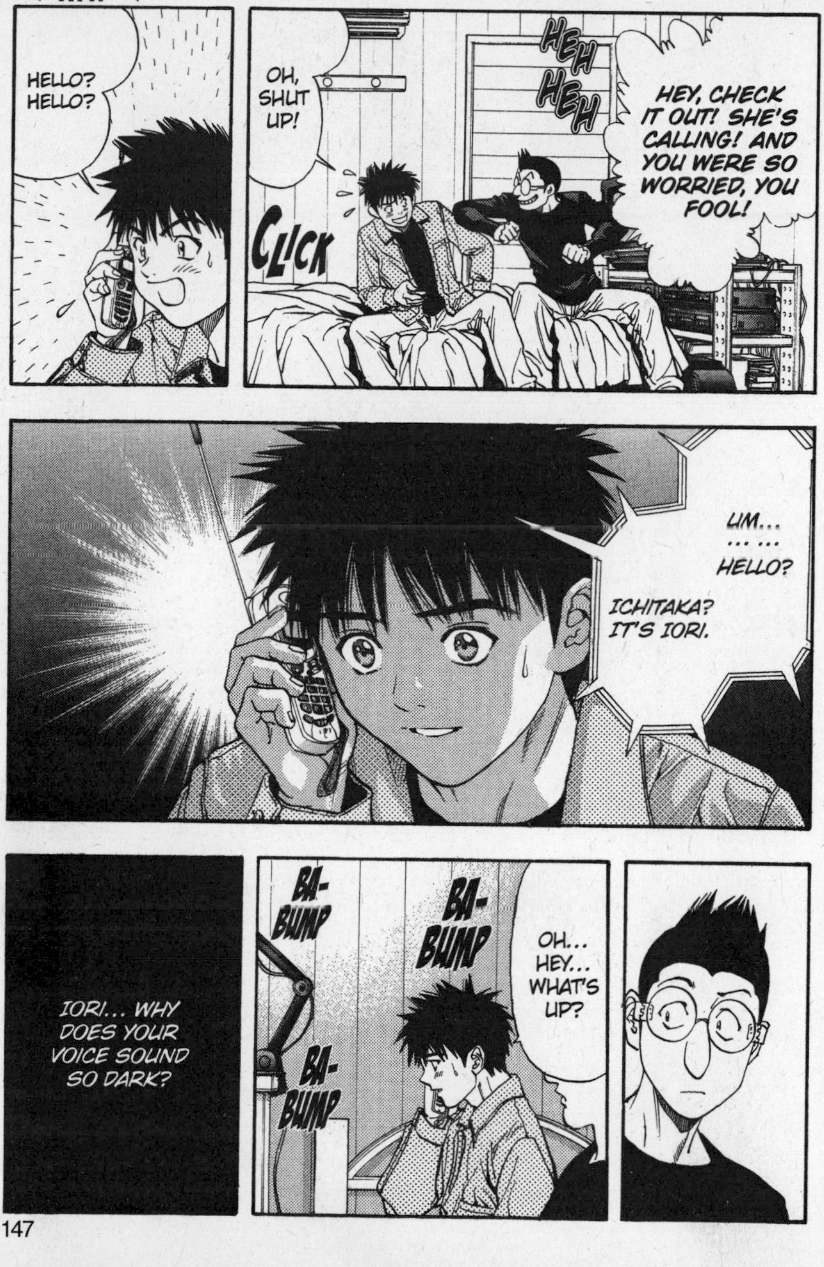
HEH HEH
HEY, CHECK IT OUT! SHE'S CALLING! AND YOU WERE SO WORRIED, YOU FOOL!
OH, SHUT UP!
CLICK
HELLO? HELLO?
UM... ... ... HELLO?
ICHITAKA? IT'S IORI.
BA-BUMP
BA-BUMP
OH... HEY... WHAT'S UP?
BA-BUMP
IORI... WHY DOES YOUR VOICE SOUND SO DARK?

I"s

アイズ

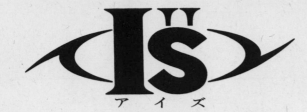

Chapter 92: Intuition

READ THIS WAY

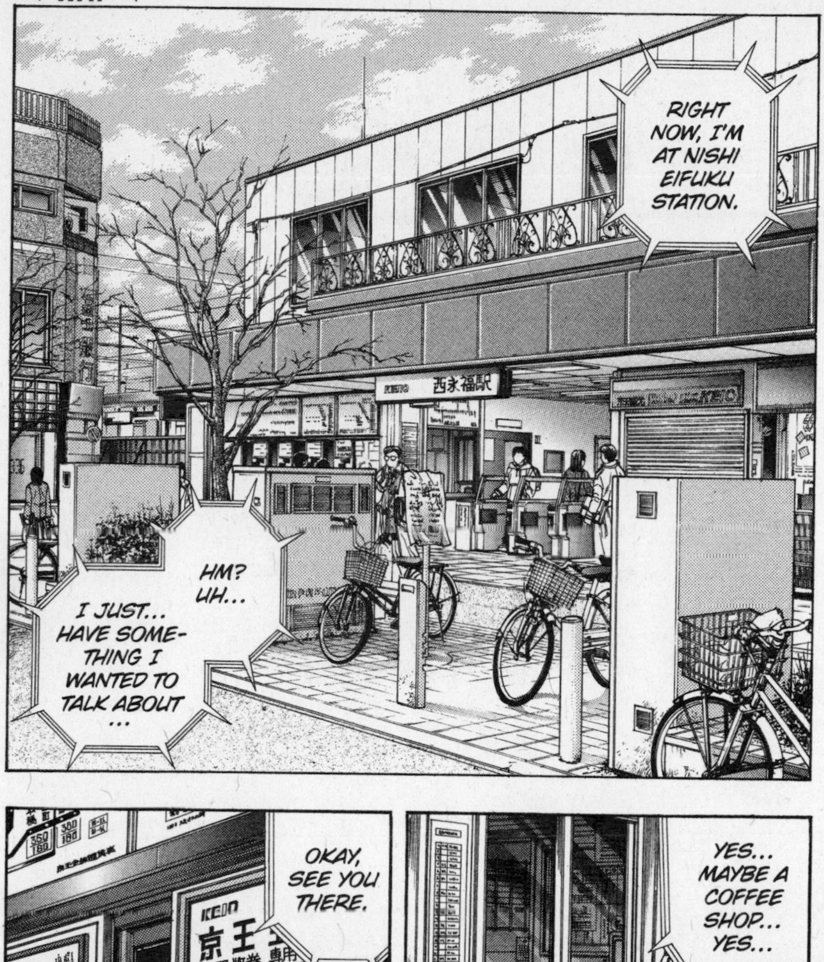
RIGHT NOW, I'M AT NISHI EIFUKU STATION.
HM? UH...
I JUST... HAVE SOME-THING I WANTED TO TALK ABOUT ...
西永福駅

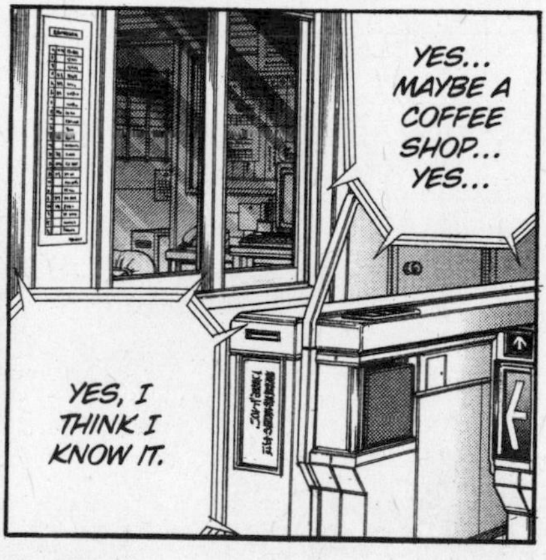
YES... MAYBE A COFFEE SHOP... YES...
YES, I THINK I KNOW IT.

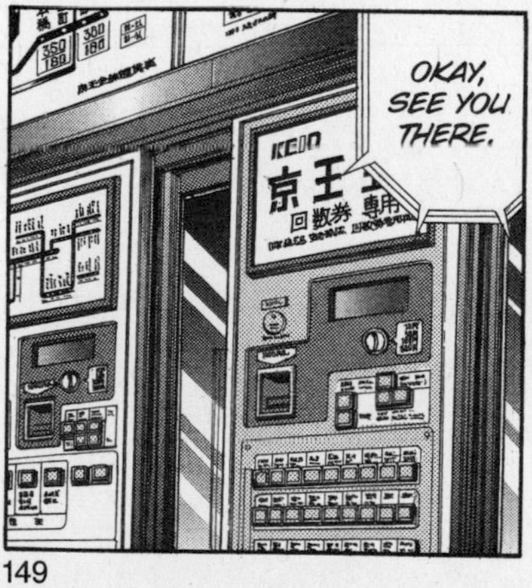
OKAY, SEE YOU THERE.
KEIO
京王
回数券 専用

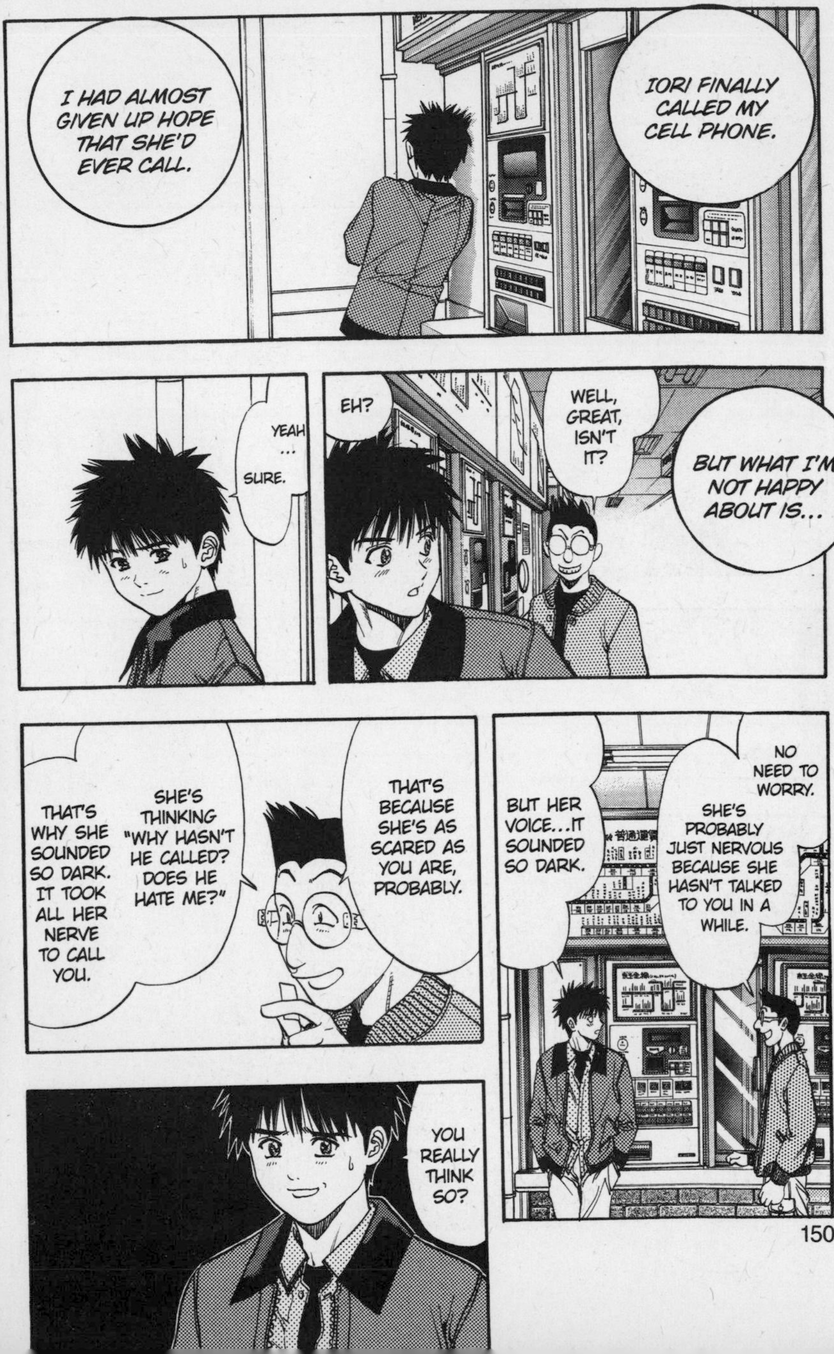
IORI FINALLY CALLED MY CELL PHONE.
I HAD ALMOST GIVEN UP HOPE THAT SHE'D EVER CALL.
BUT WHAT I'M NOT HAPPY ABOUT IS...
WELL, GREAT, ISN'T IT?
EH?
YEAH... SURE.
NO NEED TO WORRY.
SHE'S PROBABLY JUST NERVOUS BECAUSE SHE HASN'T TALKED TO YOU IN A WHILE.
BUT HER VOICE...IT SOUNDED SO DARK.
THAT'S BECAUSE SHE'S AS SCARED AS YOU ARE, PROBABLY.
SHE'S THINKING "WHY HASN'T HE CALLED? DOES HE HATE ME?"
THAT'S WHY SHE SOUNDED SO DARK. IT TOOK ALL HER NERVE TO CALL YOU.
YOU REALLY THINK SO?

READ THIS WAY

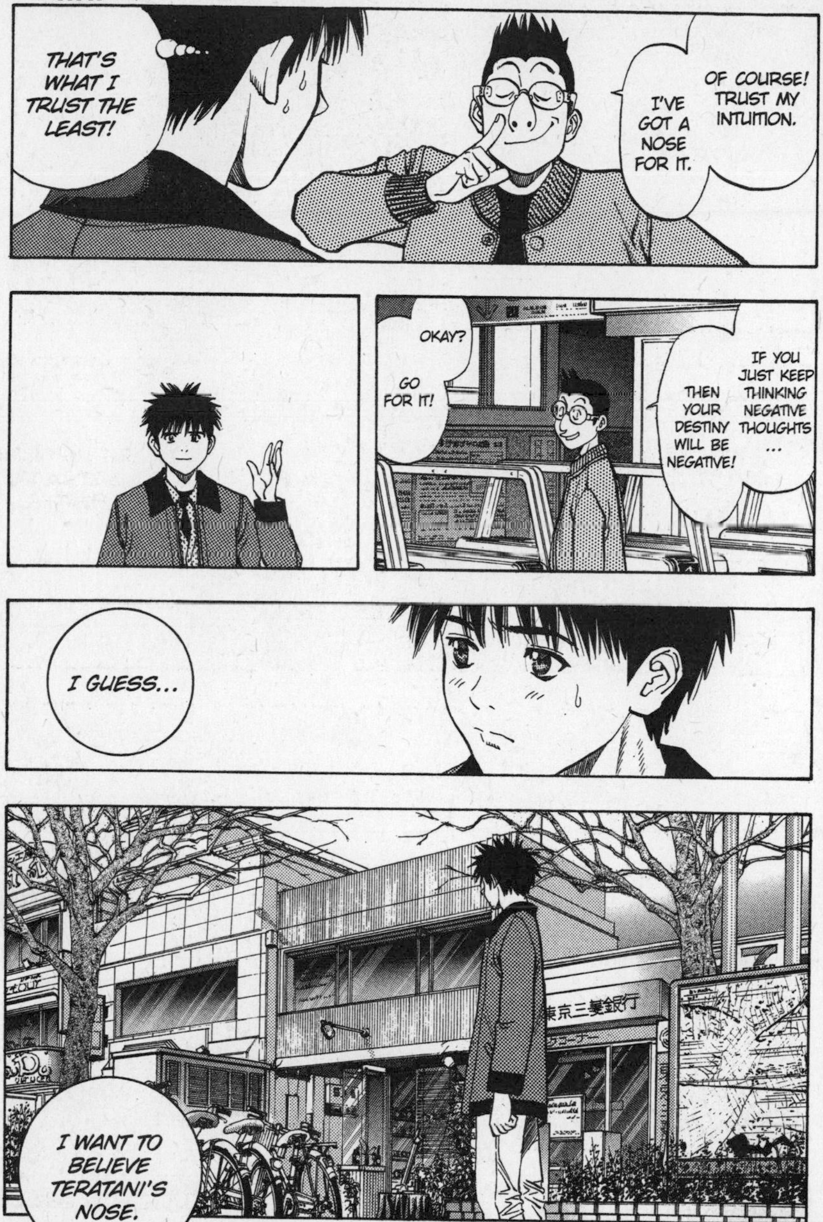
OF COURSE! TRUST MY INTUITION.
I'VE GOT A NOSE FOR IT.
THAT'S WHAT I TRUST THE LEAST!
IF YOU JUST KEEP THINKING NEGATIVE THOUGHTS ...
THEN YOUR DESTINY WILL BE NEGATIVE!
OKAY?
GO FOR IT!
I GUESS...
東京三菱銀行
I WANT TO BELIEVE TERATANI'S NOSE.

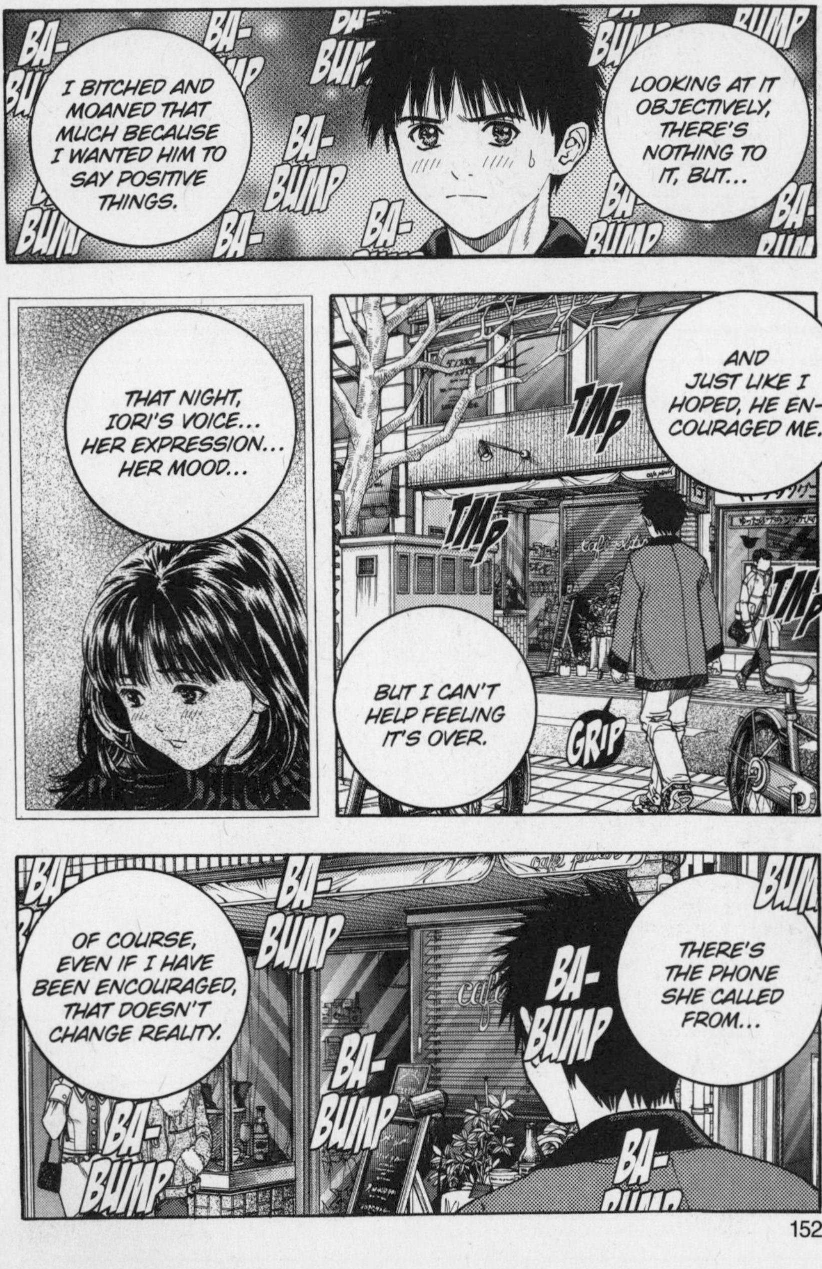
BA-BUMP
LOOKING AT IT OBJECTIVELY, THERE'S NOTHING TO IT, BUT...
BA-BUMP
BA-BUMP
I BITCHED AND MOANED THAT MUCH BECAUSE I WANTED HIM TO SAY POSITIVE THINGS.
BA-BUMP
AND JUST LIKE I HOPED, HE ENCOURAGED ME.
TMP
TMP
TMP
BUT I CAN'T HELP FEELING IT'S OVER.
GRIP
THAT NIGHT, IORI'S VOICE... HER EXPRESSION... HER MOOD...
THERE'S THE PHONE SHE CALLED FROM...
BA-BUMP
BA-BUMP
BA-BUMP
OF COURSE, EVEN IF I HAVE BEEN ENCOURAGED, THAT DOESN'T CHANGE REALITY.
BA-BUMP

READ THIS WAY

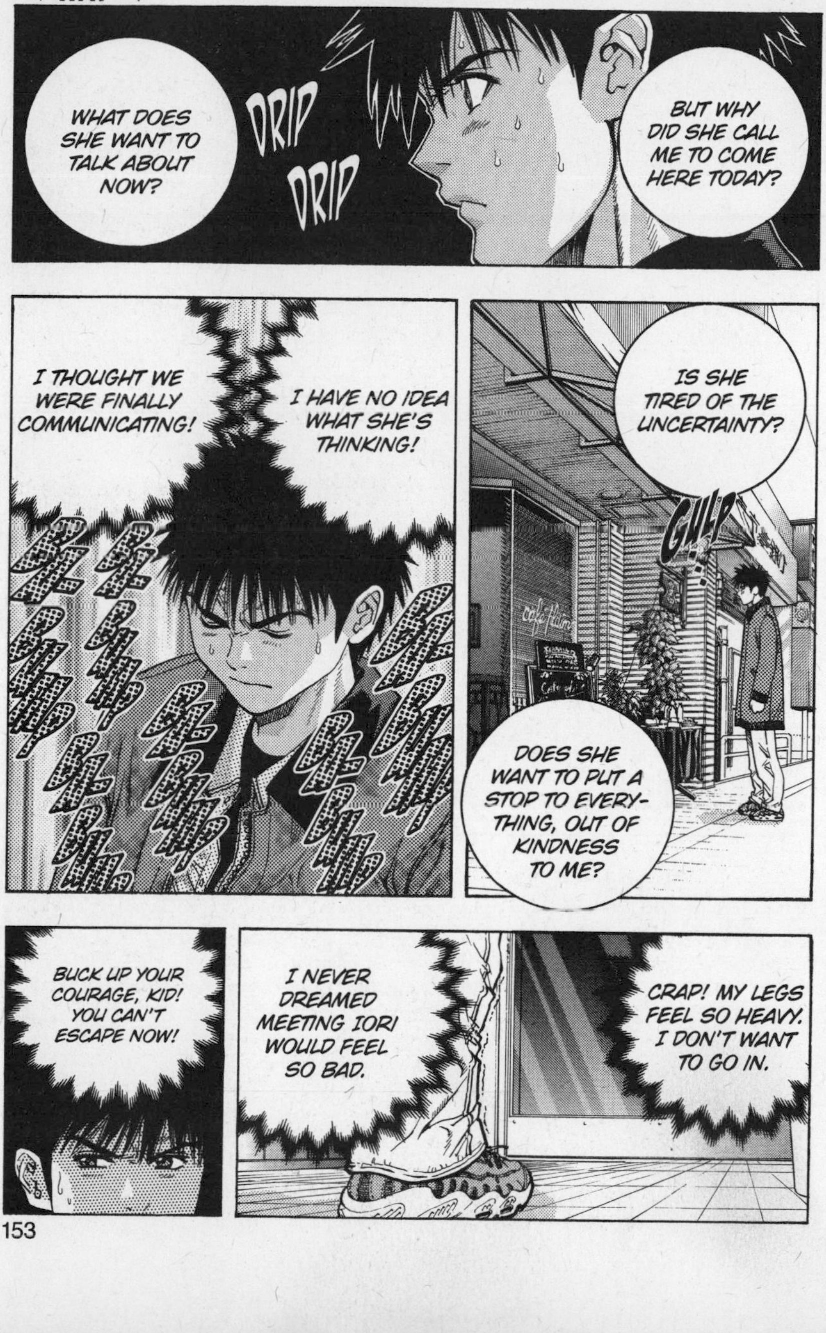
BUT WHY DID SHE CALL ME TO COME HERE TODAY?
DRIP DRIP
WHAT DOES SHE WANT TO TALK ABOUT NOW?
IS SHE TIRED OF THE UNCERTAINTY?
GULP
DOES SHE WANT TO PUT A STOP TO EVERY-THING, OUT OF KINDNESS TO ME?
I HAVE NO IDEA WHAT SHE'S THINKING!
I THOUGHT WE WERE FINALLY COMMUNICATING!
CRAP! MY LEGS FEEL SO HEAVY. I DON'T WANT TO GO IN.
I NEVER DREAMED MEETING IORI WOULD FEEL SO BAD.
BUCK UP YOUR COURAGE, KID! YOU CAN'T ESCAPE NOW!

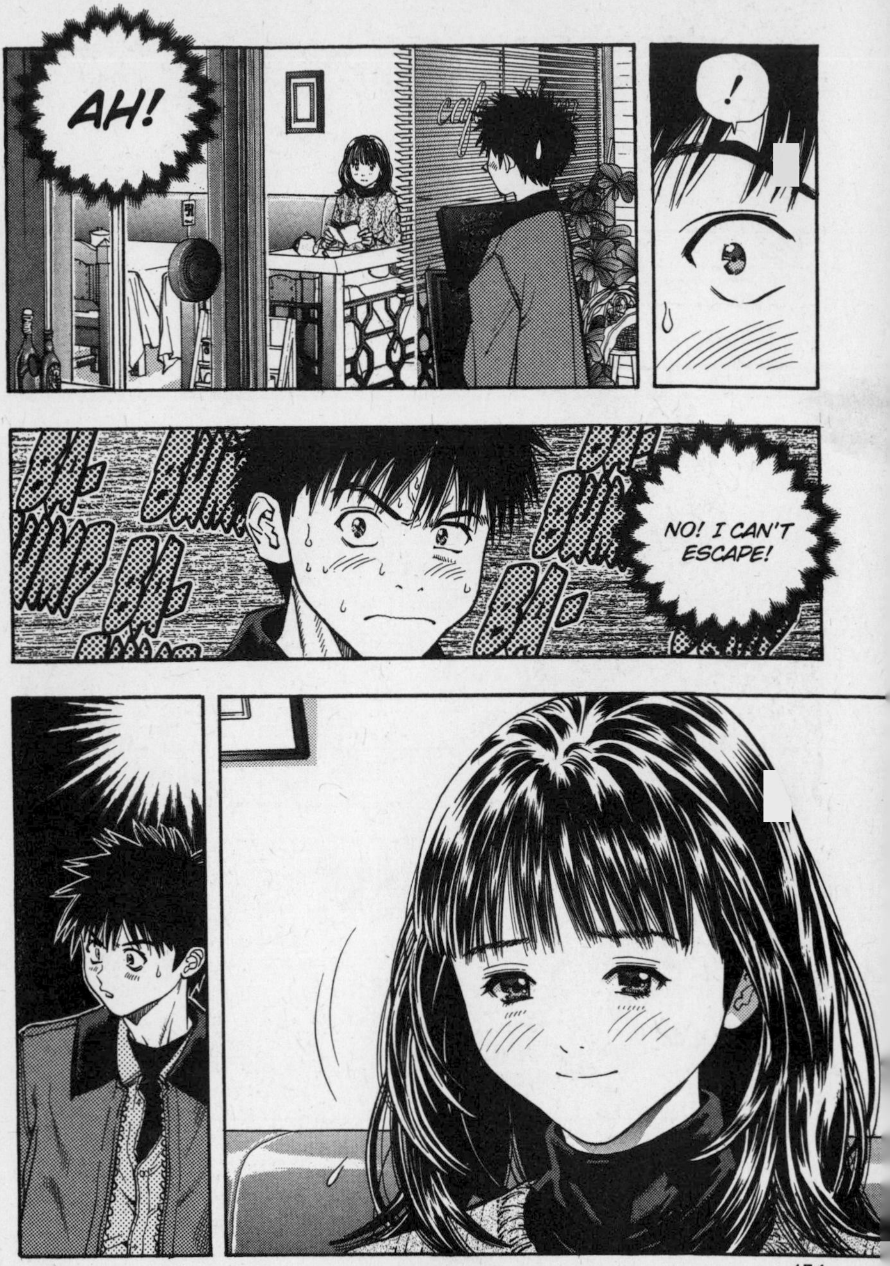
!
AH!
NO! I CAN'T ESCAPE!

READ THIS WAY

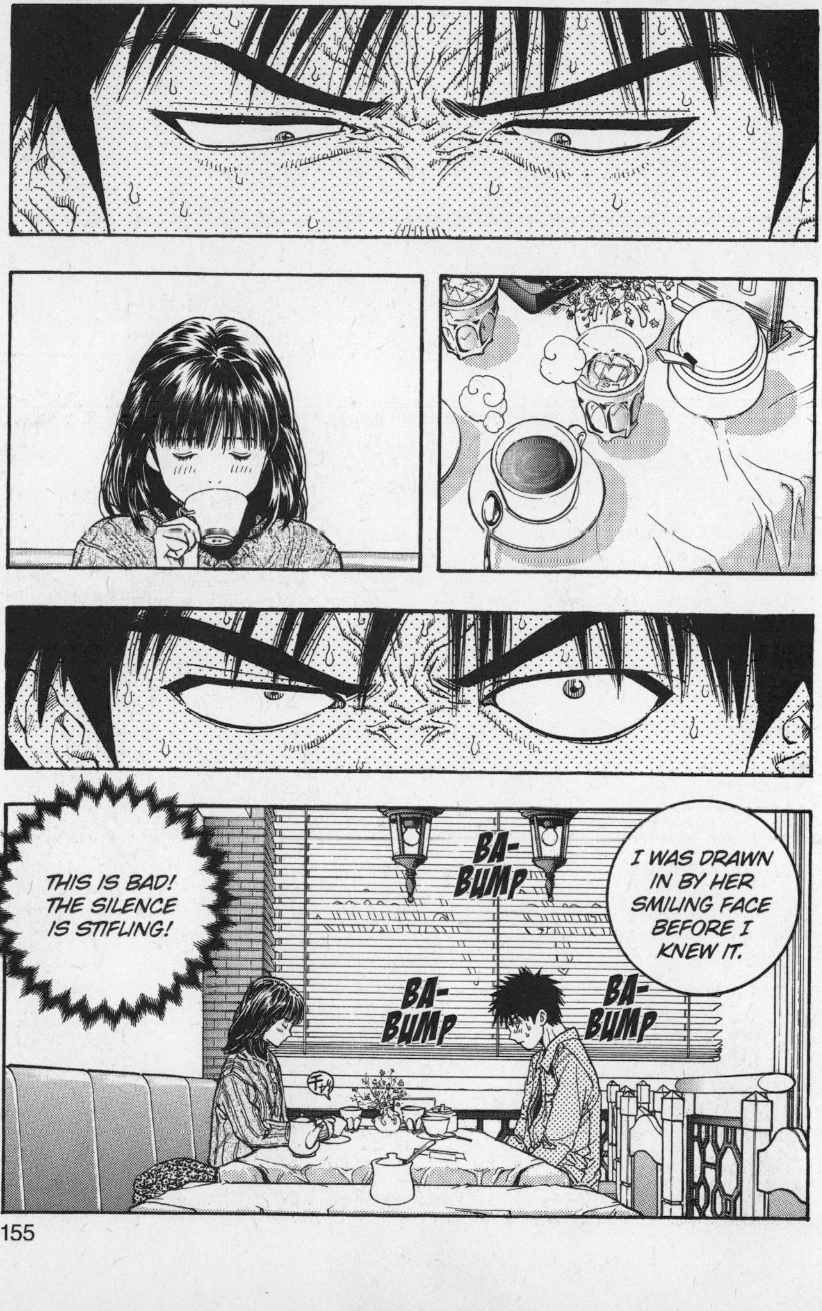
I WAS DRAWN IN BY HER SMILING FACE BEFORE I KNEW IT.
BA-BUMP
BA-BUMP
THIS IS BAD! THE SILENCE IS STIFLING!
BA-BUMP

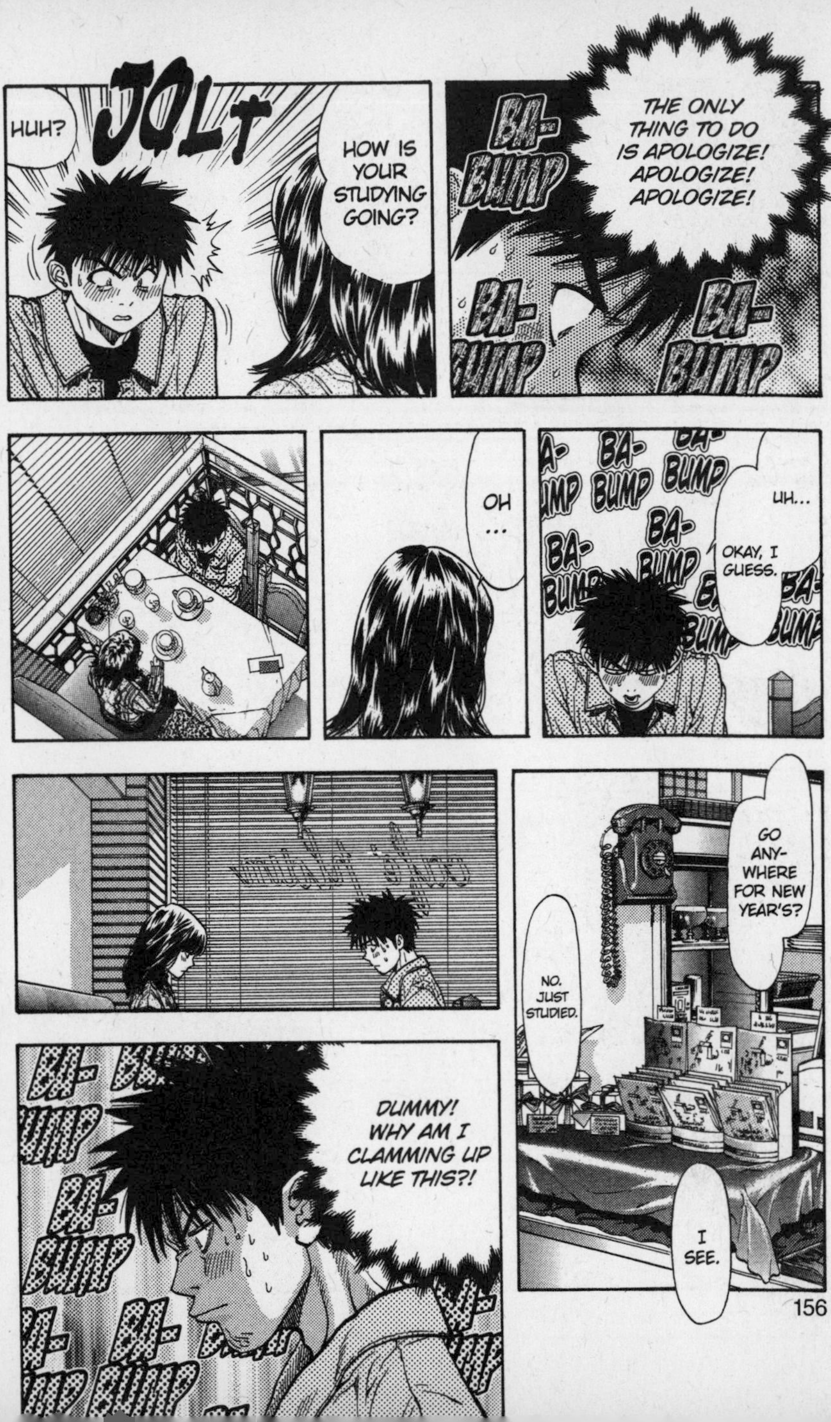
THE ONLY THING TO DO IS APOLOGIZE! APOLOGIZE! APOLOGIZE!
BA-BUMP
BA-BUMP
BA-BUMP
HOW IS YOUR STUDYING GOING?
JOLT
HUH?
BA-BUMP
BA-BUMP
BA-BUMP
BA-BUMP
UH...
OKAY, I GUESS.
OH ...
GO ANYWHERE FOR NEW YEAR'S?
NO. JUST STUDIED.
I SEE.
DUMMY! WHY AM I CLAMMING UP LIKE THIS?!

READ THIS WAY

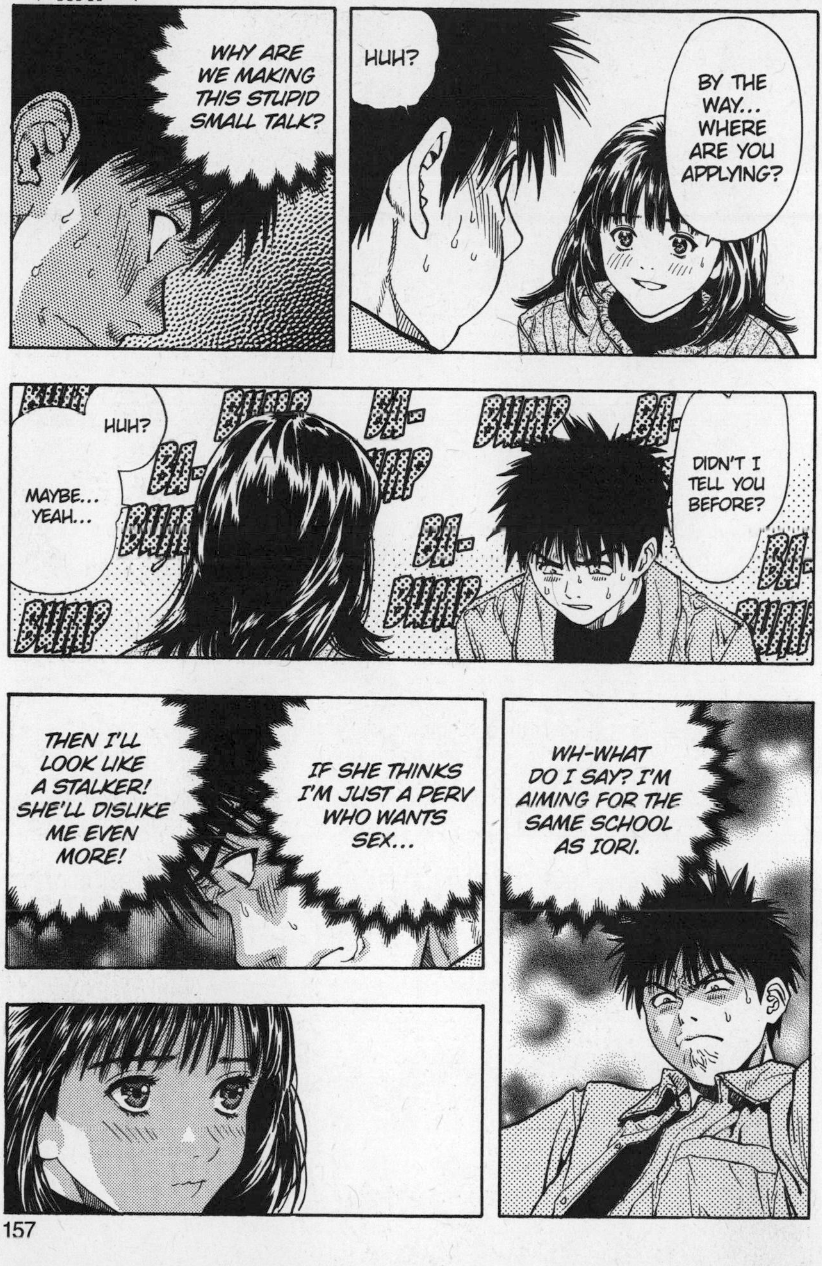
BY THE WAY... WHERE ARE YOU APPLYING?
HUH?
WHY ARE WE MAKING THIS STUPID SMALL TALK?
DIDN'T I TELL YOU BEFORE?
HUH?
MAYBE... YEAH...
WH-WHAT DO I SAY? I'M AIMING FOR THE SAME SCHOOL AS IORI.
IF SHE THINKS I'M JUST A PERV WHO WANTS SEX...
THEN I'LL LOOK LIKE A STALKER! SHE'LL DISLIKE ME EVEN MORE!

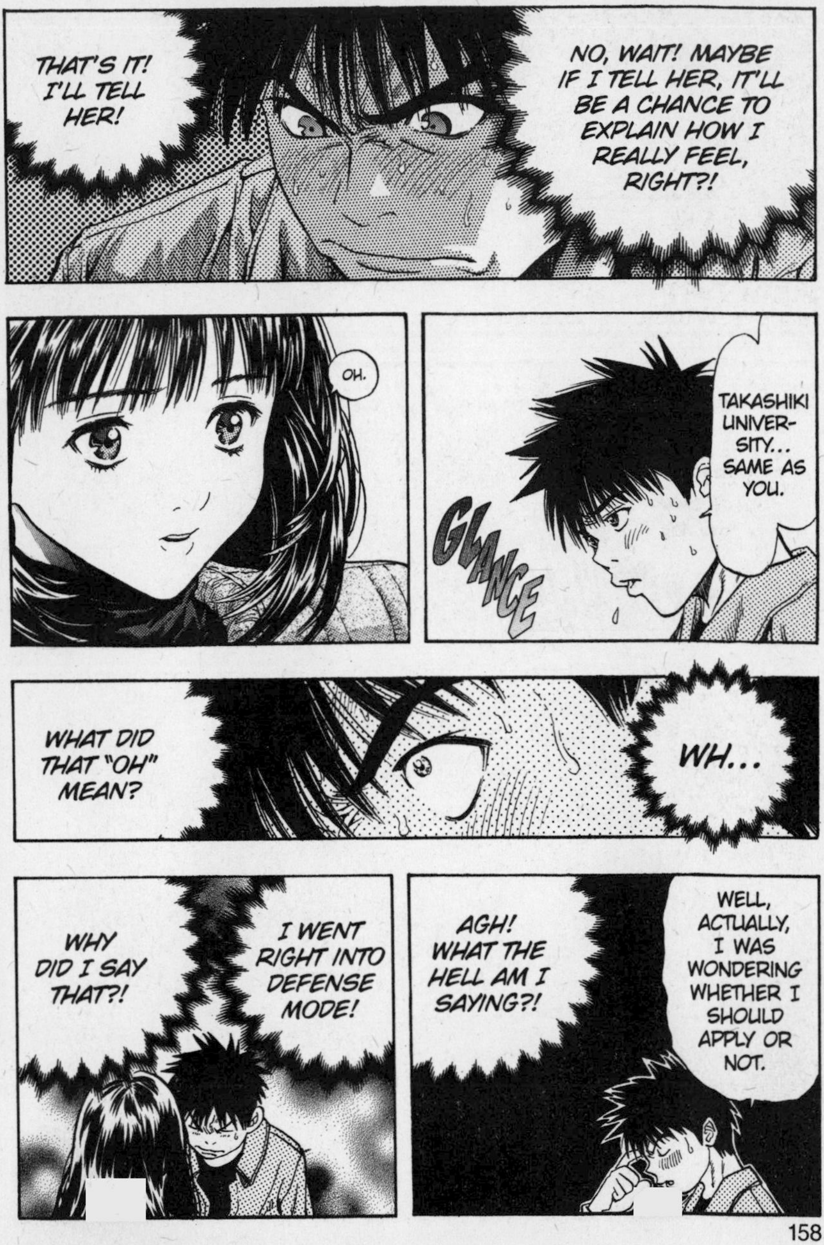
NO, WAIT! MAYBE IF I TELL HER, IT'LL BE A CHANCE TO EXPLAIN HOW I REALLY FEEL, RIGHT?!
THAT'S IT! I'LL TELL HER!
TAKASHIKI UNIVER-SITY... SAME AS YOU.
GLANCE
OH.
WH...
WHAT DID THAT "OH" MEAN?
WELL, ACTUALLY, I WAS WONDERING WHETHER I SHOULD APPLY OR NOT.
AGH! WHAT THE HELL AM I SAYING?!
I WENT RIGHT INTO DEFENSE MODE!
WHY DID I SAY THAT?!

READ THIS WAY

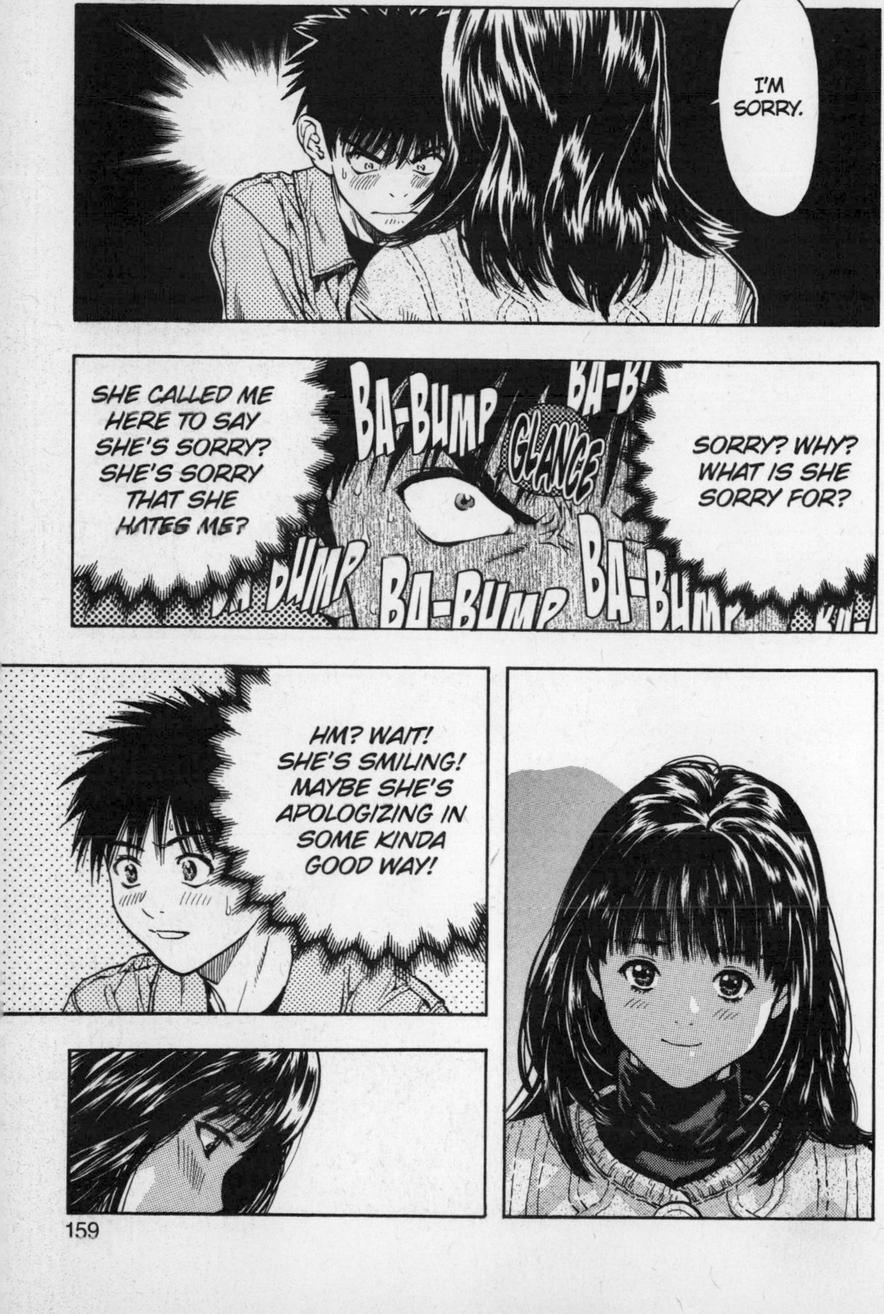
I'M SORRY.
BA-BUMP
GLANCE
SORRY? WHY? WHAT IS SHE SORRY FOR?
SHE CALLED ME HERE TO SAY SHE'S SORRY? SHE'S SORRY THAT SHE HATES ME?
BA-BUMP
HM? WAIT! SHE'S SMILING! MAYBE SHE'S APOLOGIZING IN SOME KINDA GOOD WAY!

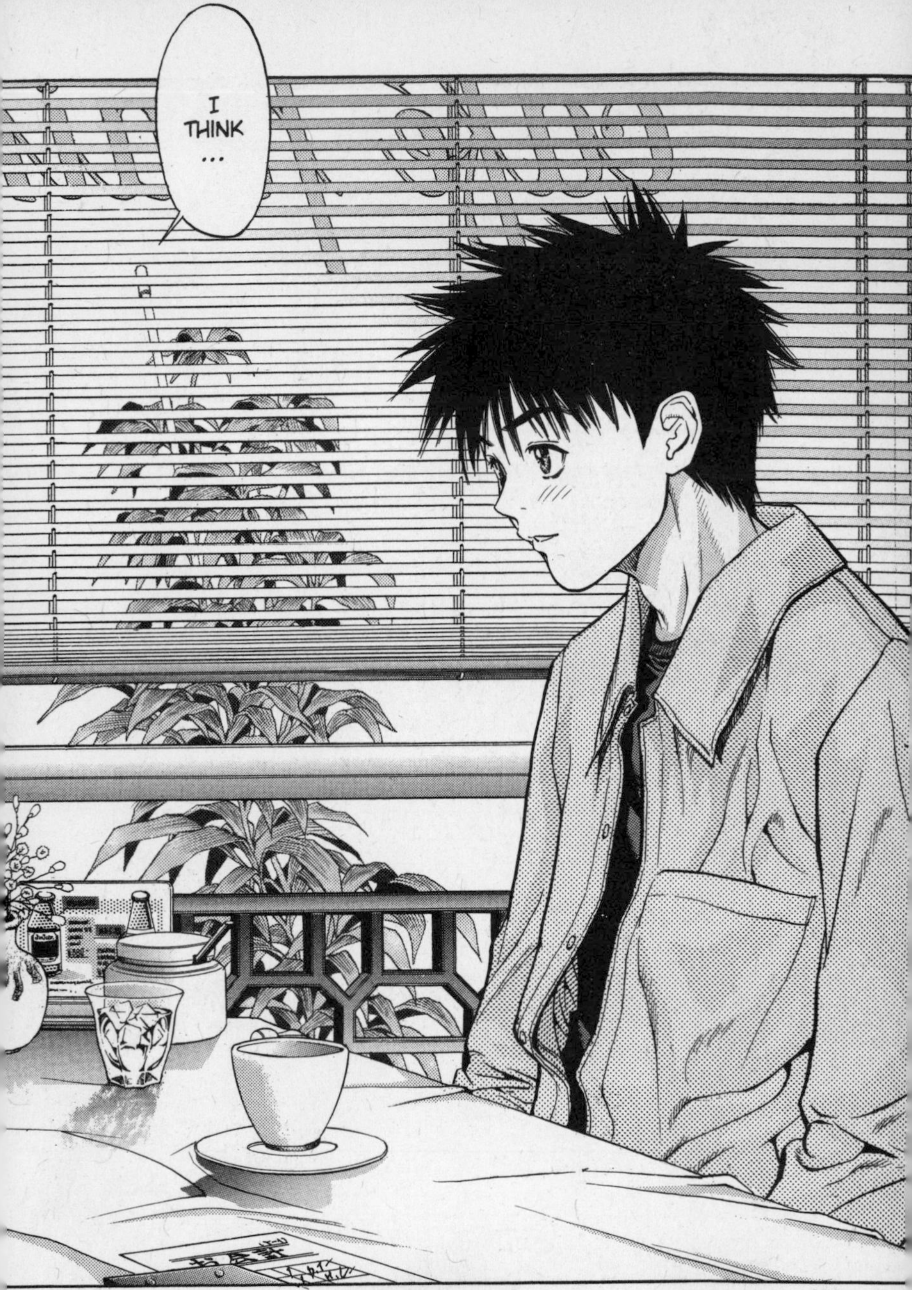
I THINK ...

READ THIS WAY

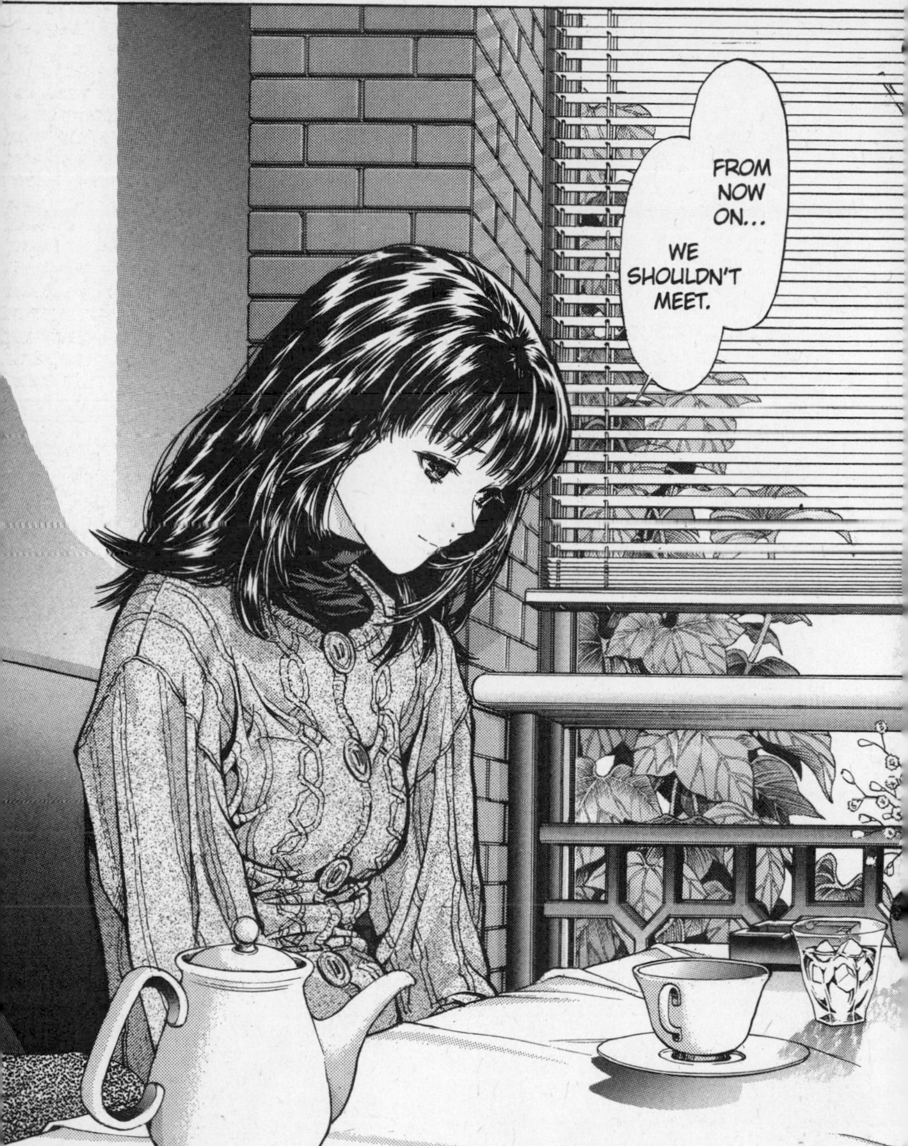
FROM NOW ON... WE SHOULDN'T MEET.

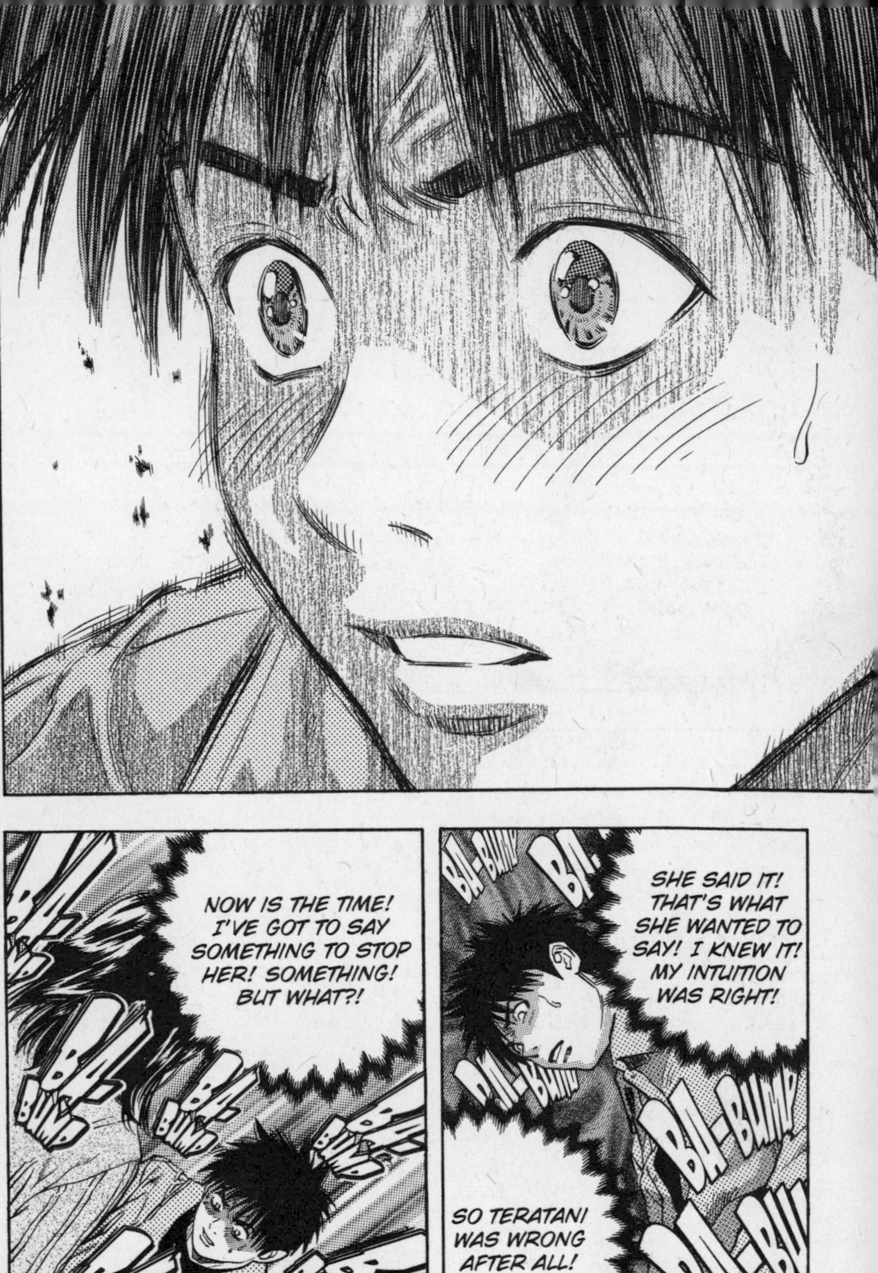
SHE SAID IT! THAT'S WHAT SHE WANTED TO SAY! I KNEW IT! MY INTUITION WAS RIGHT!
BA-BUMP
SO TERATANI WAS WRONG AFTER ALL!
NOW IS THE TIME! I'VE GOT TO SAY SOMETHING TO STOP HER! SOMETHING! BUT WHAT?!

READ THIS WAY

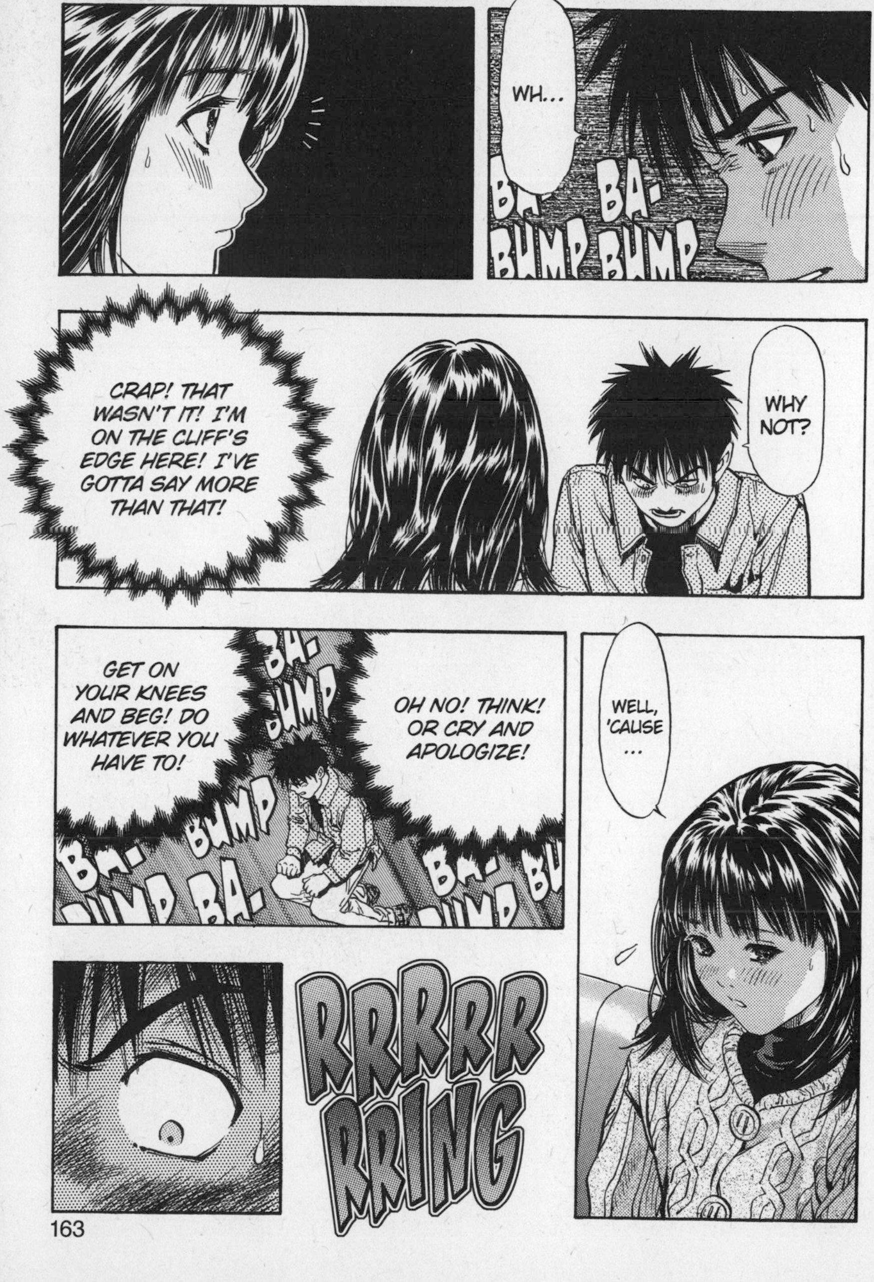
WH...
BA-BUMP
BA-BUMP
WHY NOT?
CRAP! THAT WASN'T IT! I'M ON THE CLIFF'S EDGE HERE! I'VE GOTTA SAY MORE THAN THAT!
WELL, 'CAUSE ...
OH NO! THINK! OR CRY AND APOLOGIZE!
BA-BUMP
GET ON YOUR KNEES AND BEG! DO WHATEVER YOU HAVE TO!
BA-BUMP
BA-BUMP
BA-BUMP
BA-BUMP
RRRRR RRING

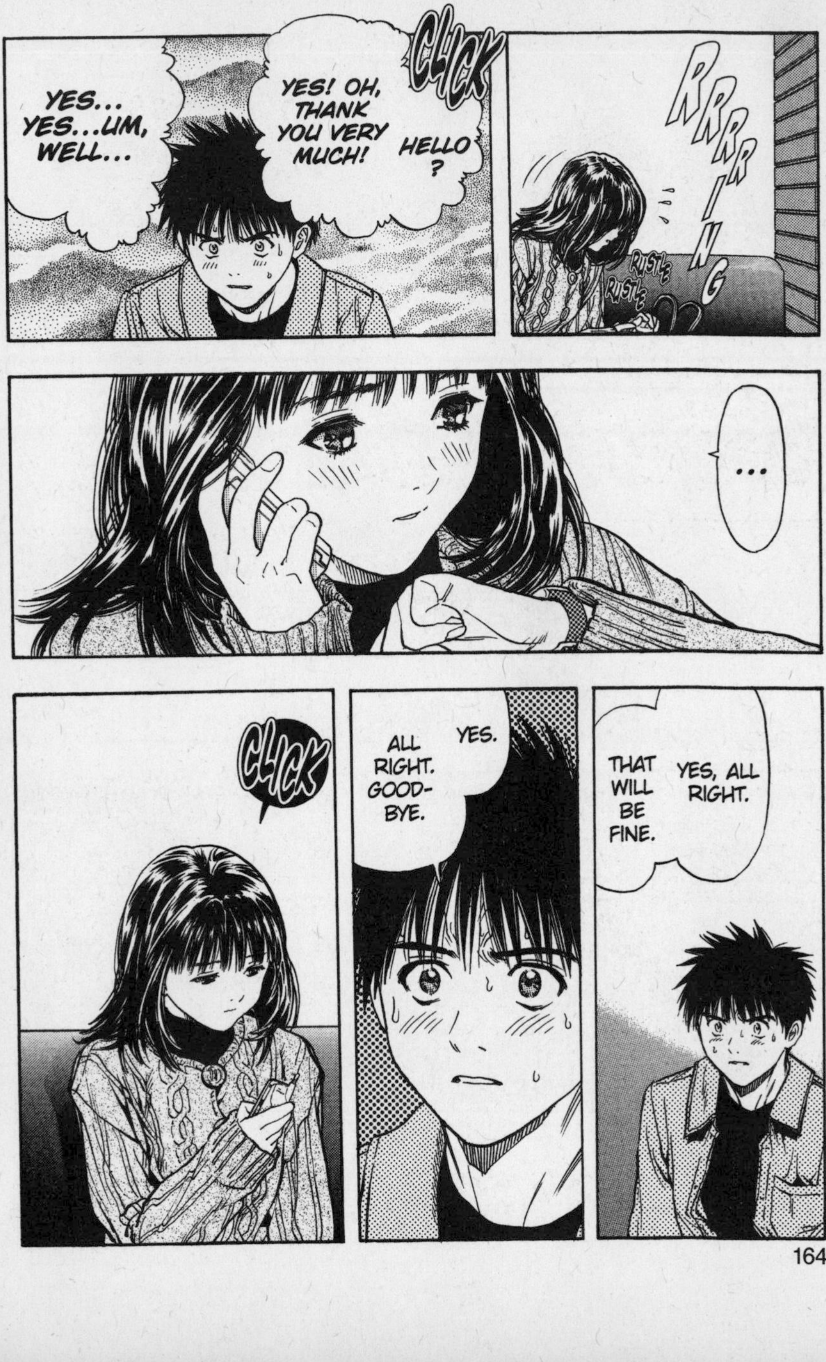
RRRRING
RUSTLE
RUSTLE
CLICK
HELLO?
YES! OH, THANK YOU VERY MUCH!
YES... YES...UM, WELL...
...
YES, ALL RIGHT.
THAT WILL BE FINE.
YES.
ALL RIGHT. GOOD-BYE.
CLICK

READ THIS WAY

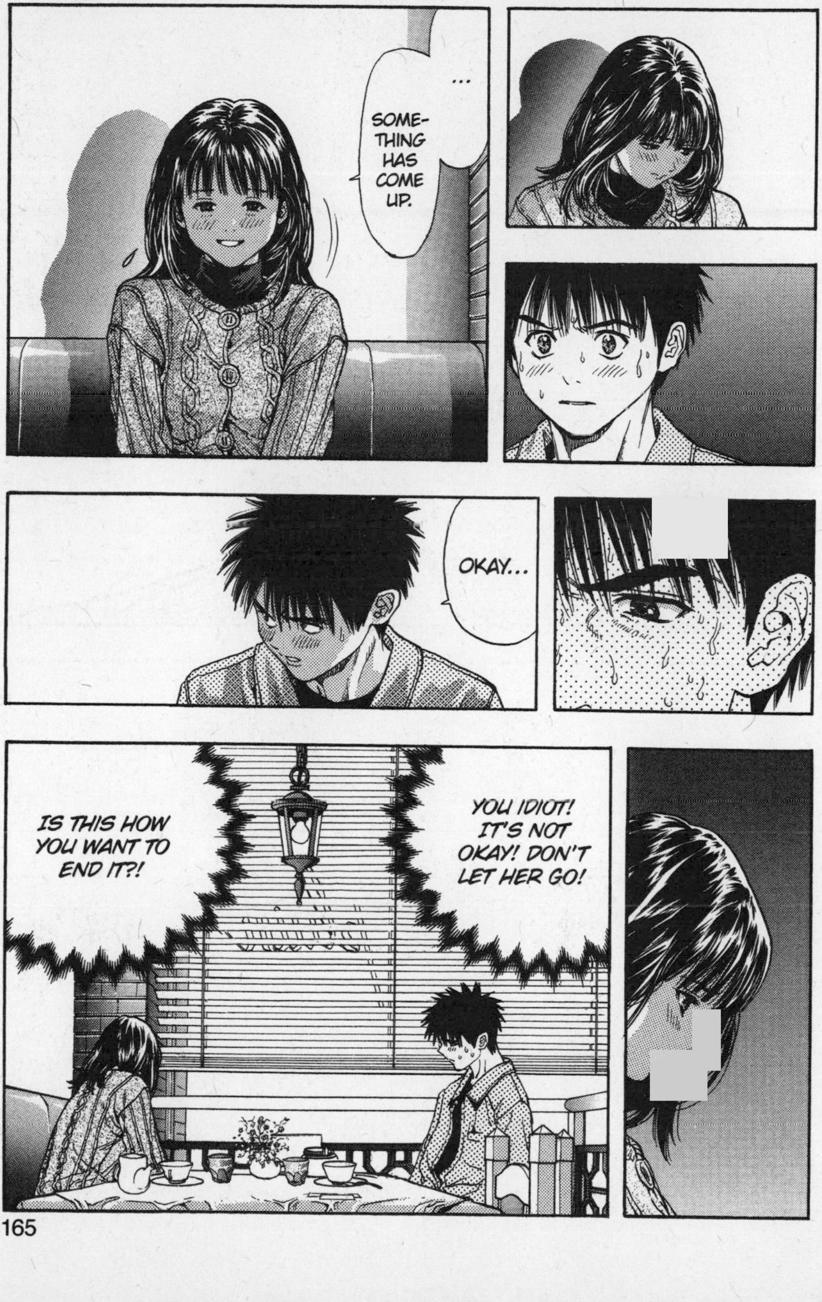
...
SOME-THING HAS COME UP.
OKAY...
YOU IDIOT! IT'S NOT OKAY! DON'T LET HER GO!
IS THIS HOW YOU WANT TO END IT?!

Chapter 93:
Just the Same Way

SEE YOU LATER.

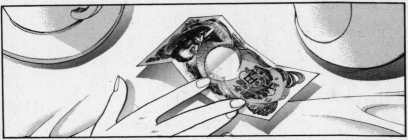

YOU DON'T NEED...

...TO PAY...

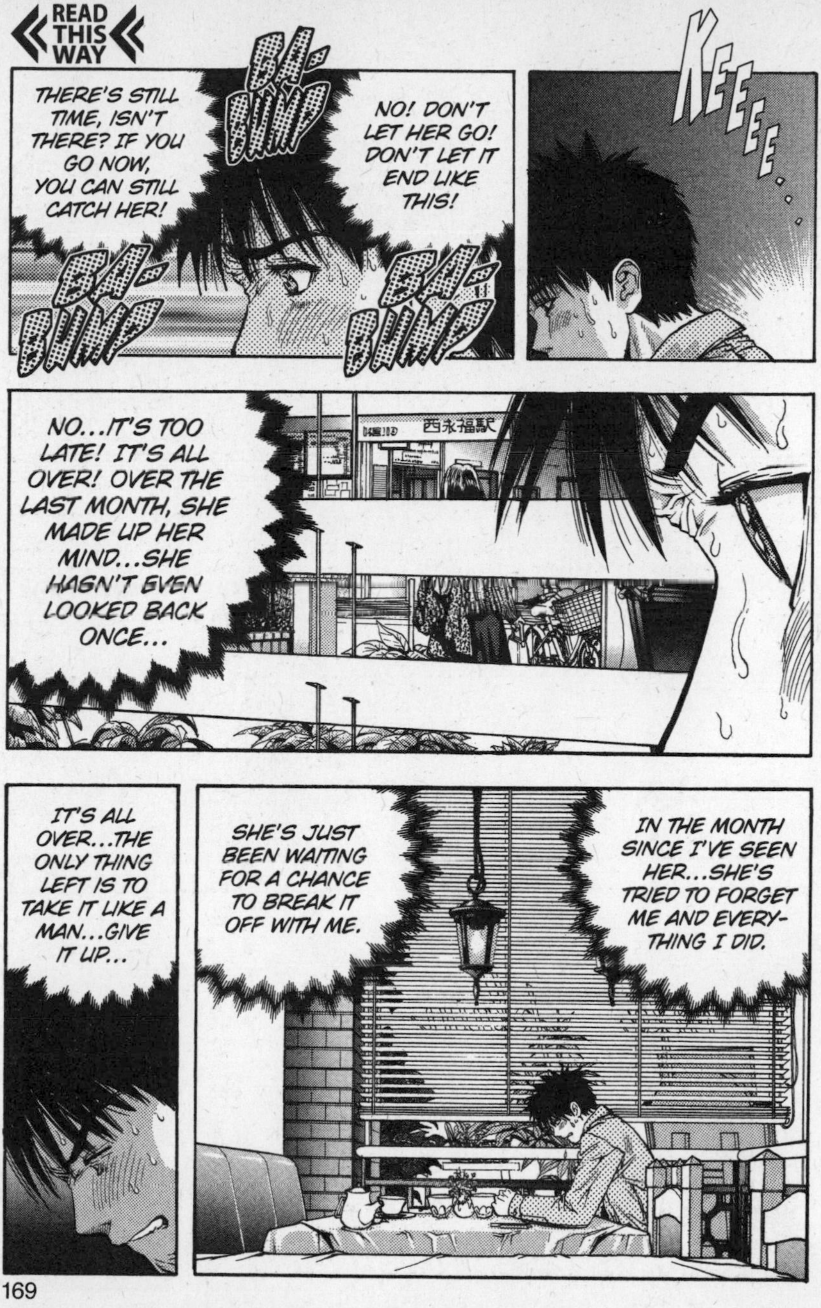
READ THIS WAY
KEEEE...
BA-BUMP
NO! DON'T LET HER GO! DON'T LET IT END LIKE THIS!
BA-BUMP
THERE'S STILL TIME, ISN'T THERE? IF YOU GO NOW, YOU CAN STILL CATCH HER!
BA-BUMP
西永福駅
NO...IT'S TOO LATE! IT'S ALL OVER! OVER THE LAST MONTH, SHE MADE UP HER MIND...SHE HASN'T EVEN LOOKED BACK ONCE...
IN THE MONTH SINCE I'VE SEEN HER...SHE'S TRIED TO FORGET ME AND EVERY-THING I DID.
SHE'S JUST BEEN WAITING FOR A CHANCE TO BREAK IT OFF WITH ME.
IT'S ALL OVER...THE ONLY THING LEFT IS TO TAKE IT LIKE A MAN...GIVE IT UP...

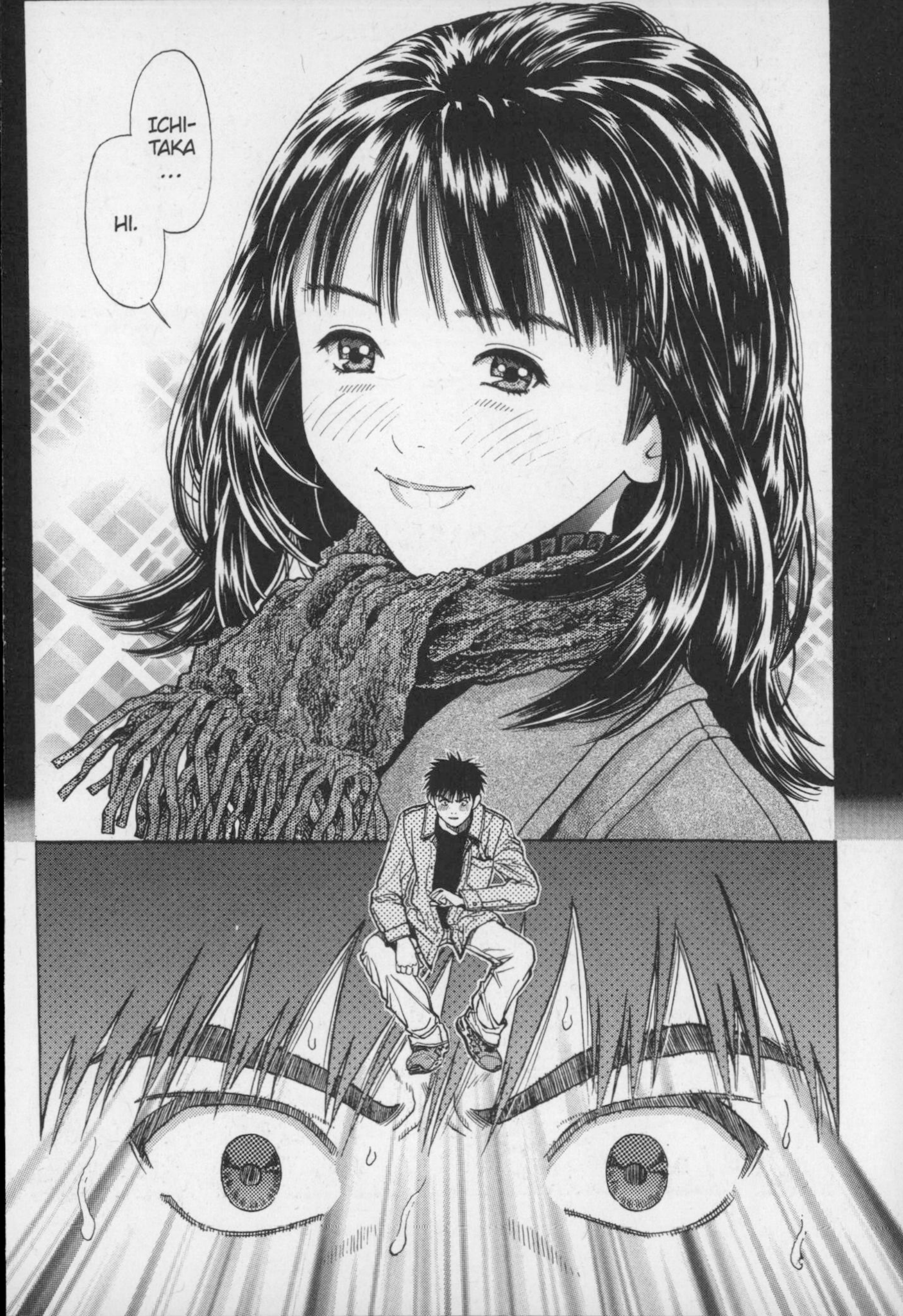
ICHI-TAKA...
HI.

READ THIS WAY

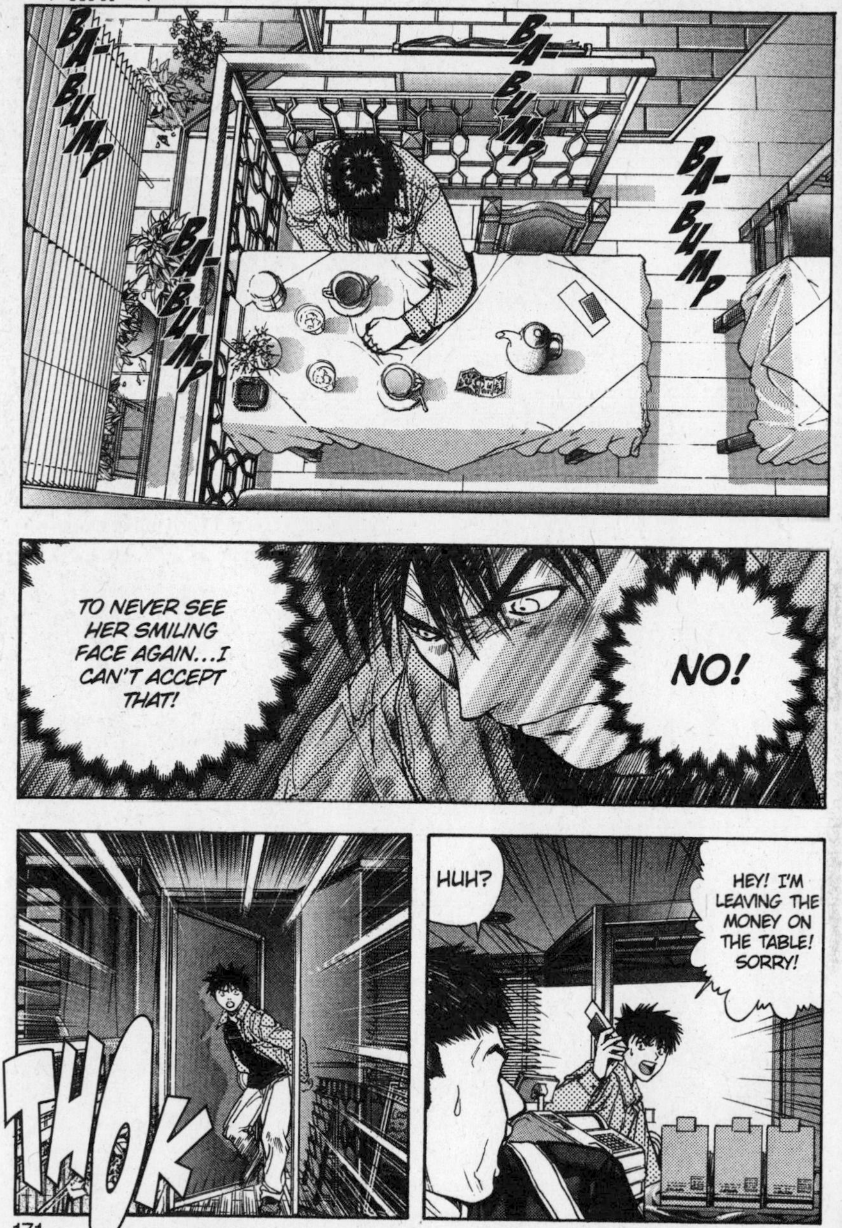
BA-BUMP
BA-BUMP
BA-BUMP
BA-BUMP
NO!
TO NEVER SEE HER SMILING FACE AGAIN...I CAN'T ACCEPT THAT!
HEY! I'M LEAVING THE MONEY ON THE TABLE! SORRY!
HUH?
THOK

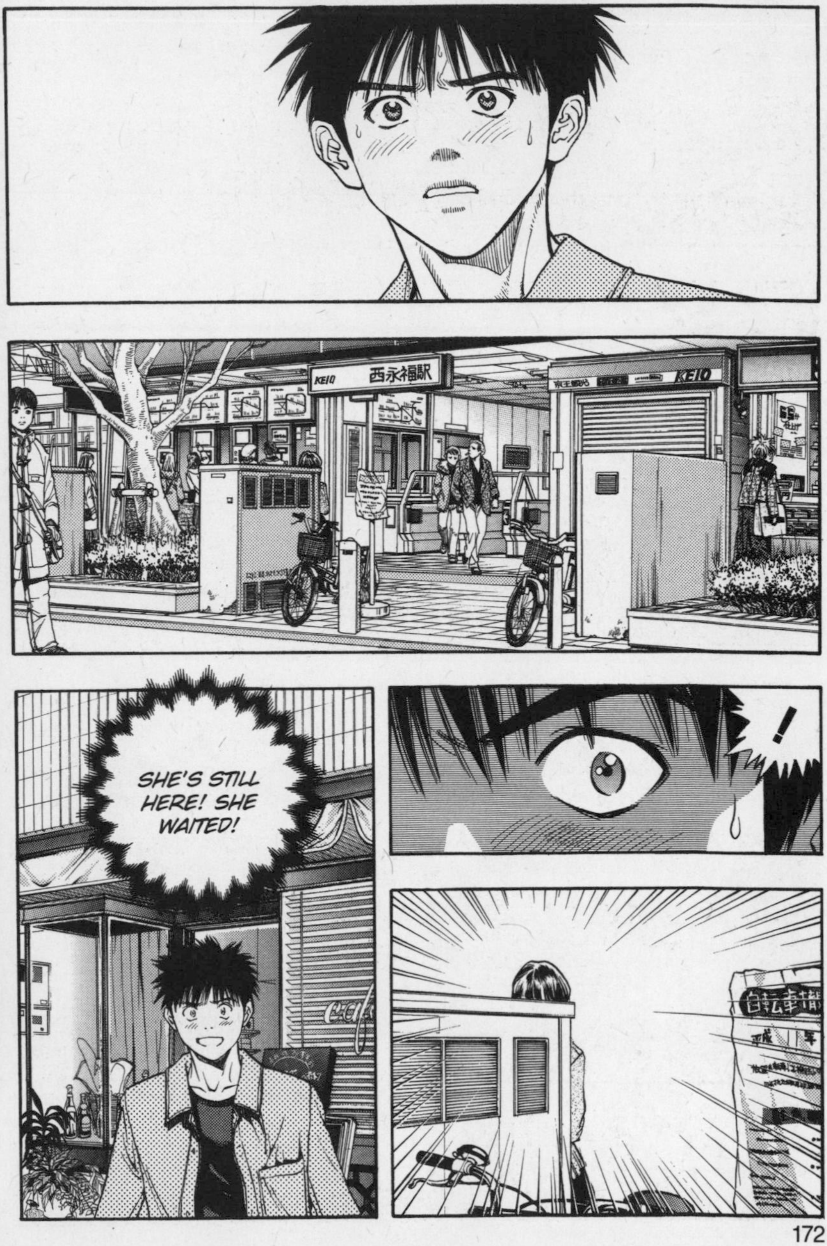
KEIO
西永福駅
KEIO
!
SHE'S STILL HERE! SHE WAITED!

READ THIS WAY

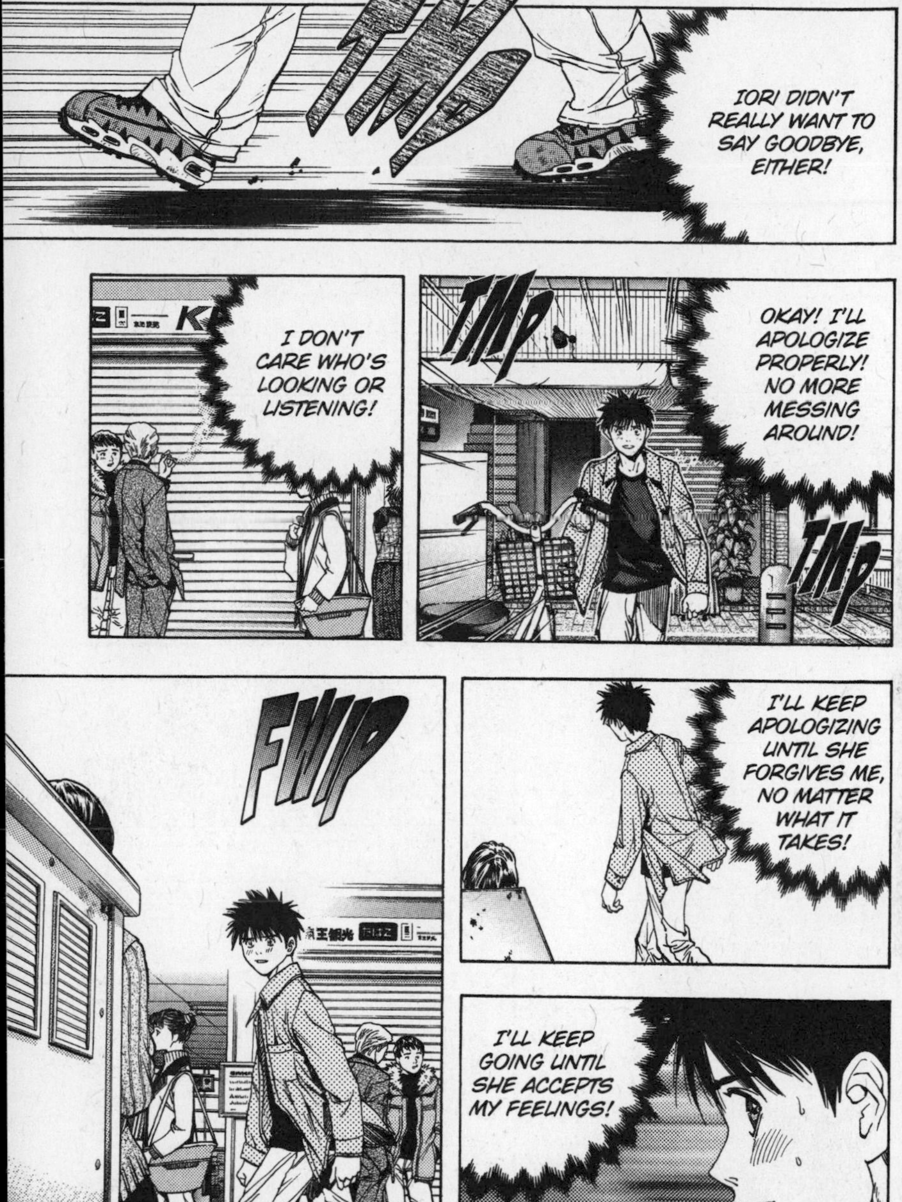

TMP
IORI DIDN'T REALLY WANT TO SAY GOODBYE, EITHER!
TMP
OKAY! I'LL APOLOGIZE PROPERLY! NO MORE MESSING AROUND!
TMP
I DON'T CARE WHO'S LOOKING OR LISTENING!
I'LL KEEP APOLOGIZING UNTIL SHE FORGIVES ME, NO MATTER WHAT IT TAKES!
I'LL KEEP GOING UNTIL SHE ACCEPTS MY FEELINGS!
FWIP

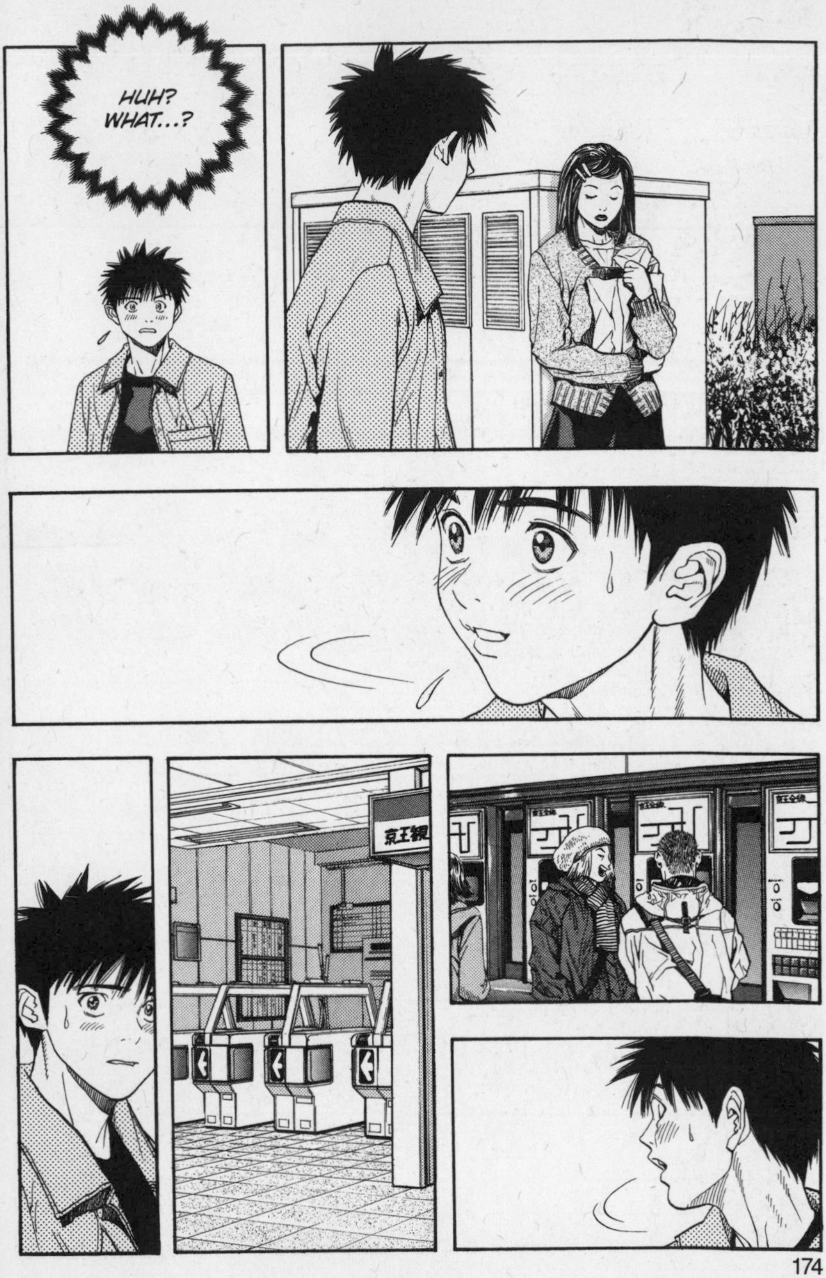
HUH? WHAT...?
京王線

READ THIS WAY

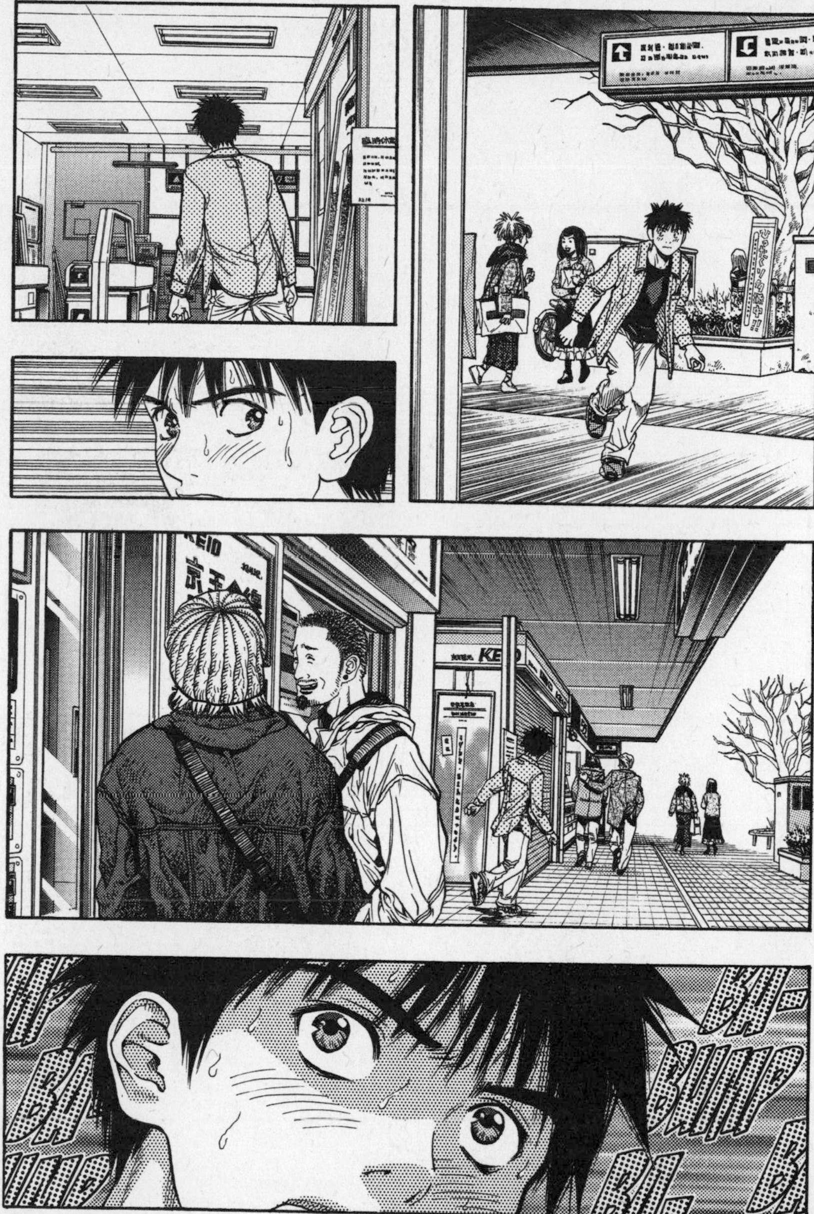
KEIO
KEIO
BA-BUMP
BA-BUMP

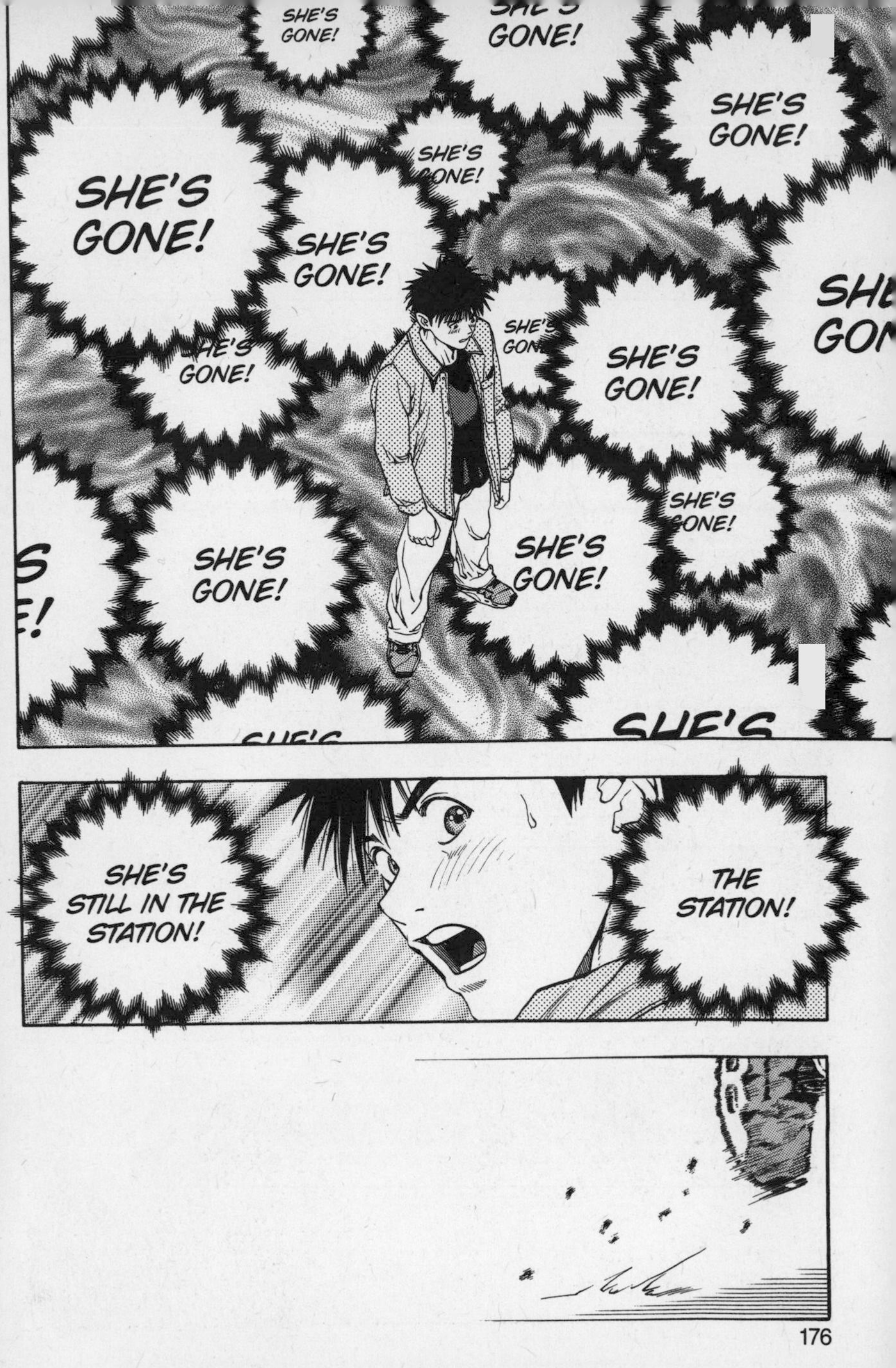
SHE'S GONE!
GONE!
SHE'S GONE!
SHE'S GONE!
SHE'S GONE!
SHE'S GONE!
SHE'S GONE!
SHE'S GONE!
SHE'S GONE!
SHE'S GONE!
THE STATION!
SHE'S STILL IN THE STATION!

READ THIS WAY

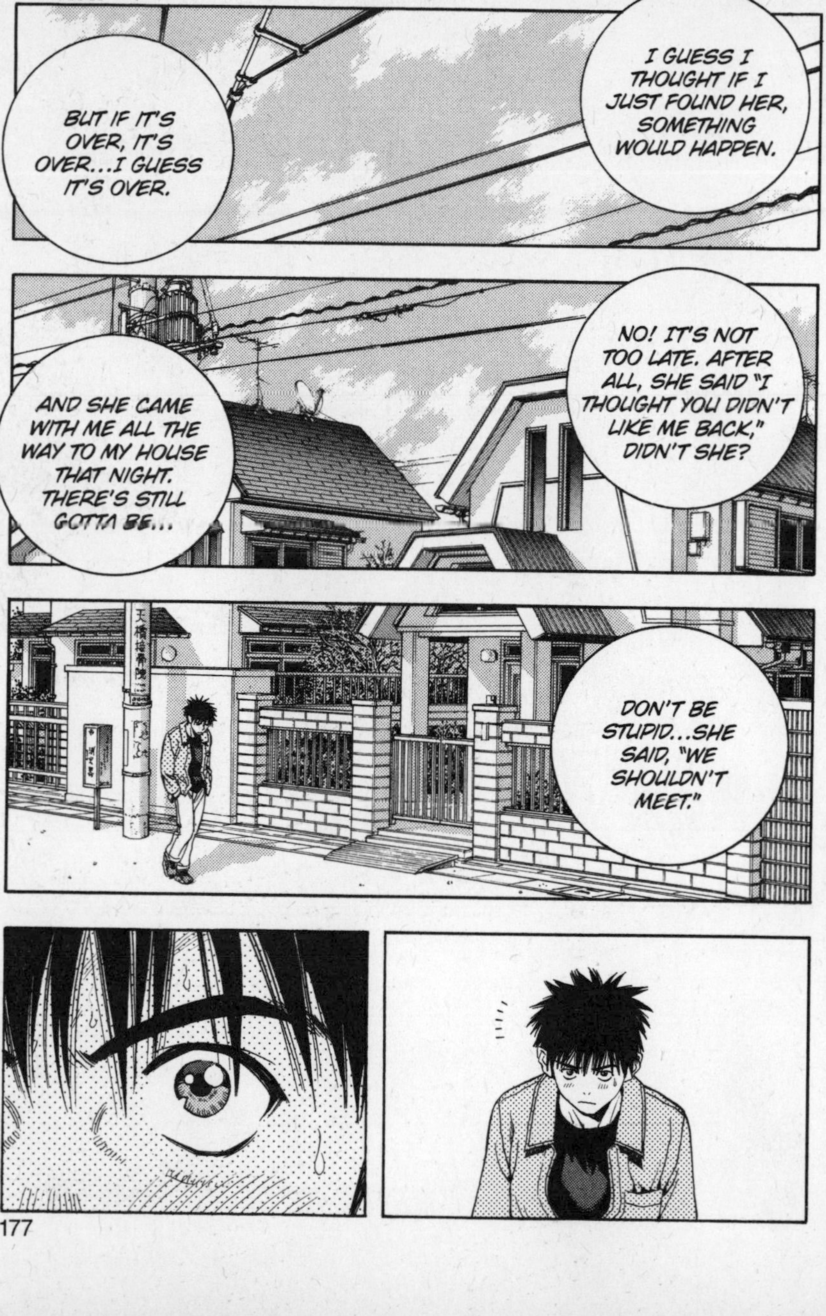

I GUESS I THOUGHT IF I JUST FOUND HER, SOMETHING WOULD HAPPEN.
BUT IF IT'S OVER, IT'S OVER...I GUESS IT'S OVER.
NO! IT'S NOT TOO LATE. AFTER ALL, SHE SAID "I THOUGHT YOU DIDN'T LIKE ME BACK," DIDN'T SHE?
AND SHE CAME WITH ME ALL THE WAY TO MY HOUSE THAT NIGHT. THERE'S STILL GOTTA BE...
DON'T BE STUPID...SHE SAID, "WE SHOULDN'T MEET."

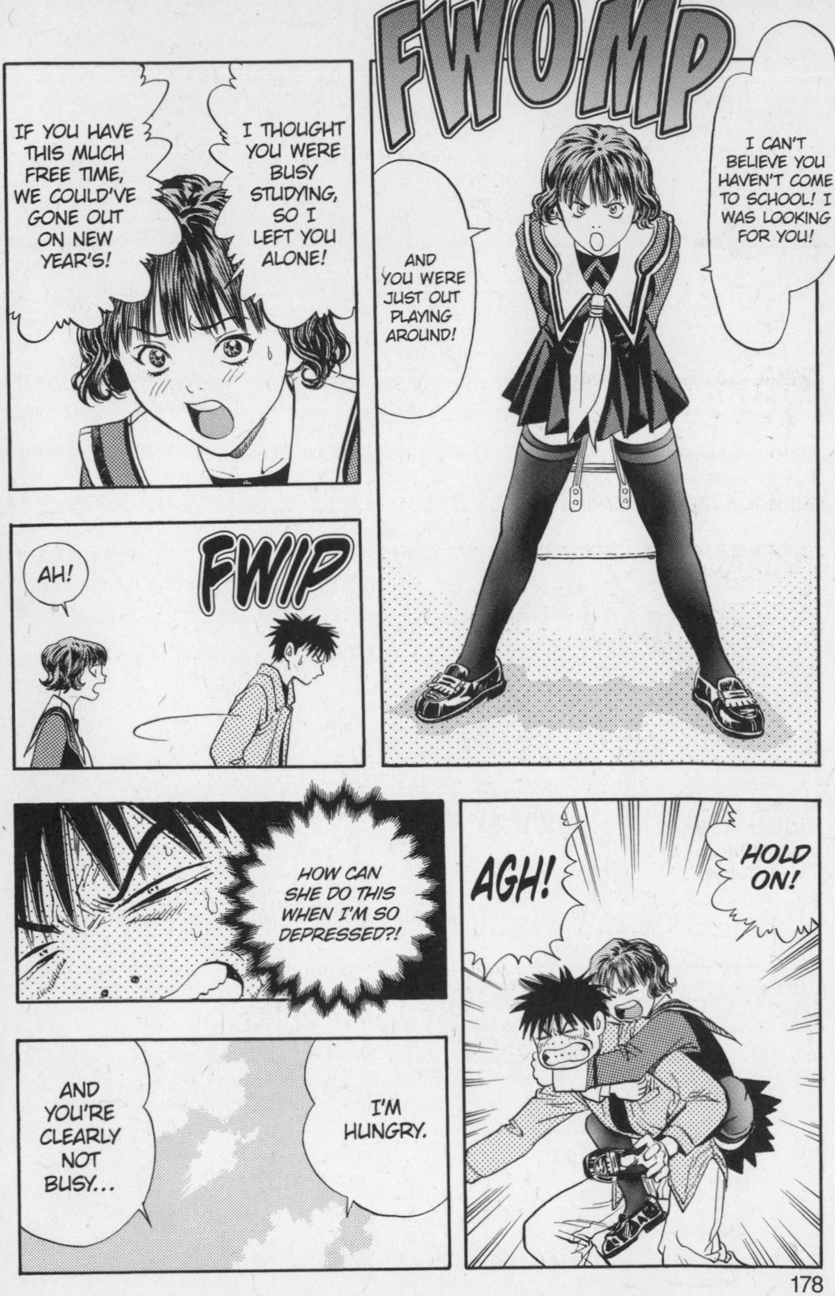
FWOMP
I CAN'T BELIEVE YOU HAVEN'T COME TO SCHOOL! I WAS LOOKING FOR YOU!
AND YOU WERE JUST OUT PLAYING AROUND!
I THOUGHT YOU WERE BUSY STUDYING, SO I LEFT YOU ALONE!
IF YOU HAVE THIS MUCH FREE TIME, WE COULD'VE GONE OUT ON NEW YEAR'S!
FWIP
AH!
HOLD ON!
AGH!
HOW CAN SHE DO THIS WHEN I'M SO DEPRESSED?!
I'M HUNGRY.
AND YOU'RE CLEARLY NOT BUSY...

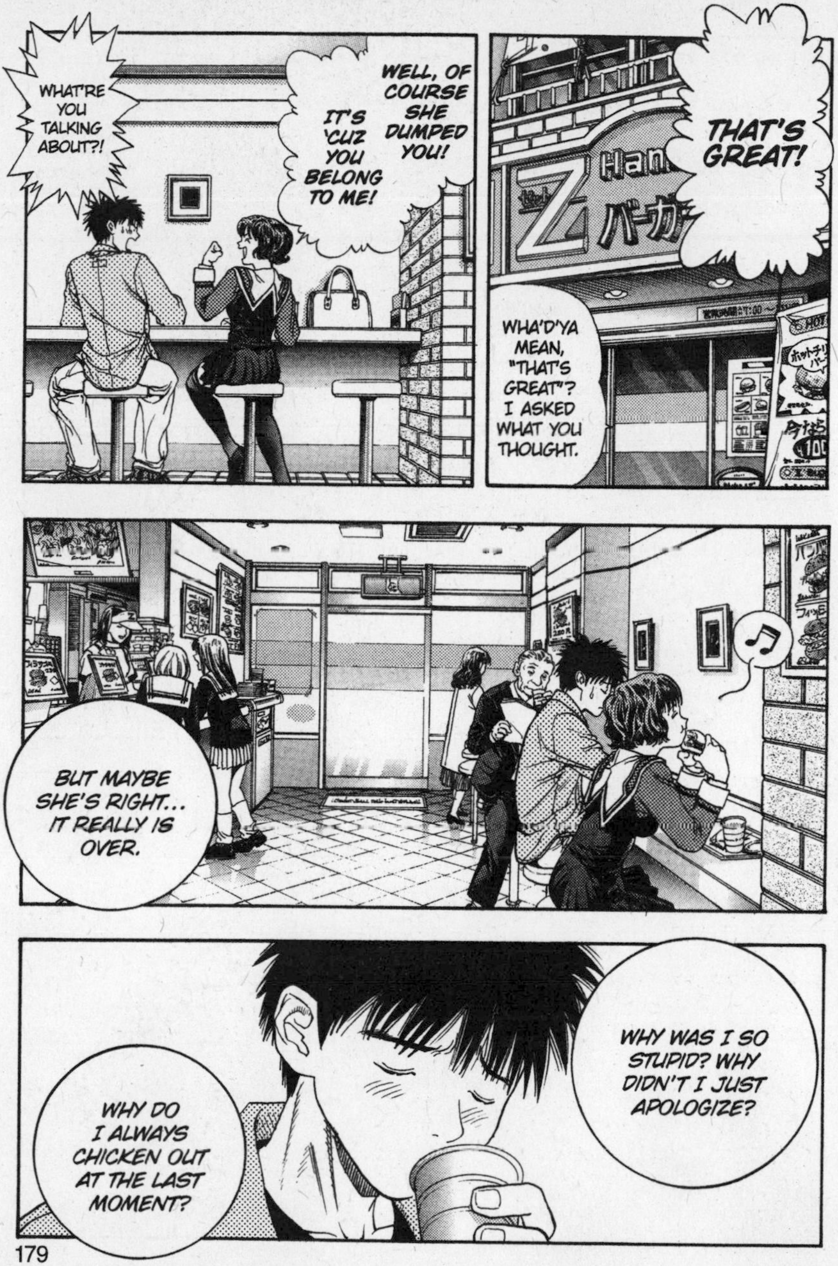
THAT'S GREAT!
WHA'D'YA MEAN, "THAT'S GREAT"? I ASKED WHAT YOU THOUGHT.
WELL, OF COURSE SHE DUMPED YOU! IT'S 'CUZ YOU BELONG TO ME!
WHAT'RE YOU TALKING ABOUT?!
BUT MAYBE SHE'S RIGHT... IT REALLY IS OVER.
WHY WAS I SO STUPID? WHY DIDN'T I JUST APOLOGIZE?
WHY DO I ALWAYS CHICKEN OUT AT THE LAST MOMENT?

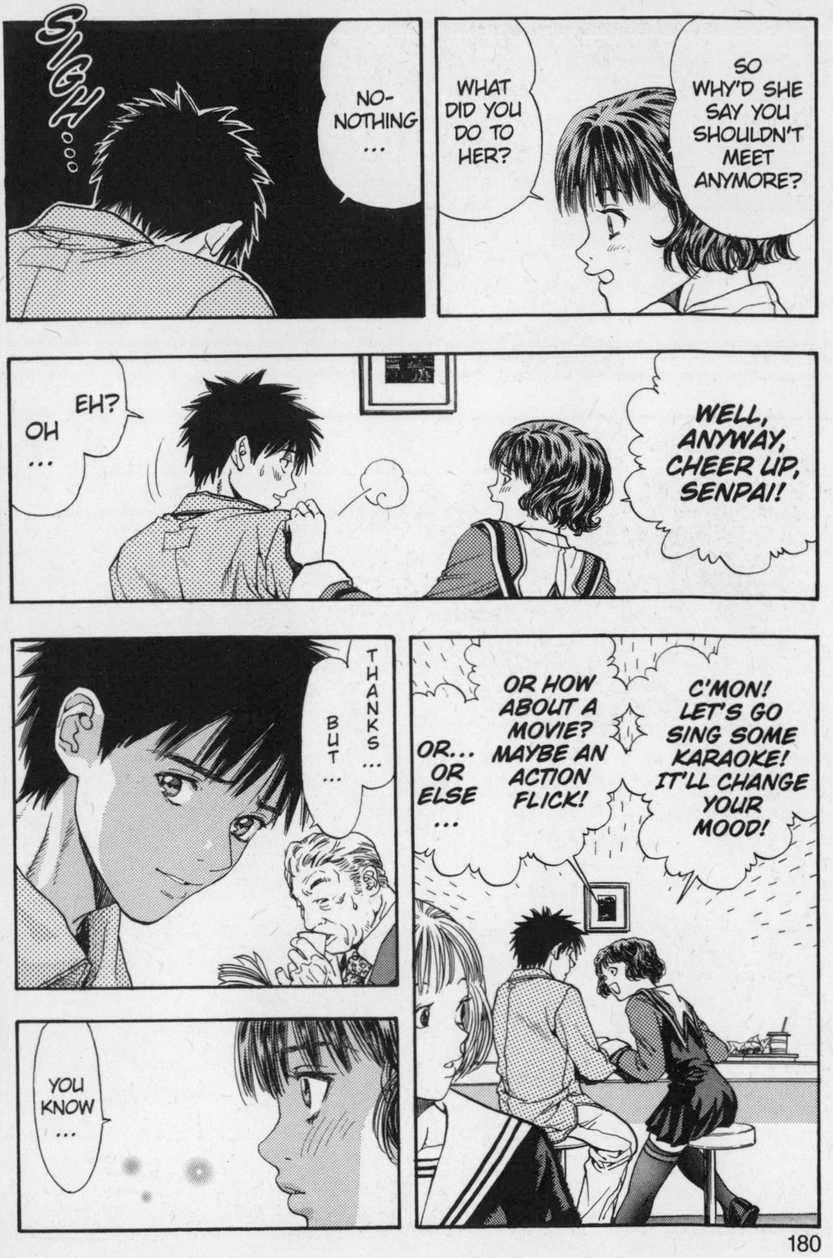
SO WHY'D SHE SAY YOU SHOULDN'T MEET ANYMORE?
WHAT DID YOU DO TO HER?
NO-NOTHING ...
SIGH...
WELL, ANYWAY, CHEER UP, SENPAI!
EH?
OH ...
C'MON! LET'S GO SING SOME KARAOKE! IT'LL CHANGE YOUR MOOD!
OR HOW ABOUT A MOVIE? MAYBE AN ACTION FLICK!
OR... OR ELSE ...
THANKS ...
BUT ...
YOU KNOW ...

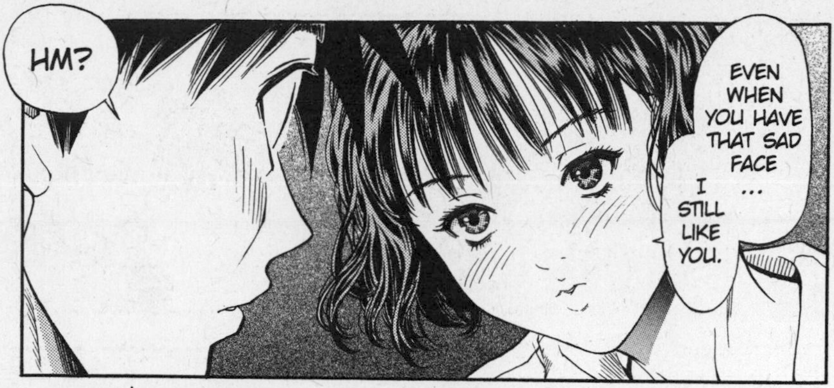
EVEN WHEN YOU HAVE THAT SAD FACE ...
I STILL LIKE YOU.
HM?

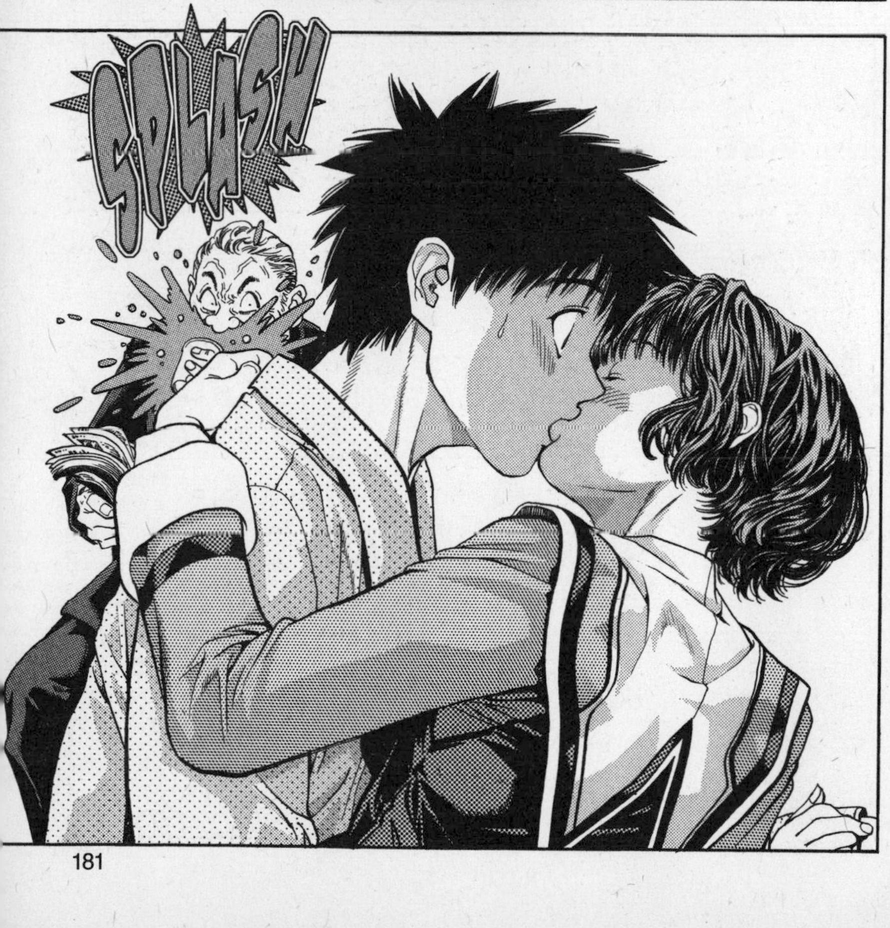
SPLASH

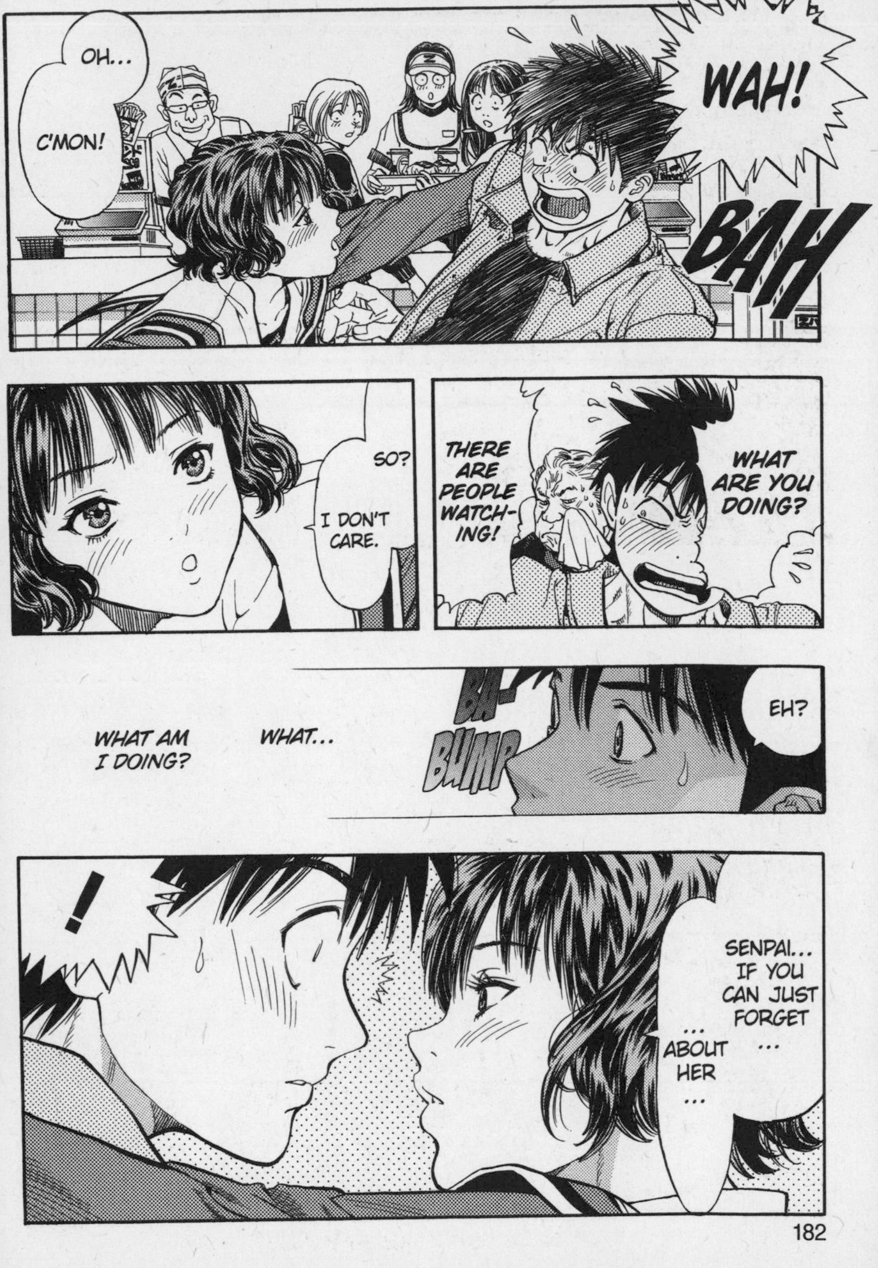
WAH!
BAH
OH...
C'MON!
WHAT ARE YOU DOING?
THERE ARE PEOPLE WATCHING!
SO?
I DON'T CARE.
EH?
BA-BUMP
WHAT...
WHAT AM I DOING?
SENPAI... IF YOU CAN JUST FORGET ...
... ABOUT HER ...
!

READ THIS WAY

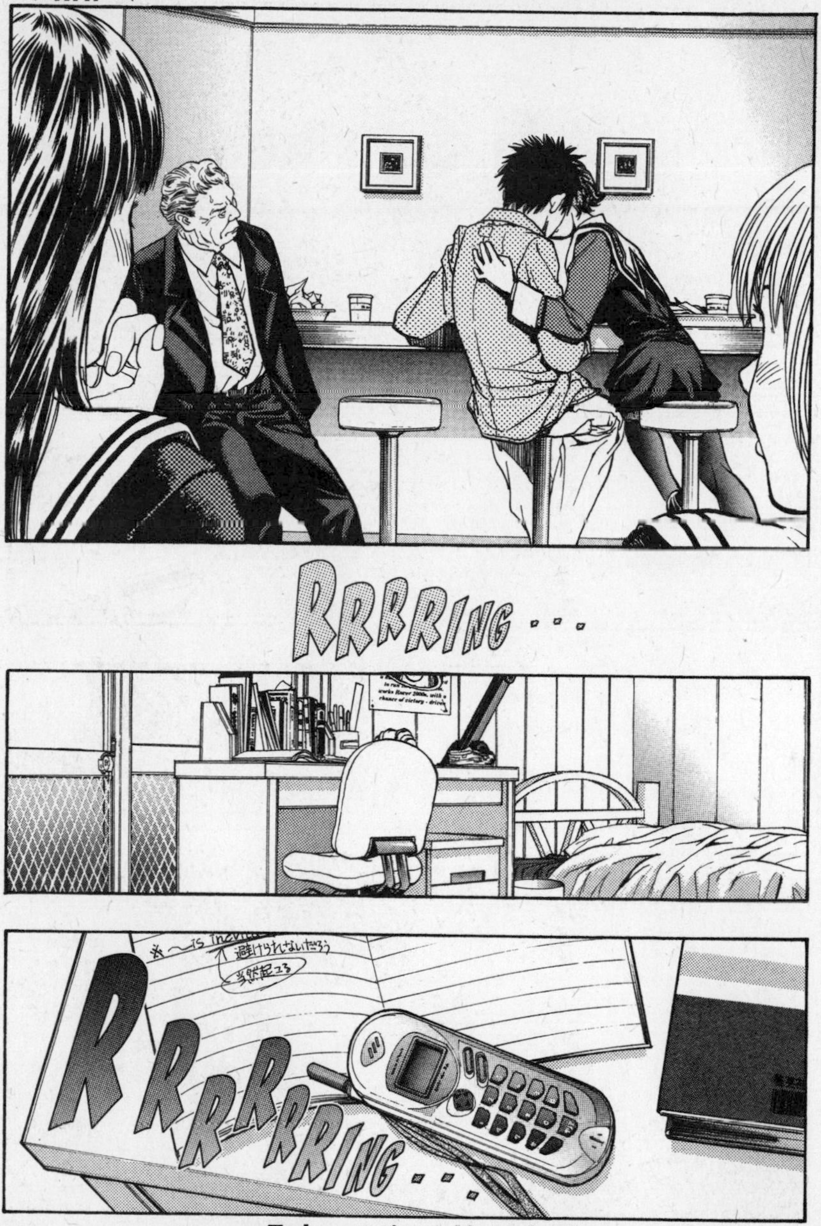
RRRRING...
RRRRRRING...

To be continued in Vol. 11!

アイズ

I"s Illustration
Collection

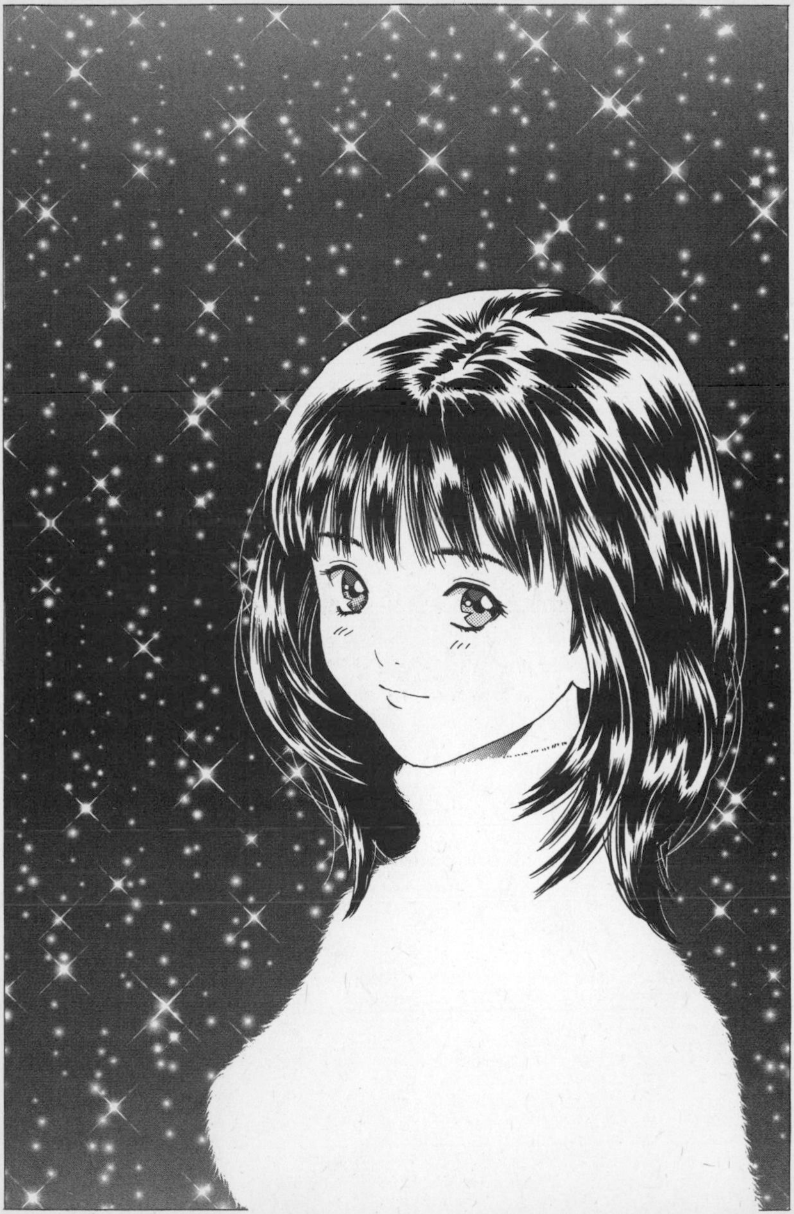

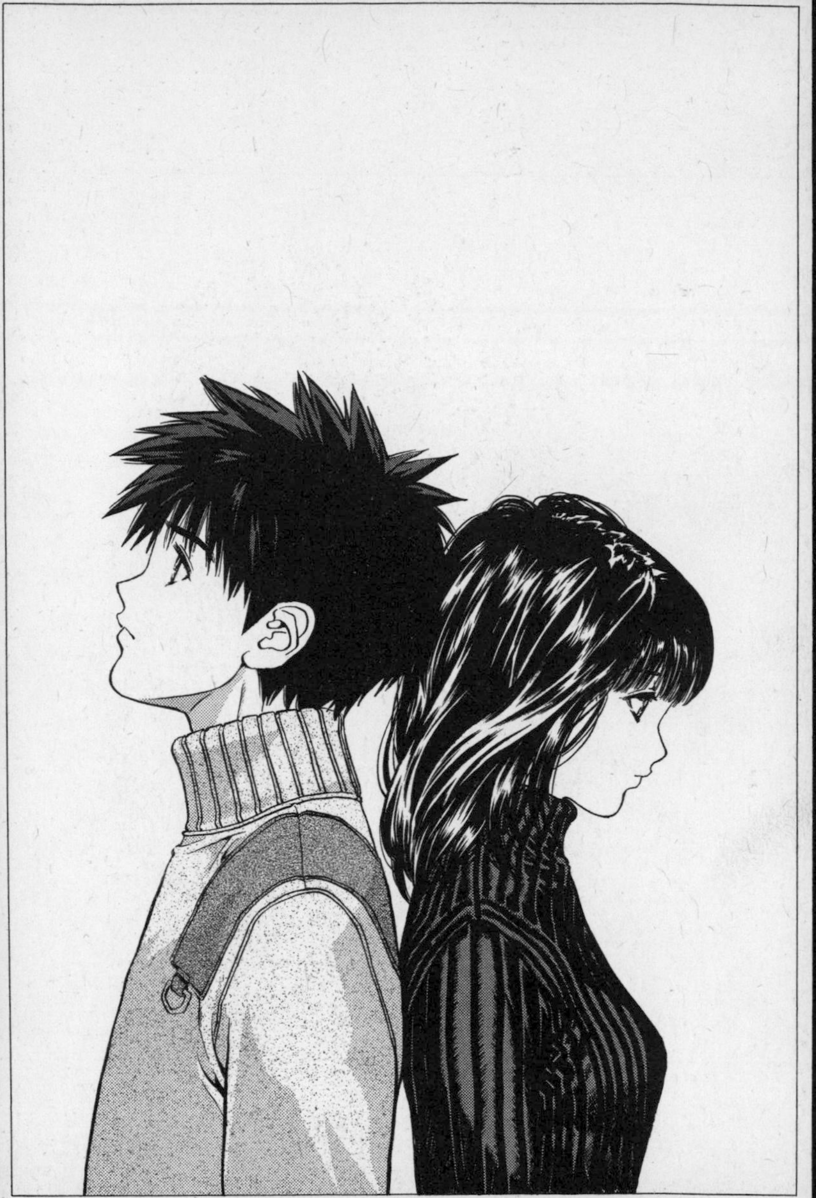

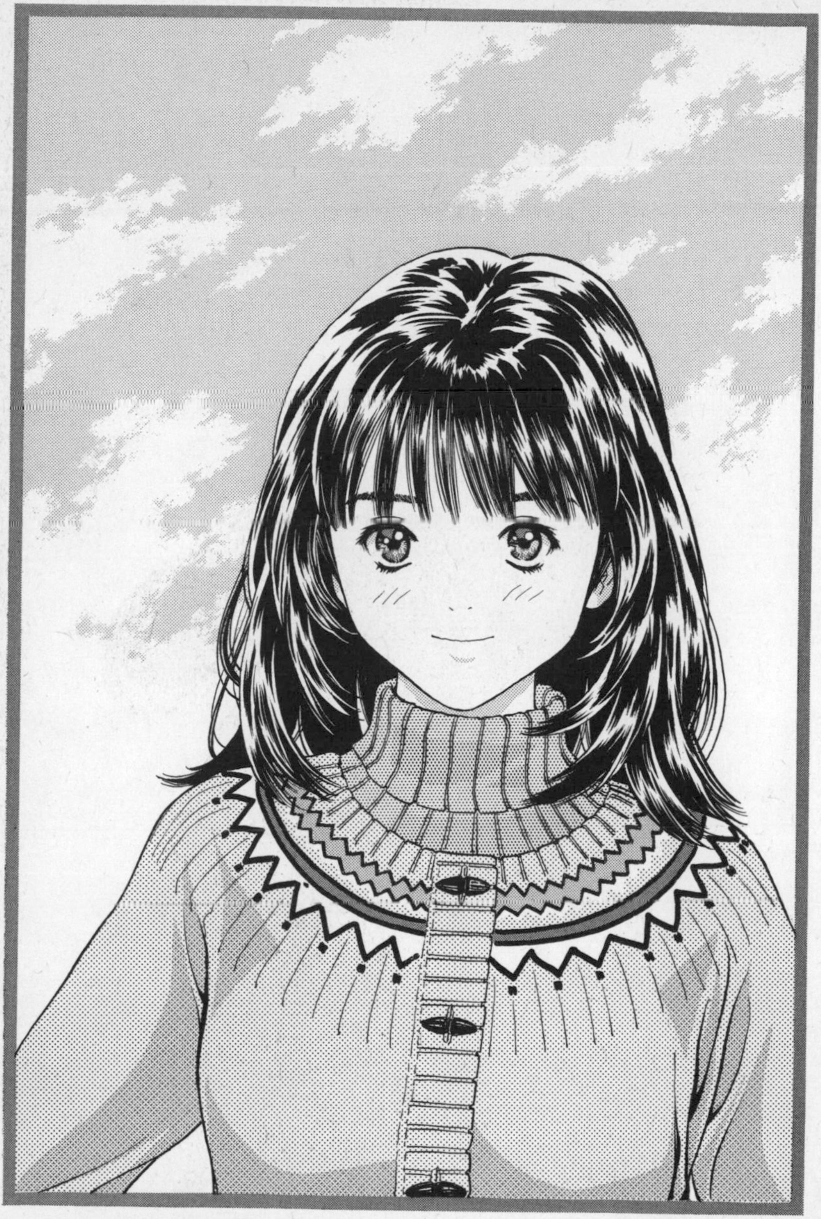

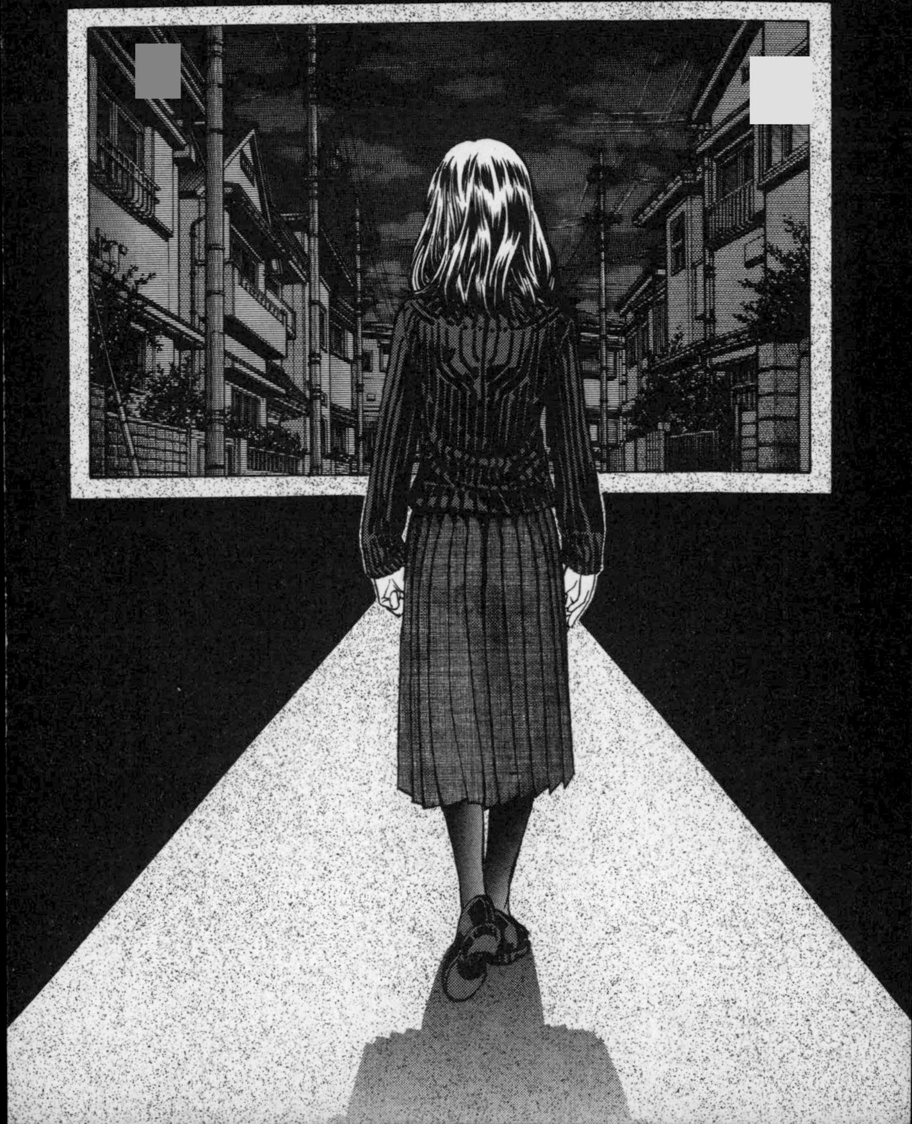

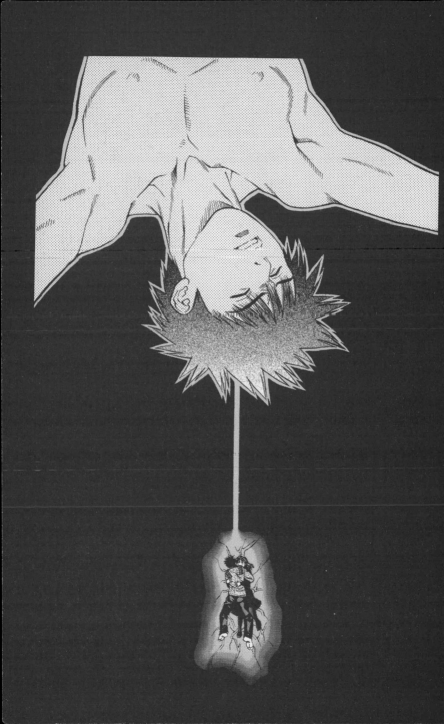

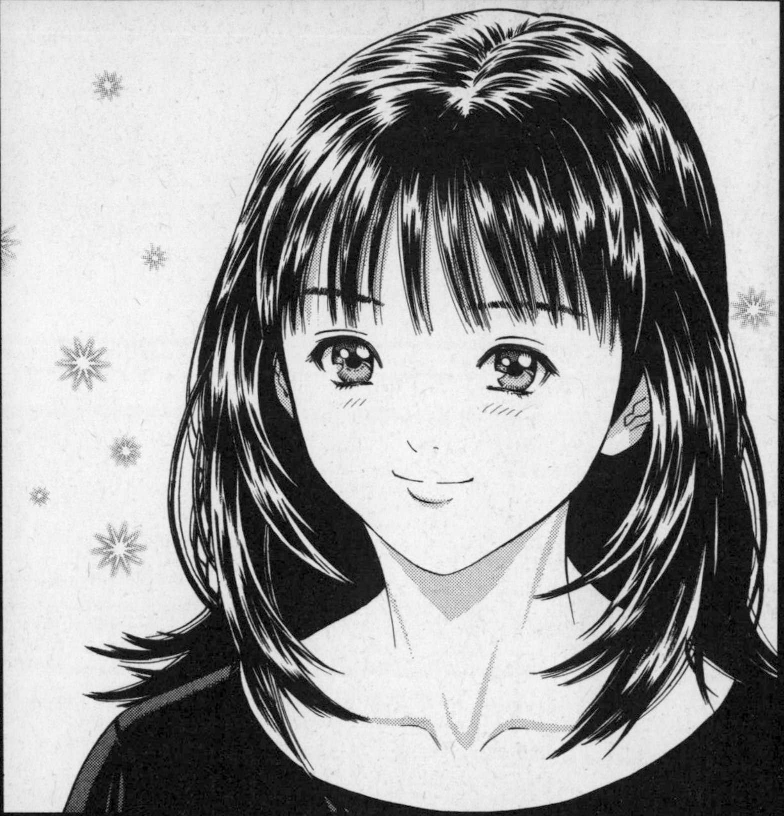

NEXT VOLUME PREVIEW

Things are changing fast for Ichitaka, with high school graduation and college entrance exams fast approaching. Just when he thinks Iori has completely rejected him, he finds it's not that simple. Her career is beginning to take off, and everyone around her is pressuring her not to get involved with boys. Meanwhile, Izumi is still as determined as ever to get Ichitaka for herself. With their school days coming to an end, Ichitaka must decide how to take control of his life.

Available in January 2007

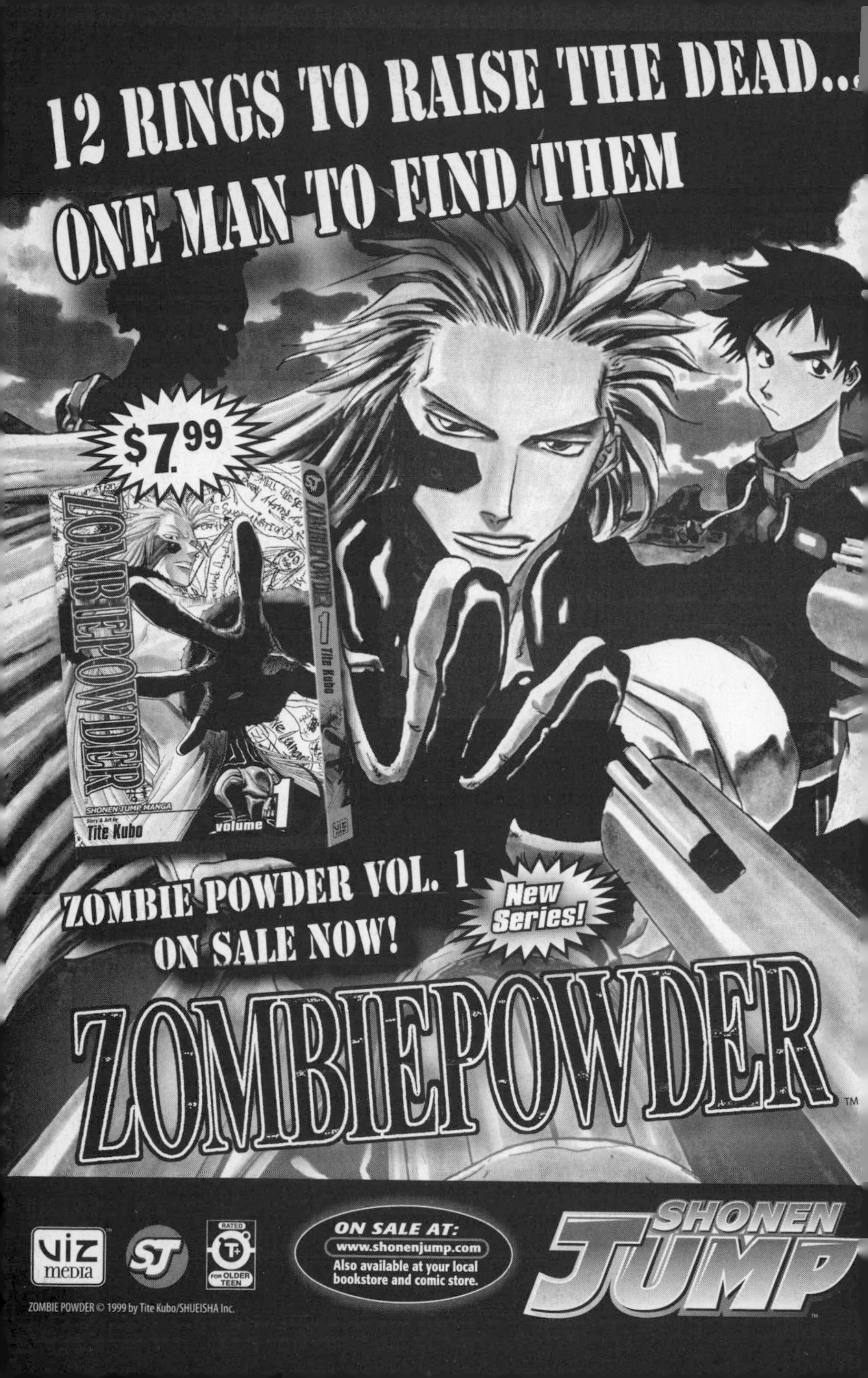
12 RINGS TO RAISE THE DEAD...
ONE MAN TO FIND THEM
$7.99
ZOMBIEPOWDER
SHONEN JUMP MANGA
Story & Art by
Tite Kubo
volume 1
ZOMBIE POWDER VOL. 1
ON SALE NOW!
New Series!
ZOMBIEPOWDER™
ON SALE AT:
www.shonenjump.com
Also available at your local bookstore and comic store.
SHONEN JUMP
ZOMBIE POWDER © 1999 by Tite Kubo/SHUEISHA Inc.

Rurouni Kenshin
™
Novel
$9.99
The popular manga is now available as a novel!
Rurouni Kenshin
RUROUNI KENSHIN
VOYAGE TO THE MOON WORLD
Original Concept by Nobuhiro Watsuki
Written by Kaoru Shizuka
translated by Cindy Yamauchi & Mark Giambruno
SHONEN JUMP FICTION
ON SALE AT:
www.shonenjump.com
Also available at your local bookstore and comic store.
RUROUNI KENSHIN -MEIJI KENKAKU ROMANTAN- MAKI NO ICHI © 1996 by Nobuhiro Watsuki, Kaoru Shizuka/SHUEISHA Inc.

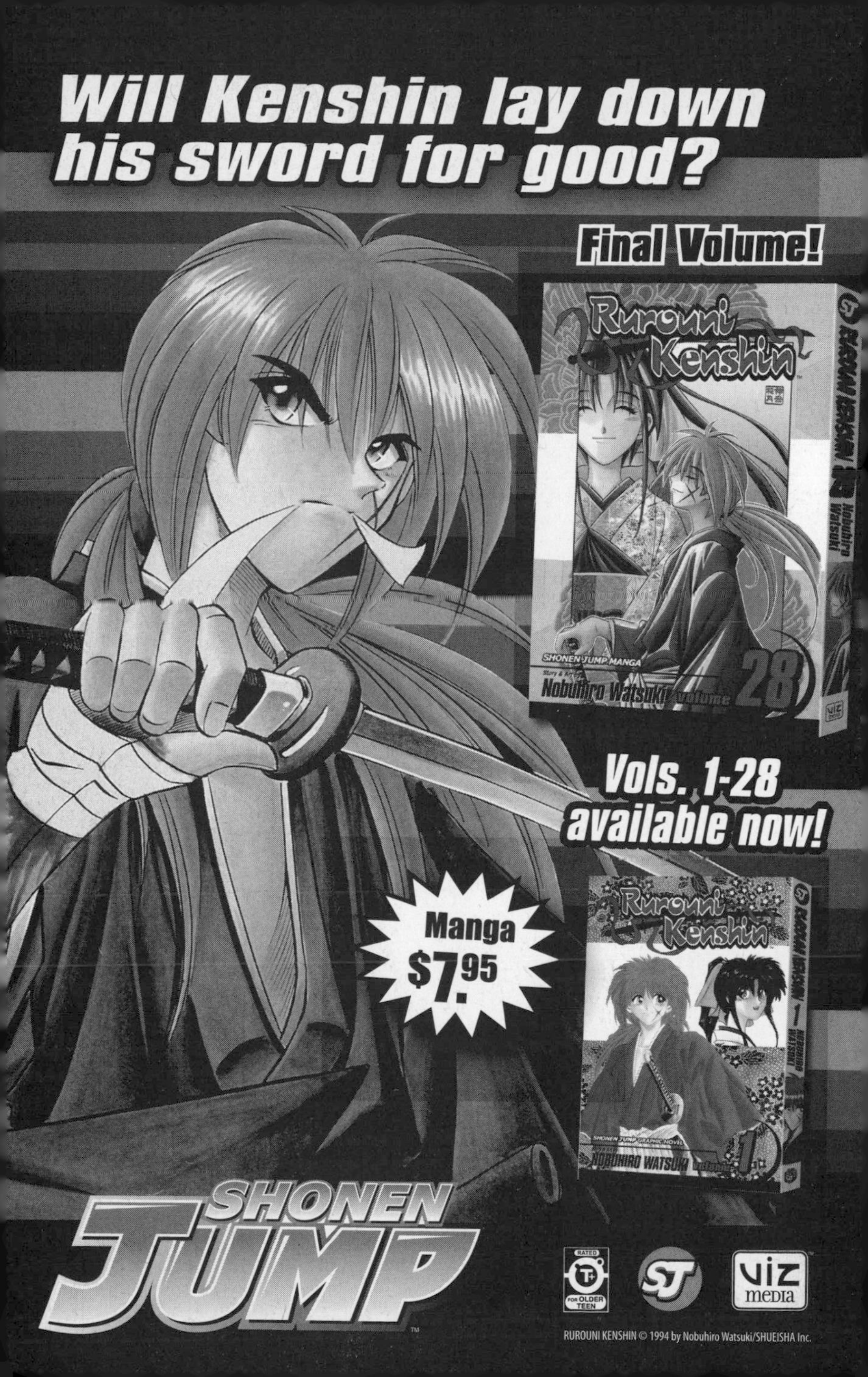
Will Kenshin lay down his sword for good?
Final Volume!
Rurouni Kenshin
SHONEN JUMP MANGA
Nobuhiro Watsuki volume 28
Vols. 1-28 available now!
Manga $7.95
Rurouni Kenshin
NOBUHIRO WATSUKI
SHONEN JUMP
RATED T+ FOR OLDER TEEN
SJ
VIZ media
RUROUNI KENSHIN © 1994 by Nobuhiro Watsuki/SHUEISHA Inc.

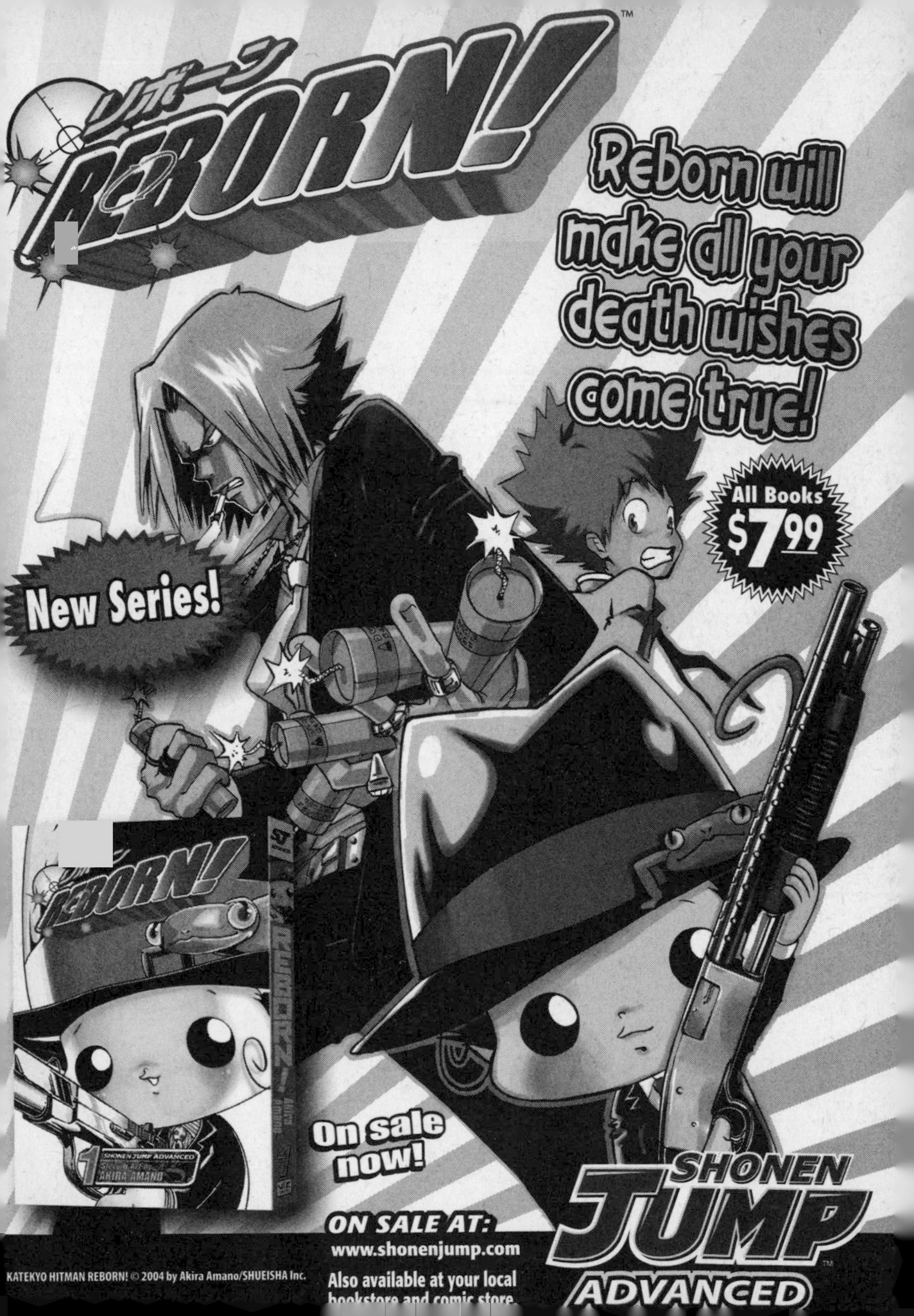
リボーン
REBORN!
Reborn will make all your death wishes come true!
All Books $7.99
New Series!
REBORN!
SHONEN JUMP ADVANCED
AKIRA AMANO
On sale now!
ON SALE AT:
www.shonenjump.com
Also available at your local bookstore and comic store.
SHONEN JUMP ADVANCED
KATEKYO HITMAN REBORN! © 2004 by Akira Amano/SHUEISHA Inc.

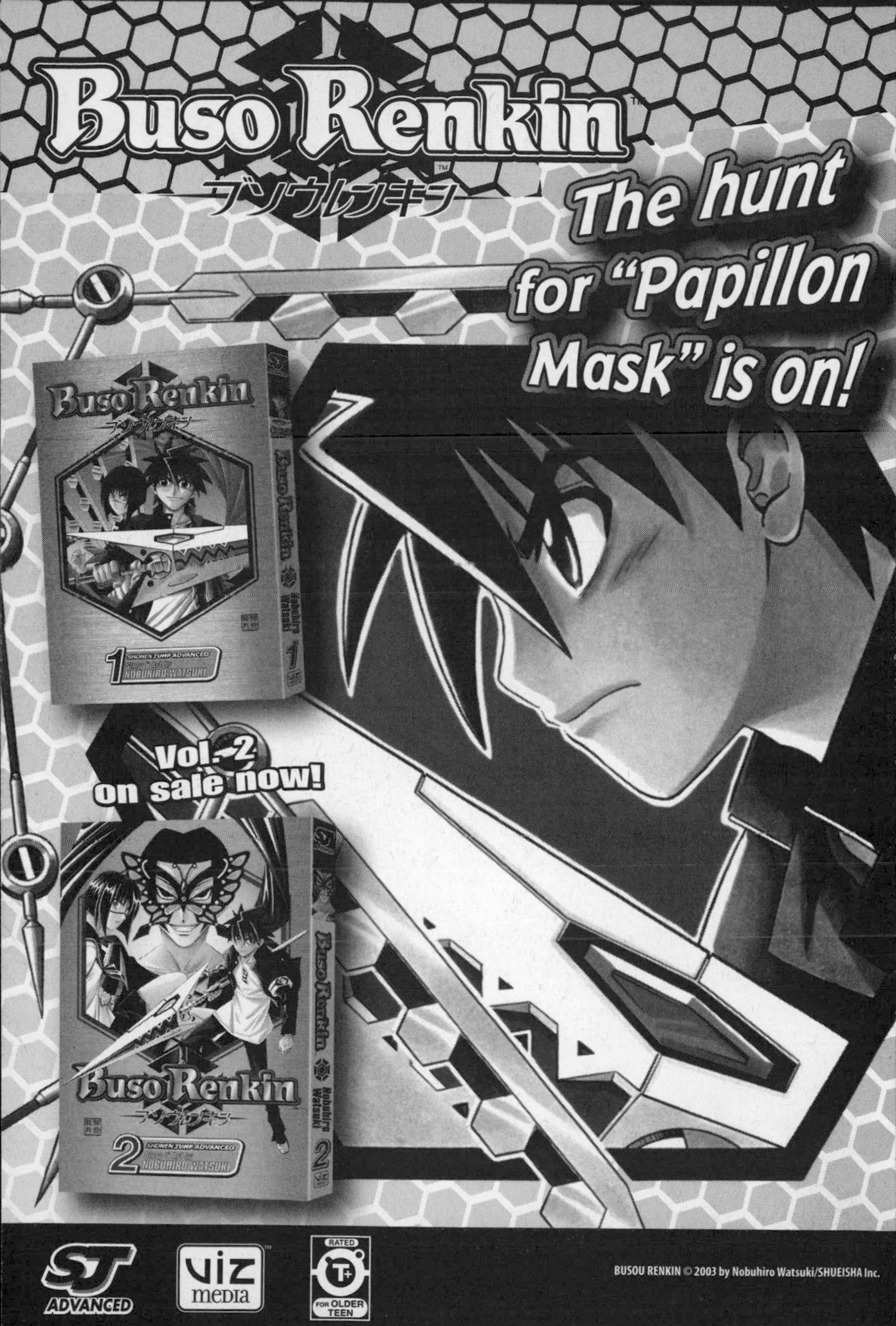

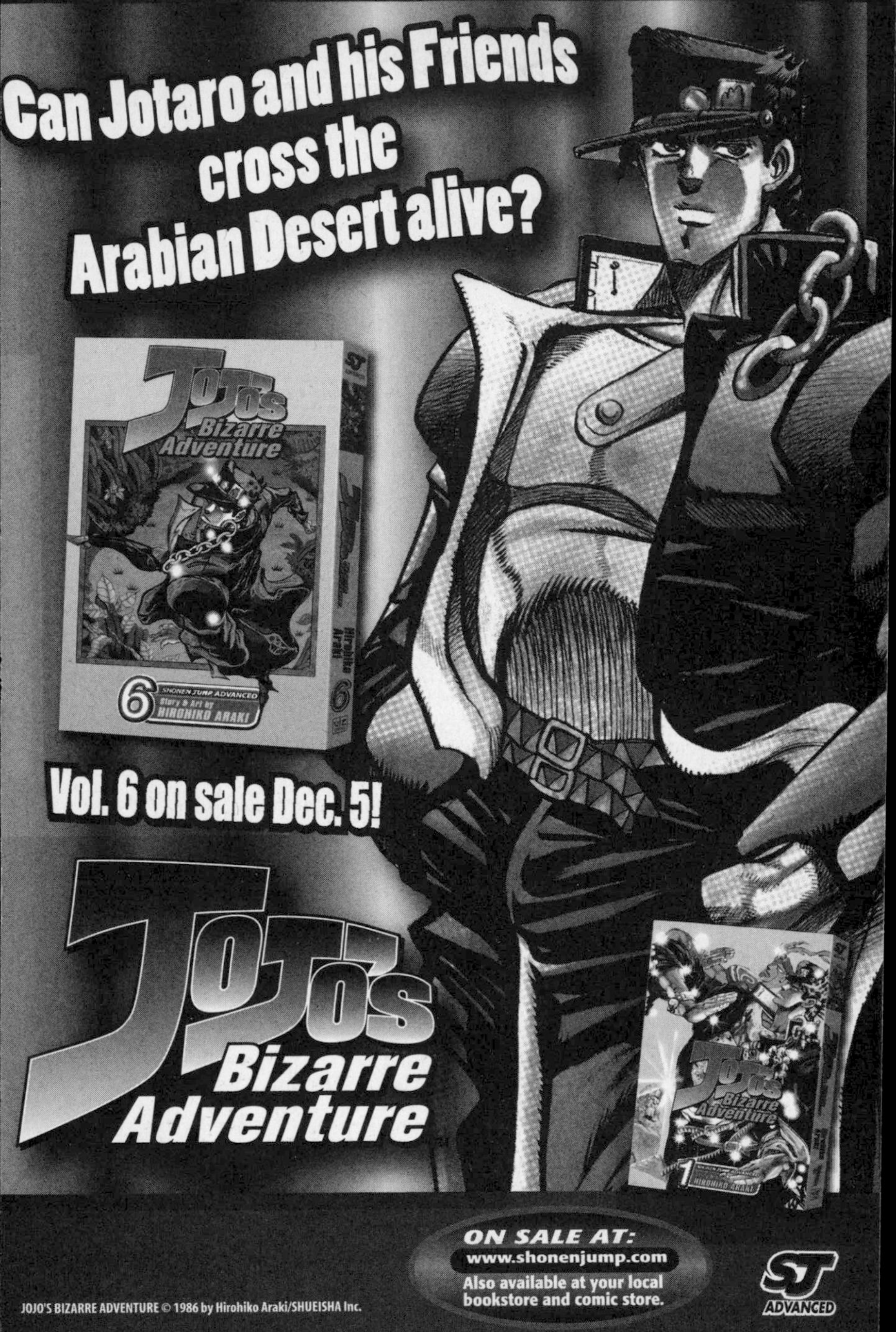
Can Jotaro and his Friends cross the Arabian Desert alive?
JoJo's Bizarre Adventure
6 SHONEN JUMP ADVANCED Story & Art by HIROHIKO ARAKI
Vol. 6 on sale Dec. 5!
JoJo's Bizarre Adventure
ON SALE AT:
www.shonenjump.com
Also available at your local bookstore and comic store.
SJ ADVANCED
JOJO'S BIZARRE ADVENTURE © 1986 by Hirohiko Araki/SHUEISHA Inc.

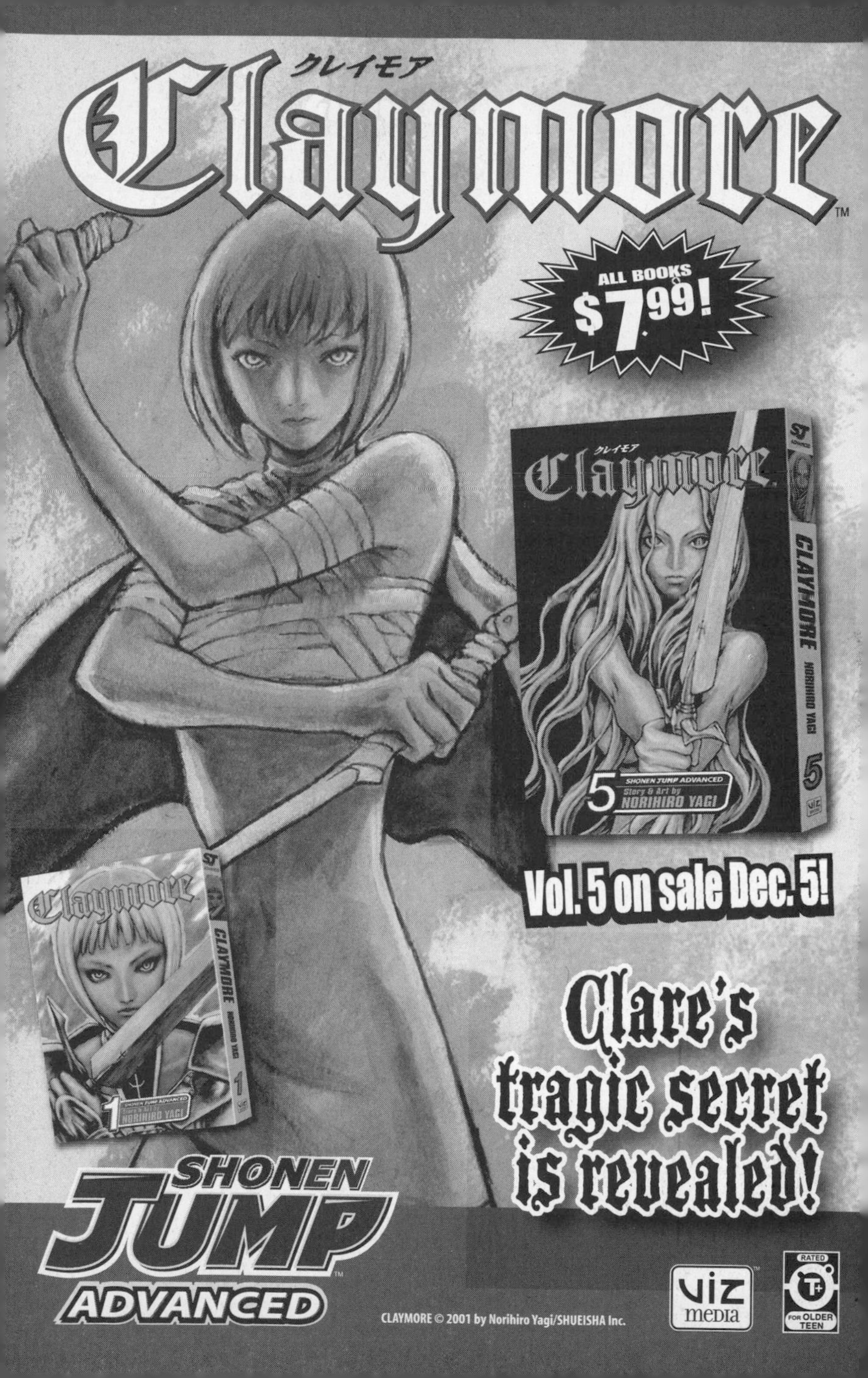

クレイモア
Claymore™
ALL BOOKS $7.99!
クレイモア
Claymore
CLAYMORE
NORIHIRO YAGI
5
5 SHONEN JUMP ADVANCED
Story & Art by NORIHIRO YAGI
Vol. 5 on sale Dec. 5!
Claymore
CLAYMORE
NORIHIRO YAGI
1
1 SHONEN JUMP ADVANCED
NORIHIRO YAGI
Clare's tragic secret is revealed!
SHONEN JUMP ADVANCED™
CLAYMORE © 2001 by Norihiro Yagi/SHUEISHA Inc.
viz media
RATED T+ FOR OLDER TEEN

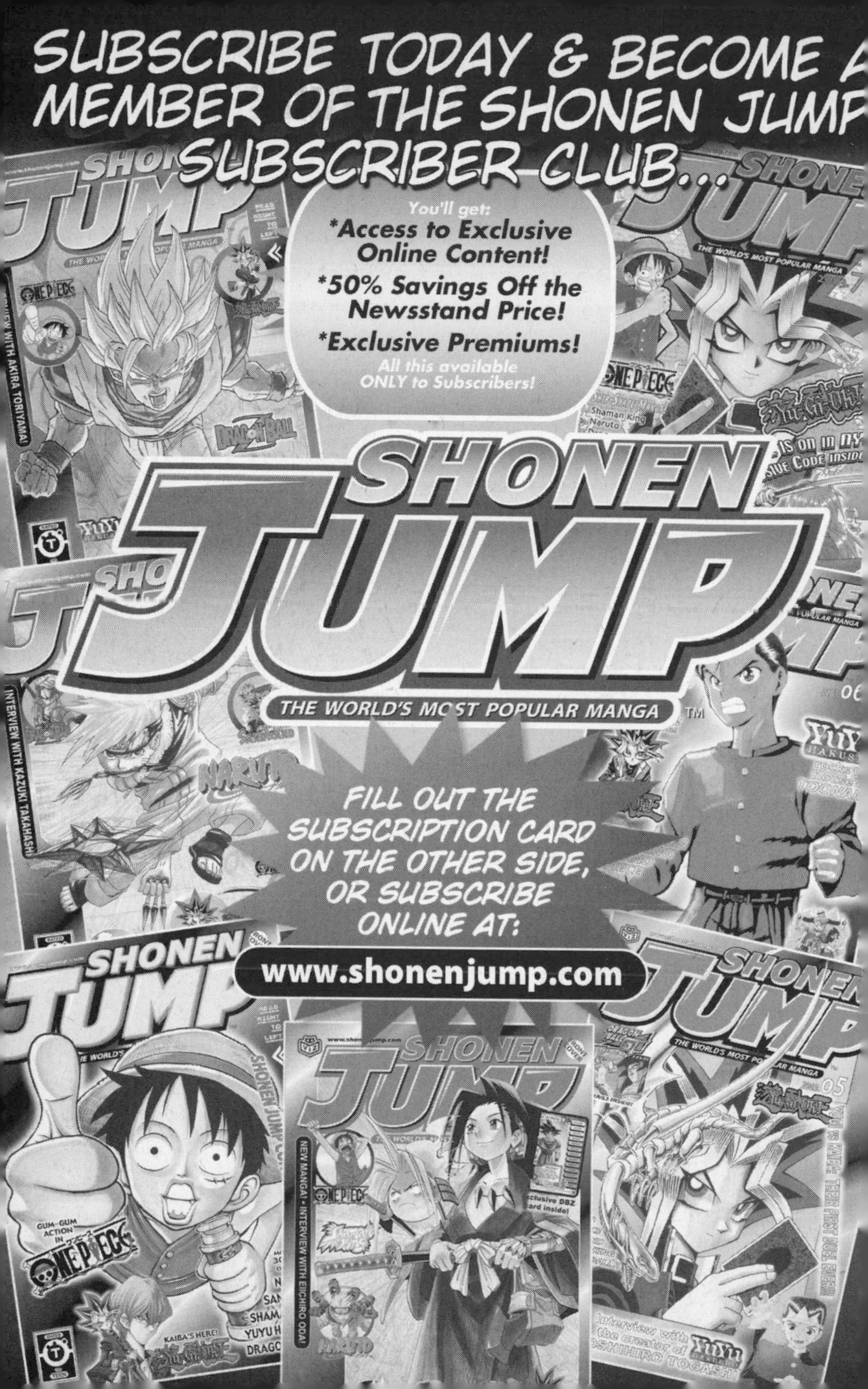
SUBSCRIBE TODAY & BECOME A
MEMBER OF THE SHONEN JUMP
SUBSCRIBER CLUB...
You'll get:
*Access to Exclusive Online Content!
*50% Savings Off the Newsstand Price!
*Exclusive Premiums!
All this available ONLY to Subscribers!
SHONEN JUMP
THE WORLD'S MOST POPULAR MANGA ™
FILL OUT THE SUBSCRIPTION CARD ON THE OTHER SIDE, OR SUBSCRIBE ONLINE AT:
www.shonenjump.com